Language and Legal Interpretation in International Law

OXFORD STUDIES IN LANGUAGE AND LAW

Oxford Studies in Language and Law includes scholarly analyses and descriptions of language evidence in civil and criminal law cases as well as language issues arising in the area of statutes, statutory interpretation, courtroom discourse, jury instructions, and historical changes in legal language.

Speak English or What?: Codeswitching and Interpreter Use in New York City Small Claims Court
Philipp Sebastian Angermeyer

Law at Work: Studies in Legal Ethnomethods
Edited by Baudouin Dupret, Michael Lynch, and Tim Berard

Speaking of Language and Law: Conversations on the Work of Peter Tiersma
Edited by Lawrence M. Solan, Janet Ainsworth, and Roger W. Shuy

Discursive Constructions of Consent in the Legal Process
Edited by Susan Ehrlich, Diana Eades and Janet Ainsworth

From Truth to Technique at Trial: A Discursive History of Advocacy Advice Texts
Philip Gaines

Discourse, Identity, and Social Change in the Marriage Equality Debates
Karen Tracy

Translating the Social World for Law: Linguistic Tools for a New Legal Realism
Edited by Elizabeth Mertz, William K. Ford, and Gregory Matoesian

Conceptions in the Code: How Metaphors Explain Legal Challenges in Digital Times
Stefan Larsson

Deceptive Ambiguity by Police and Prosecutors
Roger Shuy

Legal Integration and Language Diversity: Rethinking Translation in EU Lawmaking
C.J.W. Baaij

Legal Translation Outsourced
Juliette R. Scott

Shallow Equality and Symbolic Jurisprudence in Multilingual Legal Order
Janny H.C. Leung

Strategic Indeterminacy in the Law: Linguistic Tools for New Legal Realism
David Lanius

Translating the Social World for Law: Linguistic Tools for a New Legal Realism
Elizabeth Mertz, William K. Ford, and Gregory Matoesian

Confronting the Death Penalty: How Language Influences Jurors in Capital Cases
Robin Conley Riner

Language and Legal Interpretation in International Law

EDITED BY ANNE LISE KJÆR

and

JOANNA LAM

OXFORD
UNIVERSITY PRESS

OXFORD
UNIVERSITY PRESS

Oxford University Press is a department of the University of Oxford. It furthers the University's objective of excellence in research, scholarship, and education by publishing worldwide. Oxford is a registered trade mark of Oxford University Press in the UK and certain other countries.

Published in the United States of America by Oxford University Press
198 Madison Avenue, New York, NY 10016, United States of America.

Library of Congress Cataloging-in-Publication Data
Names: Kjær, Anne Lise, editor. | Lam, Joanna, editor.
Title: Language and legal interpretation in international law /
Anne Lise Kjær, Joanna Lam.
Description: New York : Oxford University Press, 2022. |
Series: Oxford studies in language and law |
Includes bibliographical references and index.
Identifiers: LCCN 2021033938 (print) | LCCN 2021033939 (ebook) |
ISBN 9780190855208 (hardback) | ISBN 9780190855222 (epub) |
ISBN 9780190855215 | ISBN 9780190855239
Subjects: LCSH: International law—Language. | Law—Europe—Language.
Classification: LCC KZ1285.5 . L36 2022 (print) |
LCC KZ1285.5 (ebook) | DDC 341.01/4—dc23
LC record available at https://lccn.loc.gov/2021033938
LC ebook record available at https://lccn.loc.gov/2021033939

DOI: 10.1093/oso/9780190855208.001.0001

1 3 5 7 9 8 6 4 2

Printed by Integrated Books International, United States of America

CONTENTS

CONTRIBUTORS

Lucie Pacho Aljanati is a lecturer of legal and economic translation at Barcelona's Universitat Pompeu Fabra. She holds primary degrees in translation and interpreting (Instituto Superior San Bartolomé, Argentina, and Pompeu Fabra University, Spain) and a double MA in European law, Area of Freedom, Security, and Justice (Toulouse 1 Capitole University, France) and European integration (Autonomous University of Barcelona, Spain). In 2015 she obtained an international doctoral distinction with a dual PhD in translation studies (University of Geneva) and international relations and European integration (Autonomous University of Barcelona). She has extensive experience as a translator, simultaneous interpreter, and project manager, and has participated in the first phase of the LETRINT project (Legal Translation in International Institutional Settings) at the University of Geneva's Transius Centre.

Martina Bajčić is Assistant Professor at the Law Faculty of the University of Rijeka, a member of the Institute of European and Comparative Law, and the Jean Monet Inter-University Centre of Excellence Opatija. She holds a PhD in linguistics, a Master's degree in European integration law and a Diploma in language and law from the Case Western Reserve University (Cleveland, Ohio). Her research and teaching interests are in the area of (EU) legal terminology and cognition, multilingual aspects of EU law, legal interpretation, and institutional translation. She has authored and co-edited publications in the field of law and language and corpus translation studies, and participated in several international research projects in the field of EU law and language. She is a member of the International Language and Law Association, ILLA.

Adam Dyrda completed his PhD at Jagiellonian University, Cracow, Poland in 2012. In 2018, he obtained a degree of doctor habilitatus on the basis of his monograph on the metaphilosophical underpinnings of theoretical disagreements in jurisprudence. He is an Associate Professor in the Department of Legal Theory at Jagiellonian University. His research interests include neopragmatism, epistemology, ethics of belief, general jurisprudence, and legal realism. In recent years Dr

Dyrda has worked on 'holistic pragmatism' developed by Morton G. White (1917–2016) and on the contemporary reinterpretations of American legal realism. In 2020, as a Fulbright scholar, Dr Dyrda visited the University of California-Irvine to work on the project entitled 'Ethics of Institutional Beliefs'. The project combined epistemological and ethical inquiries over the status of 'institutional beliefs', namely beliefs (or attitudes, intentions, etc.) regarding the existence and functioning of social and legal institutions.

Tomasz Gizbert-Studnicki is Emeritus Professor of Law, Jagiellonian University, Cracow, Poland. He was head of the Department of Legal Theory (1988–2018), Chairman of the Board of the Jagellonian Research Centre 'Law, Language, Philosophy', a fellow of the Alexander-von-Humboldt Stiftung, University of Goettingen (1985–7), a member of the Executive Committee of International Association of Legal and Social Philosophy (1995–9), and Chairman of the Editorial Board of the Journal of the Polish Section of IVR. He is author of three books and numerous articles (in Polish, English, German and French) on various topics of legal theory, including the language of law, legal interpretation, legal argumentation, and methodological problems of jurisprudence.

Anne Lise Kjær is a Professor of Legal Linguistics and a senior researcher at the Centre of Excellence for International Courts (iCourts) at the Faculty of Law, University of Copenhagen. She has a Master's degree in translation of languages for special purposes from Copenhagen Business School and a PhD in the phraseology of German legal language. Her present research focuses on the role that language(s) play(s) in the development and interpretation of international law. She has investigated the European Court of Human Rights, the Court of Justice of the European Union, and the International Criminal Tribunal for the former Yugoslavia. She has also analysed Scandinavian Supreme Courts with a view to identifying how they translate and transplant European Human Rights concepts into the languages and reasoning of their own case law. She applies a combination of research methods, including, but not limited to, discourse analysis, translation studies, and corpus linguistics. She is on the steering committee of the International Language and Law Association, ILLA.

Joanna Lam is Professor WSR at the Centre of Excellence for International Courts (iCourts) and Director of Study Hub for International Economic Law and Development (SHIELD), Faculty of Law, University of Copenhagen, She is also affiliated with Kozminski University and serves as the Chair of the Nordic-Asian Forum for International Economic Law. Lam graduated from Harvard Law School and the University of Warsaw (*summa cum laude*), and holds doctoral and habilitation degrees in legal studies. A former Fulbright Fellow, she completed visiting appointments at, *inter alia*, Harvard Law School (2004–5 and 2007–8), UNIDROIT (2006), University of California, Berkeley (2008), and Renmin University (2013).

Her recent research focuses on legal interpretation in international arbitration; on the role of international economic law in facilitating green transition; and on reform of investor-state dispute resolution.

Chang-fa Lo is Permanent Representative of Taiwan to the WTO. He was Justice of Taiwan's Constitutional Court, Chair Professor and Distinguished Professor at National Taiwan University (NTU), Dean of NTU College of Law, and Director of Asian Center for WTO and International Health Law and Policy of NTU College of Law. In this last capacity, he launched two English journals, *Asian Journal of WTO and International Health Law and Policy* (SSCI-listed) and *Contemporary Asia Arbitration Journal* (ESCI-listed). As Dean of the NTU College of Law, he also launched an English journal, *NTU Law Review* (TSCI-listed). He was a panelist of two WTO disputes (DS332 and DS468), and a member of the Permanent Group of Experts. He received an SJD degree from Harvard. He is author/editor of twenty-one books and author of 120 journal papers and book chapters. He has received important academic awards, including the National Chair Professorship Award. His fields include WTO, human rights, and international health law.

Marcin Matczak is an Associate Professor at the University of Warsaw and a partner in DZP, one of the largest Polish law firms. His academic interests cover legal theory and legal philosophy. His publications include articles and books on theories of legal interpretation, judicial reasoning, and judicial formalism, with special focus on the application of philosophy of language in legal philosophy. He has been involved in the recent Polish constitutional crisis, first as attorney representing NGOs before the Constitutional Tribunal, and later as a commentator on Verfassungsblog (verfassungsblog.de).

Karolina Ristova-Aasterud is a Full Professor at the Faculty of Law 'Iustinianus Primus' University SS. Cyril and Methodius (UKIM) in Skopje, North Macedonia. She holds an LLB (UKIM, 1994), an LLM in international and comparative law ('with distinction', Georgetown University, USA, 2000), an MSc in Political Science (UKIM, 2008) and a PhD in law (UKIM, 2010). Her teaching and research interests are in the area of jurisprudence, political theory, feminism, and EU studies (EU enlargement and EU parliamentary dimension). She has published over forty scholarly articles in English, Macedonian, and Serbo-Croatian. Her notable work in English includes book chapters in *Women's Access to Political Power in Post-Communist Europe* (ed. R. E. Matland and K. A. Montgomery, Oxford University Press, 2003); *Law, Politics and the Constitution: New Perspectives from Legal and Political Theory* (ed. A. Geisler, M. Hein, and S. Hummel, Peter Lang, 2014); and *Promoting Gender Equality Abroad: An Assessment of EU Action in the External Dimension* (ed. T. Kruessmann and A. Ziegerhofer, LIT Verlag, 2017). She also served as Member of Parliament in the Assembly of the Republic of Macedonia from 2002 to 2006.

Izabela Skoczeń obtained her PhD from the Faculty of Law and Administration at the Jagiellonian University in Cracow. In 2017 she took up employment with the Cracow Faculty of Law and Administration. She is the author of a number of papers on the intersection of legal theory and philosophy of language, some of which have been published in journals such as the *International Journal for the Semiotics of Law*. Her book *Implicatures within Legal Language* appeared in the Springer Law and Philosophy series in 2019. She is a member of the interdisciplinary Jagiellonian Centre for Law, Language, and Philosophy as well as the Guilty Minds Lab at the University of Zurich.

Lawrence M. Solan is Don Forchelli Professor of Law and Director of Graduate Education at Brooklyn Law School in New York and holds both a law degree and a PhD in linguistics. His scholarly works are largely devoted to exploring interdisciplinary issues related to law, language, and psychology, especially in the areas of statutory and contractual interpretation, the attribution of liability and blame, and linguistic evidence. He is director of Brooklyn Law School's Center for the Study of Law, Language, and Cognition, and his acclaimed book, *The Language of Judges*, is widely recognized as a seminal work on linguistic theory and legal argumentation. His most recent books are *The Language of Statutes: Laws and their Interpretation*, published by the University of Chicago Press in 2010, *The Oxford Handbook of Language and Law*, co-edited with Peter Tiersma and published in 2012, and *Speaking of Language and Law: Conversations on the Work of Peter Tiersma*, co-edited with Janet Ainsworth and Roger Shuy and published by Oxford University Press in 2015. He has authored numerous articles and book chapters, and regularly lectures in the United States and abroad.

Tomasz Stawecki, is Professor at the Faculty of Law and Administration, at the University of Warsaw. He specializes in legal theory and philosophy of law. His research covers also legal ethics, constitutional, and comparative law. He graduated from University of Warsaw, and completed research stays in Oxford, Washington, Florence, and Moscow. He is an author or co-author of about 100 publications, mostly in Polish, including a study on constitutional interpretation as co-author and co-editor (2014). He has been a member of the International Association for Legal and Social Philosophy (IVR) since 1994. He was President of the Polish Section (2006–10), and member of the Executive Committee of IVR (2011–19). Tomasz Stawecki has also been very active in legal practice as a counsel in international law firms in Warsaw (1991–2016), and since 2016 as a judge at the Voivodship Administrative Court in Warsaw.

Julian Udich is a legal officer with the German Federal Ministry of Justice and Consumer Protection, Berlin. He studied at Bucerius Law School in Hamburg, Germany, and passed both State Exams in German Law (2011 and 2016). He was a PhD candidate and research and teaching assistant at Bucerius Law School, where he concentrated on the field of public international law, treaty law, interpretation, and conflict of norms. His present work concerns domestic and European migration and asylum law.

Güneş Ünüvar is a Senior Research Fellow at Max Planck Institute for International, European and Regulatory Procedural Law in Luxembourg, and Of Counsel at Özgür Ünüvar Bakiler Attorney Partnership in Ankara, Turkey. He obtained his PhD in 2016 from the University of Copenhagen, and his LLM from Vrije Universiteit Brussel in 2012. He was a Carlsberg Foundation Postdoctoral Research Fellow at the Centre of Excellence for International Courts (iCourts) at the Faculty of Law of the University of Copenhagen (2017–2021), and Visiting Research Fellow at Columbia Law School (2016). His research focuses on international economic adjudication, with a particular focus on international investment law and its *raison d'etre*.

Jaroslav Větrovský is an Assistant Professor of International Law at the University of West Bohemia, Faculty of Law, the Czech Republic. He holds a Master's degree in Law (University of West Bohemia, 2005), Human Rights Law (University of Strasbourg, 2008), and Ph.D. in International Law (Pan-European University, 2012). His present research focuses on general concepts of public international law and their intersections with 20th century philosophical ideas and movements (analytical philosophy, phenomenology, philosophy of mind). His recent publications include a study on intentionality in international criminal law entitled '*Mens Rea*, Intentionality and Wittgenstein's Philosophy of Psychology' (*Philosophical Foundations of International Criminal Law: Correlating Thinkers.* Eds. M. Bergsmo and E. J. Buis, Torkel Opsahl Academic EPublisher, 2018).

Bartosz Wojciechowski is an Associate Professor at the University of Łódź, Director of the Center for Theory and Philosophy of Human Rights, and a member of the editorial boards of *International Journal for the Semiotics of Law* (Springer), *The Intellectum: A Journal of Generating Understanding* (Greece), *Przegląd Sejmowy* (the journal of the Sejm of the Republic of Poland), and *Folia Iuridica Universitatis Lodziensis*. He is an international expert in the EU-funded project 'Pravo-Justice' (European Justice for Ukraine) and a judge of the Supreme Administrative Court (head of the Faculty of European Law). He has published several co-edited books, as well as articles on legal interpretation, judicial discretion, interculturality, and morality of law.

Ezgi Yildiz works at the Global Governance Center at the Graduate Institute, Geneva, as a Senior Researcher for the project Paths of International Law: Stability and Change in the International Legal Order (PATHS), funded by the European Research Council. She holds a PhD in International Relations with a Minor in International Law (*summa cum laude avec félicitations du jury*) from the Graduate

Institute, Geneva. She conducts interdisciplinary research on international relations and international law, and specializes in international courts, human rights, and ocean governance. Prior to joining the PATHS team, she was a Postdoctoral Fellow at the Carr Center for Human Rights Policy at Harvard Kennedy School and a Visiting Fellow at the Minda de Gunzburg Center for European Studies at Harvard University. Her forthcoming book *Between Forbearance and Audacity: How the European Court Redefined the Norm Against Torture and Inhuman or Degrading Treatment* will appear with Cambridge University Press in 2022. She has published several articles in, inter alia, *European Journal of International Law, Temple International and Comparative Law Journal,* and *Journal of Human Rights Practice.*

Introduction

The dynamics of law and language in the interpretation of international legal sources

ANNE LISE KJÆR AND JOANNA LAM

I.1. Introduction

Legal interpretation has occupied legal practice and theory for centuries. Ever since Plato's *Laws*, the question of what the law is—and who or what determines the meaning of laws—has been one of the central issues of legal philosophy. In the history of legal theory, the answers to those questions have differed, with emphasis either on the legislator, the text, or the judge, reflecting also the different methods of interpretation adopted in the different legal cultures of the world.

Recent scholarly developments in law's neighbour disciplines have brought about changes in the understanding of legal interpretation. The linguistic turn in philosophy of the twentieth century, as well as pragmatist trends in contemporary linguistic research, focusing on the interpreters' reception and application of the legislative text rather than its content, has significantly changed the theory of interpretation. The emergence of new streams within social and cultural studies pointing to the importance of the context of any interpretive event has also significantly influenced the approaches, methods, and imagery adopted by legal practitioners and scholars interested in the issue of legal interpretation.

Until recently the linguistic turn has not affected the theory and practice of international law and international courts, which have maintained a predominantly positivist interpretive tradition.[1] However, this has gradually changed over the past decades with the new types of challenges for adjudicators that intensifying globalization processes in law have created. The changes are observable on the

[1] See, similarly, Daniel Peat and Matthew Windsor: 'Playing the Game of Interpretation. On Meaning and Metaphor in International Law', in Andrea Bianchi, Daniel Peat, and Matthew Windsor, eds., *Interpretation in International Law* (2015), 3.

Anne Lise Kjær and Joanna Lam, *Introduction* In: *Language and Legal Interpretation in International Law.*
Edited by: Anne Lise Kjær and Joanna Lam, Oxford University Press. © Oxford University Press 2022.
DOI: 10.1093/oso/9780190855208.003.0001

institutional level, with an increasing proliferation of international courts and tribunals acting in contexts which are politically and legally less well-defined than in case of national courts. The vague legislative basis of adjudication has forced international judges and arbitrators to take on the role of legislators who, to a certain extent, establish legal rules and principles themselves while deciding cases brought before them.

Besides the judicial activism and the dynamic interpretation style (that have turned international adjudicators into writers rather than readers of the law), globalization has also affected the practice of legal interpretation in other ways. Acting across a multiplicity of languages and legal traditions, comparative law, legal translation, and multilingual interpretation have become necessary elements in the interpretive practice of international courts and tribunals.

The purpose of this book is to cast light on the workings of language in international legal interpretation in the context of contemporary processes of globalization. We take an explicit interdisciplinary perspective, which includes both legal theories of interpretation and linguistic theories of meaning, and both legal philosophy and the philosophy of language. This book treats the subject as it appears within and across different legal fields—international economic law, human rights law and international criminal law, EU law, and international arbitration. It also includes more general perspectives on international legal interpretation, among them comparative law, multilingualism, and legal translation.

The intended audience is a readership consisting of both lawyers and linguists interested in the workings of language in law and legal interpretation—or, in other words, the growing disciplinary fields of legal linguistics, legal rhetoric, and legal semiotics. Academics specializing in international law, as well as practitioners faced with the challenges and changes of globalization processes, belong to the audience as well.

I.2. Language, translation, and multilingual interpretation in international law

The relationship between language and law is regularly described as one of dependency: 'Law is a profession of words', as David Mellinkoff famously wrote in the preface of his book *The Language of the Law* (1963).[2] 'Most of the encounters that we have with the law are language events: meetings and interactions with lawyers, confrontations with the police, appearances in court.'[3] Add a philosophical

[2] David Melinkoff, *The Language of the Law* (1963).

[3] Michael Freeman and Fiona Smith, 'Law and Language: An Introduction', in Michael Freeman and Fiona Smith, eds., *Law and Language: Current Legal Issues* (2013), 7.

perspective, '[l]aw is guidance through language, whether the language of statutes, judicial decisions, constitutional provisions, contracts, or wills',[4] and you can easily conclude that the '[p]airing of language and law seems so natural'.[5]

The study of language and law as a separate discipline is young. David Mellinkoff counts as one of the first authors investigating legal language systematically forty-five years ago.[6] The more recent blossoming of interest in the field has been triggered by, among other things, 'the rise of interdisciplinary work in the study of law' and the 'tremendous foothold that linguistics has taken in the intellectual world'—that is, by the linguistic turn in the social sciences.[7]

With widespread international cooperation and the globalization of the economy, law today transgresses not only the boundaries of national legal systems but also the languages in which concepts and rules law are expressed. Consequently, issues of legal translation and linguistic diversity penetrate the everyday practice of many lawyers, even within the confines of their domestic legal systems. When national lawyers apply legal texts phrased in languages other than their own, they are confronted with the difficulties of interlingual understanding, and when they interpret legislative texts set up in more than one official language, they have to deal with the pitfalls of multilingual interpretation.

Thus, with globalization, translation of legal texts, as well as multilingual interpretation, has become essential to the practice of law. This is why in the present book we investigate legal interpretation of international law also from the point of view of language, translation, and multilingualism.

I.2.1. Language and legal interpretation

Some legal systems traditionally attach more importance to the language and wording of legislative texts than others. In common law jurisdictions, the plain meaning rule (or literal rule) dictates that judges rely on a non-contextual understanding of the language used in legal texts, the idea being that when the text is unambiguous, the words are to be interpreted according to their ordinary meaning.[8] Similarly, the canons of interpretation in civil law traditions, when strictly followed, require the interpreter to take his or her starting point in the text as it is worded, before the context, history, and purpose of the legislative text are considered.[9] Even if

[4] Brian Bix, 'Legal Interpretation and the Philosophy of Language', in Lawrence Solan and Peter Tiersma, eds., *The Oxford Handbook of Language and Law* (2012), 145.

[5] Lawrence Solan and Peter Tiersma, 'Introduction', in Lawrence Solan and Peter Tiersma, eds., *The Oxford Handbook of Language and Law* (2012), 1.

[6] Freeman and Smith, 'Law and Language', 1.

[7] Solan and Tiersma, 'Introduction', 1.

[8] Freeman and Smith, 'Law and Language', 5.

[9] Winfried Brugger, 'Legal Interpretation, Schools of Jurisprudence, and Anthrophology: Some Remarks from a German Point of View', *The American Journal of Comparative Law*, 42 (1994), 395, 396.

considerable differences exist between German and French law, it is safe to say that, theoretically, judges in both systems are generally bound by the language of the text, unless it is unclear or its application would lead to absurd results.[10]

In Scandinavian legal systems, interpreters traditionally rely more on the intent of the legislator as expressed in the *travaux préparatoires*, and a pragmatic approach to legal interpretation is dominant. In the words of Zweigert and Kötz, 'the realism of Scandinavian lawyers and their sound sense of what is useful and necessary in practice'[11] set Scandinavian legal systems apart from the civil law systems of the European continent. What matters to Scandinavian legal interpreters is whether or not the solution to the legal issue at hand is reasonable and effective, not the exact wording of the legislative text.

However, in legal practice lawyers and judges across legal traditions mostly include aspects other than the strict wording of the legislative text in their interpretative endeavour, and the theoretical differences between them are less obvious on a practical level. For example, Bell, an English legal scholar, has studied deliberations of judges in French courts and concluded that English law and French law may not be so different after all.[12] What ties together the interpretation practice of judges is that they are more interested in reaching a conclusion than in studying in a systematic manner the linguistic features (wording and grammar) of the legal texts.

Paradoxically, one can assert that the language of legal texts attracts the interpreter's attention only when it is unclear, thus making room for multiple interpretations or not making sense at all. When unclear, the language of the law ceases to be law's silent companion and becomes the subject of dispute, rather than being the source that enables the interpreter to resolve a dispute. In such cases, interpreters may still believe that a smooth functioning of the relationship between language and law is the rule, admitting that errors and intentional vagueness do occur, but otherwise sticking to the idea that language is a reliable medium through which law can be expressed.

However, in multilingual legal systems, when unclarity is regularly caused by divergence between language versions, even though each of them are phrased clearly, blind trust in the text is challenged. This is why, in this book on interpretation in international law, it is necessary to include a linguistic perspective on legal interpretation. Language scholars, being specialists in the workings of language, shed light on the reasons why language is not a mere instrument that lends itself to automatic text production and text reception. All language use is inherently interpretive, but

[10] Claire M. Germain, 'Approaches to Statutory Interpretation and Legislative History in France', *Duke Journal of Comparative & International Law*, 13 (2003), 195, 201.

[11] Konrad Zweigert and Heinz Kötz, *An Introduction to Comparative Law*, tr. Tony Weir (3rd edn, 1995), 285.

[12] John Bell, 'English Law and French Law—Not so Different?', *Current Legal Problems*, 48 (1995), 63–101.

as famously stated by Gadamer in his seminal book *Truth and Method*, interpretation across linguistic differences illustrates this more convincingly than interpretive endeavours in monolingual encounters: 'Where a translation is necessary, the gap between the spirit of the original words and that of their reproduction must be taken into account. It is a gap that can never be completely closed.'[13]

I.2.2. Language and translation in international law

In monolingual legal contexts, especially within the confines of culturally homogenous legal systems, the idea that there is a 1:1 relationship between language and law can more easily be upheld than in multilingual legal systems that cross cultures. Once law must be expressed in more than one language, it turns out that the interaction between law and language is more complicated than a monolingual outlook can lead one to assume. Legal languages are not nomenclatures which can name legal concepts uniformly across the socio-political and cultural contexts in which they are rooted. This is why congruence between the language versions of multilingual legal texts is an ideal which cannot be achieved. Moreover, when legislative drafting requires translation from one legal language into another, the drafter is faced with the fundamental problem which has preoccupied Western translation scholars for centuries (at least since Cicero, see Robinson[14]): should one translate the text in a manner that ensures fidelity to the source language (SL) or rather translate in accordance with the conventions of the target language (TL) to ensure the comprehensibility of the text to the target language audience?

Most translation scholars support TL orientation—see, for example, the work by Susan Šarčević[15]—whereas Baaij[16] recommends SL orientation. However, the choice between TL and SL orientation does not solve the special problem of multilingual law, viz. that all language versions of legislative texts are equipped with equal authenticity, and none of them are to be considered to be the source language version. From the point of view of translation theory, one could even claim that translation of EU law is not translation at all[17] and that the differences between source and target language conventions are irrelevant for determining the legal meaning, which must be attached to all language versions uniformly.[18]

[13] Hans-Georg Gadamer, *Truth and Method* (2006), 386.

[14] Douglas Robinson, *Western Translation Theory from Herodotus to Cierco* (2014).

[15] See especially Susan Šarčević, *New Approach to Legal Translation* (1997).

[16] Cornelis J. W. Baaij, *Legal Integration and Language Diversity: Rethinking Translation in EU Lawmaking* (2018).

[17] Anne Lise Kjær, 'Legal Translation in the European Union: A Research Field in Need of a New Approach', in Krzysztof Kredens and Stanislaw Gozdz-Roszkowski, ed., *Language and the Law: International Outlooks* (2007), 69–95.

[18] Anne Lise Kjær, 'Nonsense: The CILFIT Criteria Revisited from the Perspective of Legal Linguistics', in Henning Koch Ulrich Haltern, and Joseph H. H. Weiler, eds., *Europe: The New Legal*

When one considers the difficult relationship between law and language in the drafting and interpretation of EU law, it becomes apparent that the division of labour between lawyers and linguists is not as straightforward as one would think. The common understanding among linguists is that they are dealing with the language of legal texts, not with the legal norms laid down by the texts. The common expectation among lawyers is that translators provide a copy of a legal text in another language without changing the meaning of the text. In other words, linguists translate language; lawyers interpret law. Lawyers are engaged with the meaning of law, translators merely with the language of law.

However, this is a false distinction. As the example of EU law shows, one might just as well claim the opposite of the common understanding: linguists translate legal meaning; lawyers interpret legal language. Thus, McAuliffe adequately describes the *hybridization* of law and language that results from the peculiarities of translation and interpretation in EU law:

> While it is accepted that there is approximation involved in translation and thus in EU law, it is also accepted that those who use that law will acknowledge that exact transpositions of concepts are impossible to achieve, yet will understand the 'EU meaning' of those concepts—that is, EU law is, quite simply, a new legal language.[19]

Ultimately, the hybridization of law and language in EU law entails a shift in the way one can understand the interdependency of law and language and the relationship between translation and interpretation. Language *creates* law, the use of linguistic formulas transforms case-law into 'law',[20] and prior linguistic choices and linguistic precedent[21] determine the way EU legislation and EU judgments may be translated and interpreted.

I.2.3. Language and multilingual interpretation

Article 33 of the Vienna Convention on the Law of Treaties determines the rules of interpretation of treaties authenticated in two or more languages. The basic

Realism: Essays in Honour of Hjalte Rasmussen (2010), 297–316; Anne Lise Kjær, 'The Theoretical Perspectives of Legal Translation in the EU: The Paradoxical Relationship between Language, Translation, and the Autonomy of EU law', in Susan Šarčević, ed., *Language and Culture in EU Law: Multidisciplinary Perspectives* (2015), 91–107.

[19] Karen McAuliffe, 'Translation at the Court of Justice of the European Communities', in Frances Olsen, Alexander Lorz, and Dieter Stein, eds., *Translation Issues in Language and Law* (2009), 106.

[20] Urška, Šadl, 'Case—Case-law—Law: Ruiz Zambrano as an Illustration of How the Court of Justice of the European Union Constructs Its Legal Arguments', *European Constitutional Law Review*, 9 (2013), 205.

[21] Karen McAuliffe, 'Precedent at the Court of Justice of the European Union: The Linguistic Aspect', in Michael Freeman and Fiona Smith, eds., *Law and Language: Current Legal Issues* (2013), 483–93.

principle is that all texts are equally authoritative, and that none of them prevails in case of divergence between them. Moreover, if the texts diverge, the meaning which best reconciles the texts, 'having regard to the object and purpose of the treaty', shall be adopted. The Vienna Convention thus prescribes a combination of the textual and teleological interpretation methods.

In an early study on multilingualism in international law, Tabory[22] comprehensively analysed the development of multilingualism during the twentieth century and discussed some of the problems of multilingual interpretation which were not covered by the final wording of the Vienna Convention. Though discussed during the debates in the Internal Law Commission drafting the convention, no clear answer was given in the final text to the question of comparison of the official language versions: can the interpreter rely only on one language version or is he or she obliged always to consult all language versions?[23]

Multilingual interpretation has attracted increasing attention during the past decades, and due to the conspicous linguistic regime of the EU, with twenty-four official languages, interpretation of EU legislation has been subject to extensive scrutiny. Fascination with the EU's multilingualism has been spurred by the Court of Justice of the European Union's own case law governing the interpretation of EU law. In the well-known *CILFIT* judgment, para. 18–19, the court indirectly gives an answer to the question asked by Tabory and takes it a step further.

In the *CILFIT* judgment the Court states that the characteristic features of community law as a supranational legal order in its own right gives rise to particular difficulties which national courts have to take into account when they tend to believe that the text of an EU provision is clear. On the one hand, interpretation of community law provisions involves a comparison of the different language versions and, on the other hand, the concepts and terminology used in community law differ from those used in the law of the member states. The equal authenticity of the language versions, combined with the unity and uniqueness of EU law, causes an interpretive puzzle. National interpreters are obliged to attach meaning to the texts of community law *above* any of the language versions and *without* paying attention to the wording in any of them (for an in-depth analysis of the *CILFIT* judgment, see, for example, Rasmussen, Van Calster, and Kjær[24]).

Among many other important works on multilingualism and multilingual interpretation in EU law, the interdisciplinary studies by the Scandinavian researchers Paunio[25] and Derlén[26] should be highlighted. Both studies are doctoral theses that

[22] Mala Tabory, *Multilingualism in International Law and Institutions* (Sijthoff & Noordhoff, 1980).

[23] Tabory, *Multilingualism*, 195ff.

[24] Hjalte Rasmussen, 'The European Court's Acte clair Strategy in C.I.L.F.I.T or: "Acte clair, of course!" But What Does It Mean?' *European Law Review*, 9 (1984), 242; Geert van Calster, 'The EU's Tower of Babel—The Interpretation of Multilingual Texts by the European Court of Justice', in Ami Barav and Derrick Wyatt, eds., *Yearbook of European Law—1997* (1997); Kjær, 'Nonsense'.

[25] Elina Paunio, *Legal Certainty in Multilingual EU Law: Language, Discourse and Reasoning at the European Court of Justice* (2013).

[26] Mattias Derlén, *Multilingual Interpretation of European Union Law* (2009).

integrate knowledge from several disciplinary domains in their analyses of multilingual interpretation. While Derlén focuses on the extent to which national courts consider all language versions when interpreting EU law—as required by the Court of Justice of the European Union in the *CLIFIT* judgment—Paunio is interested in formulating a theory that can explain why the language communities of the member states trust and accept EU law in spite of the uncertainty caused by its multilingualism.

In a review article, Bengoetxea pertinently described the consequences of multilingualism for legal interpretation:

> The legal text, the provision, contains norm candidates, and the interpretation determines the norm for the instant case. This theory [the 'no ordinary meaning' thesis] is much clearer in multilingual law, where the different language versions can potentially contain different norms, but a common, shared, harmonised or superimposed meaning is extracted from them all to create the EU norm.[27]

At the end of the day, multilingualism forces the interpreter to reflect on the language of law and the extent to which it is possible to depend on it when interpreting a piece of legislation. The choice between *Text* or *Telos* becomes more urgent when the language versions of the text points in different directions. You cannot *not* rely on the language of the text—but you cannot trust it either! Or, as Leung puts it in a recent book on legal multilingualism, the only certain thing about interpretation of multilingual legislation, is its uncertainty.[28]

I.3. Theories of legal interpretation and international law

I.3.1. The shifting paradigm of legal interpretation: From the syllogistic model to the dynamic theories of legal interpretation

The linguistic turn, initiated in the twentieth century, has resonated strongly with legal studies, leading to formulation and reformulation of a number of theories, aimed at capturing the particular importance of the law as a phenomenon functioning within and through language. The conceptual development and

[27] Joxerramon Bengoetxea, 'Text and Telos in the European Court of Justice. Four Recent Tales on the Legal Reasoning of the ECJ', *European Constitutional Law Review*, 11 (2015), 184, 209.

[28] Janny H. C. Leung, *Shallow Equality and Symbolic Jurisprudence in Multilingual Legal Orders* (2019), 183.

proliferation of various approaches to law as a linguistic phenomenon have been particularly visible in the field of legal interpretation. Processes of legal interpretation have always been perceived as critical to the social functioning of the law. In particular, such interpretive processes which lead to binding outcomes, that is, those that form a part of adjudicatory activity, have for centuries been acknowledged as essential in this regard.

This well-established perception of legal interpretation as a crucial component of adjudicatory activity has led many theorists to focus on safeguards, which should be provided and observed in order to eliminate the arbitrariness of this process and the resulting threat to such values as legal certainty and predictability. In continental legal doctrine, this has been famously expressed by Charles Montesquieu, who postulated that judges should serve merely as 'the mouth that pronounces the words of the law'[29] not bestowed with powers to alter its content or impact. In this approach, the role of judges is perceived as ceremonial and elevated, but also passive (Montesquieu characterized them as 'inanimate beings'[30]).

The Montesquieuan approach, embedded in his doctrine of strong separation of powers within the state, seeks to minimize adjudicatory discretion. It has served as a point of reference for a number of syllogistic theories of legal interpretation, which perceive processes of legal rendition as a series of formalized operations, aimed at the discovery of the objectively existing 'true meaning' of the text of legal instrument. This is followed by the transmission of the discovered meaning to the disputants and to non-parties of the dispute (i.e. to the society). The described process is not conducted in a free manner, but guided by a set of authoritative, interpretative directives, organized in a hierarchical way, so as to ensure stability and accuracy of the procedure, as well as its standardization (allowing for repetition of both the process and the results, and hence increasing legal certainty).

Similar concepts of legal interpretation, perceiving it as a heavily guided path to uncovering the actual meaning of legal text, have also been formulated under other sets of philosophical assumptions. In the common law tradition, the doctrine of legal textualism, developed on the basis of US constitutional law, has been highly influential. Syllogistic models of legal interpretation, based on the discovery of the ordinary meaning of legal text (and allowing for a number of authorized deviations therefrom), along with relevant sets of interpretive directives and guidelines, have also been created under the auspices of legal positivism. Finally, it has also been argued that the theories aimed at discovery of the 'true meaning' of a legal instrument (existing independently from the interpreter) include not only textual models but also intentionalist ones, in which the original object to be discovered and conveyed to the audience is the will of the legislator.

[29] Charles de Secondat Montesquieu *The Spirit of the Laws* (1989), 163.

[30] Montesquieu, *The Spirit of the Laws*.

The persisting popularity of the syllogistic models of legal interpretation has been attributed to their suggested ease of practical application: the adjudicator performing a series of predetermined operations is presumed to arrive at the desired goal. However, many commentators have raised objections, based on the inaccuracy of such depictions of textual interpretative processes in general, and legal interpretation in particular, as potentially largely mechanical. They have also argued that such representations of interpretative activity are indeed counterfactual, as adjudicators rarely choose to rely on the outcomes of the primarily positive application of the main guiding principles without checking the results (and potentially modifying influence) of other interpretive considerations.

These reservations have served as a basis for a number of theories of legal interpretation, which assume a non-syllogistic, dynamic character to the process. This group of theories, as emphasized by Eskridge, Frickey, and Garret,[31] focuses on legal interpretation as a process of meaning-making, in which the role of adjudicator is not reduced to serving merely as a vehicle for the pre-existing meaning of the norms. The acknowledgement of discursive character of legal interpretation has been expressed by theorists representing such diverse streams of legal theory as hermeneutics, analytical jurisprudence, jurislinguistics, and deconstructivism. The roots of these approaches have been sought in the nineteenth-century German legal historical school and the concept of *Rechtsfindung*, opposing the Montesquieuan, textual ideal of legal exegesis.[32] The linguistic turn in twentieth-century philosophy and jurisprudence, the expansion of studies on openness of language, and the development of semiotics have brought further inspirations to this field.

I.3.2. Legal interpretation in international adjudication

The significant growth of interest in legal interpretation in the twentieth century originated in studies of national courts and reflections on the role of the judge in the domestic context. In the historical perspective, arguments have also been raised about systemic and institutional particularities, leading to differences between the French school of legal exegesis and the German contextual approach, or between the civil law and common law interpretive approaches. However, the expansion of international law and of international adjudicatory institutions after World War II has added a new, notable dimension to studies on legal interpretation. On many occasions, the echoes of debates, conducted in the domestic context about the desired nature of legal interpretation, can also be found in international adjudication, where the sequentialist approach to the application of Article 31.1 of the

[31] William Eskridge Jr., Philip Frickey and Elizabeth Garrett, *Legislation and Statutory Interpretation* (2000), 211ff.

[32] Hugues Rabault, *L'interprétation des normes: l'objectivité de la méthode* (1997), 10.

Vienna Convention on the Law of Treaties (VCLT) has been contrasted with a holistic one.[33] However, processes of legal interpretation conducted by international courts and tribunals (ICTs) cannot be reduced to a simple transfer of techniques, methods and approaches developed in the national context.

The common will of the states plays a decisive role in the creation of instruments of public international law, as well as in the establishment and upkeep of ICTs. As Ingo Venzke remarks, this 'myth of origin',

> the common narrative according to which international law owes its existence and normativity to the consent of its subjects, serves as a crucial, primary source of legitimacy for the ICTs. At the same time, the embedment of the ICTs in non-national sources should be emphasised, as the powers of international courts (including competences for conducting legal interpretation) are allocated in international treaties.[34]

In this regard, international commercial arbitration (ICA), driven and institutionalized primarily by private actors, as well as investor-state arbitration (ISDS) of a mixed, public-private character, should be noted as areas where the abovementioned 'myth of origin' by consent of the states functions in a specific manner. It is, however, not absent from these fields[35] and, as recent projects, such as the establishment of a Multilateral Investment Court (to replace the dispersed system of ad hoc investor-state arbitration) demonstrate, it may also be of growing importance. It is indeed the postulated reform of ISDS that has led commentators to consider, to what extent the establishment of an international court for investor-state disputes would increase uniformity and coherence of legal interpretation in this field and—as a consequence—lead to higher legal certainty.[36]

[33] Laura Nielsen, *The WTO, Animals, and PPMs* (2007), 200–1. See also in general Evandro Menezes de Carvalho, *Semiotics of International Law: Trade and Translation* (2011).

[34] Ingo Venzke, *How Interpretation Makes International Law: On Semantic Change and Normative Twists* (2012).

[35] Emmanuel Gaillard, *Legal Theory of International Arbitration* (2010), 25; Joanna Jemielniak, *Legal Interpretation in International Commercial Arbitration* (2014), 211ff.

[36] See, for example, Susan D Franck, 'The Legitimacy Crisis in Investment Treaty Arbitration: Privatizing Public International Law Through Inconsistent Decisions', *Fordham Law Review* 73 (2005), 1521; Andreas Bucher, 'Is There a Need to Establish a Permanent Reviewing Body?', in Emmanuel Gaillard, ed., *The Review of International Arbitral Awards* (2008), 285; Benedict Kingsbury and Stephan Schill, 'Investor-State Arbitration as Governance: Fair and Equitable Treatment, Proportionality, and the Emerging Global Administrative Law', in A. J. Van den Berg, ed., *50 Years of the New York Convention* (2010), 18; Shai Dothan and Joanna Lam, 'A Paradigm Shift? Arbitration and Court-Like Mechanisms in Investors' Disputes', in Güneş Ünüvar, Joanna Lam, and Shai Dothan, eds., *Permanent Investment Courts: The European Experiment. European Yearbook of International Economic Law* (2020), 19.

I.3.3. Legal interpretation and autonomization of international courts and tribunals

The role played by ICTs in promoting uniformity of legal interpretation in supranational, regional, and international settings has been long acknowledged by commentators. Whereas these adjudicatory bodies have acquired notable autonomy in developing and promoting universalizing tendencies in legal interpretation, their interplay with national courts is a nuanced process, which cannot be characterized as imposing interpretative preferences onto domestic institutions in regard to the interpretation of national law. As explained in the context of the European Court of Human Rights (ECtHR) and the CJEU, this can be attributed to diversity of means by which enforcement of international obligations can be achieved, and to interpretative discretion, which national courts retain in this regard:

> The subsidiarity of international scrutiny of human rights, the national margin of appreciation, procedural autonomy of national legal orders, all these are mechanisms of international adjudication allowing national courts to keep control over the process of interpreting national law.[37]

As noted above in the context of the postulated ISDS reform, the use of legal interpretation as an instrument of growing autonomization of ICTs, and as a token of their independence from immediate political influences, has been an object of praise. This interpretative autonomy and the 'semantic authority'[38] of international adjudicatory institutions have been acknowledged as factors stabilizing the international legal order. However, this is not necessarily a commonly shared perspective, as recent years have also brought a backlash against international courts, as well as such anti-institutional actions as the obstruction of appointments to the Appellate Body of the World Trade Organization (WTO AB) by the United States, effectively disabling the WTO AB. The notable scope of interpretive autonomy, acquired by international courts, may be difficult to reconcile with resistance against supranational legal orders and multilateral initiatives. The ICTs' 'myth of origin', rooted in the consent of international community, and giving way to the further, autonomous growth of these institutions, has thus been seriously challenged.

I.4. Structure of the book

The present book addresses the phenomena described above by demonstrating how ICTs in different areas of law conduct processes of legal interpretation, what tools

[37] Joanna Jemielniak and Przemysław Mikłaszewicz, 'Capturing the Change: Universalising Tendencies in Legal Interpretation', in Joanna Jimielniak and Przemysław Mikłaszewicz, eds., *Interpretation of Law in the Global World: From Particularism to a Universal Approach* (2010), 2.

[38] Venzke, *How Interpretation Makes International Law.*

they use to this end and how said processes further resonate with different groups of actors: the disputants, the states, the domestic courts, the international community. It examines methods and directives of legal interpretation used by the courts and scrutinizes whether their development relates to the interpretative repertory, applied in the domestic setting, and to what extent international adjudicatory bodies have indeed established original tools for conducting legal interpretation.

The book is subdivided into three parts. The individual parts and chapters of the book cover different aspects of the interpretation of international law. Together, they form a coherent whole ensured with a shared focus on the linguistic turn in interpretation theory: interpretation as a discourse practice performed by judges in language and on the basis of language.

Part I consists of papers that treat legal interpretation from the perspective of language theories and is subdivided into two subparts: Part I.1, which is concerned with defining what legal interpretation is; and Part I.2, which deals with legal interpretation as a discursive practice performed by judges. Part II takes the linguistic turn in interpretation theory a step further and focuses on the role that multilingualism and translation have for interpretation in international law. Finally, Part III covers interpretation theory and practice in specific areas of international law (commercial law, trade law, human rights law, and international criminal law), thus elucidating the influence that diverse legal contexts have on interpretation issues.

Each part consists of chapters written by highly profiled researchers with outstanding positions in their respective research fields and by talented young scholars who are in the beginning of their careers but whom the editors count as rising stars.

I.4.1. Part I: Theoretical perspectives

I.4.1.1. What is legal interpretation? International legal interpretation between law and legal discourse

The chapters in this part provide theoretical insights into different aspects of interpretive activity in the context of adjudication. The perspectives of domestic courts, international arbitration, and international courts are represented to offer a nuanced view of challenges that these adjudicatory bodies face in the interpretation of internationally shared legal concepts.

Tomasz Stawecki is professor at the Faculty of Law and Administration, University of Warsaw, and a renowned expert in the field of legal theory. He combines academic expertise with ajudicatory experience as a judge at the Voivodship Administrative Court in Warsaw. In his chapter he discusses a non-obvious concept of 'Legal interpretation as a solution to disputes over the validity of laws.' Stawecki argues that, while *prima facie* distinct, the issues of legal interpretation cannot be separated from the problems of validity of the law, for several reasons. He demonstrates how both matters are interconnected at the level of theoretical discourse, as can be seen in debates on, *inter alia,* what the law is, how it should be applied by the courts, and what the source of obligation to observe it is. Stawecki also discusses how both sets of considerations are present in adjudicatory practice. He further examines whether theoretical concepts developed in this regard on the grounds of domestic judicial practices can be applied in the context of international courts and tribunals.

The problems of adjudication in an international setting lie at the core of the chapter by *Adam Dyrda and Tomasz Gizbert-Studnicki*, professors of legal theory at the Faculty of Law and Administration of the Jagiellonian University. In their chapter, entitled 'Do legal concepts travel?', the authors explore the functional aspects of such basic legal concepts as 'ownership', 'contract', and 'negligence', which they characterize as substantive multicultural concepts (SMCs). By exploring the field of international commercial arbitration, they observe that despite essential differences between various legal systems, lawyers from diverse jurisdictions are nevertheless successful in using SMCs in mutual communication. Dyrda and Gizbert-Studnicki formulate four hypotheses to explain this phenomenon, by pointing to such factors as the reliance of certain SMCs on supranational standards; the transfer of some SMCs to *lex mercatoria* from domestic legislation; the relative lack of determinacy by other, domestically embedded legal concepts in the case of some SMCs; and the orientation towards the (shared) outcome of application of the SMCs rather than towards differences in their conceptual grounding.

Marcin Matczak is professor of legal theory at the University of Warsaw with years of experience as a practising lawyer. The resulting deep understanding of processes of adjudication permeates his chapter 'The semantics of openness: Why references to foreign judicial decisions do not infringe the sovereignty of national legal systems'. In it, Matczak identifies a notable gap between legal theory and domestic adjudicatory practice. He challenges the popular view that, as national law is an outcome of sovereign lawmaking activity, its interpretation should not be affected by foreign judicial decisions. The author confronts this theory with the adjudicatory practice of citing foreign decisions, widespread among municipal courts in different states. Matczak's response to this evident disparity is a proposal to replace the prevalent, author-centred semantic internalism, focusing on the intention of the specific, domestic lawmaker. He proposes to apply instead the theory of semantic externalism, pursuant to which meaning is sought in the relationship between language and external reality. He also argues that this theoretical perspective offers a common epistemological platform for adjudicatory practices in various states, as well as allows for an explanation of the practices of judicial citations across jurisdictions.

In the chapter 'Who forges the tools? The methods of interpretation between interpretive discourse and positive norms of law', the author *Julian Udich*, affiliated with the German Federal Ministry of Justice and Bucerius Law School, explores the problem of establishing an accepted set of methods of interpretation of public international law, as commonly recognized instruments for construing the meaning of its norms. Udich acknowledges the role of interpretive rules enshrined in Articles 31–33 of the VCLT in this regard, but he also points to their limitations (such as the non-exhaustive character of the list or the lack of information on interrelations between the methods). The author seeks to address this lacuna and proposes to treat the methods of interpretation 'not as norms, but as the result of a meta-discourse accompanying any interpretation of norms of PIL'. To this end, he examines various aspects of the functioning of said discourse and highlights the influence of ICTs in different interpretive sub-systems.

I.4.1.2. Who does legal interpretation? Legal interpretation as judicial activity

This part of the book focuses on the functional aspects of legal interpretation as an integral part of decision-making processes conducted by adjudicators. The chapters discuss interpretive approaches and techniques adopted by judges, and formulate theoretical proposals for setting the limits of judicial discretion in regard to legal interpretation.

Bartosz Wojciechowski combines academic expertise as professor of legal theory at the University of Łódź with adjudicatory practice as a judge of the Polish Supreme Administrative Court. This combination of theoretical and practical insight is visible in his chapter 'Balancing interpretation rules as the element of judicial discretion'. Wojciechowski focuses on vague legal terms and general clauses and argues that the process of the operative interpretation of these types of terms can serve as a model for balancing rules of interpretation (with the latter characterized as *the* exercise of judicial discretion). Acts of judicial discretion are presented as instances of legal interpretation essentially irreducible to the constraints of syllogistic models of interpretation. The author draws examples from case law analysis to argue that the transition from the simple, sequential approach to legal interpretation to the discursive model is indeed taking place. He also advocates a Dworkinian version of the latter, postulating the social awareness of a judge and his or her deep immersion in legal culture.

The issue of limits of judicial interpretation in regard to instruments of international law is the topic of the chapter authored by *Jaroslav Větrovský*, assistant professor of international law at the Faculty of Law, Pan-European University in Bratislava. Větrovský's paper is entitled 'Interpretation of international treaties and the role of Articles 31 and 32 of the Vienna Convention on the Law of Treaties: A Wittgensteinian perspective'. The author draws inspiration from late works of Ludwig Wittgenstein to approach the issue of treaty interpretation from a new angle. He employs concepts developed in Wittgensteinian philosophy of language. He, *inter alia*, refers to the concept of language-games in order to overcome the dichotomy of the concept of legal interpretation as a discovery of meaning of the legal text and that of legal interpretation understood as a process of creation of meaning.

I.4.2. Part II: Language and translation in the interpretation of international law

The chapters in this part elucidate the way the language and languages of legislation influence interpretation of law. The four chapters describe different aspects of the role that language and multilingualism in particular play in legal interpretation and reflect the disciplinary and cultural perspectives that the authors represent.

In *Lawrence M. Solan*'s chapter 'Interpreting multilingual laws: Some costs and benefits' his background as an American lawyer and a professor of law at an American law school clearly shapes his argument. While most European scholars tend to be concerned about the costs of multilingualism in the EU, especially with a view to legal certainty and predictability, Solan focuses on the benefits of multilingualism. His main argument is that multilingual laws help the interpreter in cases of doubt: when one language version is unclear, a comparison with the other language versions may cast light on the content that the legislature had in mind when drafting the law. As Solan puts it, 'the absence of a single text protects interpretation against judicial reliance on linguistic accidence'. Coming from a monolingual legal culture, it is clear to the reader that Solan envies his European Union colleagues that they can employ the method of 'Augustinian interpretation', as he calls it, that is, the possibility of comparing the language versions in order to identify the purpose of the law.

Martina Bajčić is an assistant professor at the Faculty of Law at the University of Riejeka and a linguist specializing in the field of terminology studies. In her chapter 'On the conceptualization of meaning in legal interpretation', her main objective is to show that a cognitive terminological approach can provide clarity to the process of legal interpretation. One of her main points is that the Court of Justice of the European Union (CJEU), when interpreting EU law, 'proceeds from the concept, and not from the term as its linguistic denotation' and generally relies on a prototype theory of meaning which recognizes the fuzzy nature of legal concepts and allows for a dynamic interpretation style. By doing so, the court avoids attaching too much weight to the terminology of the individual language versions of multilingual EU law and avoids favouring one language version over the others for the benefit of legal certainty.

Lucie Pacho Aljanati holds degrees in both law and legal translation. Her chapter 'Multilingual interpretation by the CJEU in the Area of Freedom, Security, and Justice' is a case study of the CJEU's application of multilingual interpretation in judgments belonging to one particular legal field (the Area of Freedom, Security and Justice). It turns out that the court applied multilingual interpretation in only ten out of the 177 judgments analysed (5.64% of the cases). Moreover, the court did not use comparison of the language versions in a consistent manner. Aljanati identifies three different purposes of comparison: (1) a comparison which treats divergence between the language versions as a problem of interpretation; (2) a comparison which uncovers divergence but does not treat it as a problem of interpretation; and (3) a comparison which concludes that even if the language versions are not divergent, a teleological interpretation is necessary to cope with the ambiguity of the text. As a translator, Aljanati's special interest is to identify instances of divergence between the language versions which are due to translation errors that could have been avoided.

In *Anne Lise Kjær*'s chapter, 'Translation of judgments of the European Court of Human Rights into non-official languages: The politics and practice of European multilingualism', the focus is on the inherent multilingualism of the European Human Rights System (the European Convention on Human Rights [ECHR] and the ECtHR). The judgments of the ECtHR are produced in the two official languages only, English and French. While multilingualism was never an issue in the discussions leading to the adoption of the ECHR, the founding fathers did have concerns about the implementation of the convention in the states. However, not until the beginning of the reform process at the turn of the century was translation of ECtHR judgments into non-official languages put on the agenda in the dialogue between the human rights system and the member states. It was introduced into the reform discourse under the heading of member states' implementation of the convention and their knowledge and understanding of the court's case law. The chapter traces the development of translation arguments in the reform discourse and discusses the possible reasons why translation into languages other than English and French was not an issue until the court faced challenges from the member states in the early 2000s.

I.4.3. Part III: Interpretation in special areas of international law

I.4.3.1. International Trade, Investment and Commercial Law

This part of the book discusses the role of interpretive activity in all three fields of international economic law (trade law; investment treaty law and arbitration; and international commercial law and arbitration). The chapters examine decision-making processes and case law in these respective fields to demonstrate how they have contributed to the development and consolidation of substantive norms in this quickly evolving area of international law.

The author of the next chapter, *Chang-fa Lo*, combines academic experience as professor at National Taiwan University with judicial practice in a national setting (as justice of the ROC Constitutional Court), as well as in an international one (as a WTO panellist). Lo's paper focuses on the issue of 'Fundamental values being introduced into the treaty interpretation process under the WTO beyond semantic finding of conveyed meaning'. He argues that in international law, legal interpretation should be guided not only by a search for linguistic and logical meaning of the text of the treaty but also by a set of fundamental values. Drawing examples from WTO case law, Lo demonstrates how such values (further categorized into internal/external values and domestic/universal ones) are used by interpreters. He also demonstrates how the inclusion of external values as interpretive considerations in the interpretation of international treaties (including the WTO agreements) is not only feasible and useful but also necessary and does not jeopardize legal predictability and certainty.

Joanna Lam's chapter 'Legal interpretation and adjudicatory activism in international commercial arbitration' discusses the issue of creative aspects of legal interpretation and limits thereof. The author is Professor WSR at iCourts and Director of Study Hub for International Economic Law and Development (SHIELD) at the Faculty of Law, University of Copenhagen. Her chapter examines the problem of 'adjudicatory activism', understood as reaching decisions by the courts and arbitral tribunals through a recourse to considerations lying outside the scope of applicable law (which can be done either as exercise of adjudicatory discretion or as act in excess of its limits). The research perspective of legal semiotics informs the chapter, and consequently the assumption that every process of legal interpretation is a process of meaning-making is adopted. In this vein, arbitral case law analysis is conducted, illustrating how exercises of adjudicatory activism by arbitrators have led to the formulation and consolidation of substantive rules.

Izabela Skoczeń is postdoctoral researcher at the Department of Legal Theory, Jagiellonian University, Krakow. Her chapter, entitled 'Is a legal implicature only in the eye of the beholder?', focuses on the problem of the interpretation and application of provisions of the 1980 Vienna Convention for the International Sale of Goods (CISG) in the adjudicatory practice of courts and arbitral tribunals. Skoczeń argues that linguistic arguments, used by the adjudicatory bodies in CISG cases, are adopted in a secondary manner, only after a general, politically oriented decision about the interpretive outcome has been reached (despite official claims to the contrary). In particular, the recourse to Article 8 of the CISG, as indicated by the courts and arbitral tribunals, serves a decorative function, and the choice of the CISG as governing law can be characterized as a conversational implicature in the sense proposed by Grice. The author claims that, while the official discourse of adjudicatory bodies is ostensibly consistent with the Gricean theory of communication, the described interpretive practice contradicts said theory.

The last chapter in this part examines the problem of the interpretation of one of the key principles in investment treaty law. Its author, *Güneş Ünüvar*, is a Senior Research Fellow at Max Planck Institute for International, European and Regulatory Procedural Law (Luxembourg). In 'The vague meaning of the Fair and Equitable Treatment principle in investment arbitration and new generation clarifications', Ünüvar demonstrates how the adjudicatory activity of arbitral tribunals has played a decisive role in shaping this (nowadays prevalent) legal standard. The author presents this gradual development and clarification of the Fair and Equitable Treatment (FET) principle as a context for further crystallization of this legal concept in 'new wave' free trade agreements, such as CETA. FET provisions in these agreements, in Ünüvar's opinion, constitute a new quality in investment treaty law and further enhance the coherence of the legal interpretation of the principle.

I.4.3.2. Human rights law and international criminal law

The two chapters in this section of the book illustrate that a proper understanding of legal interpretation in international law should include the broader sociopolitical and historical context in which a legislative text was drafted and interpreted across time and space. Thus, the papers show how the formal legal discourse of courts and tribunals is influenced over time by the discourses prevailing in other parts of society and how the formal legal discourse develops and changes accordingly.

Ezgi Yildiz, a political scientist and legal scholar, in her chapter 'Interpretative evolution of the norm prohibiting torture and inhuman or degrading treatment under the European Convention', traces the origin of two fundamental human rights norms. She shows how the evolution of the norms may be explained in a three-level contextual model comprising the sociopolitical context, the institutional set-up of the European Convention system and the prevailing view on torture at a given time. This contextual analysis of the ECtHR's interpretation of convention concepts reveals that the dynamic interpretation style of the court results in a transformation of the meaning of the concepts over time, but that the meaning does not develop in a linear progression.

In her chapter 'Crimes against women in armed conflicts: Judicial activism and feminist legal interpretation as key factors in the reconstruction of concepts of international humanitarian law', the lawyer and political scientist *Karolina Ristova-Aasterud* examines the development and reconstruction of the meaning of certain international humanitarian law concepts. She argues that the development can be explained by two factors: first, the judicial activism of the two ad hoc tribunals, the International Criminal Tribunal for the former Yugoslavia (ICTY) and the International Criminal Tribunal for Rwanda (ICTR); and second, the activism of the feminist 'interpretive community', which has organized a common fight against the gender bias in international humanitarian law. The main conclusion of the paper is to the effect that feminist discourse has had considerable impact on the semantic and conceptual understanding of crimes against women. However, the fight against gender bias has not yet been won, and Ristova-Aasterud concludes that the best safeguard against backlash is to maintain a fair gender representation in international courts.

References

Baaij, Cornelis J. W., *Legal Integration and Language Diversity: Rethinking Translation in EU Lawmaking* (Oxford, 2018).

Bell, John, 'English Law and French Law—Not so Different?', *Current Legal Problems*, 63 (1995).

Bengoetxea, Joxerramon, 'Text and Telos in the European Court of Justice. Four Recent Tales on the Legal Reasoning of the ECJ', *European Constitutional Law Review*, 11 (2015), 184–216.

Bix, Brian, 'Legal Interpretation and the Philosophy of Language', in Lawrence Solan and Peter Tiersma, eds., *The Oxford Handbook to Language and Law* (Oxford, 2012), 145.

Brugger, W., 'Legal Interpretation, Schools of Jurisprudence, and Anthrophology: Some Remarks from a German Point of View', *The American Journal of Comparative Law*, 42 (1994), 395–421.

Bucher, A., 'Is There a Need to Establish a Permanent Reviewing Body?', in Emmanuel Gaillard, ed., *The Review of International Arbitral Awards* (Juris Publishing, 2008).

Derlén, Mattias, *Multilingual Interpretation of European Union Law* (Kluwer Law International, 2009).

Dothan, Shai and Joanna Lam, 'A Paradigm Shift? Arbitration and Court-Like Mechanisms in Investors' Disputes', in Güneş Ünüvar, Joanna Lam, and Shai Dothan, eds., *Permanent Investment Courts: The European Experiment. European Yearbook of International Economic Law* (Dordrecht, 2020), 1–25.

Eskridge Jr., William, Philip Frickey and Elizabeth Garrett, *Legislation and Statutory Interpretation* (New York, Foundation Press, 2000).

Franck, S. D., 'The Legitimacy Crisis in Investment Treaty Arbitration: Privatizing Public International Law Through Inconsistent Decisions', *Fordham Law Review*, 73 (2005), 1521.

Freeman, Michael and Fiona Smith, 'Law and Language: An Introduction', in Michael Freeman and Fiona Smith, eds., *Law and Language. Current Legal Issues* (Oxford, 2013), 1–7.

Gadamer, Hans Georg, *Truth and Method* (London, 2006).

Gaillard, E., *Legal Theory of International Arbitration* (Leiden; Boston MA, 2010).

Germain, C. M., 'Approaches to Statutory Interpretation and Legislative History in France', *Duke Journal of Comparative & International Law*, 13 (2003), 195–206.

Jemielniak, Joanna and Przemysław Mikłaszewicz, 'Capturing the Change: Universalising Tendencies in Legal Interpretation', in Joanna Jemielniak and Przemysław Mikłaszewicz, eds., *Interpretation of Law in the Global World: From Particularism to a Universal Approach* (Dordrecht, 2010), 1–27.

Jemielniak, Joanna, *Legal Interpretation in International Commercial Arbitration* (Farnham; Burlington, 2014).

Kingsbury, Benedict and Stephan Schill, 'Investor-State Arbitration as Governance: Fair and Equitable Treatment, Proportionality, and the Emerging Global Administrative Law', in A. J. Van den Berg, ed., *50 Years of the New York Convention* (Alphen aan den Rijn , 2010), 5–68.

Kjær, Anne Lise, 'Legal Translation in the European Union: A Research Field in Need of a New Approach', in Krzysztof Kredens and Stanislaw Gozdz-Roszkowski, eds., *Language and the Law: International Outlooks* (Peter Lang, 2007), 69–95.

Kjær, Anne Lise, 'Nonsense: The CILFIT Criteria Revisited from the Perspective of Legal Linguistics', in Henning Koch, Ulrich Haltern, and Joseph H. H. Weiler, eds., *Europe: The New Legal Realism: Essays in Honour of Hjalte Rasmussen* (Djøf/Jurist- og Økonomforbundet, 2010), 297–316.

Kjær, Anne Lise, 'The Theoretical Perspectives of Legal Translation in the EU: The Paradoxical Relationship Between Language, Translation, and the Autonomy of EU law', in Susan Sarcevic, ed., *Language and Culture in EU Law: Multidisciplinary Perspectives* (Routledge, 2015), 91–107.

Leung, Janny, *Shallow Equality and Symbolic Jurisprudence in Multilingual Legal Orders* (Oxford, 2019).

McAuliffe, Karen, 'Translation at the Court of Justice of the European Communities', in Frances Olsen, Alexander Lorz, and Dieter Stein, eds., *Translation Issues in Language and Law* (Basingstoke, 2009), 99–115.

McAuliffe, Karen, 'Precedent at the Court of Justice of the European Union: The Linguistic Aspect', in Michael Freeman and Fiona Smith, eds., *Law and Language: Current Legal Issues* (Oxford, 2013), 483–92.

Melinkoff, David, *The Language of the Law* (New York, 1963).

Menezes de Carvalho, Evandro, *Semiotics of International Law: Trade and Translation* (Berlin; Heidelberg, 2011).

Montesquieu, C. d. S., translated and edited by Anne M. Cohler, Basia Carolyn Miller, Harold Samuel Stone, *The Spirit of the Laws* (Cambridge; New York, 1989).

Nielsen, Laura, *The WTO, Animals, and PPMs* (Leiden, 2007).

Paunio, Elina, *Legal Certainty in Multilingual EU Law: Language, Discourse and Reasoning at the European Court of Justice* (Farnham, 2013).

Peat, Daniel and Matthew Windsor, 'Playing the Game of Interpretation: On Meaning and Metaphor in International Law', in Andrea Bianchi, Daniel Peat, and Matthew Windsor, eds., *Interpretation in International Law* (Oxford, 2015).

Rabault, H., *L'interprétation des normes: l'objectivité de la méthode* (Paris, 1997).

Rasmussen, Hjalte, 'The European Court's Acte clair Strategy in C.I.L.F.I.T or: 'Acte clair, of course!' But What Does It Mean?', *European Law Review*, 9 (1984), 242–59.

Robinson, Douglas, *Western Translation Theory from Herodotus to Cierco* (2014).

Šadl, Urška, 'Case—Case-law—Law: Ruiz Zambrano as an Illustration of How the Court of Justice of the European Union Constructs Its Legal Arguments', *European Constitutional Law Review*, 9 (2013), 205–29.

Šarčević, Susan, *New Approach to Legal Translation* (Kluwer Law International, 1997).

Solan, Lawrence and Peter Tiersma, eds., *The Oxford Handbook to Language and Law* (Oxford, 2012).

Solan, Lawrence and Peter Tiersma, 'Introduction', in Lawrence Solan and Peter Tiersma, eds., *The Oxford Handbook to Language and Law* (Oxford, 2012), 1–9.

Tabory, Mala, *Multilingualism in International Law and Institutions* (Sijthoff & Noordhoff, 1980).

Van Calster, Geert, 'The EU's Tower of Babel—The Interpretation of Multilingual Texts by the European Court of Justice', in Ami Barav and Derrick Wyatt, eds., *Yearbook of European Law—1997* (Oxford, 1997).

Venzke, Ingo, *How Interpretation Makes International Law: On Semantic Change and Normative Twists* (Oxford, 2012).

Zweigert, Konrad and Heinz Kötz, *An Introduction to Comparative Law*, trans. Tony Weir (3rd edn, Oxford, 1995).

PART I

THEORETICAL PERSPECTIVES

1. What is legal Interpretation? International Legal Interpretation Between Law and Legal Discourse

1

Legal interpretation as a solution to disputes over the validity of laws

TOMASZ STAWECKI

1.1. Validity of law—interpretation of law—paradigm of law

The issue of the validity of the law seems completely unimportant to studies of legal semiotics. After all, semiotics is the study of the language as a real cultural subject, while validity is very often perceived as a kind of convention.[1] Legal semiotics combines semantic, structural, and functional analyses of the legal discourse with the results of social and legal studies. The studies in semiotics will, therefore, concentrate on the theory and practice of interpreting the law,[2] but not really on decisions regarding the validity of the law. If, however, we analyse the problems of interpretation of the law in greater detail, it transpires that their distinctiveness from the matter of the validity of the law is not at all obvious.

First of all, both of these types of issue are interwoven in the theoretical discourse, namely in disputes on, *inter alia,* what the law is, how we can identify it, how it should be applied by the courts, and why we are obliged to take heed of it. Critics of legal positivism and their contemporary adversaries focused for over half a century on issues of the validity of the law, since it is necessary to specify the legal grounds referred to in the imperious decision (e.g. judicial decision) and to determine its content.[3] Today, however, in disputes on the so-called rule of recognition, the conclusion is drawn that 'the notion of 'contributor to legal content' or 'determinant of

[1] Ronald Dworkin, *Law's Empire* (1998), 94–95; see also Leslie Green, 'Positivism and Conventionalism', *Canadian Journal of Law and Jurisprudence,* 12/1 (January 1999), 36ff.

[2] Joanna Jemielniak, *Legal Interpretation in Commercial Arbitration* (2014), 49ff.

[3] Andrei Marmor, 'The Nature of Law', in Edward N. Zalta, ed., *The Stanford Encyclopedia of Philosophy* (Winter 2011), http://plato.stanford.edu/archives/win2011/entries/lawphil-nature/; the same ideas are developed in Marmor's *Social Conventions: From Language to Law* (2009).

Tomasz Stawecki, *Legal interpretation as a solution to disputes over the validity of laws* In: *Language and Legal Interpretation in International Law.* Edited by: Anne Lise Kjær and Joanna Lam, Oxford University Press. © Oxford University Press 2022. DOI: 10.1093/oso/9780190855208.003.0002

legal content' is a much broader notion than that of legal validity'.[4] Jules L. Coleman suggests that, in today's jurisprudence, there is a shift in the interest of researchers from the area of the validity of the law towards broader methods of determining the content of the law. Coleman, commenting on Ronald Dworkin's theory, notes also the regularity which is significant for the wider jurisprudential discourse: in his early work (for example, in *The Model of Rules*), Dworkin was still moving around within the framework of the paradigm which encompassed the notion of the validity of the law. In Dworkin's later books, however, especially *Law's Empire*, the idea of the validity of the law is completely absent. Dworkin does not ask the questions which legal positivists ask when building on H. L. A. Hart's thoughts.[5] Coleman acknowledges that this is precisely one of the consequences of 'the interpretive turn' which started in the mid-1980s. For example, if the notion of principles, which differs from the notion of rules, were to be introduced into legal thought, the matter of the binding character of law has to be seen in a way which is different from that which was developed by the traditional theory of the law:

> Dworkin argues that countenancing moral principles as binding legal sources—and not merely as discretionary standards—undermines [fundamental] tenets [of legal positivism]. If moral principles can be legally binding, then they are legal standards; but principles are not rules, and so the *Model of Rules*—the claim that all legal standards are rules—cannot be sustained. If certain moral principles are legally binding, then they are binding as principles, and so in virtue of their status as principles, which is to say that their claim to legal authority depends on their substantive merits; but if the substantive morality or merit of a principle is (or can be) a condition of legality (at least for some legally binding norms), then the Separability Thesis—the claim that morality cannot be a condition of legality—must likewise fall. So too the Rule of Recognition . . .[6]

In addition, the matter of the relationship between interpretative practices and the traditional issue of the binding character of the law is not just limited to disputes by the rule of recognition proposed by Hart. This relationship is key to establishing what we understand at all by the law and how we perceive its application. It is worth noting that, for more than fifty years, the application of the law has frequently been presented as a process of making partial decisions in European civil-law countries, which lead to a final decision, for instance, a court judgment. According to some authors, the typical model position is the model of the decision-making process, as

[4] Jules L. Coleman, *Legality and the Legal Content: Some Preliminaries* (2008), 40.

[5] Coleman, *Legality and the Legal Content*, 11.

[6] J. L. Coleman, 'Constraints on the Criteria of Legality', *Legal Theory*, 6 (2000), 172.

presented by Jerzy Wróblewski, consisting of the application of the law in a specific case. This model contains six major stages: (1) the determination of the validity and applicability of the relevant rule of substantive law, (2) determination of the meaning of this rule in a manner precise enough for its use in deciding the case (interpretation), (3) the acceptance as proven of the facts of the case . . . , (4) subsumption (the so-called 'drawing' of the facts to the standard), (5) establishing the legal consequences of the proven facts of the case on the basis of the respective provision of the law, and (6) formulation of the final decision.[7] At this point, we are not interested in all the components of the judicial decision-making process, although care should be taken to distinguish the decision on the validity of the legal norms from the interpretative decision. Again, the problem of the validity of the law is combined with the problem of interpretation of the law, although it is relatively separate.[8]

Therefore, when legal interpretation in the practice of international courts is analysed, the relationship between these two elements of the process of applying the law must be noted. Even if the majority of legal philosophers focused on the positive law, understanding this as just 'central elements in the concept of law' (as referred to by Hart[9]), the 'borderline cases of the law', such as Community (i.e. EU) law or new *lex mercatoria*,[10] can become interesting to the proponents of the semiotics of the law. Judicial decisions on the basis of new and less elaborated forms of the law can prove to be just as important, just like the principles designed by Ronald Dworkin have become important legal standards. Adjudication requires that a decision be made about the validity and applicability of specific norms. Therefore, problems of legal validity should not be entirely beyond the scope of interest to legal semiotics.

The considerations below are not intended to describe the discussion around the relationship between the validity of the law and its interpretation within or at the level of the theory of the law. I do not intend to repeat or argue with the assertions of J. L. Coleman and other authors. However, I would like to show that legal practice in national courts (common courts, administrative courts, and constitutional courts), and partially in the Court of Justice of the European Union, developed solutions similar to those which are proposed by the theory of the law after the interpretative turn. The requirements of legal coherence, as well as efficiency of judicial activity, have led to similar results to those of the philosophical and theoretical reflection on the nature of the law. Therefore, the objective of my chapter is to demonstrate

[7] Jerzy Wróblewski, *The Judicial Application of Law*, ed. Zenon Bankowski and Neil MacCormick (1992), 31.

[8] Other authors apply similar reasoning. Aharon Barak emphasizes that the legal meaning of a specific legal text set out in the process of interpretation and the validity of the applied rule are two distinct elements of judicial decision-making. Aharon Barak, *Purposive Interpretation in Law* (2005), 395.

[9] H. L. A. Hart, *The Concept of Law* (2nd edn, 1997), 17.

[10] Jemielniak, *Legal Interpretation in Commercial Arbitration*, 149ff.

how the interpretational activity of judges influences the paradigm of the law shared among many contemporary lawyers (including academics) in Europe.

The conclusion, which, in my opinion, arises from this practice, relates to Coleman's argument: the development of new standards of interpreting the law, especially the so-called constitution-conforming interpretation and EU law-conforming interpretation of domestic law, has led to issues of validity of the law being pushed into the background. In other words, the interpretative turn in legal theory has resulted in declining interest among judges in the problems of validity of the law in favour of focusing on issues of interpretation. This is not only an important change in practice, but also a significant change in the modern paradigm of the law. I also have no doubt that this is important to the reflection on the interpretation of the law in international commercial arbitration.

1.2. The Radbruch Formula as a standard of a judicial decision

As the starting point for analysing issues of validity of the law and interpreting the law, I selected the so-called Radbruch Formula, which is well known to European lawyers. It was used not only immediately after 1945, among other occasions, in Nuremberg, but also after 1990 in the cases of 'the Berlin Wall shooters' (German border guards).[11] It also seemed to be a practical tool for shaping the processes of applying the law in post-Communist countries.[12] Perhaps even the Radbruch Formula, for example, in the version developed by Robert Alexy,[13] could also be used in liberal-democratic political systems to identify and prevent injustices.[14]

In order to check the hypothesis that the interest of researchers has shifted from the problems of the validity of the law towards problems of interpretation, I leave Gustav Radbruch's various interpretations and assessments of his philosophy of the law outside the scope of the chapter's considerations. I am interested in Radbruch's Formula as a theoretical instrument in the hands of judges. Are judges in societies which accept the principles of liberal-democratic regimes eager to reach out for Radbruch's Formula, and are the claims of the scholar from Heidelberg perceived

[11] Rudolf Geiger, 'The German Border Guard Cases and International Human Rights', *European Journal of International Law*, 9 (1998), 540ff. See also case at ECtHR: *Streletz, Kessler and Krenz v. Germany*, 34044/96, 35532/97, 44801/98, 22.3.2001.

[12] Jirí Pribán, *Legal Symbolism: On Law Time and European Identity* (2007), 161ff.

[13] Robert Alexy, 'A Defence of Radbruch's Formula', in *Recrafting the Rule of Law: The Limits of Legal Order* (1991), 15–40. See also Brian Bix, 'Robert Alexy, Radbruch's Formula and the Nature of Legal Theory', *Rechtstheorie*, 37 (2006), 139–46.

[14] Robert Alexy, *The Argument from Injustice: A Reply to Legal Positivism* (2002); Vivian Grosswald Curran, 'Law's Past and Europe's Future', *German Law Review*, 6/2 (2005), 501ff.

to be an important tool for settling cases entangled in axiological conflicts in judges' professional practice? The first impression is that it seems reasonable for the answer to these questions to only be negative. How can this be explained? I claim that the cause and the internal justification of the judicial scepticism towards Radbruch's position is the acceptance of different ways of reasoning, in particular, different ways of interpreting the law and justifying interpretative decisions.

I have taken the liberty of making the reservation that my paper is in nature an overview, which requires detailed elaboration. Therefore, I am trying to refer to Radbruch's original statements and positions expressed in court judgments rather than ready interpretations of legal theory. However, I believe that such a reflection can become a footnote in discussion of the changes in the dominant paradigm of the application of the law.[15]

Assessment of the extent to which Radbruch's Formula is used in the judicial application of the law and the context which determines the attitude to this concept requires that attention be drawn to its main components. It is usually accepted in the literature on the philosophy of the law that Radbruch's Formula consists of three basic claims. They have been discussed repeatedly in the literature, so I am presenting them as briefly as possible. They are (1) the claim about the gross conflict between the law and justice as the decisive criterion for challenging the validity of the law (*Unerträglichkeitsthese*), (2) the claim of the lack of legality (from the very beginning) of grossly unjust statutes (*Verleugnungsthese*), and (3) the claim about the defencelessness of lawyers against barbarian law (*Wehrlosigkeitsthese*).[16]

Radbruch formulates the first claim as follows: 'the conflict between justice and legal certainty may well be resolved in this way: the positive law, secured by legislation and power, takes precedence, even when its content is unjust and fails to benefit the people, unless the conflict between statute and justice reaches such an intolerable degree that the statute as a "flawed law" must yield to justice'.[17]

The radicalism of the conviction that a grossly unjust law is invalid gives rise to several specific problems. First of all, the basic difficulties related to the implementation of Radbruch's Formula apply to two different issues—normativity

[15] Krzysztof Pałecki, ed., *Neutralization of Values in Law* (2013), 372–3.

[16] Gustav Radbruch, 'Statutory Lawlessness and Supra-Statutory Law (1946)', *Oxford Journal of Legal Studies*, 26/1 (2006), 1–11; Stanley L. Paulson, 'Radbruch on Unjust Laws: Competing Earlier and Later Views?' *Oxford Journal of Legal Studies*, 15 (1995), 489ff; Stanley L. Paulson, 'On the Background and Significance of Gustav Radbruch's Post-War Papers', *Oxford Journal of Legal Studies*, 26/1 (2006), 17–40; and Brian Bix, 'Radbruch's Formula and Conceptual Analysis', *American Journal of Jurisprudence*, 56/1 (2011), 45–57.

[17] Radbruch, 'Statutory Lawlessness and Supra-Statutory Law', 7; Paulson, 'On the Background and Significance of Gustav Radbruch's Post-War Papers', 26.

and competence.[18] The former involves the establishment of the boundary between 'ordinary injustice' not causing a derogation to the norm and 'gross injustice' which incites such an effect. It is emphasized that *lex iniustissima* qualifies a legal norm as being invalid, not only as 'unjust' or 'bad'.[19] It is interesting, however, that the qualification of 'gross injustice' is not analysed as a problem of the interpretation of the law.[20] The latter issue involves the answer to the question already asked by Hobbes: who actually sets the boundary, which, if crossed, means that *Unerträglichkeitsthese* (or, to use another term, *Quis judicabit*) applies, and with what effect—*ex nunc* or *ex tunc*? It could be argued that philosophers of the law mainly see a normative problem in the Radbruch Formula, while judges focus on competence issues.

That Radbruch emphasizes the strict relationship, and perhaps even identifies justice and equality under the law, may be of some importance to the response to the questions posed above. Therefore, Radbruch considers justice as a necessary feature of positive law itself, which is the work of the lawmaker. In this respect, we adjudicate on the validity of the law. However, justice in the process of the judge applying the law is rather 'slowness/ subservience to the law'. The justness of the law is not the same as the rightness of a court judgment.

As I previously suggested, the fact that the assessment of the 'injustice' of the law requires an interpretation of the law, including the assessment of its ethical values, is also not appreciated.[21] Perhaps this is the effect of the impact of legal positivism on Gustav Radbruch's thoughts. By assuming that legal certainty is the fundamental value of the law, legal positivism has reduced the other two pillars of the law, namely purposefulness and justice, to the role of supplementary interpretational criteria. The law is usually clear—as was believed—and does not require detailed interpretation.[22] The assurance of the justice and purposefulness of the law is, therefore,

[18] Jerzy Zajadło, *Formuła Radbrucha. Filozofia prawa na granicy pozytywizmu prawniczego i prawa natury* [Radbruch's Formula: Legal Philosophy at the Border between Legal Positivism and Natural Law Theory] (2001), p. 110.

[19] Paulson proposes a similar classification of '*unrichtiges Recht*' when writing about *false law*. Paulson, Radbruch on Unjust Laws', 491.

[20] This is probably because of Radbruch's concept of legal interpretation as limited to legal texts, and not covering the analysis of facts.

[21] Some commentators on Radbruch remind us that problems with interpretation of unjust law have been noticed by judges. See Julian Rivers, 'The Interpretation and Invalidity of Unjust Laws', in *Recrafting the Rule of Law: The Limits of Legal Order* (1991), 40ff; and Paulson, 'On the Background and Significance of Gustav Radbruch's Post-War Papers', 28. The interdependence of interpretation and validity of the law is not, however, regarded as a fundamental issue.

[22] On the other hand, 'gross injustice' is also clear and obvious: Paulson cites interesting reasoning of a German court, dated 1968: '"[L]egal" provisions from the National Socialist period can be denied validity when they are so clearly in conflict with fundamental principles of justice that a judge who wished to apply them or to recognize their legal consequences would be handing down a judgment

the task of the lawmaker, and the courts cannot either consider or question this. Therefore, Radbruch's Formula seems to leave an open door for judges who are prepared to depart from it.

It should be added that Radbruch's second claim focuses on the lack of legal character of grossly unjust statutes. Radbruch proposes that, in certain situations, the norms which are formally dressed in the robes of the law should be considered as not deserving of being called the applicable law from the outset. This is a challenge (*Verleugnung*) to the legal character of the norm from the very beginning.[23]

Finally, Radbruch's third claim is that positivism makes lawyers defenceless against barbarian law. Positivism, by its conviction that a 'statute is a statute', incapacitated lawyers in Nazi Germany and made them defenceless with respect to statutes of an arbitrary and criminal nature. Similarly, positivism is unable to justify the validity of statutes by their own strength. Positivism believes that the validity of statutes is already proven by their effectiveness. Coercion can perhaps be justified by force, but never duty and validity. However, if a lawyer argues his role from a formal position, for instance, from the fact of being a judge, it is easy to lose this ethical aspect or treat it less seriously.

Other affirmative or critical comments on Radbruch's concept are also possible. However, from our point of view, of greatest importance is the emphasis that his formula, especially its first two claims, places on the problem of the validity of the law. Strictly speaking, it focuses on the establishment of the premises and circumstances of law's invalidity. In the conditions of the philosophy of the law from the beginning of the twenty-first century, oscillating around the problems of rational legal discourse, the concept of 'statutory lawlessness' may, however, be a starting point for discussions on other issues: the establishment, application, interpretation, as well as observance of the law.[24]

1.3. Problems of interpretation of statutes in Radbruch's philosophy of the law

Gustav Radbruch's concentration on the matter of the validity of the law was not incidental and was related to the method in which this author understood the issue of applying the law, including interpreting the law. In this respect, Radbruch's position seems to be typical of German legal thought in the first quarter of the

of non-law rather than of law'. Paulson, 'On the Background and Significance of Gustav Radbruch's Post-War Papers', 27.

[23] Radbruch's two claims are complementary, although Paulson mentions that they *overlap*. Paulson, 'Radbruch on Unjust Laws', 491.

[24] Jerzy Zajadło, 'Formuła Radbrucha—geneza, treść, zastosowanie' [Radbruch's Formula: The Origin, Content and Applicability], *Państwo i Prawo*, no. 6 (2000), 31.

twentieth century. After all, it was rooted in the theory of the Free Law School (*Freirechtsschule*).[25] Radbruch was inspired by the work of Hermann Kantorowicz, just like Hans Kelsen,[26] and was considered an ardent promoter of this thought. Therefore, according to Radbruch, who wrote the 'Introduction to Jurisprudence' (*Einführung in die Rechtswissenschaft*) in 1910,[27] the judge should primarily be independent and impartial: 'The *judge* sitting on the bench is nothing but an engine of subsumption, a judgement machine, a legal automaton . . . , devoid of individuality'.[28]

However, the application of the law is not an obvious process of referring to specific facts. According to Radbruch, a judge may arrive at a clear and non-conflicting decision in any foreseeable case through the simple application of the law only if the lawmaker clearly anticipated and settled every case which could be thought of as without internal contradictions. The judge's decision is not always determined; on the contrary, it is frequently a result of his rational, albeit discretionary, power. However, the effect of the judicial decision primarily depends on the lawmaker's work.

When commenting on the role of the judge and the process of interpreting statutes, Radbruch points out that a lawyer has three tasks with respect to a statute: interpretation, construction, and systemization. However, interpretation does not involve the determination of the actual will of the lawmaker, but 'the thought embodied in the spiritual product itself, regardless of whether anyone consciously included this thought in this given product'.[29] In the *Legal Philosophy*, Radbruch adds an important explanation to his concept of the nature of the interpretation of legal texts: 'The interpreter may understand the law better than its creators understood it; the law may be wiser than its authors—indeed, it must be wiser than its authors. The thoughts of the authors of a law necessarily have gaps, cannot always avoid obscurities and contradictions; yet the interpreter must be able to derive a clear and uncontradicted decision from the law in any conceivable legal case.'[30]

[25] According to Grosswald Curran, 'At the beginning of the twentieth century, [Radbruch] had been a proponent of the innovative Free Law School'; Grosswald Curran, Law's Past and Europe's Future', 497.

[26] Frank Kantorowicz Carter, 'Gustav Radbruch and Hermann Kantorowicz: Two Friends and a Book—Reflections on Gnaeus Flavius' *Der Kampf um die Rechtswissenschaft* (1906)', *German Law Review*, 7/7 (2005), 657ff; Stanley L. Paulson, 'Formalism, "Free Law," and the "Cognition" Quandary: Hans Kelsen's Approaches to Legal Interpretation', *University of Queensland Law Journal*, no. 27 (2009), 20–3.

[27] Eighth edition published in 1928.

[28] Expression based on Polish edition (translation by Czesław Znamierowski) of Gustav Radbruch, *Wstęp do prawoznawstwa* [Introduction to Jurisprudence] (1924), 133.

[29] Radbruch, *Wstęp do prawoznawstwa*, 236. Cf. Gustav Radbruch, 'Legal Philosophy (1932)', in *The Legal Philosophies of Lask, Radbruch, and Dabin*, trans. Kurt Wilk (1950), 145–6.

[30] Radbruch, 'Legal Philosophy', 141–2.

Radbruch grants a judge with wide discretionary power. He focusses, however, only on the content of the judicial decision, not on the validity of specific pieces of legislation. Therefore, the interpretation of the law appears not to have any connection with the decision about whether to apply certain norms or not.

After 1945, Radbruch came to the conclusion that the judge not only applies the law but must also make it the subject of constant assessment from the point of view of justice. 'Complete consideration of the law' took on a distinctly axiological dimension. A judicial decision should, therefore, be—in today's language—functionally related to the values constituting the foundation of the law. This is because when a law is the source of evil, the judge should refuse to use it, because it does not qualify for consideration as a law. As I mentioned, the assessment of the 'injustice' of the law requires its interpretation in terms of assessing its ethical value, the interpretation of the content, which—we assume—is linguistically clear,[31] and not its interpretation understood as determination of an individual norm, which can be applied in a specific case.[32] In this sense, the author of the essay 'Statutory Lawlessness and Over-statutory Law' does not develop the analytically oriented theory of legal reasoning and does not modify his earlier 'discretionary' attitude to the directives on interpretation, but rather emphasizes his professional sensitivity in combining the ability to acquire knowledge (*episteme*) with virtue (*arete*). A judge's key task in the process of applying the law since the mid-twentieth century has been, therefore, to perceive values, rather than force his own hierarchy of them.

1.4. Radbruch's Formula in the Polish courts

Radbruch's idea of the law is highly esteemed in the Polish philosophy of the law. However, if the case law of the Polish courts and tribunals were to be traced from the mid-twentieth century on, it is difficult not to get the impression that judges were reluctant to reach out for the Radbruch Formula. This is evidenced not only by the procedurally final and politically significant facts: neither the executioners of the soldiers of the Home Army (*Armia Krajowa*), nor those who were guilty of the death of the workers in Gdańsk in December 1970, nor the originators and key executioners of martial law in 1981–1983 and other political crimes stood before a court. The law has not become the basis for effectively imposing liability. Whether

[31] According to the post-war works of Hans Kelsen, this type of interpretation of the norms only appears in the case where there are no general norms that can be applied to a given case. However, this is a form of lawmaking. Cf. Hans Kelsen, *General Theory of Law and State,* trans. A. Wedberg (1948), 145.

[32] The interpretation of the law should also not be considered a process of a political struggle to impose a specific understanding of the law on other groups. Cf. H. Dębska, 'Legal Doxa as a Form of Neutralization of Values in the Law: The Case of Constitutional Tribunal Judgments', in Krzysztof Pałecki, ed. *Neutralization of Values in Law,* 312.

this was a consequence of the profoundly immoral content of the applicable law or defects in the process of applying the law is a matter of dispute. The objectives of the law, however, were not achieved in this respect, and the public belief is that the practice of the courts did not result in the materialization of the principle of justice.

Polish judges did not adopt Radbruch's Formula as a guiding maxim of conduct with respect to a grossly unjust law. Some approved Radbruch's Formula as a moral standard for assessing positive law but considered specific regulations as not deserving to be dismissed. Other judges regretted that the Polish judicature is departing from Radbruch's Formula and, consequently, is failing to bring about the materialization of the idea of the law: the elemental balance between legal certainty, purposefulness, and justice.[33] However, Adam Strzembosz, a Supreme Court judge and an historian of the judiciary, summed up these attitudes in the spirit of the third claim making up Radbruch's Formula:

> Over the years . . . Polish science was dominated by the doctrine of legal neopositivism which, replacing the primitive theory of the law as a tool in the battle of the classes, legitimized every law which was correctly enacted and promulgated. This theory played an inglorious role [in 1981–1988], because it was an excuse for those judges who, out of cowardice or opportunism, ruthlessly applied the regulations of martial law. Even today, in response to the allegation that they issued strict sentences for activities commonly considered not only admissible, but also serving the common good, they say they were applying the law.[34]

Likewise, a review of the case law of the Polish courts in recent years does not suggest that judges have been referring to Radbruch's Formula.[35] While commenting on the provisions of the Criminal Procedures Code (Article 440), the Supreme Court explained that a 'gross injustice . . . is one which particularly seriously breaches the public sense of justice', adding, 'If a judgment is so unfair for the accused, it is possible to change it in the appeal instance'.[36] The subject of the judicial assessment is, therefore, a seriously incorrect (flawed) judicial decision but not the legal grounds for this decision. It can, therefore, be assumed that judges do not treat the interpretation of the law as a broad and complex task, encompassing the assessment of the

[33] See the viewpoint of Ewa Łętowska, a judge of the Constitutional Tribunal, expressed in her dissenting opinion to the judgment dated 27 October 2010, case no. K 10/08.

[34] M. Stanowska and Adam Strzembosz, *Sędziowie warszawscy w czasie próby 1981–1988* [Warsaw Judges in the Time of Test: 1981–1988] (2005), 293.

[35] However, Radbruch's Formula is cited in the decisions of the Grand Chamber of the European Court of Human Rights in the case *Streletz, Kessler and Krenz v. Germany*.

[36] Judgment of the Supreme Court (of Poland) dated 1 October 2008, case no. V KK 261/08.

regulations in terms of justice, rightness, and equality, and do not relate interpretation and validation issues to themselves.

1.5. Interpretation of the law as a method of avoiding *lex iniustissima* consequences

The above-cited examples of the poor acceptance of Radbruch's Formula in Poland should not be treated as a simple continuation of the pre-war legal positivism or as a fundamental resistance by judges to the natural law argument of the invalidity of an unjust law. It can be assumed that the reasons for the judicial attitudes lie elsewhere: in the visualization of the role of language in the process of the functioning of the law, especially its application and interpretation. Since the end of the 1950s, legal science in Europe including, to some extent, in Poland, has been trying to take into account the change referred to as the linguistic turn. It was acknowledged that the belief in legal certainty, which is the consequence of careful legislation and trueness to the procedures, is fallacious.[37] The theory of the law dealt much more intensively with vagueness and ambiguity, including its unintentional and highly unavoidable open texture.[38] A generation later, there was an interpretative turn in the philosophy of the law, sometimes referred to as the 'hermeneutic turn',[39] as well as the discovery of discourse as a unique way of communicating, which simultaneously creates and changes the social world.

In principle, judges are quite resistant to philosophical novelties. Two more detailed concepts of interpreting the law were of huge, if not key, importance: an interpretation in conformity with Community law (with the directives, with the law of the European Union), sometimes also referred to as 'conforming interpretation' ('conform-interpretation') or 'harmonious interpretation of domestic law',[40] as well

[37] On European understanding of legal certainty in particular in connection with the rule of law, see James R. Maxeiner, 'Legal Certainty: A European Alternative to American Legal Indeterminacy?', *Tulane Journal of International and Comparative Law*, 15/2 (2007), 541ff.

[38] See, for example, Tomasz Gizbert-Studnicki, 'Types of Vagueness, in: The Reasonable as Rational? On Legal Argumentation and Justification', in Werner Krawietz, Robert S. Summers et al., ed., *Festschrift for Aulis Aarnio* (2000), 135–44.

[39] See, for example, D. Kennedy, 'The Turn to Interpretation', *Southern California Law Review*, 58 (1985), 251ff; William N. Eskridge, Jr, 'Gadamer/Statutory Interpretation', *Columbia Law Review*, 90 (1990), 609–81; Kenneth J. Kress, 'The Interpretive Turn', *Ethics*, 97 (1987), 834–60.

[40] See, for example, Joanna Jemielniak and Przemysław Mikłaszewicz, 'The Interpretation of National Law in Conformity with EU Law: A New Method of Interpretation to Serve the Effectiveness of the *Acquis communautaire*', in Joanna Jemielniak and Przemysław Mikłaszewicz, ed., *Interpretation of Law in the Global World: From Particularism to a Universal Approach* (2010), 4ff. Another term for 'EU law conforming interpretation' is 'sympathetic interpretation'. Cf. Stephen Weatherill, *Cases and Materials on EU Law* (6th edn, 2003), 163.

as the interpretation of statutes in conformity with the Constitution ('pro-constitutional interpretation of the law'). Both concepts were developed in the judgments of the courts and in the science of the law in Western Europe, but both have won major recognition in Poland. Initially, each of these positions also assumed a hierarchical conflict of norms and, consequently, the derogation from (lack of application of) the respective lower norm. There was even a change in the development of each of these theories whereby, instead of repealing a flawed norm (a national law which is inconsistent with European law or a statute which is inconsistent with the Polish Constitution), the principle was accepted that, in the event of non-conformity of norms, there is no need to discard the lower norm, but, through the interpretation of the law, it can be given such a meaning that it can be applied in accordance with the higher norms. An interpretation which is in conformity with European law or the Constitution has become an alternative to derogation. This is because the interpretation of the law, as a process of understanding the law and a key tool in its application, gives grounds for not accepting a formula which leads to the lack of validity of controversial legal norms.

The key hypothesis to this outline can be formulated in this sense: contemporary concepts of the interpretation of the law enable the restriction of the validation radicalism that can be derived from Radbruch's Formula. If it turns out that some regulation deserves to be considered *lex iniustissima,* the judge does not need to make a decision not to apply a norm arising from a formally applicable regulation, which is rather difficult for him and usually controversial, but can respect the general will of the lawmaker by applying a dubious regulation as well as it can possibly be reconciled with other rules or legal standards which are binding on him.

A brief analysis of the said views of the interpretation of the law can be presented as an illustration of this argument.

1.6. Interpretation of national law in conformity with Community law

The principles of interpreting national law with Community law (the law of the European Union) developed in parallel with the basic principles of the legal order of the European Community. The legal (academic) doctrine played a role in this respect, but decisions of the European Court of Justice (ECJ) were of key importance. The fundamental principles of EU law and its development are well known. Therefore, it is worth devoting most attention to those judgments of the ECJ which correspond to Radbruch's Formula.

The starting point was traditional. In *Costa (Flaminio) v. ENEL (Ente Nazionale Energia Elettrica)* (case 6/64) in 1964, the ECJ held that, in the event of a conflict between national law and Community law, the given state should change its legislation and pay any compensation.[41] This meant that the ECJ accepted a monistic concept of the law and, simultaneously, for the first time, the principle of primacy of Community law over national law. Therefore, national judges are obliged to apply Community norms as having priority and not as laws which need to be transformed or incorporated into national law.[42] The application of national law which is in conflict with Community law is ruled out. This could resemble Radbruch's Formula: *lex iniustissima* [i.e. incompatible with Community law] *non est lex*. Of course, in the case law of the ECJ, qualified, 'gross' non-conformity of national law with Community law was not analysed, while the ECJ did not rule on or even mention the invalidity of national law. However, it required that it not be applied in a situation of conflict.

The principle of the primacy of Community law understood in this way was related to the second fundamental principle of the European order: the principle of the direct effect of Community law. All national courts are obliged to directly and promptly implement clear and unconditional rules of Community law, even if they are in conflict with national laws or even constitutions.[43] The principle of direct effect was later developed in the formula of the full effectiveness of Community law (*effet utile*)—the obligation to act in order to achieve the Community's real objectives and not just the letter of the law.

The concept of the primacy of Community law was strengthened even more in a judgment of the ECJ about a dozen years later in *Public Finance Administration v. Simmenthal SpA*. The ECJ held that national judges faced with the conflict between national law, whatever its nature, and Community law must ignore—must shut their eyes—to national law:[44]

> any provision of a national legal system . . . which might impair the effectiveness of community law by withholding from the national court having

[41] The judgment in *Costa v. ENEL* was neither the first nor the only one. However, early judgments of the ECJ determined the situation of citizens facing a conflict between national law and Community law to a minor extent. Cf. P. Craig and G. de Búrca, *EU Law: Text, Cases, and Materials* (3rd ed., 2003), 231.

[42] 'The validity of a Community instrument or its effect within a Member State cannot be affected by allegations that it strikes at either the fundamental rights as formulated in that State's constitution or the principles of a national constitutional structure' (emphasis added). Cf. Josephine Steiner and Lorna Woods, *EU Law* (10th edn, 2009), 89. This was confirmed, *inter alia*, by the judgments of the ECJ in joined cases 9/65 and 58/65 *San Michele v. High Authority*. I leave, however, the discussion initiated by the well-known decision of the German Constitutional Court: *Internationale Handelsgesellschaft mbH (Solange I)* [1974] 2 CMLR 540.

[43] The assumption of clarity of EU law is not absolute. There was a discussion whether effectiveness of Community law is a sufficient justification for insisting that a *prima facie* case of a Community law right must take precedence over a clear-cut right under national law. The careful conclusion was that legal certainty may (not necessarily must) be a reason to take clarity of provisions into account. Cf. Stephen Weatherill and Paul Beaumont, *EU Law* (1999), 195.

[44] Steiner and Woods, *EU Law*, 91.

> jurisdiction to apply such law the power to do everything necessary at the moment of its application to set aside national legislative provisions which might prevent community rules from having full force and effect are incompatible with those requirements which are the very essence of community law. . . . a national court which is called upon, within the limits of its jurisdiction, to apply provisions of community law is under a duty to give full effect to those provisions, if necessary refusing of its own motion to apply any conflicting provision of national legislation, even if adopted subsequently, and it is not necessary for the court to request or await the prior setting aside of such provision by legislative or other constitutional means.[45]

When reading the justification to the judgment of the ECJ, it is difficult not to get the impression that we are dealing with a repetition of the first and second claims comprising Radbruch's Formula: national law which is incompatible with Community law is not (applicable) law, while simultaneously it is the 'higher' law that determines the standard of actions of the addresses of the law.

One more important principle was derived from the judgment in the *Simmenthal* case: even if a constitutional court (tribunal) is appointed in a Member State, which has the task of resolving conflicts between statutes and the Constitution or acts of a lower order and statutes, the court of law (i.e. a court other than the constitutional court) has an absolute duty to ensure the effectiveness of Community law without waiting for an appropriate ruling of the constitutional court.[46] In a way, we encounter the ECJ's response to the doubt raised by the third claim constituting Radbruch's Formula: a national judge[47] should not take the attitude of defencelessness in the conflict between the two orders; he cannot hide behind the usually required procedures, the longevity of the wait for an answer to a question of law. He should apply Community law as the European *übergesetzliches Recht*.

Commentators point out that the exclusion of the principle of *lex posterior derogat legi priori* with respect to the intersection of Community law with national law inevitably raises the association of experiences in the Nuremberg trials or the trials of the 'Berlin Wall shooters': in the event of a conflict between two legal orders, the principle of non-retroactivity should not constitute an obstacle to achieving justice.[48]

[45] *Amministrazione delle Finanze dello Stato v. Simmenthal SpA*, case 106/77) [1978]: http://eur-lex.europa.eu/legal-content/EN/TXT/HTML/?uri=CELEX:61977CJ0106&from=EN.

[46] Cf. Craig and de Búrca, *EU Law*, 282.

[47] Later, the principle of applying Community law was also extended to other types of public authority, especially the bodies of administration.

[48] On the problems of non-retroactivity as a condition for legal certainty in ECJ decisions, see Steiner and Woods, *EU Law*, 149–51, and Weatherill, *Cases and Materials on EU Law*, 162–3.

In the process of the evolution of Community law, as well as the formation of the principles of the pro-Community interpretation of national law, namely the interpretation of statutes in conformity with the EU directives, the case of *Sabine von Colson and Elisabeth Kamann v. Land Nordrhein-Westfalen* [1984] (case 14/83) was of ground-breaking importance. The case concerned two skilled women who were applying for a job in a male prison in North Rhine-Westphalia. The ECJ ruled that although the directive providing for the imposition of sanctions for the breach of the discrimination prohibition left Member States free to choose between various good solutions for achieving its objectives, it required that the state choose a solution that provided appropriate, effective, and adequate compensation for the damage caused. The national court is responsible for interpreting and applying the national law selected for implementing the directive in conformity with the requirements of Community law *as far as possible* and within the powers assigned to the court in national law, including its discretionary power.[49] Therefore, what matters is the attainment of the objectives of Community law and not only formal compliance of national law with the directive.

Furthermore, national courts need to interpret national law 'in the light of the content and objective of the directive', even if its provisions do not have a direct effect. Even so, we are facing a fundamental change with respect to the standards developed in *Costa v. ENEL* and later cases: the national court should not reject national law despite its non-compliance, even partial, with the Community standard, but should apply national law, adjusting it accordingly. Adjustment involves choosing—from among all possible and non-absurd meanings of the regulation being interpreted—such a meaning as fits into the semantic framework of the wording and is consistent with the objective of the directive.[50] This is precisely the essence of the interpretational paradigm shift: it is the interpretation and not the derogation from a flawed law which plays the key role, even if we were to restrict our reflection to the sphere of applying the law.

The principle of interpreting national law in conformity with Community law was developed through further judgments of the ECJ, as well as being specified in

[49] 'According to the third paragraph of article 189: a directive shall be binding, as to the result to be achieved . . . but shall leave to the national authorities the choice of form and methods. Although that provision leaves member states to choose the ways and means of ensuring that the directive is implemented, that freedom does not affect the obligation imposed on all the member states to which the directive is addressed, to adopt, in their national legal systems, all the measures necessary to ensure that the directive is fully effective, in accordance with the objective which it pursues' (from http://eur-lex.europa.eu/legal-content/EN/TXT/HTML/?uri=CELEX:61983CJ0014&from=EN). Cf. Steiner and Woods, *EU Law*, 125.

[50] Certain inspirations for that kind of reasoning may be found in German legal philosophy, particularly in the studies on the 'limits of interpretation' (*Auslegunggrenze*). See Matthias Klatt, *Theorie der Wortlautgrenze. Semantische Normativität in der juristischen Argumentation* (2004). In English, see Matthias Klatt, *Making the Law Explicit: The Normativity of Legal Argumentation* (2008), 33ff.

greater detail by decisions of the national courts. In particular, in *Marleasing*,[51] the ECJ adamantly emphasized that the national courts need to interpret national law in the light of the relevant provisions of the directives, regardless of whether national law was adopted in order to implement the directive, or whether it was earlier or later than the directive, in other words. This is important, because, for a long time, several Member States, including, for example, the United Kingdom, did not accept the principle that an earlier law should also be interpreted in accordance with the directive. The time for accepting a law which takes precedence as a criterion for assessing subordinate (national) law, as in Nuremberg in 1946, was again not considered decisive.[52]

In other decisions, including in Pfeiffer,[53] the principle of interpreting national law in conformity with the directives was related to the need to ensure the legal protection of individuals and the need for the full effectiveness of Community law. In this way, it was highlighted that the pro-Community interpretation is of an alternative nature with respect to the concept of the direct effect and the state's liability for damages, which was formulated in the early decisions of the ECJ, with *Costa v. ENEL* at the helm. The argument voiced in this outline, namely interpretation as an alternative to derogation, was emphasized there.

1.7. Interpretation in compliance with the Constitution

Turning from ECJ judgments to the constitutional system of law in a Member State is fully justified by the subject of our analysis. It is also a continuation of previous reflections. Decision-making processes within the structure of national courts are the other side of the coin: a domain for making EU law fully effective.[54]

As I mentioned at the beginning of this chapter, the idea or principle of interpreting statutes (and other legal acts) in conformity with the Constitution, sometimes also known as the 'interpretation of the law in compliance with the Constitution' (in German, *verfassungskonforme Auslegung*) or the 'pro-Constitutional interpretation of the law', is the next example of the practice of moving from a dispute about validity to a dispute about meaning. It was and is the subject of numerous disputes. In addition, this principle is evolving; it is changing its form.[55] The analysis of the

[51] *Marleasing SA v. La Comercial International de Alimentacion SA* (case C-106/89) [1990].

[52] Certain limits on the interpretation of EU law standards were developed by the ECJ in its judgments of the 1990s. Cf. Steiner and Woods, *EU Law*, 126.

[53] *Pfeiffer Grosshandel GmbH v. Lowa Warenhandel GmbH* [1999] (case I 2835).

[54] Cf. Adam Bodnar, 'Comment on Katharina Pabel—The Right to an Effective Remedy in a Polycentric Legal System', *German Law Journal*, 6 (2005), 1617–1622; available at http://www.germanlawjournal.com/index.php?pageID=11&artID=659.

[55] This concept was developed by the German Federal Constitutional Court after 1953.

statements from the representatives of the legal doctrine, as well as the positions expressed by the judges in the justifications of judgments and in other forms, demonstrates that two 'camps', academic and judicial, are relatively separate. Each of these is also differentiated internally: in particular, the interpretations by the Constitutional Tribunal and by the Supreme Court substantially differ from each other. However, some significant regularity can be seen.

A simplified interpretation of this special type of interpretation can frequently be encountered in the literature constituting the works of legal doctrine. It is claimed that, because of the recognition of the normative nature of the Polish Constitution, the provisions of the law should be interpreted in such a way that the interpreted statutes are not in conflict with the norms expressed in the Constitution. In this context, the method of operation of the interpreter qualifies as a form of systemic interpretation of the law: if a clear legal norm cannot be established on the basis of the linguistic interpretation, reference is then made to other normative acts, in particular the Constitution, as a result of which a non-controversial interpretational decision can be made.[56] The norm arising from an act of a higher order means, however, that the norm expressed directly in the lower-order act is modified. In such a simplified approach, the principle of interpretation of statutes in conformity with the Constitution matches the traditional theories of interpreting the law but seems to be a doctrinal *superfluum*. Moreover, reflection on interpretation of law includes no references to the problem of validity of law or particular statutes.

If we are to analyse deeply Polish development of interpretative methods and policies, we can easily find that much more detailed and more precise understanding of the principles of interpretation in conformity with the Constitution was proposed by the Constitutional Court after enactment of the Constitution of 2 April 1997. However, this concept has taken on various forms in its rulings. In the earliest rulings (1998–2002), this idea was connected directly with the concept of the so-called interpretative judgments.[57] This principle was also associated with the presumption of constitutionality of statutes and the idea of legal certainty. Importantly, there was no mention of a 'principle' of interpretation in conformity with the Constitution, especially in 1997–2003, but of the specific 'technique

[56] On the traditional concept of systemic interpretation, see Wróblewski, *The Judicial Application of Law*, 100–3.

[57] The idea of 'interpretative judgements' was discussed even before 1997. Lech Garlicki explains that 'initially, the Polish system had made a distinction between "interpretative decisions" and "interpretative resolutions" of the Constitutional Court. The former represents a type of judgment on the constitutionality of a statute and follow the Italian pattern of *sentenza* interpretative. The latter were issued by the Constitutional Court in the exercise of its other competence, namely, the establishment of 'universally binding interpretation of statutes'. The 1997 Constitution abolished the procedure of 'interpretative resolutions', but, at the same time, it provided that the 'judgments of the Constitutional Court [i.e. decisions concerning constitutionality of statutes] are final and universally binding'. Lech Garlicki, 'Constitutional Courts versus Supreme Courts', *I•CON*, 5/1 (2007), 59.

for interpreting statutes', or 'method of interpretation'. It was accepted that, if the linguistic formulation of the provision under consideration enables the establishment of such an understanding of this regulation, which would allow for the acknowledgement that it is in compliance with the Constitution, there is no direct need to rule that such a provision is inconsistent with the Constitution. The application of the technique of interpreting an act in compliance with the Constitution should take priority, because it corresponds to the presumption of the constitutionality of statutes. It was assumed that if two or more non-absurd interpretations of certain provisions (contested before the Constitutional Tribunal) were possible, the Tribunal would look for such an interpretation which is consistent with the Constitution.[58]

The principle arises from the above concept presented by the Constitutional Court that can be referred to as pragmatic minimalism of intervention: if it is possible to avoid finding unconstitutionality, then that is what is to be held. At the same time, this pragmatic minimalism of the Constitutional Tribunal required the acknowledgement of the interpretational nature of the rulings of the constitutional court. Consequently, the adoption of methods of interpretation in accordance with the Constitution was in fact the rule that the regulation under review will be considered compatible with the Constitution, but only on condition that this provision is understood in the manner indicated in the sentence of the judgment. Only in this way (in this sense) can this provision apply to both bodies of administration (central or local governments) and the courts.

The nature of the 'method of interpretation in accordance with the Constitution' as applied in Poland may be explained by comparison with the theory of adjudication formulated by Ronald Dworkin. Dworkin assumes that even in the hard cases, there is only 'one right answer' with the best fit to the case in question. However, 'the method of interpretation in conformity with the constitution' lacks the distinction between the conclusive rules and inconclusive principles and, therefore, the clear idea of grading, balancing, or weighing of the principles of the law.[59] The concept of the constitutional interpretation of statutes implicitly assumes a significant amount of decision-making discretion by the Constitutional Tribunal in deciding which of

[58] Garlicki points out that the idea of choosing from different possible meanings was not an obvious method of interpretation: 'Ordinarily, [the constitutional] court would follow the interpretation already established in the jurisprudence of the supreme court. Sometimes, however, the constitutional court may be confronted with multiple possible interpretations and may be tempted to indicate which one is constitutionally correct'. Garlicki, 'Constitutional Courts versus Supreme Courts', 48–49.

[59] Ronald Dworkin, *Taking Rights Seriously* (1977), 22ff. The interpretation of statutes in accordance with the constitution does not also fit into the theory of balancing of principles as a process of optimization, developed by Robert Alexy. The former is focused on the hierarchical relation between interpreted laws, not so much on their content as it is required for the purposes of distinguishing 'principles'. Cf. Robert Alexy, 'Balancing, Constitutional Review, and Representation', *I·CON*, 3/4 (2005), 572–81.

the possible interpretations of the contested statutory provisions is in compliance with the Constitution and which is not. Ronald Dworkin, as is known, did not accept discretionary powers of judges even in so-called difficult cases.

The concept and the practice of 'interpretative judgments' as developed by the Constitutional Tribunal has encountered criticism from the judges of the Supreme Court.[60] They argued that the rulings of the Constitutional Tribunal are only binding on the courts by the fact that the given regulation is consistent with the Constitution, but not with regard to the direction of its interpretation. The judges of the Supreme Court openly refused to apply interpretative judgments of the Constitutional Tribunal.[61] They referred to the constitutional principle of the independence of judges: judges are only subject to the Constitution and statutes, but not the rulings of the Constitutional Tribunal. However, the Constitutional Tribunal rejected such an interpretation of the principles of the constitutional interpretation of statutes as being erroneous. According to the judges of the Constitutional Tribunal, the arguments of the proponents of the position presented by the Supreme Court would lead to an unreasonably large amount of discretion in the process of interpreting the provisions of statutes by the courts of law and the administrative courts, therefore—it can be said—to the idea of legal certainty in the name of enigmatically understood justice being challenged.[62]

In the middle of the first decade of the twenty-first century, both the main judges of the courts and tribunals, as well as the representatives of the legal doctrine were looking for ways to mitigate or eliminate the conflict between the positions represented by the Constitutional Tribunal and the Supreme Court, as well as the Supreme Administrative Court. One of the most inspiring and convincing was the concept formulated by Ewa Łętowska of a multi-centric legal system arising from the multiplicity and institutional distinctiveness of each of the courts and tribunals.[63] The author of this concept also derives postulates on the interpretation of the law and the interpretation of the constitution from the description of certain relationships between the main courts in Poland, as well as between them and the supranational courts (CJ EU and ECtHR): a mutually benevolent interpretation based on split spheres of jurisdiction according to the Roman and civil-law principle of *quoad usum*. This concept aroused a great deal of interest in the theory

[60] A theoretical controversy quickly transformed into a conflict ('war of courts') between two supreme judicial institutions. Cf. Garlicki, 'Constitutional Courts versus Supreme Courts', 59–60, 63.

[61] The Supreme Court's position was expressed, *inter alia*, in the resolution dated 17 December 2009, case no. III PZP 2/09.

[62] It has to be considered that the lines of reasoning of the Constitutional Tribunal and the Supreme Court were different: 'The Tribunal reads the text in order to evaluate the constitutionality of the norm, whereas courts of general jurisdiction also read the texts, but they do so in order to 'isolate the norm of individual application'. Ewa Łętowska, 'Multicentricity of the Contemporary System of Law and Its Consequences', *The Polish Foreign Affairs Digest*, 2/15 (2005), 107–16.

[63] Łętowska, 'Multicentricity of the Contemporary System of Law and Its Consequences'.

of the law,[64] although acknowledgement among the judges was limited and rather concealed.

Another important argument in the controversies on interpretative judgments was presented by the Constitutional Tribunal in 2005, in the general information on the activity of the Tribunal. The Constitutional Tribunal upheld its defence of the interpretative judgments and emphasized that 'wherever it is possible to use this method, there are no grounds for declaring the unconstitutionality of a statute'. By that statement, the Tribunal returned to the originally known idea: interpretation might be a solution enabling the court (Constitutional Tribunal) to avoid a decision questioning the validity of certain statutory provisions.

An additional change in the Constitutional Tribunal's position was primarily the declaration that, in its rulings, the Constitutional Tribunal follows the principle of respecting the uniform interpretation consolidated in court judgments, especially in the judgments of the Supreme Court and the Supreme Administrative Court. The Tribunal accepted that frequently the content of laws is finally developed in the process of their application by the bodies designated for this. If it is obvious that a specific method of understanding a provision of a statute has already become consolidated, especially if it is unambiguously and authoritatively expressed in the rulings of the Supreme Court or the Supreme Administrative Court, the Tribunal considered that this provision has precisely such content.[65]

Certain commentators understood this position, in a way, not as a tactical move by the Tribunal, but as a reference to the concept of the so-called 'living law', according to which the content of a legal norm is only assessed in the light of its application. However, other authors pointed out that the rejection of the uniform interpretation of laws, which are consolidated in the judgments of the courts of law, would give rise to serious procedural problems. Acknowledging such a uniform interpretation as simply an erroneous interpretation would prevent a party from claiming rights on the basis of a constitutional complaint, because it would undermine the argument that the laws were in conflict with the Constitution.

The next component of the evolution of the concept of interpreting statutes in conformity with the Constitution was the change in the function of this concept. Statements of the Constitutional Tribunal can be found, both from individual adjudicating panels and the Tribunal as a whole, in which the said type of interpretation is not so much a programmed element of the Constitutional Tribunal's

[64] See, for example, Marek Zirk-Sadowski, Mariusz Golecki, and Bartosz Wojciechowski, eds., *Multicentrism as an Emerging Paradigm in Legal Theory* (2009).

[65] Garlicki summarizes the position of the Tribunal: 'Of course, the court always has the competence to invalidate a statute. One of the grounds for such invalidation may be that the practice of the ordinary courts has constructed the statute in a manner incompatible with the constitutional interpretation established by the constitutional court. But such a drastic option may be exercised only in exceptional circumstances'. Garlicki, 'Constitutional Courts versus Supreme Courts', 67.

adjudicating policy, as a specific argument used by the Constitutional Tribunal when ruling on the provision in question. Invoking this argument enables the Tribunal to limit a complex ethical argument, especially the considerations regarding the possible understandings of such fundamental constitutional values as equality before the law and social equality as a form of justice. It is obvious that these values are implemented by very many states of affairs. In such cases, the Tribunal checks whether the provision under review can be reconciled with any of the uncontroversial methods of making fundamental values real or whether the provision of the Constitution expressing such a value is an adequate pattern (basis) of control.

The Tribunal found that not only does its own slightly abstract pragmatic minimalism of the intervention (as mentioned above) apply to such a position, but so does judicial passivism or purely judicial restraint. This is because the Constitutional Tribunal acknowledged that it is certainly not appointed to replace the lawmaker in the role of the entity shaping social policy and the detailed procedures of pursuing it.[66] Such a view of the principle of interpretation in accordance with the Constitution also means that an investigation into whether we are dealing with *lex iniustissima* is abandoned.

In recent years, the Constitutional Tribunal has been indicating further important aspects of the practice of interpreting statutes in compliance with the Constitution. The Constitutional Tribunal primarily emphasizes a further function of this principle: it should be a necessary component of the process of arriving at an interpretative and final decision of the Tribunal on the unconstitutionality of the contested provisions. This is because the Constitutional Tribunal recalls that a judgment about the unconstitutionality of a provision is treated as the *ultima ratio* and should always be preceded by an attempt to interpret it in compliance with the Constitution. Therefore, it is possible to reconstruct an important argument of the Constitutional Tribunal: the review of the validity of norms cannot be ruled out in the activities of the constitutional court, but emphasis should be placed on the interpretation of the law, rather than on the validation problem.

The concepts of interpretation of national law in accordance with the directives and the constitutional interpretation of laws have evolved in recent years, which does not change the fact that they are still the subject of numerous disputes in legal doctrine and the judgments of the courts. In relatively few cases do judges combine them with disputes on fundamental legal values: justice, equality, legal security, and

[66] The statement on the lack of intention to 'replace the lawmaker' is a reference to the ideal of Hans Kelsen describing a constitutional court as a 'negative legislator'. Some of today's most activist courts provide legislators with positive formulas for rescuing the laws from unconstitutionality. Cf. Wojciech Sadurski, 'Judicial Review in Central and Eastern Europe: Rationales or Rationalizations?', *Israel Law Review*, 42/3 (January 2009), 500ff. See also Alec Stone Sweet, *Governing with Judges* (2000), 135.

so on. If anything, ties are mentioned together with the procedural values, setting rules, and the principles of applying the law in accordance with the idea of the rule of law. So is the idea of the relationship with Radbruch's Formula suggested in this outline reasonable?

The answer to such a question can be 'yes and no'. There are sufficiently numerous examples showing that the interpretation of the law allows judges to avoid advocating a particular position taken ethically in a proclaimed judgment. Highlighting the primacy of the linguistic interpretation, emphasizing the role of systemic interpretation, and even reaching out to Community law, in particular positive law, or the Constitution, can be a method of avoiding taking a position on the axiologically 'sensitive' issue.[67] Interpretative, as well as argumentative, practice can follow in the footsteps of lawyers, who—as Jeremy Bentham used to say—'like a conjurer, draw from the same fountain bitter waters, or sweet, as he pleases'.

On the other hand, the interpretation of the concept of 'conforming interpretation' forces the legal decision to conduct and, to a major extent, to disclose the reasoning for choosing such a meaning of the disputed provision which is the closest possible to these 'higher standards'. In such a case, the judge is forced to demonstrate that his decision was made because of the interpretation of the statute 'in the light of the objective and the wording of the directive' or the Constitution. It is impossible to avoid even a limited discourse, especially in the case of an interpretation which is compliant with the Constitution, in which many of the provisions directly express key social values. This probably happens where the validity of the law is treated as the determination of legitimated and not just legal obligations in their formal sense. A Polish author writing about the cases of the 'shooters from the Berlin Wall' clearly indicates that only such an assessment of the acts performed made it possible to challenge the provisions ruling out the illegality of issuing and executing the criminal instructions (commands), and to convict the perpetrators.[68]

It should also be remembered that the concepts of the 'conforming interpretation' constitute a response to the collapse or even weakening of two important legal myths: the myth of the fundamental semantic clarity of acts of law and the myth of the social inter-subjective obviousness of values such as justice, especially when

[67] This opinion has been supported by the empirical study on the Constitutional Tribunal's adjudication. Cf. Tomasz Stawecki, Wiesław Staśkiewicz, and Jan Winczorek, *Between Polycentrism and Fragmentation: The Impact of Constitutional Tribunal Rulings on the Polish Legal Order* (2009); available at http://www.ey.com/PL/en/Industries/Government---Public-Sector/Debate_Constitutional-Tribunal. Marek Zirk-Sadowski described the model of adjudication as 'soft Kelsenism'. Cf. Marek Zirk-Sadowski, 'Soft Kelsenism versus Multicentrism: Some Remarks on Theoretical Foundation of European Law', in Zirk-Sadowski, Golecki, and Wojciechowski, *Multicentrism as an Emerging Paradigm in Legal Theory*, 51–68.

[68] Sebastian Sykuna, 'High-Tech Weapons and the Protection of Human Rights during Humanitarian Interventions', in M. Barczewski, R. Warner, M. Miłosz, eds., *Selected Papers on High Technology Law* (2006), 122.

we are dealing with *lex iniustissima*. The observation of various manifestations of worldview and ethical pluralism, reinforced by the awareness of the problem of incommensurability of legal values;[69] the discussions around various hard cases; and the difficulty of achieving a consensus around specific solutions or standards, especially Rawls's overlapping consensus, show us that the simple system of eliminating 'non-conforming' norms is just as difficult to apply as it is ineffective in pursuing a good and socially legitimated law. In this context, it can be accepted that the interpretation of the law can provide an alternative to the practical use of such concepts as Radbruch's Formula and can actually defend the addressees of the law against legal formalism and oppressiveness.

References

Alexy, Robert, 'A Defence of Radbruch's Formula', in Dyzenhaus, David, ed., *Recrafting the Rule of Law: The Limits of Legal Order* (Oxford and Portland, 1991), 15–39.

Alexy, Robert, 'Balancing, Constitutional Review, and Representation', *International Journal of Constitutional Law*, 3/4 (October 2005), 572–81.

Alexy, Robert, *The Argument from Injustice: A Reply to Legal Positivism* (Oxford, 2002).

Barak, Aharon, *Purposive Interpretation in Law* (Princeton and Oxford, 2005).

Bix, Brian, 'Radbruch's Formula and Conceptual Analysis', *American Journal of Jurisprudence*, 56/1 (2011), 45–57.

Bix, Brian, 'Robert Alexy, Radbruch's Formula and the Nature of Legal Theory', *Rechtstheorie*, 37 (2006), 139–46.

Bodnar, Adam, 'Comment on Katharina Pabel—The Right to an Effective Remedy in a Polycentric Legal System', *German Law Journal*, 6 (2005), 1617–22. Available at: http://www.germanlaw journal.com/index.php?pageID=11&artID=659.

Coleman, Jules L., 'Constraints on the Criteria of Legality', *Legal Theory*, 6 (2000), 171–183.

Coleman, Jules L., *Legality and the Legal Content: Some Preliminaries* (Warsaw, 2008), 39–58.

Craig, P. and G. de Búrca, *EU Law: Text, Cases, and Materials* (3rd ed., Oxford, 2003).

Dębska, H., 'Legal Doxa as a Form of Neutralization of Values in the Law: The Case of Constitutional Tribunal Judgments', in Krzysztof Pałecki, ed. *Neutralization of Values in Law* (Warsaw, 2013), 303–351.

Dworkin, Ronald, *Law's Empire* (Oxford and Portland, 1998).

Dworkin, Ronald, *Taking Rights Seriously* (London, 1977).

Eskridge, William N., Jr, 'Gadamer/Statutory Interpretation', *Columbia Law Review*, 90 (1990), 609–81.

Garlicki, Lech, 'Constitutional Courts versus Supreme Courts', Oxford University Press and New York University School of Law: *I•CON*, 5/1 (2007), 44–68.

Geiger, Rudolf, 'The German Border Guard Cases and International Human Rights', *European Journal of International Law*, 9/3 (1998), 540–9.

Gizbert-Studnicki, Tomasz, 'Types of Vagueness, in: The Reasonable as Rational? On Legal Argumentation and Justification', Werner Krawietz, Robert S. Summers et al., eds., *Festschrift for Aulis Aarnio* (2000), 135–44.

[69] Cf. Nien-hê Hsieh, 'Incommensurable Values', in Edward N. Zalta, ed., *The Stanford Encyclopedia of Philosophy* (Fall 2008), http://plato.stanford.edu/archives/fall2008/entries/value-incommen surable/.

Green, Leslie, 'Positivism and Conventionalism', *Canadian Journal of Law and Jurisprudence*, 12/1 (January 1999), 35–52.

Grosswald Curran, Vivian, 'Law's Past and Europe's Future', *German Law Review*, 6/2 (2005), 483–512.

Hart, H. L. A., *The Concept of Law* (2nd edn, Oxford, 1997).

Hsieh, Nien-hê, 'Incommensurable Values', in Edward N. Zalta, ed., *The Stanford Encyclopedia of Philosophy* (Fall 2008), http://plato.stanford.edu/archives/fall2008/entries/value-incommensurable/.

Jemielniak, Joanna, *Legal Interpretation in Commercial Arbitration* (Farnham, 2014).

Jemielniak, Joanna and Przemysław Mikłaszewicz, 'The Interpretation of National Law in Conformity with EU Law: A New Method of Interpretation to Serve the Effectiveness of the *Acquis communautaire*', in Joanna Jemielniak and Przemysław Mikłaszewicz, ed., *Interpretation of Law in the Global World: From Particularism to a Universal Approach* (New York: Springer Publishing Company, 2010).

Kantorowicz Carter, Frank, 'Gustav Radbruch and Hermann Kantorowicz: Two Friends and a Book—Reflections on Gnaeus Flavius' *Der Kampf um die Rechtswissenschaft* (1906)', *German Law Review*, 7/7 (2005), 657–700.

Kelsen, Hans, *General Theory of Law and State*, trans. A. Wedberg (Cambridge, MA, 1948).

Kennedy, D., 'The Turn to Interpretation', *Southern California Law Review*, 58 (1985), 251–73.

Klatt, Matthias, *Making the Law Explicit: The Normativity of Legal Argumentation* (Oxford, 2008).

Klatt, Matthias, *Theorie der Wortlautgrenze. Semantische Normativität in der juristischen Argumentation* (Baden-Baden, 2004).

Kress, Kenneth J., 'The Interpretive Turn', *Ethics*, 97 (1987), 834–60.

Łętowska, Ewa, 'Multicentricity of the Contemporary System of Law and Its Consequences', *The Polish Foreign Affairs Digest*, 2/(2005), 107–16.

Marmor, Andrei, 'The Nature of Law', in Edward N. Zalta, ed., *The Stanford Encyclopedia of Philosophy* (Winter 2011), http://plato.stanford.edu/archives/win2011/entries/lawphil-nature/.

Marmor, Andrei, *Social Conventions: From Language to Law* (Princeton and Oxford, 2009).

Maxeiner, James R., 'Legal Certainty: A European Alternative to American Legal Indeterminacy?', *Tulane Journal of International and Comparative Law*, 15/2 (2007), 541–609.

Pałecki, Krzysztof, ed., *Neutralization of Values in Law* (Warsaw, 2013).

Paulson, Stanley L., 'Formalism, "Free Law," and the "Cognition" Quandary: Hans Kelsen's Approaches to Legal Interpretation', *University of Queensland Law Journal*, 27/2 (2009), 7–39.

Paulson, Stanley L., 'On the Background and Significance of Gustav Radbruch's Post-War Papers', *Oxford Journal of Legal Studies*, 26/1 (2006), 17–40.

Paulson, Stanley L., 'Radbruch on Unjust Laws: Competing Earlier and Later Views?' *Oxford Journal of Legal Studies*, 15/3 (1995), 489–500.

Pribán, Jirí, *Legal Symbolism: On Law Time and European Identity* (Farnham, 2007).

Radbruch, Gustav, 'Legal Philosophy (1932)', in *The Legal Philosophies of Lask, Radbruch, and Dabin*, trans. Kurt Wilk (Cambridge, MA, 1950).

Radbruch, Gustav, 'Statutory Lawlessness and Supra-Statutory Law (1946)', *Oxford Journal of Legal Studies*, 26/1 (2006), 1–11.

Radbruch, Gustav, *Wstęp do prawoznawstwa* (Warszawa, 1924).

Rivers, Julian, 'The Interpretation and Invalidity of Unjust Laws', in Dyzenhaus David, ed., *Recrafting the Rule of Law: The Limits of Legal Order* (Oxford and Portland, 1991), 40–65.

Sadurski, Wojciech, 'Judicial Review in Central and Eastern Europe: Rationales or Rationalizations?', *Israel Law Review*, 42/3 (January 2009), 500–27.

Stanowska, M. and Adam Strzembosz, *Sędziowie warszawscy w czasie próby 1981–1988* (Warszawa, 2005).

Stawecki, Tomasz, Wiesław Staśkiewicz, and Jan Winczorek, *Between Polycentrism and Fragmentation: The Impact of Constitutional Tribunal Rulings on the Polish Legal Order*

(Warszawa: Ernst & Young, 2009), Available at: http://www.ey.com/PL/en/Industries/Government---Public-Sector/Debate_Constitutional-Tribunal.
Steiner, Josephine and Lorna Woods, *EU Law* (10th edn, Oxford, 2009).
Stone Sweet, Alec, *Governing with Judges* (Oxford, 2000).
Sykuna, Sebastian, 'High-Tech Weapons and the Protection of Human Rights during Humanitarian Interventions', in M. Barczewski, R. Warner, M. Miłosz, eds., *Selected Papers on High Technology Law* (Chicago–Gdańsk, 2006).
Weatherill, Stephen, *Cases and Materials on EU Law* (6th edn, Oxford and New York, 2003).
Weatherill, Stephen and Paul Beaumont, *EU Law* (London, 1999).
Wróblewski, Jerzy, *The Judicial Application of Law*, ed. Zenon Bankowski and Neil MacCormick (Dordrecht, 1992).
Zajadło, Jerzy, *Formuła Radbrucha. Filozofia prawa na granicy pozytywizmu prawniczego i prawa natury* (Gdansk, 2001).
Zajadło, Jerzy, 'Formuła Radbrucha—geneza, treść, zastosowanie' [Radbruch's Formula: The Origin, Content and Applicability], *Państwo i Prawo*, no. 6 (2000), 25–42.
Zirk-Sadowski, Marek, Mariusz Golecki, and Bartosz Wojciechowski, eds., *Multicentrism as an Emerging Paradigm in Legal Theory* (Berlin, 2009).
Zirk-Sadowski, Marek, 'Soft Kelsenism versus Multicentrism: Some Remarks on Theoretical Foundation of European Law', in Marek Zirk-Sadowski, Mariusz Golecki, and Bartosz Wojciechowski, *Multicentrism as an Emerging Paradigm in Legal Theory* (2009), 51–68.

2

Do legal concepts travel?

ADAM DYRDA AND TOMASZ GIZBERT-STUDNICKI

2.1. Introduction: The 'deixis' of arbitration

Let us start with a few trivial observations. International commercial arbitration is a cross-cultural enterprise, and the parties involved usually come from different countries. Arbitrators, as a rule, are of nationalities different from those of the parties, the venue of arbitration very frequently differs from the place of performance of contract, the applicable law is often unrelated to the domiciles of the parties and to the venue of arbitration, the language of arbitration is usually not the native tongue of the arbitrators, and so on.[1] This paper aims to investigate how such a cross-cultural context (the specific 'deixis') of the decision-making process may influence the interpretation of certain basic legal concepts. We will deal only with selected problems, and our analysis will be analytical rather than empirical. In addition, our goal is to formulate questions that should be answered and hypotheses that should be tested, as opposed to proposing definite solutions or explanations.

We intend to investigate the interpretation of concepts that are not specific to any legal system but are used by all developed legal systems; in particular, we explore concepts including 'ownership', 'contract', and 'negligence'.[2] Let us call such concepts 'substantive multicultural concepts' (SMCs). The fact that different legal systems use the same term or its equivalent in another language (e.g. the English 'contract', French '*contrat*', German '*Vertrag*') does not necessarily mean

[1] Compare the detailed analysis of the issue of the national aspects of arbitration in Joanna Jemielniak, *Legal Interpretation in International Commercial Arbitration* (2014), 2–8.

[2] We will not analyse 'formal legal concepts', such as 'right', 'power', and 'immunity'. For the distinction between substantive and formal concepts, see Tomasz Gizbert-Studnicki and Mateusz Klinowski, 'Are Legal Concepts Embedded in Legal Norms?' *International Journal for the Semiotics of Law*, 25/4 (2012), 556.

Adam Dyrda and Tomasz Gizbert-Studnicki, *Do legal concepts travel?* In: *Language and Legal Interpretation in International Law*. Edited by: Anne Lise Kjær and Joanna Lam, Oxford University Press. © Oxford University Press 2022.
DOI: 10.1093/oso/9780190855208.003.0003

that such a term expresses the same concept.[3] The meaning of such concepts should initially be derived from the applicable law of a particular jurisdiction. The rules of specific legal systems (taken together with the conceptions developed in jurisprudence and the case laws of a particular country) define 'ownership', 'tort', or 'contract', particularly in terms of what the truth conditions are for statements of the type 'X is the owner of Y' and 'X and Y are bound by a contract'. Such truth conditions are, at least to a certain extent, specific to a given legal system. Conversely, however, lawyers from different jurisdictions are usually successful in communicating through the use of such concepts. Although the SMCs that they apply are jurisdiction-specific, these lawyers display a strong conviction that they are talking about the same ideas, and they typically achieve mutual understanding and draw common reasonable conclusions. These goals are especially important in international commercial arbitration, in which arbitrators who frequently come from different jurisdictions are compelled to make a unified decision, sometimes on the basis of the concepts of a legal system that is alien to all of them. How can this paradox be explained?

To put it in a more general sense, a question that arises is whether our current stock of concepts is adequate for meaningful communication across legal traditions and cultures.[4] The answer to this question is important for at least two issues. The first, which is of theoretical importance, is whether a genuinely general jurisprudence is possible. We will not focus on this issue because we have in mind a more practical matter. That is, the second issue that emerges in the context of international arbitration is the possibility of reaching understanding amongst arbitrators with foundations rooted in different jurisdictions, legal cultures, and traditions. Such understanding is achieved in most cases given that international arbitration generally works well. Our questions, therefore, are rather of the Kantian sort: how is common understanding possible, and what are the limits of such understanding?

We do not believe that these questions have only one general answer, but rather several partial answers. These answers must refer to several issues that we want to analyse in more detail. Before proceeding, we discuss certain methodological assumptions.

[3] We will not discuss the problems of double intermediacy, particularly linguistic intermediacy, in the application of national law. See Jemielniak, *Legal Interpretation in International Commercial Arbitration*, 64–7.

[4] This is a paraphrase of a question formulated by William Twining, 'Have Concepts, Will Travel: Analytical Jurisprudence in a Global Context', *International Journal of Law in Context* (2005), 7.

2.2. Methodological assumptions (an ideal arbitrator and the emic vs. etic approach)

First, we assume that the questions we raise are not understood as empirical questions. An empirical survey based on the investigation of arbitration proceedings and particular decisions (including dissenting opinions) may be interesting for the purpose of determining how arbitration tribunals arrive (or why they fail to arrive) at a common understanding of relevant concepts. Conducting such research would probably be difficult given the confidentiality of proceedings and files, but empirical research is not what we have in mind. As previously stated, our task is analytical. For the purpose of this chapter, therefore, we adopt the image of an 'ideal' or 'perfect' arbitrator. Actual arbitrators are encumbered by numerous fact-based limitations. They do not possess full knowledge of their respective national laws, *lex mercatoria* (LM), and supranational standards; they may not have mastered the canons and rules of interpretation; they may have limited knowledge of the facts of a case; they may not have full mastery of the language of arbitral proceedings; and they may not be totally impartial. In what follows, we will not include any such limitations and weaknesses of actual arbitrators in our discussion and instead speak of ideal or perfect arbitrators, who are absolutely free of the aforementioned deficiencies. Furthermore, we assume that such arbitrators are fully rational and that the decision-making process is not subject to time limitations.

Second, a useful approach in further analysis is to employ certain methodological tools that were initially developed for linguistics and then applied in cultural anthropology. What we have in mind here is the distinction between two possible approaches to alien cultures, namely, the distinction between the emic and etic approaches.[5] Emic and etic perspectives are conceived of as theoretical devices intended for the purposes of linguistics and anthropology, but we believe no obstacles stop us from using them in practical contexts wherein comparing various cultures is necessary, especially when such cultures clash.

In cultural anthropology, an emic perspective is defined as the internal perspective of a researcher, who strives to describe a particular culture in terms of the self-understanding of the members of this culture. By contrast, an etic perspective pertains to the external perspective of a comparativist researcher, who attempts to describe phenomena in terms of general, external standards and categories that apply across cultures.[6] In other words, the emic approach investigates how local people think,

[5] Marvin Harris, 'History and Significance of the Emic/Etic Distinction', *Annual Review of Anthropology*, 5 (1976), 329–50.

[6] Michael Morris, Kwok Leung, Daniel Amies, and Brian Lickel, 'Views from Inside and Outside: Integrating Emic and Epic Insights about Culture and Justice Judgments', *The Academy of Management Review*, 24/4 (October 1999), 781.

how they perceive their rules of behaviour, and what holds meaning for them. The etic approach focuses on what a researcher considers important from the perspective of comparative research on other cultures. The etic approach analyses culture in terms that can be applied across cultures and attempts to be 'culturally neutral' in that it excludes ethnocentric and cultural limitations or biases.

In the attempt to apply the emic/etic distinction to our problem of interpreting SMCs, the following questions arise: (1) should an ideal arbitrator adopt the etic or the emic approach? (2) what would be the practical consequences of adopting either approach? and (3) is a purely emic or a purely etic approach workable?

At first glance, the emic approach is the more suitable of the two. If the subject matter of a dispute is governed by a national law, the arbitrators should attempt to understand such governing law in terms of the respective legal culture and not in terms of their own culture(s). To put it colloquially, they should put themselves in the shoes of a domestic judge with a foundation rooted in the national legal culture and decide on a case in the manner in which it would be decided by such a judge. Otherwise, these arbitrators may be held accountable for making the wrong decision or for incorrectly applying the governing law. Becoming a cultural insider necessitates that arbitrators adopt an emic perspective.

We do not believe, however, that such a conclusion is justified. It presupposes that the parties entering into an arbitration agreement intend to incite potential disputes, which would be resolved as they would by the state courts of a respective jurisdiction. We do not regard this intention as generally ascribable to the parties. To the contrary, the parties decide on an arbitration mechanism of dispute resolution because they want to avoid the resolution of potential disputes by state courts. They decide on international arbitration out of a desire to eliminate the biases of a particular legal culture. They prefer supranational resolutions that should be detached from the 'internal point of view' (to use H. L. A. Hart's terminology) that is characteristic of particular national jurisdictions. The genuine internal point of view of a supranational arbitrator cannot be coextensive with that of a national judge, which, by definition, corresponds to an emic perspective.

This does not mean, however, that adopting a purely etic approach should be recommended. If a national legal system is (expressly or tacitly) selected by parties, then the intention of the parties is to have their potential disputes resolved in accordance with the rules of this particular system. Adopting a purely etic approach may result in the disregard of such intention, because this perspective drives arbitrators to abandon certain important features of a legal culture or to re-interpret the content of legal rules in terms of general categories that are alien to this culture.[7]

[7] Compare Jemielniak, *Legal Interpretation in International Commercial Arbitration*, 63, for the distinction of three possible approaches to interpretation from this perspective.

From our perspective, therefore, an integrative emic–etic approach should be adopted. The methodology of cultural anthropology currently maintains that emic and etic insights may be integrated and that the interplay of both may facilitate the comprehensive understanding and explanation of cultural phenomena; these goals can be realized provided that a researcher applies both approaches in a conscious and reflexive manner and is aware of the limitations of these approaches.[8] We believe the same applies to practical problems arising in the context of international commercial arbitration.

2.3. Selected problems with an integrative emic–etic approach

Applying an integrative emic–etic approach is by no means easy, both for theoretical and practical reasons. In particular, difficulties arise in connection with the application of the emic approach. As indicated above, the main problem is that our knowledge of law is necessarily parochial, because our foundations are rooted in a particular legal culture, and we think in terms of our cultures and our concepts of law.[9] This limitation applies not only to actual arbitrators, but also to ideal or perfect arbitrators. Law is a cultural phenomenon. A necessary hermeneutic truth is that an appropriate understanding of law is possible only in a context that considers a specific legal culture in its entirety. When we examine an alien legal system, we do so necessarily from the perspective of our concept of law. Therefore, our perception of such a system is always, to some extent, parochial—a limitation that cannot be eliminated.[10]

Let us go back to our question of how arbitrators with foundations rooted in various jurisdictions can arrive at a common conclusion. Our contention is that such a goal is achieved through the integrated emic–etic approach applied by ideal arbitrators.

First, it is not true that all SMCs are exclusively jurisdiction-specific. One of the authors of this chapter argued elsewhere against the so-called *embedding theory (ET) of SMCs.*[11] This theory maintains that the meaning of such concepts is fully determined by the rules of a respective national law; it particularly asserts that SMCs are equivalent to a set of inferential links that are defined by the rules of a national law. Therefore, any legal concept is only a useful abbreviation of a set of inferential links and can be easily eliminated.[12]

[8] Morris, Leung, Amies, and Lickel, 'Views from Inside and Outside', 794.

[9] Joseph Raz, 'On the Nature of Law', *Archiv für Rechts- und Sozialphilosophie*, 82 (1996), 4.

[10] We take here the position of a moderate legal relativism. See Twining, 'Have Concepts, Will Travel', 8.

[11] Gizbert-Studnicki and Klinowski, 'Are Legal Concepts Embedded in Legal Norms?', 553–62.

[12] Alf Ross, 'TûTû', *Scandinavian Studies in Law* (1957), 139–53.

The main argument developed against ET is based on the observation that certain (but not all) SMCs appear not only at the level of national legislation, but also at the level of supranational laws (European law, international law, and human rights law). Such supranational laws serve as benchmarks for assessing national legislation. This benchmarking gives rise to two issues. First, SMCs are not equivalent to the sets of inferential links determined by a national law because a supranational law also contributes to the content of SMCs. Second, the interpretation of SMCs must take into account supranational laws, which determine at least certain basic features of the concepts; supranational laws also, therefore, determine which specific basic truth conditions for statements that refer to SMCs are common to all jurisdictions. Thus, arbitrators from different jurisdictions share such truth conditions, the specific extent of such sharing being the degree to which the content of SMCs overlaps with that of a supranational law. Despite the peculiarities of national legislation, a supranational law determines, at least partially, the core meaning of certain SMCs. If the national law contains specific inferential links that are inconsistent with these core SMC meanings, then such inferential links must be rejected. This discussion indicates that interpreting such SMCs involves the use of emic and etic perspectives.

Second, certain SMCs have 'travelled' from national legislation to LM. LM is an ambiguous designation, but we will not discuss its various meanings because of space limitations.[13] Referring to LM, we have in mind not so much a body of codes and conventions (e.g. UNIDROIT, the Uniform Customs and Practice for Documentary Credits, INCOTERMS), which are applicable only if the contract between disputing parties refers to them (or in certain cases, does not explicitly exclude their application). Our interest revolves around a set of more or less informal customs, rules, and principles developed in commercial practice, *inter alia* via arbitral case law that is based on the authority of a state or international organization. LM is sometimes subject to private codifications. As Tamanaha states, '[t]ransnational commercial practice and the intent of the parties, not state law, provides the primary guidance to the arbitrators' interpretation of the contracts'.[14] Tamanaha also notes that '[t]ransnational commercial practice developed a set of rules with respect to international transactions which are to a certain extent depoliticized and legal-system indifferent'.[15] We may say that only one LM exists at the global scale, although its boundaries are unclear, and some of its components may be vague or underdetermined. Therefore, although arbitrators come from different jurisdictions, they share a common set of customs, rules, and principles, which are not specific to given national legislation. This situation frequently facilitates the common understanding of matters that are subject to arbitration and enables the

[13] See Jemielniak, *Legal Interpretation in International Commercial Arbitration*, 149–74.

[14] Brian Tamanaha, *A General Jurisprudence of Law and Society* (2001), 126.

[15] Tamanaha, *A General Jurisprudence of Law and Society*, 126.

resolution of a dispute.[16] Involving LM in the interpretation of SMCs is an instance of the etic approach.

Nevertheless, reference to supranational legal standards that partially define SMCs and prevail over national ones and reference to LM as a set of informally developed standards, rules, and principles that do not originate from particular legislation only partially explains why arbitrators with foundations rooted in different legal cultures usually reach a common understanding of the SMCs relevant to the issues that give rise to an arbitration dispute. Why do such references constitute only a partial explanation?

Several factors can be attributed to such partiality. The basic one is that a dispute is usually (unless the arbitration agreement provides otherwise) to be decided on the basis of a national law (either directly indicated in a contract or selected on the basis of conflicts in laws and rules). Therefore, the concepts of this national law are decisive. Supranational standards do not apply to all the legal concepts of a national law. In the first place, they apply to concepts that are directly or indirectly linked to universal human rights (e.g. due process of law, autonomy, or ownership), but do not apply to many others, including numerous SMCs. Furthermore, supranational standards do not always define SMCs in detail and refer only to selected basic features; that is, they determine the 'essence' of such concepts, but leave very many specific matters to national legislation. If a dispute is related to such specific matters, reference to supranational standards would be unhelpful to dispute resolution. For example, a national regulation that provides for the right of one party to a contract to settle a dispute with the other party by the party's unilateral arbitrary decision would be in breach of the supranational standards of due process of law and fairness; therefore, the arbitrators would most probably declare such a contractual clause void and ineffective, even if it is not explicitly prohibited by the applicable national law. Conversely, the details of an appropriate mechanism for pre-arbitral methods of resolving a dispute between parties are left to national legislation.

In addition, certain concepts are either totally jurisdiction-specific because they do not have any direct equivalents in other jurisdictions (e.g. the concept of 'perpetual usufruct'—'*użytkowanie wieczyste*' in Polish law—which is only very roughly similar to '*Erbbaurecht*' in German law or 'leasehold' in English law) or are specific to a certain type of jurisdiction (e.g. 'beneficial ownership' in common law, which to our knowledge, does not have any direct equivalent in jurisdictions of the civil law world). By contrast, certain concepts that appear in practically all jurisdictions have similar meanings in all common law systems but different connotations in civil

[16] Joanna Jemielniak and Przemysław Miklaszewicz, 'Introduction', in Joanna Jemielniak and Przemysław Miklaszewicz, ed., *Interpretation of Law in the Global World: From Particularism to a Universal Approach* (2010), 62. Compare also Jemielniak and Miklaszewicz, 'Introduction', 17, who write '[t]he continuing quest for determining a possible common core of diverse legal systems has been the driving force of the *lex mercatoria* through arbitral case law, as well as via private codification efforts'.

law systems. These meanings are only very roughly equivalent (e.g. the concepts of 'trust', 'tort', and, probably, 'negligence'). As far as LM is concerned, its rules, standards, and principles contain only a limited number of concepts, in the first place linked to the trade of goods and services (e.g. delivery, payment, and delay). Even if shared by arbitrators, LM concepts, therefore, do not allow for a solution to all jurisdiction-specific interpretation problems that may arise in connection with dispute resolution.

When we attempt to familiarize ourselves with the law of an alien jurisdiction, we are in principle unable to fully overcome the limitations that stem from our cultural roots and our understanding of our own cultures. We may exert our best efforts and endeavour to understand the concepts of an alien culture, but the difficulty is that most concepts cannot be thoroughly understood in isolation. Most concepts of any legal system form a network, in which the meaning of one concept depends, to a small or huge extent, on the meaning of others. A common-law attorney can attempt to understand the German or Polish concepts of a contract only if he/she is familiar, on one hand, with the broader concepts of a legal action ('*Rechtsgeschäft*', '*czynność prawna*') and, on the other hand, with the concept of declaration of will and the concept of defects of declarations of will. Such an attempt also depends on the lawyer's familiarity with the concepts of various deficiencies of declarations of will (invalidity, suspended ineffectivity, voidability, and so on). To our knowledge, the concept of a contract in common-law jurisdictions is part of a different conceptual framework. Frequently, in the context of international commercial arbitration, arbitrators must answer the question 'is this a valid contract'? Formulating a response necessitates a thorough understanding of not only the very concepts of the contract, but also all related concepts.[17] This requirement indicates that the emic, rather than the etic, approach is appropriate.

This perspective applies to most, but not all, legal concepts. Certain concepts are relatively isolated in the sense that their meaning does not greatly depend on the meaning of other related concepts. As it appears, this observation may serve as (at least) a partial explanation of the phenomenon described by Twining, that is, the phenomenon that some legal concepts 'travel well', whereas others 'travel badly'.[18] A concept travels well if it can be used with reasonable clarity and precision across various kinds of boundaries, including boundaries between jurisdictions. A concept travels badly if its use is, for some reason, confined to a specific jurisdiction or type of jurisdiction (e.g. civil-law or common-law jurisdictions) and cannot be directly applied with respect to an alien legal culture.

[17] Jemielniak, *Legal Interpretation in International Commercial Arbitration*, 134, draws attention to 'false friends', namely, legal concepts that seem to have direct counterparts in other legal systems but are not freely exchangeable. Examples are the concept of 'contract law' and addressing the issue of unforeseeable circumstances.

[18] Twining, 'Have Concepts, Will Travel', 8ff.

2.4. Which concepts travel well?

Twining analyses three examples of concepts that travel well.[19] His first example is irrelevant to the purpose of this paper given that it refers to fundamental legal concepts as analysed by Hohfeld. In this paper, we deal only with SMCs, and Hohfeldian concepts are formal and unsubstantive. Twining's second example refers to the concept of 'imprisonment', which is relevant on a cross-border basis pursuant to the UN Standard Minimum Rules of Treatment of Prisoners (1955). The third example—a surprising one—is the concept of 'corruption'. Unfortunately, the last two examples have very little (if at all) to do with international commercial arbitration and will, therefore, not be comprehensively discussed. Relevant to our topic, however, is a feature common to both. That is, the last two concepts are relatively isolated in the sense that grasping their meaning does not require the determination of relationships between them and many other legal concepts (as is the case with the concept of 'contract' indicated above). This isolation does not mean, of course, that these concepts are precise and clear-cut. To the contrary, many borderline cases may arise, but the core meaning of both concepts appears to be insensitive to their application across various legal cultures.

Twinning's concern is of a theoretical nature given that his question is whether a truly general jurisprudence is possible. Our question is more practical because we are interested in the understanding of alien concepts by arbitrators in the context of dispute resolution. An observation worth noting, however, is that the direct relationship between 'travelling well' and 'being relatively isolated' from the entire conceptual scaffold of a particular legal culture may be caused by the almost absolute dependence of the legal meaning (use) of the term that refers to a particular concept (e.g. the concept of corruption) on the core ordinary language meaning of that term. In other words, a particular concept may be a good traveller if the conceptual baggage it carries is somehow limited. Every traveller knows that a small and light pack results in a comfortable journey. Thus, simple concepts that do not have a long doctrinal history are good candidates for travel. Such concepts do not need to be 'translated' within the entire conceptual scaffold (including doctrinal controversies) but are translated in a manner very similar to that applied in the simple ordinary language concepts to which they stay closely connected.

To sum up, our hypothesis is that the concepts that are interlinked in any given legal system with many other legal concepts travel badly in the sense that an outsider will experience difficulties in grasping their meaning. The appropriate interpretation of such concepts necessitates the adoption of the emic approach. By contrast, the concepts that are at least relatively isolated from other legal concepts travel well in the sense that they are easily accessible to an individual whose foundation is rooted

[19] Twining, 'Have Concepts, Will Travel', 8ff.

in a different legal culture. The only condition is that in both cultures—the emigrant (the culture *from which* the concept travels) and the immigrant (the culture *to which* the concept travels)—a concept should be relatively isolated; that is, it should be simple and connected to its easily translatable ordinary language counterpart.[20] The distinction between concepts that travel well and those that travel badly is not a logical dichotomy. Whether a concept travels well or travels badly is a matter of degree. Therefore, our third explanatory point related to our basic question is that reaching a common understanding of an SMC that is 'isolated' in the sense indicated above is an easy task.

Unfortunately, perhaps most of the crucial SMCs that are relevant to the context of international commercial arbitration travel badly. As indicated above, the fundamental concept of 'contract' is probably in all legal systems embedded in a network of related concepts specific to a given legal system or a given type of legal system (for continental legal systems, such concepts as declaration of will, invalidity, voidance, and so on). The same perhaps applies to another crucial concept, the concept of 'tort'. Therefore, the distinction between SMCs that travel well and those that travel badly does not provide a fully satisfactory answer to our question of how arbitrators come to a common conclusion, even if such a conclusion depends heavily on the understanding of a concept specific to the applicable law. This deficiency exists, notwithstanding cultural differences, differences in jurisdictions of origin, and the application of laws that may be alien to all arbitrators.

2.5. Additional explanation: Incompletely theorized outcomes

Let us come to our final explanatory point. Additional explanation may be sought if we examine legal systems and cultures from a different angle. What we have in mind here is a perspective that does not concentrate on cross-cultural similarities and differences amongst legal concepts, but on the outcomes that are generated by the application of various cultural-specific concepts to one and the same case (or similar cases). We are particularly interested in the approach proposed in the theory of comparative law by Markesinis (which we deem equally applicable to scopes that are beyond the interest of comparative law).[21] The starting point of

[20] To use Ludwig Wittgenstein's metaphor, good travellers are those concepts that are not exclusively determined by complicated and specific forms of life and are, therefore, able only to play a role in language games performed with this form. Rather, given their simplicity, being a relatively stable element of one form of life, they can be found in other, even very distinct, forms of life. Thus, they can be applied in different language games performed in the context of even very distant forms of life.

[21] Basil Markesinis, 'Unity or Division: The Search for Similarities in Contemporary European Law', *Current Legal Problems*, 54 (2001), 591–617.

this approach is to look into cases and not concepts. As Markesinis indicates, 'the observer is comparing familiar situations and is not confused by structures, terminology, or concepts that are either untranslatable or, if apparently easy to translate, they are misleading'.[22] Markesinis presents a brief comparison of the German concept of 'tort' with respective common-law concepts. 'Tort' in German law is closely linked to the concept of '*Rechtswidrigkeit*' ('illegality'), which is historically derived from the Roman concept of *iniuria*. *Rechtswidrigkeit* is determined by reference to the content of explicit legal rules or by reference to *boni mores*. *Rechtswidrigkeit* is a necessary condition for ascribing liability in the torts of German law. No similar concept can be found in the Anglo-American tort of negligence, which is linked to a more general concept of 'duty of care'. As Markesinis states, '[t]he comparison of two systems through their concepts is thus . . . off-putting. This is because . . . you cannot find the concept, notion or architecture you are looking for which is so self-evident to your foreign colleague'.[23] However, if one examines outcomes (content of judicial decisions related to similar cases in both jurisdictions), one will notice that these outcomes closely resemble one another, notwithstanding major conceptual differences. Different concepts may conceal similar solutions, and similar concepts may hide differences.

This mechanism of comparing legal outcomes proposed by Markesinis resembles Sunstein's idea of 'incompletely theorized agreements' that are achieved in political discourse when no shared background (a common comprehensive doctrine or set of value-laden concepts) on which such an agreement can be based exists.[24] This agreement is 'incompletely theorized' because the parties to a dispute do not share a background theory (conceptual scaffold); the parties nonetheless achieve the same result whilst relying on particular, usually conflicting, theories. Such a strategy for achieving agreement, which we may call 'concretization and consequencealization', is a reverse of 'abstraction', which recommends abstracting a concept (i.e. its conceptions) from competing theories and identifying the basic assumptions (values) on which a theory rests (the general concept itself); eventually, a consensus is built upon the recognition of this shared set of cultural assumptions.[25] The strategy of abstraction presupposes that the concept in question 'travels well' (at least to the extent to which travel is possible when an immigrant concept as a valid passport for such travel presents a simple understanding or meaning that can be determined by a rough reference to the background elements on whose basis such concept functions in both immigrant and emigrant cultures), whereas the opposite strategy does not provide such a presupposition.

[22] Markensinis, 'Unity or Division', 593.

[23] Markensinis, 'Unity or Division', 594.

[24] Cass S. Sunstein, 'Practical Reason and Incompletely Theorized Agreements', in E. Ullmann-Margalit, ed., *Reasoning Practically* (2000), 106–22.

[25] Such a procedure is developed by J. Rawls, for example, in *Political Liberalism* (1993), 7, passim.

As previously mentioned, different concepts may conceal similar solutions. The question that arises is why outcomes are identical or similar. We argue that the similar outcomes reached in jurisdictions with different conceptual schemes are in the last instance based on either similar policy considerations or a sole reference to acceptable outcomes by parties that do not share political considerations. The outcomes based on the first option would be an effect of the abstraction strategy and would, therefore, be similar to the former explanation of a concept as a 'good traveller', although for different reasons. In this case, such outcomes will not be the concepts but the warmly welcomed results. Of course, we use the category 'policy considerations' (for lack of a better term) in a very broad sense. In particular, this category includes the goals to be achieved by the implementation of legal rules, the ethical values that underlie legal rules, and the prudential rules applied in adjudication. The same goals may be achieved, and the same values may be protected by different rules based on different conceptual frameworks. To the extent to which various legal orders have a common or similar ethical background, they provide for different ways of achieving the same outcome. Technically, such legal orders differ, but they are substantially similar as far as basic purposes and values are concerned. If lawyers with foundations rooted in different legal cultures are confronted with a case, they may apply different conceptual schemes and, therefore, structure the issues to be solved in different ways. In most cases, however, the outcome will be the same, provided that the policy considerations of each of the legal orders are similar. Practically speaking, reference to shared policy considerations may be conceived of as a very common base for achieving agreement amongst arbitrators in cases wherein the concepts at stake are very bad travellers. Nevertheless, we cannot theoretically exclude the conclusion that the resolution in very difficult cases will be merely based on the coincidence of the outcomes of seriously diverging policies. This possibility is merely theoretical insofar as it is connected to a practical problem, that is, how in such circumstances a decision will be justified.[26]

[26] It may be claimed that if each arbitrator (assuming three arbitrators, A_1, A_2, and A_3) reaches the same outcome O by using different tools and considerations [$P(A_1)$, $P(A_2)$ and $P(A_3)$, respectively], the justification of a decision can be presented either in a 'weak' disjunctive form, $\{ P(A_1) \vee P(A_2) \vee P(A_3) \} \rightarrow O$, or in a 'strong' conjunctive form, $\{ P(A_1) \wedge P(A_2) \wedge P(A_3) \} \rightarrow O$. The weak form would exactly resemble the process of heuristics but would also allow the risk that the particular, conflicting reasons that arbitrators had whilst reaching the outcome would be unsatisfactorily appreciated; conversely, the strong form may be counter-intuitive for someone who cannot accept that contradictory premises can generate one outcome (another plausible argument is that in such case, each outcome would be the right outcome, according to the logical rule that $\{X, -X\} \rightarrow Y$, where Y is 'whatever'). This argument is the last point that eventually (at least in the case of justification of the decision), some common elements of A_1, A_2, and A_3 have to be found and underlined; these elements are roughly referred to as 'policy considerations'.

2.6. Final reflections

The above conclusion may serve as a partial explanation of our problem, provided that a certain pre-condition is satisfied. This condition is that the legal cultures involved have fundamentally similar legal backgrounds. The question of whether this pre-condition is satisfied is an empirical one given that determining an answer necessitates a careful investigation of the values that underlie various legal cultures. Perhaps particular cultures that fall under this perspective are similar in certain aspects and different in others. We may suppose, for example, that in the sphere of public law, numerous differences exist because the political philosophies that prevail in different legal cultures may be distinct. Conversely, a plausible assumption is that the ethical backgrounds of different legal cultures in the sphere of private law are similar. Leaving aside any exotic legal cultures and considering only those that belong to the family of Western law, we may observe a fundamental convergence of basic values in private law. Thus, a common justification for the decision of arbitrators naturally arises. Private law is based on the principles of human freedom and autonomy; it is based on the principle of protecting the justified expectations of parties and on the general principle of fairness. Although these values and principles may be (and actually are) implemented in a legal order in many different ways through various conceptual frameworks, a fundamental convergence is in place. Therefore, notwithstanding divergences of conceptual schemes, which may be (and actually are) specific to a legal order, the application of these schemes generates identical or closely related outcomes. However, in cases where the cultural backgrounds of arbitrators are so unusual that no substantial common principles of policy can be indicated as bases for shared outcomes, arbitrators will have to formulate an interpretation in such a way that such interpretation can count as a shared background to justify their decisions. This goal will be possible not because of substantial ethical values of any kind, but because of the role arbitrators are supposed to play in arbitration. This role, being accepted by the parties involved, can be conceived of as a general, procedural, and (only in this sense, ethical) shared assumption that enables the resolution of a case.

References

Gizbert-Studnicki, Tomasz and Mateusz Klinowski, 'Are Legal Concepts Embedded in Legal Norms?' *International Journal for the Semiotics of Law*, 25/4 (2012), 553–62.

Harris, Marvin, 'History and Significance of the Emic/Etic Distinction', *Annual Review of Anthropology*, 5 (1976), 329–50.

Jemielniak, Joanna, *Legal Interpretation in International Commercial Arbitration* (2014).

Jemielniak, Joanna and Przemysław Miklaszewicz, 'Introduction', in Joanna Jemielniak and Przemysław Miklaszewicz, ed., *Interpretation of Law in the Global World: From Particularism to a Universal Approach* (Berlin, Heidelberg 2010).

Markesinis, Basil, 'Unity or Division: The Search for Similarities in Contemporary European Law', *Current Legal Problems*, 54 (2001), 591–617.

Morris, Michael, Kwok Leung, Daniel Amies, and Brian Lickel, 'Views from Inside and Outside: Integrating Emic and Epic Insights about Culture and Justice Judgments', *The Academy of Management Review*, 24/4 (October 1999), 781–96.

Rawls, John, *Political Liberalism* (New York, 1993).

Raz, Joseph, 'On the Nature of Law', *Archiv für Rechts- und Sozialphilosophie*, 82 (1996), 1–25.

Ross, Alf, 'TûTû', *Scandinavian Studies in Law* (1957), 139–53.

Sunstein, Cass S., 'Practical Reason and Incompletely Theorized Agreements', in E. Ullmann-Margalit, ed., *Reasoning Practically* (Oxford, 2000), 106–22.

Tamanaha, Brian, *A General Jurisprudence of Law and Society* (Oxford, 2001).

Twining, William, 'Have Concepts, Will Travel: Analytical Jurisprudence in a Global Context', *International Journal of Law in Context* (2005), 5–40.

3

The semantics of openness

Why references to foreign judicial decisions do not infringe the sovereignty of national legal systems

MARCIN MATCZAK

3.1. Introduction

The traditional approach to legal language and its interpretation is author-centred: the author is thought to give the text its meaning, so it is the author's intention that is given primacy in the interpretive process. The author is thus the source of the text's normativity, and his or her will is sovereign. Consequently, if a court applies a legal text to a case at hand, it applies the author's will to the case. The judge is the author's agent and functions as an extension of his/her power.

This traditional approach constitutes an obstacle for the free use of a foreign court's decisions within a national jurisdiction: a foreign verdict quoted in a national judicial context seems to undermine the independence of the national law. Lacking support from the national author, the foreign verdict does not have any precedential weight and, therefore, lacks power. Any normativity the verdict can claim comes from the foreign sovereign whose text was originally applied. Consequently, the use of foreign judicial decisions in national jurisdictions cannot be reconciled with the sovereign-author approach.

Despite this, quoting foreign verdicts in national adjudication is a common practice in many jurisdictions. Something must change to reconcile theory with practice. In this chapter, I argue on the basis of modern externalist semantics (the Barwise-Perry situational semantics and Ruth Millikan's theory of language) that a non-intentional, text-centred approach to language provides a justification for referring to foreign court verdicts without the risk of infringing a national legal system's sovereignty.

In what follows I first present the source of the controversy concerning the use of foreign court verdicts in national jurisdictions. Then I explain that this controversy is strictly connected with a particular concept of authority built around a lawmaker

Marcin Matczak, *The semantics of openness* In: *Language and Legal Interpretation in International Law*.
Edited by: Anne Lise Kjær and Joanna Lam, Oxford University Press. © Oxford University Press 2022.
DOI: 10.1093/oso/9780190855208.003.0004

perceived as a speaker whose intention governs the meaning of the legal text. In opposition to this concept, derived from the assumptions of semantic internalism, I propose an externalist approach to legal language and argue that this alternative approach allows for reconciling the use of the foreign court verdicts with the authority of domestic jurisdictions. In the conclusion, some guidelines are proposed according to which judges could evoke foreign rulings in their decisions.

3.2. Delegalization of the law? Semantic internalism vs. semantic externalism

In 2009, the Polish Constitutional Tribunal issued a ruling assessing the compliance of the obligation to fasten seatbelts in cars with the constitutional principle of freedom and the right to privacy. It quoted rulings issued in similar cases by the supreme courts of the states of Iowa, Illinois, and Washington, and also referred to similar rulings by the Austrian and German constitutional courts. Similar cases exist in which Polish courts have utilized foreign case law or doctrine in their rulings.[1]

One possible reaction to such a practice is to condemn it, holding that it infringes the sovereignty of the national legal system. Schauer and Wise consider referring to foreign case law as a judge's use of extra-textual, non-legal data. In their opinion, the use of such data is impermissible and should be treated as a 'delegalization of the law'.[2]

I believe that the position of Schauer and Wise is erroneous: citing foreign rulings and referring to foreign literature does not constitute a delegalization of the law. To the contrary, it is a practice which is completely justifiable and even desirable. The reasons for such decidedly negative opinions on citing foreign rulings stem from accepting an approach to legal text focused on the sovereign as the author of that text and on the intention of the sovereign-author as a principal factor forming its meaning. This approach assumes that the author's state of mind, in particular his or her knowledge and intentions, are key factors giving meaning to the language (the text). For this reason, identifying the author's state of mind, and in particular,

[1] 'Applying here the previously expressed principle of the beginning of the course of time-barring, the conclusion must be reached that the time-barring of an acquisition for the benefit of the recipient commences at the moment a donor's legacy is opened. This view is also represented in French legal doctrine (cf. Daniel Ripert, *Traité pratique du droit civil*, vol. III, ed. 1928, p. 667)' (ruling SN II CR 1178/57). 'The classification of factoring performed by a statistical authority should be deemed as substantively correct, as attested to by, for example, hypotheses in German case law and doctrine. In Germany . . . the ruling of the Federal Financial Court of 10 December 1981 was of fundamental importance to the taxation of VAT factoring. (G. Reiter, Factoring und Umsatzsteuer, Betriebs-Berater No. 28/82)' (ruling I SA/Wr 2887/99).

[2] F. Schauer and V. J. Wise, 'Nonlegal Information and the Delegalization of Law', *Journal of Legal Studies*, 29/1 (January 2000), 495–515.

discovering his or her intention, is the main task faced by those who interpret his or her statements.

What is the consequence of this approach? The normativity of a legal text is seen to derive from the will of its author: the author is perceived as sovereign. Consequently, when the legal text is applied by a judge in a specific instance, the judge applies the will of the sovereign in resolving the case. In this approach, the judge is an agent of the lawmaker, an extension of his will.

This approach clearly presents an obstacle to the use of foreign rulings in domestic jurisdictions: a clash of sovereignty. As emanations of a foreign sovereign-author, foreign rulings cannot be reconciled with the will of the domestic sovereign. In fact, they seem to infringe the independence of the domestic legal system. In light of this, the 'delegalization' argument is understandable.

The traditional approach to legal language presented above is known in the philosophy of language as 'semantic internalism'. This approach holds that internal mental processes, in particular, a speaker's intention, are the principal factors constituting meaning. The idea of semantic internalism is clearly presented by Barwise and Perry:

> Some theories stress the power of language to classify minds, the mental significance of language, and treat the classification of events as derivative. Thus John Locke held that words, in their primary signification, stand for ideas. They stand for objects in the world derivatively, since the ideas stand for those objects.[3]

Semantic internalism, thus understood, supports the conviction that a source of meaning is the thought of the author and the ideas present in his or her mind. Internalism, however, is not the only semantic concept formulated by the philosophy of language. Another concept of meaning which rivals internalism is semantic externalism. Barwise and Perry explain it thus: 'A second approach is to focus on the external significance of language, on its connection with the described world rather than the describing mind. Sentences are classified not by the ideas they express, but how they describe things to be.'[4]

Putnam has encapsulated semantic externalism in his well-known phrase 'Meanings just ain't in the head'.[5] Externalism assumes that it is not the intention or knowledge of a speaker that determines the meaning of words, but the features of the state of affairs to which those words refer. As Brink discusses, externalism argues that 'language users interact with their natural and social environment in certain

[3] J. Barwise and J. Perry, *Situations and Attitudes* (1983), 3–4.

[4] Barwise and Perry, *Situations and Attitudes*, 4.

[5] H. Putnam, 'The Meaning of "Meaning"', *Minnesota Studies in the Philosophy of Science*, 7 (1975), 131–93.

ways; in particular they introduce terms (e.g. names and general terms) to pick out interesting features of their environment'.[6]

The main focus of semantic externalism, then, is the world which surrounds us, the reality which is external to our minds, and not the internal state of our mind—ideas, intentions, or our understanding of reality. In seeking the basis of meaning, externalism directs its attention towards the external world, attempting to determine in what way our words and sentences classify the state of affairs treated as fragments of reality. Again, Barwise and Perry state as follows: 'Meaning's natural home is the world, for meaning arises out of the regular relations that hold among situations—bits of reality'.[7]

As conceived in semantic externalism, meaning consists in the relatively stable relation which comes to exist between linguistic signs and states of affairs—situations and events. That relation is visible in the instances of use of a given sign: the instances of use create a historical chain, beginning from the moment of the first use and extending through time. Each further use of that linguistic sign is a repetition of that previous relation. As semantic externalists emphasize, 'The meaning of a human language consists of an intricate relation M between utterance events and other aspects of objective reality, a relation entirely determined by the way the linguistic community uses the language'.[8]

The existence of a relation between instances of use of the language and fragments of reality is confirmed by Ruth Millikan, who points out that a constitutive factor of meaning is the historically conceived co-occurrence between the word and the world (reality). The chains of use of a given linguistic sign create what are known as lineages[9] or reproductively established families.[10] These are sets of individual uses of a given linguistic sign, and the individual elements of those sets—tokens—remain in a mapping relation with the world. As Millikan writes,

[6] D. O. Brink, 'Semantics and Legal Interpretation: Further Thoughts', *Canadian Journal of Law and Jurisprudence*, 2/2 (July 1989), 182. An interesting externalist position applied to jurisprudence can be also found in the German literature; see D. Busse, *Recht als Text: Linguistische Untersuchungen zur Arbeit mit Sprache in einer gesellschaftlichen Institution* (1992).

[7] Barwise and Perry, *Situations and Attitudes*, 16.

[8] Barwise and Perry, *Situations and Attitudes*, 17.

[9] Millikan writes, 'The phenomenon of public language emerges, I believe, not as a set of abstract objects, but as a real sort of stuff in the real world, neither abstract nor arbitrarily constructed by the theorist. It consists of actual utterances and scripts, forming crisscrossing lineages.' See Ruth Millikan, *Language: A Biological Model* (2005), p. 38.

[10] Millikan writes, 'tokens of a written English word "dog" that have been reproduced by Xerox, by various people's hands (each hooked to a somewhat differently programmed nervous system), and by various kinds of printing presses are all members of a single reproductively established family. Similarly, if a parrot says "hello", granted that he copied from an English speaker's tokens of "hello", his token is a member of the same reproductively established family as are the speaker's tokens of "hello"'. Millikan, *Language, Thought and Other Biological Categories* (1984), 23.

> These [mapping rules] are rules in accordance with which a critical mass of sentences have mapped onto affairs in the world in the past, thus producing correlation patterns between certain kinds of configurations of sentence elements and certain kinds of configurations in the world.[11]

Configurations of semantic elements and configurations of elements of reality enter into a relation which, as stated, is relatively stable historically. This stability results from the fact that further uses of linguistic signs repeat earlier uses by copying—not only by using the same sign, but by using that sign in the same or a similar context of reality. By complying with previous usage, a language user remains in a state of deference to it.[12] This deference is similar to the legal situation of precedence. Each further user of a linguistic sign is bound by earlier uses and, in this way, maintains the stability of the semantic relation between the language and the world.

The question may arise as to why previous ways of referring to the world through language should have any normative significance for future references. The explanation lies in the idea of 'proper function' proposed by Millikan (1984). She indicates that a lineage is created by a certain function being fulfilled by the relation between the word and the world, which equates with the relation M (in Barwise and Perry's notation). Naming a state of affairs in a particular way constitutes a certain value for society, to the extent that the name is applied consistently to states of affairs having the same properties. An example is provided by the word 'danger': its application to states of affairs that possess the feature of 'being dangerous' is of obvious value to the society using that language. Through the precise, consistent use of the word, a given society can avoid risks. This means that the proper use of the word 'danger' has a specific 'survival value'[13] for a given society. That value is dependent, however, on the correct use of the word concerned. If careless members of a society begin using the word 'danger' heedlessly, as a joke or in some other improper way, the word will lose its survival value. The cause of that loss will be the absence of a relation between the word and a state of affairs having certain properties. Without the relation M, the word 'danger' loses its proper function. That is why it is so important for a society to take care that words are used properly, that every use of a given word corresponds to the right state of affairs.[14]

[11] Millikan, *Language, Thought and Other Biological Categories*, 99–100.

[12] A. Rauti, 'Multiple Groundings and Deference', *The Philosophical Quarterly*, 62/246 (January 2012), 317–36.

[13] Millikan, *Language, Thought and Other Biological Categories*.

[14] Millikan's 'survival value' should not be understood in a narrow, biological sense. The value of a precise language is its usefulness for everyday purposes within a given society. This usefulness indirectly contributes to the evolutionary success of this society. There is no need to prove a direct relationship between the precision of language use and biological survival per se for a survival value to exist. In that approach, Millikan follows Quine; see P. Hylton, *Quine* (2010), 16–17.

Linguistic precedence and the principle of deference make it possible to maintain the relative stability of the relation M and, therefore, to maintain the proper function of individual linguistic tools. Language users cannot conduct themselves like Lewis Carroll's Humpty Dumpty, who claimed, 'When I use a word . . . it means what I choose it to mean—neither more nor less';[15] such wilful behaviour constitutes a threat to the proper function of words and, more broadly, to linguistic stability. That stability provides a measure of linguistic objectivity, even in the case of abstract or ambiguous words.

To take an example, Richard Bernstein points out that the use of the predicate 'is cruel', while not precise, is subject to certain rules. One cannot apply it, for example, to a state of affairs in which a woman helps a blind man to cross the road.[16] This results from the lineage of the predicate 'is cruel' containing states of affairs whose characteristics are very different from those of the state of affairs in which one person helps another: 'is cruel' refers to states of affairs in which the suffering of one person is deliberately caused by another person. Since that feature is not present in the state of affairs under discussion, it is not possible—in the normative sense—to use the predicate 'is cruel' in reference to that state of affairs. To put it another way, if applied to a helpful gesture, the predicate 'is cruel' will not perform its proper function in relation to the state of affairs at hand and will thereby threaten the stability of the use of that predicate.[17]

To sum up, the most important aspect of meaning brought into relief by semantic externalism is the reality standing behind a linguistic sign. The features of that reality actually determine meaning. Following the approach initiated by Kripke and Putnam,[18] a reference is determined by essential characteristics of the reality to which we refer when using words. In other words, a linguistic sign refers to that which possesses a specific internal structure, nature, or function.[19] From this perspective, one of the first externalists was probably Shakespeare:

> What's in a name? That which we call a rose
> By any other name would smell as sweet.[20]

In saying so, Shakespeare's Juliet is clearly focused on the reality behind the words and not on the words themselves. In this regard, her behaviour mirrors that of everyday language users across different languages who refer to essentially the same

[15] Lewis Carroll, *Through the Looking-Glass* (1872).

[16] R. J. Bernstein, *The Pragmatic Turn* (2010), 159.

[17] It is easy to see the relevance of Bernstein's point to legal practitioners and theoreticians, given the debate around the Eighth Amendment to the US Constitution.

[18] S. Kripke, *Naming and Necessity* (1980); Putnam, 'The Meaning of "Meaning"'.

[19] Putnam, 'The Meaning of "Meaning"'.

[20] W. Shakespeare, *Romeo and Juliet*, Act II, Scene 2.

things. 'Rose' (English), '*Die Rose*' (German), '*róża*' (Polish), and '*rosa*' (Italian) are different linguistic signs in different languages; the reality they refer to is, however, similar. In the next section, I show that this similarity makes translation across languages possible, enabling judges to share their experience across jurisdictions.

3.3. Semantic justification for judicial borrowings

We have seen that semantic externalism proposes an approach to language that is focused on reality as the object to which linguistic signs refer. This approach, as opposed to internalism, posits a non-intentional analysis of language, in other words, an analysis which focuses not on the speaker's meaning, but rather on the meaning of the language itself—sentence meaning, created by a historical lineage of instances of language use. The speaker's meaning, based on the authorial intention, is always unique to a particular text and context; the world (understood as the reality to which words refer) appears broadly similar to all nations and jurisdictions.[21] Focusing on how legal terms and concepts are applied to reality makes it possible to learn from the foreign experience and replicate it in different languages and jurisdictions. This provides a rational justification for referring to foreign verdicts.

If we transfer the externalist approach to the field of legal language, we can state that the use of language by a judge in a given ruling is an application of a linguistic sign to a certain fragment of reality. The sign applied is the language of legal acts, while the reality to which that language is applied comprises the facts of a given case. Every ruling is but one of the historical instances of referring language to reality. Such reference demonstrates the previously mentioned 'word-to-world' relation. That relation may then be repeated in another ruling that applies the linguistic signs to the same or a similar reality. It is of no importance whether the reality the judge refers to exists in one jurisdiction or another.

As conceived through semantic externalism, foreign rulings constitute elements of a lineage (Millikan) and, therefore, instances of the use of given linguistic signs (sentences and words) in reference to a specific state of reality. As such, they constitute examples of the relation between the world and language, a relation which may

[21] Two philosophical objections to the approach proposed in this chapter can be formulated: one is that there exists no objective reality (an ontological objection); another, that we do not perceive reality objectively (an epistemological objection). Either objection may undermine the conclusion that the perception of the world by different people in different jurisdictions is similar. In this chapter, I would like to avoid entering the long and complex philosophical discussion concerning the objectivity of reality and its perception. My purpose is much humbler—it is to propose a new paradigm in understanding legal language by shifting the focus from the intentions and states of mind of speakers to the states of affairs in the world to which our language refers. The question of objectivity must be answered in both cases, but the more pressing question is which reality is more objectively perceived—an internal or an external one. I would go for the latter, leaving the old philosophical discussion aside.

be repeated by another judge who applies similar terms to a similar state of affairs. Given the tendency to defer to past speakers,[22] a previous application of a linguistic sign to a state of reality may provide an argument for a further, analogous application. The fact that such a new application is to be made in another jurisdiction is insignificant since, in essence, meaning is decided by the historical relation between uses of the word and reality—and the latter is similar in all legal systems. In this way, references to previous foreign rulings may provide a source of knowledge about the correct application of language to the world.

The historical relation between the uses of the words and elements of reality needs to be seen in a broader context than a monolinguistic one. The Romance languages, for instance, comprise a broader communicative community of language users that perceive a similar reality and classify it with similar words. Given that Western legal culture has its source in Roman law and Mediterranean culture, a multilinguistic community is a natural environment for establishing the meaning of legal terms.

A good example is the use of the idea of '*proporcjonalność*' ('proportionality' in English, '*proportion*' in French[23]) in reference to the situation already cited in the ruling of the Polish Constitutional Tribunal, concerning the obligation to fasten seatbelts when driving a car. The 'word–world' relation in this case is the relation between the word 'proportionate' or the predicate 'is proportionate' (and their equivalents in other languages) and the state of affairs which can be presented as state X: 'the state of affairs in which a person's freedom is limited by the obligation to fasten a seatbelt while driving'.

The relation between the predicate 'is proportionate' and the state of affairs X has been established as a result of a series of instances in which the linguistic sign 'is proportionate' (and its Polish equivalent '*jest proporcjonalny*') has been used in reference to a state of affairs X or to a similar state of affairs. In the seatbelt ruling, we have a further instance of the use of the predicate 'is proportionate' in reference to a state of affairs X (or to a similar state). Therefore, it is justifiable for the Polish Constitutional Tribunal to refer to rulings by American courts or by the Austrian or German constitutional courts, because in all of those cases there is a similar 'word–world' relation, and the Polish Constitutional Tribunal may treat those earlier cases as linguistic precedents for a precise application of the language to the world. In effect, the Polish court may refer to instances in which other courts have qualified a state of affairs X as corresponding to the predicate 'is proportionate' to justify its own ruling on the admissibility of restricting personal freedom by imposing an obligation to fasten seatbelts.

[22] Rauti, 'Multiple Groundings and Deference'.

[23] Interestingly, some equivalents of 'proportionate' in different Western languages are not identical (see the German '*verhältnismäßig*'). This illustrates that the choice of words is ultimately arbitrary, although the reality they describe remains essentially the same.

Seen from the perspective of semantic externalism, judicial borrowings are in fact attempts to interpret the domestic legal text. That said, the interpretation in the sense of semantic externalism is not an attempt to discover the intention of the author. It rather comprises an analysis of the previous instances of using the interpreted terms and an examination of the nature of realities those terms referred to at each instance of their use. The meaning of the term is thus established by understanding what the recurring features of the reality are in each of the instances analysed. The judges' attention is focused on understanding the relation between the words and the world. If they lack a sufficient number of examples of that relation in their own language and judicial practice, they reach out to a similar practice and similar relations in other languages and jurisdictions. This practice is justified as long as the nature of the reality to which the compared terms have been applied is similar.[24]

3.4. Conclusions and guidelines for judicial borrowers

A linguistic justification supports the practice of referring to foreign rulings and doctrine without infringing the autonomy of a given jurisdiction. The practice of borrowing from foreign rulings is based on the assumption that the person interpreting the law must analyse a number of instances of the use of a term to discover what elements of reality historical users of that term have referred to. Part of that historical linguistic use is the usage made in other jurisdictions. Referring to such usage anchors contemporary interpretational decisions in previous linguistic usage.

[24] A possible criticism against the presented theory could be based on the argument that semantic externalism in general applies well to mind-independent, tangible objects (e.g. like gold or water, which are natural kinds), but cannot explain how abstract or theoretical terms (like legal terms) acquire or change meaning. A criticism of this type was presented by D. Patterson in a discussion with D. Brink (D. Patterson, 'Realist Semantics and Legal Theory', *Canadian Journal of Law and Jurisprudence*, 2/2 [July 1989], 175–9; Brink, 'Semantics and Legal Interpretation'). I find Brink's counter-arguments convincing and will not repeat them here. Two additional arguments reinforce Brink's position. First, Millikan's idea of proper function can be attributed to every linguistic instrument, including abstract and theoretical terms; as such, it has a much wider application than the classical Kripke-Putnam semantics that focused on proper names and natural kinds, and to which Patterson's criticism referred. Second, in the view of philosophical pragmatism, abstract and theoretical terms should be perceived as parts of a greater whole—a theory—that ultimately has a function with regard to an external, tangible world. This function is to solve practical problems of human beings. For instance, in law this function is to co-ordinate human behaviours. As a part of a greater set of claims, abstract and theoretical terms perform their proper function as parts of this set and ultimately link with tangible reality via other terms. To paraphrase Quine, our set of concepts faces reality not individually, but only as a corporate body.

The approach presented above requires a departure from internalist semantics, which seeks meaning through an analysis of an author's intentions. By using the approach of realistic semantics and semantic externalism, an interpreter is freed of limitations such as the time and place in which the original author lived. If what is of interest to us is the correlation between the use of a term and specific elements of reality, we can look for similarities between realities in which the term has been uttered and in which it is interpreted, and thereby, define its meaning.

The nature of reality determines the meaning of linguistic signs, and that reality is more universal than the intentions of a specific language user. Thus, in order to define the meaning of a sign, one can refer to situations in which other societies have used a similar sign to refer to a similar reality. This makes it possible to base the linguistic analysis of specific terms on arguments from the usage of similar terms by another society in reference to a similar reality. Thanks to such an approach, the valuable practice of using comparative legal arguments attains legitimacy.

For that legitimacy to be complete, however, it is necessary to create at least the framework of a methodology for using arguments from foreign rulings in court deliberations. Otherwise, there is a risk of referring to such arguments at will, and such liberty could pose the threat of uncontrolled judicial discretion. After all, not every judicial borrowing is by definition justifiable. The theoretical framework presented in this chapter, from which the following guidelines are derived, may provide the basis for a rational discourse on the justifiability of judicial borrowings:

Guideline 1: Before an argument from a foreign ruling is used, it is necessary to show the existence of a communicative community between the legal systems within which we are making borrowings.[25] Different communities tend to use terms differently, and borrowings between legal cultures based on completely different tenets (e.g. the Roman law tradition and the Islamic Sharia tradition) are unjustified.

Guideline 2: A judge must put forward arguments to the effect that those terms whose meanings he or she establishes were, in the case law tradition of both systems, used in similar factual situations and, therefore, that the practice of using one of those terms to supplement the meaning of a second is justified.[26]

[25] The existence of such a community is evident, for example, in the following ruling by the Polish Constitutional Tribunal: 'The German Union Constitutional Tribunal, ruling within common European standards for democratic states also held that a ban on or dissolution of an assembly is a final resort . . . (see ruling of 14 May 1985 in the case of a demonstration in Brokdorf, Decisions of the *Bundesverfassungsgericht*, Vol. 2/Part 1, Karlsruhe 1998, p. 299)' (ruling TK Kp 1/04) (emphasis mine).

[26] The Polish Constitutional Tribunal acted in this way in ruling on an accused's right to access case files: 'The German Federal Constitutional Court (*Bundesverfassungsgericht*, hereinafter the FCC) addressed the subject of the conditions for restricting access to case files by an accused in a situation where means of force have been used against him, among other instances in a ruling of 19 January 2006,

Guideline 3: A judge must show that the tradition of use of a given term (concept, idea, doctrine, etc.) is better elaborated than in his/her own jurisdiction and, therefore, that referring to that tradition enhances our knowledge of the meaning of the words we are interpreting.[27]

Following the above guidelines may help make the references to foreign court verdicts more orderly and, therefore, may help control discretionary judicial powers. As a consequence, those judicial borrowings will lessen the risk identified by Schauer and Wise of delegalization of the law.

A crucial assumption underlies this chapter: in legal interpretation, the authority of the text should supplant that of its author. Legal interpretation is the process of establishing the meaning of the text which binds judges, and the source of the meaning is located not in the author's intention, but in the word-to-world relation. This relation is derived from previous linguistic practice: not perceived narrowly, as a national practice, but as the practice of using similar legal terms in other languages and other legal systems. By respecting this relation, legal discourse is expanded, universalized, and ultimately strengthened.

References

Barwise, Jon and John Perry, *Situations and Attitudes* (Cambridge, MA, 1983).

Bernstein, Richard. J., *The Pragmatic Turn* (Cambridge, 2010).

Bix, Brian., 'Can Theories of Meaning and Reference Solve the Problem of Legal Determinacy?', *Ratio Juris*, 16/3 (September 2003), 281–95.

Brink, David. O., 'Semantics and Legal Interpretation: Further Thoughts', *Canadian Journal of Law and Jurisprudence*, 2/2 (July 1989), 181–91.

Burge, Tyler, 'Individualism and the Mental', *Midwest Studies in Philosophy*, 4 (1979), 73–121.

Busse, Dietrich, *Recht als Text: Linguistische Untersuchungen zur Arbeit mit Sprache in einer gesellschaftlichen Institution* (Tübingen, 1992).

Hylton, Peter, *Quine* (Oxford, 2010).

Kripke, Saul, *Naming and Necessity* (Cambridge, MA, 1980).

Millikan, Ruth, *Language, Thought and Other Biological Categories* (Cambridge, MA, 1984).

Millikan, Ruth, *Language: A Biological Model* (Oxford, 2005).

case file No. 2 BvR 1075/05. . . . The FCC adopted a similar position in an earlier ruling of 11 July 1994, case file No. 2 BvR 777/94' (ruling TK K 42/07) (emphasis mine).

[27] An example of compliance with this guideline is the following passage from a ruling of the Polish Constitutional Tribunal, in which the judges found support in an established line of precedents from other jurisdictions: 'In the case of the People vs Kohrig (ruling of 1 October 1986, No. 62719-24, 498 N.E. 2d 1158, Illinois 1986), the Illinois Supreme Court held that an order to use seatbelts does not infringe a citizen's right to privacy . . . Similar argumentation was used by the Iowa Supreme Court in the case of the State vs. Hartog . . . , and by the Washington Supreme Court . . . A ruling on the obligation to fasten seatbelts was also handed down by the Austrian Constitutional Tribunal . . . The compliance of the provisions on the obligation to fasten seatbelts with basic constitutional law was upheld by the Federal Constitutional Tribunal' (ruling TK SK 48/05).

Patterson, Dennis, 'Realist Semantics and Legal Theory', *Canadian Journal of Law and Jurisprudence*, 2/2 (July 1989), 175–9.
Putnam, Hilary, 'The Meaning of "Meaning"', *Minnesota Studies in the Philosophy of Science*, 7 (1975), 131–93.
Rauti, Antonio, 'Multiple Groundings and Deference', *The Philosophical Quarterly*, 62/246 (January 2012), 317–36.
Schauer, Frederick and Virginia J. Wise, 'Nonlegal Information and the Delegalization of Law', *Journal of Legal Studies*, 29/1 (January 2000), 495–515.
Stavropoulos, Nicos, *Objectivity in Law* (Oxford, 1996).

4

Who forges the tools?

The methods of interpretation between interpretive discourse and positive norms of law

JULIAN UDICH

Interpretation of Public International Law is no unrestrained endeavour, as the ILC's famous evaluation of interpretation resembling 'an art, not an exact science'[1] might at first sight indicate.[2] The main tools for guidance are those usually termed the methods or means of interpretation—for example, recourse to the ordinary meaning of a text, its systematic relation to other norms, a sentence's grammatical structure, or its object and purpose. Their relevance originates from the fact that only an interpretation allegedly adhering to the acknowledged methods of interpretation is considered a legitimate statement of a norm's meaning.[3] Thus, interpreters explain their reasoning by reference to those methods.[4] The usually accepted *canon* of interpretive rules is codified in Articles 31–33 of the Vienna Convention on the Law of Treaties (VCLT).[5]

However, those positive norms are able neither to provide a comprehensive list of methods,[6] nor to define the interrelations between different methods.[7] Thus, a

[1] ILC, 'Draft Articles on the Law of Treaties with Commentaries', *ILC Yearbook* (1966), Article 28, para. 4.

[2] The author wishes to thank Jens Theilen for his extremely valuable comments on a draft of this chapter and adds that the chapter and references have mainly been kept as originally presented.

[3] Robert Alexy, *Theorie der juristischen Argumentation* (2012), 273 and 300–307; IngoVenzke, *How Interpretation Makes International Law* (2012), 48.

[4] See, for example, Alexy, *Theorie der juristischen Argumentation*, 273 ff.

[5] 1155 UNTS 331. For a detailed treatment of parallel customary law, cf Oliver Dörr, 'Article 31: General Law of Interpretation', in *Vienna Convention on the Law of Treaties: A Commentary*, ed. Oliver Dörr and Kirsten Schmalenbach (2012a), Article 31, paras. 9–13 and 33–37.

[6] Cf. Dörr, 'Article 31', para. 33: 'The Convention's rules of interpretation are **not exclusive** in a way that they prevent the interpreter from applying other principles'.

[7] Notwithstanding the subsidiarity declared in VCLT Article 32 that subjects' recourse to the *travaux préparatoires* and other supplementary means to previous yet futile application of the rules in Article

Julian Udich, *Who forges the tools?* In: *Language and Legal Interpretation in International Law.* Edited by: Anne Lise Kjær and Joanna Lam, Oxford University Press. © Oxford University Press 2022. DOI: 10.1093/oso/9780190855208.003.0005

more thorough explanation as to the origins and definitions of those methods is required. At the same time, a lively discussion on interpretation endures in contemporary international law practice and doctrine[8] and mostly resolves around how methods relate to each other[9]—for example, how far norms could be harmonized by reference to external systematic and *telos*, thereby disregarding the most ordinary meaning of a norm. Furthermore, an explanation is necessary as to how the accepted methods of interpretation could be amended.

Consequently, it is necessary to sketch a methodological framework to explain certain phenomena. The framework has to explain how interpretive methods become recognized in a legal system; furthermore, it has to provide a procedure for amendments to those methods; and finally, it should be based upon the status quo of Public International Law (PIL) practice.

This chapter outlines the basis for such a framework working within PIL, which defines the methods of interpretation not as norms, but as the result of a meta-discourse accompanying any interpretation of PIL norms, which inherently defines the legitimate interpretive methods—regardless of whether the interpretative methods are made explicit or applied implicitly. The chapter first establishes some premises fundamental for this framework (section 4.1), then (section 4.2) details the function of this discourse within interpretive communities. Subsequently (section 4.3), its explanatory value as to the role of values and morals in interpretation is described. Section 4.4 concentrates on the multiplicity of PIL treaties and the interpretive influence of courts in different sub-systems.

4.1. Premises: Discretion in interpretation

The necessary premises for this framework entail a positive system of norms, where norms are primarily textual representations without a fixed meaning in detail, thereby leaving the interpreter room for discretionary choices. Furthermore, interpretation is generally subjective; therefore, the methods build on persuasion. Those premises do not preclude this framework's application under different circumstances, but their explicit definition will facilitate transparent discussion.

31; however, this hierarchy is practiced less stringently; see Oliver Dörr, 'Article 32: Supplementary Means of Interpretation', in *Vienna Convention on the Law of Treaties: A Commentary*, ed. Oliver Dörr and Kirsten Schmalenbach (Heidelberg, 2012b), para. 27 ff.

[8] See as examples of treatises on the topic only Ulf Linderfalk, *On the Interpretation of Treaties* (2010); Alexander Orakhelashvili, *The Interpretation of Acts and Rules in International Law* (2008); Richard Gardiner, *Treaty Interpretation* (2008); and ILC and Martti Koskenniemi, 'Fragmentation of International Law', UN.Doc A/CN.4/L.682 (2006), paras. 410–80.

[9] To provide an example, see the elaborate theory on different interpretive methods and their interrelation in Linderfalk, *On the Interpretation of Treaties* (in particular, 387–395 for a comprehensive collection of his rules).

4.1.1. The legal system as a positive system of norms

For the purpose of this paper, the international legal system is in principle understood as a system of positively enacted norms, which are either represented in textual form or in the more difficult cases of customary law, without an authoritative textual manifestation.

However, a caveat seems required at this point, as in contemporary international legal theory, positivism is regularly regarded with caution: neither should this premise from an ontological perspective entirely exclude morals and values from the law—the validity of norms might well be dependent on maintaining a minimal level of justice or upholding certain values, for example in the sense of Radbruch's well-known formula.[10] Thus, a *Grundnorm*[11] on a non-positivist basis may be possible.[12] Furthermore, as will be illustrated in section 4.3, morals and values indeed play a significant role in interpretation nevertheless.

Yet, the basic idea remains valid: the positive enactment of norms means that any given norm of PIL has been adopted by a decision of certain of its subjects[13] (however indirect this decision might seem in cases of customary international law[14]), instead of having been discovered as declaratory restated norms of natural law. Thus, a norm has no further content than it was born with.

4.1.2. The indeterminate nature of positive norms

This leads to the second premise: that norms that have a textual representation are no more determined than the text representing them.[15] Neither is there any non-positivistic determination of a norm, nor does the decision to adopt a certain norm by the respective norm-givers entail an a priori determination of all possible situations this norm could cover in the future.[16] Thus, any applier of law, upon interpreting a norm, has to actually construct its meaning from the words used to express it.[17]

[10] Cf. Gustav Radbruch,'Gesetzliches Unrecht und übergesetzliches Recht', *Süddeutsche Juristenzeitung*, 1 (1946), 107 and, based on his concept, Alexy, *Begriff und Geltung des Rechts* (1992), 139 ff.

[11] See Hans Kelsen, *Reine Rechtslehre* (2nd edn, 1960), 200–208; Hans Kelsen, *Allgemeine Theorie der Normen* (1979), 203 ff; Alexy, *Begriff und Geltung des Rechts*, 154 ff.

[12] Alexy, *Begriff und Geltung des Rechts*, 189, speaks about a 'normative basic norm' ('normative Grundnorm').

[13] See Kelsen, *Reine Rechtslehre*, 4–8; Kelsen, *Allgemeine Theorie der Normen* (1979), 2 and 21–24.

[14] For a traditional position, see Hans Kelsen, *Principles of International Law* (2003), 307–11.

[15] Jörg Kammerhofer, *Uncertainty in International Law* (2011), 112; Venzke, *How Interpretation Makes International Law* (2012), 54–57.

[16] Kammerhofer, *Uncertainty in International Law*, 117–119.

[17] Venzke, *How Interpretation Makes International Law*, 46.

Furthermore, unless one presupposed that language indeed was objectively determined, no inherently 'correct' meaning of a norm is identifiable.[18]

Neither can interpretation become superfluous because the language used in norms is unambiguous: any understanding of a norm's text requires interpretation[19] and furthermore—even if one disregards the increased complexity arising with multiple authentic languages[20]—every norm is itself subject to differing opinions, at least at the margins.[21]

Thus, the interpreters' task requires her to consciously decide for one interpretation and, consequently, interpretation inevitably entails discretionary choices. Any applier of law, who engages in the act of interpretation, will have to allocate meaning to those words, because no a priori definite, single meaning for any legal norm exists.[22]

4.1.3. Subjectivity of interpretation

The two previous premises directly lead to a third: any subject of law has to individually interpret the law applicable to it.[23] However, unless a subject is especially empowered by a positive norm, her interpretation of a norm is merely a subjective statement without legally binding effect on other subjects of law.[24] In PIL, most interpreters lack the authority to interpret with binding force for other subjects[25]—one take on the norm is as good as another.

The major exception concerns those comparatively rare instances where subjects are competent to issue binding decisions vis-à-vis others. This is the case of

[18] Venzke, *How Interpretation Makes International Law*, 46.

[19] Cf. Dörr, 'Article 31', para. 15.

[20] VCLT Article 33 regulates this rudimentarily; for an extensive treatment, see Hilf, *Die Auslegung mehrsprachiger Verträge* (1973).

[21] Kammerhofer, *Uncertainty in International Law*, 111–113; Venzke, *How Interpretation Makes International Law*, 46; Hart, *The Concept of Law*, 120–128; as classical contraposition is often seen de Vattel, *The Law of Nations or Principles of International Law*, iii (1916), 199.

[22] Kammerhofer, *Uncertainty in International Law*, 112; Panos Merkouris, 'Introduction: Interpretation is a Science, Is an Art, Is a Science', in Malgosia Fitzmaurice, Olufemi Elias, and Panos Merkouris, eds., *Treaty Interpretation and the Vienna Convention on the Law of Treaties: 30 Years on* (2010), 6; contra Orakhelashvili, *The Interpretation of Acts and Rules in International Law*, 285–88.

[23] See Dörr, 'Article 31', para. 18 ('every person or organ concerned with a treaty is by necessity competent to interpret it').

[24] Jan Sieckmann, *Recht als normatives System* (2009), 153 ('subjektiver Richtigkeitsanspruch'); cf. also Venzke, *How Interpretation Makes International Law*, 46–47; Kammerhofer, *Uncertainty in International Law*, 113–115; one could also read Dworkin, *Justice for Hedgehogs* (2011), 150–151 along those lines; the contraposition is taken, for example, by Orakhelashvili, *The Interpretation of Acts and Rules in International Law*, 285–288, who presupposes there is a correct meaning.

[25] Binding interpretation should be understood as an interpretation of a norm other subjects have to accept as correct.

international courts when they issue *inter partes*—and usually only *inter partes*[26]—binding judgments.[27] However, in the absence of any formal precedential binding effect of judgments,[28] vis-à-vis most subjects, a court's interpretation is as subjective as that of any other interpreter's, relying on persuasion.[29]

4.1.4. Function of interpretive methods

The concluding premise concerns the function of interpretive methods: even though interpretation is inherently subjective, it is not an endeavour without boundaries. In order to gain any practical effect, any interpretation is required to persuade other subjects that it is preferable compared to other equally possible interpretations.[30]

The methods of interpretation are meant as a first filter providing some rationalization: only if an interpretation purportedly adheres to the accepted interpretive standards of PIL will other subjects consider it as legitimate.[31] On the contrary, an interpretation deviating from methodologically accepted standards loses its persuasive value, as it disregards the common basis for the application of the law. This is because all interpreters, when applying law belonging to a certain legal system, have to subject themselves to the conditions established by this legal system.[32]

Consequently, an interpreter may explain either explicitly or implicitly which methods she applied to derive at her final interpretation.[33] By allegedly adhering

[26] See Art. 59 ICJ-Statute and Shabtai Rosenne, *The Law and Practice of the International Court 1920–2005*, iii (4th edn, 2006), 1553–1554.

[27] In contemporary PIL two other instances of binding interpretation could be identified: the authoritative interpretation by a competent organ and, arguably, self-judging norms, if one accepts their existence. For a general introduction, see Udich, 'Vital Interests', in Rüdiger Wolfrum, ed., *Max Planck Encyclopedia of Public International Law* (2013), paras. 5–10.

[28] Rosenne, *The Law and Practice of the International Court 1920–2005*, 1553.

[29] Rosenne, *The Law and Practice of the International Court 1920–2005*, 1553.

[30] Cf. also Venzke, *How Interpretation Makes International Law*, 46–49.

[31] See Venzke, *How Interpretation Makes International Law*, 48–50; also Owen M. Fiss, 'Objectivity and Interpretation', *Stanford Law Review*, 34 (1981–1982), 748 ('disciplining rules').

[32] Also Fiss, 'Objectivity and Interpretation', 745; Venzke, *How Interpretation Makes International Law*, 49.

[33] This understanding presupposes that two, maybe even three, stages of interpretation could in theory be distinguished: an interpreter's first take on a text is necessarily a process of subconscious cognitive processing of a norms text. In a second stage, the interpreter will determine the norms meaning first, by reference to its own preferred result (if any) and second, by tentatively applying the interpretive methods to the norm. Those stages are intra-subjective. The third stage then concerns the outward communication of the interpretation to other subjects: here the interpretive methods are no means for the interpreter to discover meaning, but instruments of justifying her choices. See Dörr, 'Article 31', para. 15 with reference to Schwarzenberger, 'Myths and Realities of Treaty Interpretation', *Virginia Journal of International Law*, 9 (1968), 8, distinguishing the semi-conscious first interpretation and the rational construction. Also Sieckmann, *Recht als normatives System*, 152 ('semantic interpretation').

to the acknowledged standards of interpretation, the interpreter pronounces her interpretation to be one legitimate meaning of a norm, notwithstanding the fact that competing, different, and equally legitimate interpretations remain possible. This interpretation is then received by other subjects who could either challenge its methodological soundness and thus legitimacy, or have to engage in a substantial, legal-political argument as to whether one interpretation is preferable in terms of policy. The interpreter's final aim is thus to persuade other subjects why her interpretation is preferable. As a necessary condition to this aim, the interpreter intends to interpret legitimately, since a methodologically flawed interpretation could in theory have no persuasive value whatsoever.[34]

4.2. Forging the tools: Interpretive communities and discursive definition of methods

To enable interpreters to soundly apply the interpretive methods, they have to be identifiable. Three options come into mind: first, recourse to positive norms regulating interpretation, second, a defined canon derived from any philosophical or linguistic concept, and third, the already-mentioned discursive definition.

4.2.1. The deficits of positive norms and static concepts

The first option is only at first sight a viable solution. Even though Articles 31–33 of the VCLT do exist, those norms are unable to comprehensively guide interpretation.[35] The first limitation stems from the fact that, as treaty norms, they bind only ratifying states, whereas all other states and subjects would be left with presupposed parallel norms of customary international law.[36]

Even if one concentrates on Articles 31–33, their regulations are insufficient. The core rule of Article 31 (1) has been drafted so as to permit basically every school of interpretation to reference this Article and, some scholars argue, virtually every method of interpretation could be read to be in conformity with those Articles.[37]

[34] Certainly, there are extra-legal factors which might compensate lacking persuasiveness—political or economic power—due to which a legal position might gain support regardless of its methodological soundness. Yet this could be fairly regarded the exception to the rule. Cf. also Fiss, 'Objectivity and Interpretation', 744–5; Venzke, *How Interpretation Makes International Law*, 49–51.

[35] Daniel Rietiker, 'The Principle of "Effectiveness" in the Recent Jurisprudence of the European Court of Human Rights', *Nordic Journal of International Law*, 79 (2010), 252–253; Matz, *Wege zur Koordinierung völkerrechtlicher Verträge* (2005), 278.

[36] Cf. the critical remarks on this parallel custom by Jan Klabbers, 'Virtuous Interpretation', in Malgosia Fitzmaurice, Olufemi Elias, and Panos Merkouris, eds., *Treaty Interpretation and the Vienna Convention on the Law of Treaties: 30 Years on* (2010), 24–29.

[37] Aust, *Modern Treaty Law and Practice* (2007), 232.

Therefore, those norms are themselves subject to further concretization by interpretation.[38] In particular, the relative weight of different methods—with the possible, yet practically limited exception of subsidiarity of Article 32—remains unanswered by those rules.

Those deficits would be equally true for any parallel customary international law, unless one presupposes this customary law was more precise than the written norms of the Vienna Convention—a fictional statement nowhere to be found in literature. Consequently, the mere recourse to the positive norms of interpretation is insufficient, as it would also be to hope for further clarifying norms to be adopted in due time by the states.[39]

The second option—recourse to carefully developed *canons* of interpretation developed from certain philosophical, linguistic, or other perspectives—might provide comprehensive solutions as to how interpretation should be done.[40] However, these canons fall prey to the practical impreciseness and volatility of PIL in practice: it would be hard to prove that any single concept, as promising as it might seem, has indeed been universally accepted. As long as no single school of interpretation actually is predominant, it might seem intellectually or philosophically persuasive, yet it would provide no reliable basis for interpretation in practice.

4.2.2. Discursive definition of methods

Whereas no single school of interpretation will realistically gain universal support, PIL is constantly applied and thus requires an operational collection of methods. The methodological approach suggested here builds upon this indeterminacy. Consequently, a descriptive model based on the status quo and actual practice would have to be more flexible, yet could at least approximately determine which methods are currently accepted.

With those conditions in mind, it is suggested that the methods of interpretation are defined by a discourse between all interpreters of PIL.[41] Whenever one interprets and applies PIL, the interpretation of a concrete norm includes, on a meta-level, a discursive statement as to which methods of interpretation should be permissible for all interpreters to use and how those should relate to each other. Therefore, this chapter submits that the methods of interpretation are the momentary result of an ongoing discourse, similar to the changing nature of grammatical

[38] Klabbers, 'Virtuous Interpretation', 31–32, 35.

[39] Klabbers, 'Virtuous Interpretation', 35.

[40] As just two examples for comprehensive *canons*, from a partly linguistic perspective, see Linderfalk, *On the Interpretation of Treaties* and, from a discursive perspective, Alexy, *Theorie der juristischen Argumentation*, 299–348.

[41] See also Venzke, *How Interpretation Makes International Law*, 49–50; Klabbers, 'Virtuous Interpretation', 35–36.

rules of a language. This discourse is partly explicit, whenever a subject explains its reasoning with explicit reference to the methods applied, and partly implicit, whenever only the result of interpretation is communicated (along with the contention of its methodological soundness) without sketching the methods applied.

This meta-discourse running in parallel to the application of law—and of course sometimes made explicit by reasoning on the use of methods—flexibly defines the accepted methods of interpretation and their interrelation. Consequently, no durable standard exists, but the methods are in constant semi-fluid transformation.[42]

One could now criticize such indeterminacy as this approach's potential deficit: even though certain methods will clearly define the toolboxes' core, no clear-cut answer will be found at the margins, among rarely applied methods or approaches strongly deviating from the interpretive core. However, for the informed participant the shadowy margins of accepted methods provide all necessary information: she may put those methods to use, then, with awareness that this interpretation's legitimacy is subject to challenge. Or vice versa: she may challenge any given interpretation relying on uncertain methods not only on the substantial level of political convenience and utility, but also on the previous stage of its legitimacy.

Consequently, the discursive understanding of methods requires the interpreter—both in the active role of interpreting or in the 'passive' role as addressee of interpretations—to verify the usage of methods. Therein lays a certain capacity, paired with responsibility, as any interpreter with any application of the law also partakes in the development of those methods.

4.2.3. Interpretive communities: Who participates in the discourse?

In order to further define this influence of an interpreter, it should be clarified who the relevant interpreters are. As this concept's aim is to describe the pragmatics of PIL in practice, the answer has to be wide: in principle, any single subject of PIL—and furthermore, those persons who may be subjects, but moreover are commenters, like academics, NGOs, and various others elaborating on PIL.[43]

This scope is captured by the idea of interpretive communities: all participants to a certain legal system, all subjects concerning themselves with interpretation, form an interpretive community. Originally stemming from literary studies, the concept in its narrower sense describes groups of subjects who would understand texts similarly just because of their similar education, background, and values.[44] To oversimplify, the act of textual interpretation becomes increasingly unnecessary as the

[42] Similarly, Venzke, *How Interpretation Makes International Law*, 49.

[43] See, very similarly, Dörr, 'Article 31', paras. 18–22.

[44] Stanley Fish, *Is There a Text in This Class? The Authority of Interpretive Communities* (1980), 303 ff; Johnstone, 'Treaty Interpretation', *Michigan Journal of International Law*, 12 (1990–1991), 376–77.

group's members share similar or identical understandings.[45] Such narrow concepts would most likely work if the referenced community was relatively small, for example, if it concerned only a bilateral treaty.[46]

However, PIL, with nearly 200 states, various courts, a vast number of international organizations, and numerous scholars, is too diverse to accommodate such a narrow concept: the actual differences in educational, legal, and cultural backgrounds, not to mention differing interests, preclude automatic agreement.[47] Instead, the idea of interpretive communities should be understood in a wider sense as the entire group of subjects engaged in the interpretation of either PIL in general or a special treaty in particular. All appliers of law, in general PIL any state, international court, international organization, or other subject, form this one community simply due to the fact that they define their activities to be subject to PIL. Therefore, in principle, every single subject of law, if she interprets the law, also shapes the discourse to a certain extent.[48]

Obviously, the very nature of PIL precludes a perfect discourse of equal opportunity to speak and be heard. Even though this chapter permits no extensive discussion of discourse theory,[49] one important feature is equal participation.[50] This entails equal opportunities to make one's voice heard in the discourse, as well as the impact and reception of a single opinion.[51]

At this point, the rules of the actual discourse in PIL cannot be positively described, but one has to accept that different subjects' opinions are likely to gain different weight within the community—based on factors critical legal studies and realist approaches have identified at length.[52] Yet, as an authoritative and comprehensive definition of the permissible methods through neither positive norms nor by a competent authority is in sight, the actual, although imperfect, discourse remains the only feasible solution to determine the interpretive methods. The more influential a specific participant is the stronger will her individual interpretation shape the discourse[53]—as will be seen in the case of international courts in section 4.4.

[45] Johnstone, 'Treaty Interpretation', 378–79.

[46] Cf. below IV. for interpretive special communities for individual treaties.

[47] This automatic agreement relates to the previously mentioned preliminary interpretation, which is more subconscious: if subjects are within such a narrow community, they likely derive mostly identical interpretations from a given text. Cf. also Johnstone, 'Treaty Interpretation', 378.

[48] See similarly Venzke, *How Interpretation Makes International Law*, 49.

[49] For an extensive treatment of different theories of discourse, see Alexy, *Theorie der juristischen Argumentation*, 51 ff and Jürgen Habermas, *Faktizität und Geltung*, 151–165, 272–92.

[50] Alexy, *Theorie der juristischen Argumentation*, 158–59.

[51] Alexy, *Theorie der juristischen Argumentation*, 240–42.

[52] See generally Steven R. Ratner, 'Legal Realism School', in Rüdiger Wolfrum, ed., *Max Planck Encyclopedia of Public International Law* (2007), in particular paras. 24–30 on realist approaches, and Frankenberg, 'Critical Theory' in Rüdiger Wolfrum, ed., *Max Planck Encyclopedia of Public International Law* (2010) paras. 25–36 for an overview of critical legal approaches.

[53] On authority in discourse, see also Venzke, *How Interpretation Makes International Law*, 57–62.

4.2.4. The results: What could the discourse define and change?

The interpretive community consequently defines the methods accepted for PIL in their discourse. Three functions should be fleshed out in some detail: first, how the discourse defines which methods are accepted, second their interrelation, and third, the process of amending those rules.

First, the process of defining the acceptable methods: the interpreter with every interpretation implicitly or explicitly defines how she applies methods like ordinary meaning, systematic structure, and grammatical relation of phrases, and also describes their application. In synopsis, such individual utterances thereby define which methods are permissible and furthermore specify the details of certain methodological approaches. An example relating to a single method of interpretation is how the ordinary meaning should be selected from among the different lexical options.[54]

The second function of this discourse is to define how different methods relate to each other and under which circumstances one method prevails. Thus, the subjects define, for example, the comparable weight of the ordinary meaning versus teleological arguments. Based on this perception, the provenance of certain interpretive methods can be explained. For example, contemporary PIL is usually seen as pursuing a textual approach, exemplified by the 'single rule' of VCLT Article 31 (1), thus following neither originalist tendencies, nor a purely teleological approach.[55]

Moreover, a third aspect to be explained is the amendment of those methods: the results of a discourse are by definition always subject to change and valid only at a certain point in time. Consequently, subjects might also consciously intend to exercise influence and actively bend or amend the rules by anomalously applying the interpretive methods: if one applies the rules somewhat differently, for example, that because of the perceived *telos* the most likely lexical meaning of a word may be disregarded,[56] and releases this interpretation to the community, the reception will define its influence on the discourse. If the proposal finds acceptance, it could gradually amend the applicable methods; in the example just mentioned, establishing a certain prevalence of the object and purpose over 'the' ordinary meaning. On the contrary, if the proposal is rejected, not only the specific interpretation in question would be considered illegitimate, but the existing methodological standard

[54] For different approaches to the ordinary meaning, see Orakhelashvili, *The Interpretation of Acts and Rules in International Law*, 318–38.

[55] Dörr, 'Article 31', paras. 38–9.

[56] Cf. Fiss, 'Objectivity and Interpretation', 741–44. This example is taken for the sake of the argument and does in no way intend to capture the actual status of PIL's interpretive community, which most likely would accept this proposal by a clear majority, cf. Orakhelashvili, *The Interpretation of Acts and Rules in International Law*, 343–345; with qualification, Linderfalk, *On the Interpretation of Treaties*, 227–28.

would moreover be reinforced and the proposed amendment rejected. By the same token, a subject might be inclined to establish new methodological approaches or derivatives of existing ones, for example restrictive interpretation to rules limiting sovereignty.[57] The same rationale applies here as with defining the relationship between methods.

As the processes of defining and amending the rules are inherently chaotic, often only implicit, and as any single interpretation will rarely define a method in all its aspects, following and observing the discourse entails a certain obfuscation for the observer: the more distilled the discursive statements are in their presentation, the clearer they might seem, whereas the pandemonium of individual utterances is probably incomprehensible. Yet, the more distant the perspective, the less visible are fuzzy details that actually delineate the methods' margins. Depending on how controversial an interpretation should be and what risk of being rejected an interpreter is willing to take, she will follow a more majoritarian view, or wander the uncertain margins of those methods.[58]

Such a discursive concept does not preclude that interpretive methods are formed among a certain dogmatic or philosophical model of how language and law should be structured. However, it is submitted that, given the diverse realities of PIL, any such concept would have to participate in the multiplicity of voices amounting to the accepted methods of PIL, and would have to gain such widespread acceptance that it is predominant in order to decelerate or freeze the discourse.[59]

In conclusion, it is submitted that a discursive description of how the interpretive methods are defined and amended provides an insightful tool to differentiate between the arguments about legitimate interpretation and the substantial decision the interpreter takes. Therefore, it permits to (at least) approximately define the permissible interpretive methods and their interrelation in PIL.

4.2.5. Positive norms in interpretation: The outer limits of discourse

This section should end with a comment on the function of the meagre positive norms on interpretation like those in Articles 31–33 of the VCLT have in this concept. Obviously, those norms remain valid and—within their limited sphere of application *ratione materiae* and *personae*—binding law. In parallel, interpreters argue

[57] Cf. on the method of restrictive interpretation, Dörr, 'Article 31', para. 34; Linderfalk, *On the Interpretation of Treaties*, 280–3; Orakhelashvili, *The Interpretation of Acts and Rules in International Law*, 413–21.

[58] Yet, again, special authority might help, see Venzke, *How Interpretation Makes International Law*, 62–64.

[59] Obviously, the smaller an interpretive community is, the more likely general agreement becomes, cf. below IV.

discursively about the details of the interpretive methods. It is submitted that the positive norms of interpretation serve as a boundary and define the outer limits for the discourse: as every interpretive community within PIL defines itself by reference to international law, it implicitly accepts the authority of PIL's norms, including those on interpretation. Thus, every application of law claims legality, in the sense that it purports not to violate other norms. This includes the imperative not to violate the positive norms on interpretation.[60] Consequently, any discursive statement on interpretation which is arguably violating those positive norms would be illegal, diminishing its persuasive value to zero. Therefore, the interpreter is furthermore tasked to either argue that her usage of the interpretive methods is legal under the norms of the VCLT (or parallel custom) or is in addition burdened to prove why those positive norms have been amended, for example, derogated by new customary law, and her interpretation indeed is legal under the amended laws.

To summarize the framework up to this point: it is submitted that the methods of interpretation, their interplay, and their relative weight result from a meta-discourse as to which methods are permissible. Participants in this (imperfect) discourse are all subjects[61] of PIL who engage in interpretive efforts, even though their actual influence will vary. So far, this concept tries to illustrate how the interpretive methods in PIL came into being, what their legal nature is—they are not norms, but meta-legal conventions—and consequently, how amendments of those rules are possible. In order to illustrate the explanatory value of this concept, the last parts of the paper will now address two pressing topics in PIL.

4.3. Adding substance: Morals and values

First, the role of values and morals in interpretation should be illuminated from an interpreter's perspective. Unless one assumes a non-positivist legal system that a priori defines the weight and relevance of certain morals for the law with universally binding force, the status quo in PIL is less idealistic: certain values might be recognized more or less universally, yet disagreement remains at least in the details of how those values translate into practice.

The discursive framework might also provide a starting point from which to integrate value arguments in interpretation. First, it has to be identified where values and the process of interpretation interact. The most obvious factor is that any interpreter takes choices in interpreting the law depending on her own value

[60] See Venzke, *How Interpretation Makes International Law*, 50.

[61] As well as non-subjects, as far as their utterances are considered relevant, for example, from academia.

judgements—which is equally inevitable[62] and desirable. Generally, as described before, interpretation as such is neutral, insofar as different equally sound interpretations exist. Therefore, the interpreter decides in favour of one legitimate option, to effectuate values of her choice in law. Values could in this function be termed the guidelines for the subjective interpretation.

However, interpretation could also to a certain extent limit, or at least guide, how far an interpreter may have recourse to values. Certain interpretive methods permit a more direct recourse on values, whereas others would hide the influence of choices behind other considerations: for example, would a treaty's *telos* in most cases require the interpreter to evaluate different aspects in order to identify the relevant *telos*? On the other hand, stricter approaches relying on the ordinary meaning, for example, in a sense of the most usual lexical meaning, would more seriously limit the choices to be made.

Moreover, orientation towards a certain general value or principle might become an interpretive device in its own right. The discursively defined methods can first of all now regulate at what point, for example, by reference to a norm's *telos*, value judgements become valid interpretive arguments instead of subconscious or at least implicit choices. Consequently, the interpretive community steers the influence that open reference to value arguments has over other linguistic or systematic arguments—which themselves are in no way free from considerations of value, but do not purport to pursue them openly—by tailoring the accepted methods to provide for more or less leeway and featuring or restricting more evaluative methods.

Furthermore, and this would be the strongest connection between interpretation and values, in principle an interpretive community could agree within their discourse that certain values are indeed of such importance that any interpreter is required to pursue her realization in interpreting other laws. Technically, this value-oriented interpretation would be considered one method dominating all others to a certain extent. It is doubtful whether in the general interpretive community of contemporary PIL any such values are generally accepted and allocated to this predominant status. However, it is in principle possible, and would explain from the interpretive perspective how harmonizing interpretation could be framed and explained—as far as the community accepts certain values as their 'lighthouses' for interpretation, all norms in PIL would gradually harmonize to follow their lead.

This linkage permits the bridging of morals and law to a certain extent, without necessarily adopting a non-positivist conception of law. The weight of certain values is, by definition, subject to argument. From a harmonizer's perspective,

[62] A thorough argument on this is found, from a basically non-positivist view, in Dworkin, *Justice for Hedgehogs*, 99–122 and 156.

value-oriented interpretation could thus contribute to harmonize PIL if, and insofar as, agreement on certain guiding values or principles can be found.[63]

4.4. Increased complexity: The multiplicity of regimes and courts

Another topic of concern for contemporary PIL is its fragmented, decentralized, predominantly treaty-based character. Although PIL is a single legal system, several treaties try to comprehensively regulate certain aspects of life. Thus, it should be answered, what influence different approaches on interpretation could have either to remedy or increase the effects of this fragmented structure. Mostly, the discussion is framed along the advantages of harmonization versus the internal rationality of different treaties.[64] From the perspective of the interpretive discourse, this chapter submits a certain distinction that might prove useful to distinguish different aspects of this discussion.

4.4.1. Special interpretive communities

The paper has previously only taken into account the general interpretive community that discursively defines the permissible methods of interpretation for PIL as a whole. However, this macro-perspective can as well be complemented by a closer perspective concentrating on different treaties. Those treaties do not form 'self-contained regimes' in the stricter sense but remain part of the same legal system[65]—comprehensively argued and tellingly described by Simma and Pulkowski with the picture of different planets within the same universe[66]—yet states might interpret the norms differently.

As far as interpretation is concerned, all interpreters engaging in the interpretation of a certain treaty in principle also form a sub-interpretive community, which could decide to define methods for its own regime somewhat independently from the general discourse. Those general and special communities exist side-by-side, with subjects partaking in both communities and the requisite norms being interpreted using both interpretive toolboxes.

[63] As an example of the value-oriented interpretation by the ECtHR, see Tzevelekos, 'The Use of Article 31(3)(c) of the VCLT in the Case Law of the ECtHR', *Michigan Journal of International Law*, 31 (2009–2010), 647–65.

[64] See ILC and Koskenniemi, 'Fragmentation of International Law', paras. 410–80.

[65] Simma, 'Self-Contained Regimes', *Netherlands Yearbook of International Law*, 16 (1985), 135–6; ILC and Koskenniemi, 'Fragmentation of International Law', paras. 191–4.

[66] Simma and Pulkowski, 'Of Planets and the Universe', *European Journal of International Law*, 17, 505–6.

Regularly, a special community will be indistinguishable from the general community, as neither a reason to diverge exists, nor an actually distinct discourse develops. However, the sub-community might decide to pursue a different interpretive path than the general community. Consequently, within this special interpretive community methods might be at odds with those in PIL in general, if the special community indeed amends the interpretive methods while interpreting 'their' treaty. An example could be the progressive, highly teleological, and value-oriented interpretation by the ECtHR.[67]

One reason to deviate from the general interpretive community could be to realize the treaties' *telos* more completely. Insofar as a special approach to interpretation might further this object presumably better than the methodological take prescribed by the general community, the community could therefore decide to deviate accordingly.

Comparably to *inter se* agreements in the law of treaties, those sub-community's rules would be accepted only within the sub-community. Therefore, from the general community's perspective, those methods defined by their discourse are the only accepted methods, whereas the special communities' interpretation would be considered illegitimate: both communities interpret the same norms belonging to the same legal system, yet disagree on the tools applicable to it. Therefore, the idea of multiple communities is especially suitable to frame the discussion about allegedly 'self-contained regimes', which should from an interpretive stance simply be considered as deviating methodological discourses.[68]

In order to shed some light on this distinction, the discourses have to be separable: the rebellious community engages at the same time in its sub-discourse and at the same time participates in the general discourse. Therefore, the same utterance might contribute to both discourses in parallel. However, regularly interpretive approaches that display a strong connection to a specific treaty, in particular its *telos*, would be considered as mainly focused on the sub-communities' discourse. A suitable example would be the 'living instrument' approach by the ECtHR,[69] which

[67] Tzevelekos, 'The Use of Article 31(3)(c)', 641 ff.

[68] This way of describing self-contained regimes however has to be complemented by another aspect, the application of potential conflict solution rules, for example *lex specialis* or *lex posterior*. Those rules are arguably applicable independent of interpretive methods, even though some authors merge them with interpretation (for more detail and further references, see Vranes, 'Lex Superior, Lex Specialis, Lex Posterior', *Zeitschrift für auslandisches öffentliches Recht und Völkerrecht*, 65, 391–405). However, neither the application of *lex specialis* nor other conflict solution rules provide a basis for truly self-contained regimes; see Simma and Pulkowski, 'Of Planets and the Universe', 490–492; ILC and Koskenniemi, 'Fragmentation of International Law', para. 221.

[69] Tzevelekos, 'The Use of Article 31(3)(c)', 641 ff; Rietiker, 'The Principle of "Effectiveness"', 256–260; Letsas, 'Intentionalism and the Interpretation of the ECHR', in Malgosia Fitzmaurice, Olufemi Elias, and Panos Merkouris, eds., *Treaty Interpretation and the Vienna Convention on the Law of Treaties: 30 Years on* (2010), 263.

is by its very reasoning focused on a particular treaty, the European Convention of Human Rights, and does not even purport to apply to the entirety of PIL. The general community is consequently just tasked to either consider the results of a deviating interpretation as a violation of the law or their discursive rules respectively, or acknowledge an exception from their usual methods which applies only to a certain treaty or certain types of treaties in particular. Such a subject-matter exception could frame the discussion, for example, as to why human rights treaties in general should be interpreted differently than other treaties in PIL.[70] Thus, the general community could acknowledge, given time and persuasion, that a certain regime should be treated differently.

On the contrary, the sub-community could also, by partaking in the general community, urge that their methodological approach should also be adopted for the entire PIL, therefore trying to amend the generally accepted rules. Which stance is taken is subjective, as all interpretation is, and depends on the interpreter's intent.

4.4.2. The influence of courts within special regimes

Alongside the multiplicity of treaties, a multiplicity of specialized international organizations and in particular courts and tribunals also came into being. Typically, even treaties instituting international organizations establish few organs who publicly interpret the treaty and even fewer, like courts, which are competent to interpret with (limited) binding force.

Accordingly, those organs exercise particular influence in their respective special interpretive communities: although most organs of international organizations have no competence to issue formally authentic interpretations, theirs profit from the visibility of singular organs in a treaty, and, in the case of well-used courts, also from the regular occasion to interpret their respective treaties. In regimes with a strong court, for example, the ECtHR, the ECJ, and the Appellate Body, the respective court's influence on its own interpretive community is especially significant: being the only subject with at least limited authority to adopt binding decisions, a regime's single court will significantly shape the interpretive discourse for this regime.

Therefore, the actors at the respective court (or other institution) could decide if and whether their regime's interpretation should deviate from the general interpretive community.[71] Courts within a regime have to consciously weigh how far their regime would benefit from tailor-made interpretive methods, or how far integration with other norms on an interpretative level is more reasonable than pursuing a path of separation.

[70] Dörr, 'Article 31', para. 31.

[71] Compare again the ECtHR, see Letsas, 'Intentionalism and the Interpretation of the ECHR', 270 ff; Tzevelekos, 'The Use of Article 31(3)(c)', 647 ff.

Regardless of any internally divergent interpretation, the court should take into account that the member states to the treaty might be held accountable to the results from its interpretation by third parties following the general interpretive approach. A court might thus not only further fragmentation on a substantial level, but might also in the end cause international responsibility for a member state vis-à-vis third parties, if their fulfilment of the court's treaty requires them to violate other norms of PIL or the special community also deviates from the VCLT. Those risks might regularly prevent courts within a sub-community from separating too far from the general international community, yet it should be noted that certain regimes further their internal rationalities regardless of those potential consequences.

To summarize, the influence of courts on the discourse in their respective communities is submitted to be significantly higher than of other participants to the community.[72] Therefore, those actors bear a special responsibility to evaluate whether their regime and the member states bound to it will profit from a more aligned or separated interpretive approach.

4.4.3. Reactions to fragmentation: Interaction or rejection

The impact of fragmentation of contemporary PIL, as far as interpretative approaches are concerned—contrary to other means like conflict solution rules[73]—thus partly depends on three factors: the different actors' conscientiousness of their treaty regimes, the interest to harmonize PIL in its entirety, and the claim to enrich PIL with certain values or principles.

All three factors are influenced by how the interpretive discourse defines the methods of interpretation. It has the potential to either ameliorate conflicts between different treaty regimes or further divide the gap between them: the higher interpreters value a harmonized legal system—and this is arguably a decision, not a premise from the nature of law[74]—the more leeway they might introduce for methodological approaches trying to integrate or harmonize norms of this legal system. Furthermore, as far as the community accepts certain values as interpretive guidelines, it may remedy the decentralized structure by aligning all norms towards certain goals. On the contrary, in particular, sub-communities might be tempted to favour their treaty over others and thereby limit grand scale integration. The sum of

[72] See Venzke, *How Interpretation Makes International Law*, 62–64.

[73] On the solution of normative conflicts through conflict solution rules, see, for example, ILC and Koskenniemi, 'Fragmentation of International Law', paras. 56–122, 223–323; Nele Matz, *Wege zur Koordinierung völkerrechtlicher Verträge*, 312–339; Pauwelyn (2003) pp. 361–417.

[74] Alexander Somek, 'Kelsen Lives', *European Journal of International Law*, 18/3 (2007), 415; others base it on fundamental rationalizations, for example, Matz, *Wege zur Koordinierung völkerrechtlicher Verträge*, 1; for the opposing view—harmonization as a premise of the legal system—see Alexy, *Begriff und Geltung des Rechts*, 172–73.

interpreters' choices which constitutes the discourse therefore significantly affects the potential of interpretation to remedy the effects of fragmentation.

4.5. Summary

The methods of interpretation serve as yardsticks to test the legitimacy of a particular, subjective interpretation. They are defined by a discourse inherent in any interpretation. This perspective permits the incorporation of change and acknowledges differing approaches to interpretation within different treaty regimes, all while upholding the idea of a single legal system.

Thus, as the methods of interpretation are formed as a condensate of all interpretative issuances, in principle every interpreter and particularly courts with their highlighted impact on the discourse, bears responsibility for the individual interpretation, as well as for constituting the basis of interpretation itself.

Consequently, interpretation requires any interpreter to take responsible and conscious decisions as to how interpretation should be conducted and engage in the discourse accordingly. The result will define the permissible methods and thus the discretion any applier of law has and may put to use. To borrow from Kelsen, the norm is only a frame of possible meanings.[75] Which meanings are permissible is defined by the methodological discourse. Which of those legitimate meanings should be adopted is up to the applier of law: law or methods cannot take this responsibility from him or her.

References

Alexy, Robert, *Begriff und Geltung des Rechts* (Freiburg and Munich, 1992).

Alexy, Robert, *Theorie der juristischen Argumentation* (Frankfurt, 2012).

Aust, Anthony, *Modern Treaty Law and Practice* (Cambridge, 2007).

Bernhardt, Rudolf, 'Interpretation and Implied (Tacit) Modification of Treaties', *Zeitschrift für auslandisches öffentliches Recht und Völkerrecht*, 27 (1967), 491–506.

de Vattel, Emerich, *The Law of Nations or Principles of International Law*, iii (Washington, 1916).

Dörr, Oliver, 'Article 31: General Law of Interpretation', in Oliver Dörr and Kirsten Schmalenbach, eds., *Vienna Convention on the Law of Treaties: A Commentary* (Heidelberg, 2012a), 512–70.

Dörr, Oliver, 'Article 32: Supplementary Means of Interpretation', in Oliver Dörr and Kirsten Schmalenbach, eds., *Vienna Convention on the Law of Treaties: A Commentary* (Heidelberg, 2012b), 571–86.

Dworkin, Ronald, *Justice for Hedgehogs* (Cambridge, 2011).

Fish, Stanley, *Is There a Text in This Class? The Authority of Interpretive Communities* (Cambridge, MA, 1980).

Fiss, Owen M., 'Objectivity and Interpretation', *Stanford Law Review*, 34 (1981–1982), 739–63.

[75] Kelsen, *Reine Rechtslehre*, 346–349; Kammerhofer, *Uncertainty in International Law*, 113–116.

Frankenberg, Günter, 'Critical Thgeory', in Rüdiger Wolfrum, ed., *Max Planck Encyclopedia of Public International Law* (2010) www.mpepil.com.

Gardiner, Richard, *Treaty Interpretation* (Oxford, 2008).

Habermas, Jürgen, *Faktizität und Geltung* (Frankfurt, 1998).

Hart, H. L. A., *The Concept of Law* (Oxford, 1961).

Hilf, Meinhard, *Die Auslegung mehrsprachiger Verträge* (Berlin, 1973).

ILC, 'Draft Articles on the Law of Treaties with Commentaries', *ILC Yearbook* (1966), 187–274.

ILC and Martti Koskenniemi, 'Fragmentation of International Law', UN.Doc A/CN.4/L.682 (2006).

Johnstone, Ian, 'Treaty Interpretation', *Michigan Journal of International Law*, 12 (1990–1991), 371–419.

Kammerhofer, Jörg, *Uncertainty in International Law* (London, 2011).

Kelsen, Hans, *Reine Rechtslehre* (2nd edn, Vienna, 1960).

Kelsen, Hans, *Allgemeine Theorie der Normen* (Vienna, 1979).

Kelsen, Hans, *Principles of International Law* (Clark, 2003).

Klabbers, Jan, 'Virtuous Interpretation', in Malgosia Fitzmaurice, Olufemi Elias, and Panos Merkouris, eds., *Treaty Interpretation and the Vienna Convention on the Law of Treaties: 30 Years on* (Leiden and Boston, MA, 2010), 17–37.

Letsas, George, 'Intentionalism and the Interpretation of the ECHR', in Malgosia Fitzmaurice, Olufemi Elias, and Panos Merkouris, eds., *Treaty Interpretation and the Vienna Convention on the Law of Treaties: 30 Years on* (Leiden and Boston, MA, 2010), 257–72.

Linderfalk, Ulf, *On the Interpretation of Treaties* (Dordrecht, 2010).

Matz, Nele, *Wege zur Koordinierung völkerrechtlicher Verträge* (Berlin, 2005).

Merkouris, Panos, 'Introduction: Interpretation is a Science, Is an Art, Is a Science', in Malgosia Fitzmaurice, Olufemi Elias, and Panos Merkouris, eds., *Treaty Interpretation and the Vienna Convention on the Law of Treaties: 30 Years on* (Leiden and Boston, MA, 2010), 1–13.

Orakhelashvili, Alexander, *The Interpretation of Acts and Rules in International Law* (Oxford, 2008).

Pauwelyn, Joost, *Conflict of Norms in Public International Law* (Cambridge, 2003).

Radbruch, Gustav, 'Gesetzliches Unrecht und übergesetzliches Recht', *Süddeutsche Juristenzeitung*, 1 (1946), 105–8.

Ratner, Steven, 'Legal Realism School', in Rüdiger Wolfrum, ed., *Max Planck Encyclopedia of Public International Law* (2007), www.mpepil.com.

Rietiker, Daniel, 'The Principle of "Effectiveness" in the Recent Jurisprudence of the European Court of Human Rights', *Nordic Journal of International Law*, 79 (2010), 245–77.

Rosenne, Shabtai, *The Law and Practice of the International Court 1920–2005*, iii (4th edn, Leiden and Boston, MA, 2006).

Schwarzenberger, Georg, 'Myths and Realities of Treaty Interpretation', *Virginia Journal of International Law*, 9 (1968), 1–19.

Sieckmann, Jan, *Recht als normatives System* (Baden-Baden, 2009).

Simma, Bruno, 'Self-Contained Regimes', *Netherlands Yearbook of International Law*, 16 (1985), 111–36.

Simma, Bruno and Dirk Pulkowski, 'Of Planets and the Universe', *European Journal of International Law*, 17 (2006), 483–529.

Somek, Alexander, 'Kelsen Lives', *European Journal of International Law*, 18/3 (2007), 409–51.

Tzevelekos, Vassilis, 'The Use of Article 31(3)(c) of the VCLT in the Case Law of the ECtHR', *Michigan Journal of International Law*, 31 (2009–2010), 621–90.

Udich, Julian, 'Vital Interests', in Rüdiger Wolfrum, ed., *Max Planck Encyclopedia of Public International Law* (2013), www.mpepil.com.

Venzke, Ingo, *How Interpretation Makes International Law* (Oxford, 2012).

Vranes, Erich, 'Lex Superior, Lex Specialis, Lex Posterior', *Zeitschrift für auslandisches öffentliches Recht und Völkerrecht*, 65 (2005), 391–405.

2. Who Does Legal Interpretation?
Legal Interpretation as Judicial Activity

5

Balancing interpretation rules as the element of judicial discretion

BARTOSZ WOJCIECHOWSKI

The question of legal interpretation constitutes the essence of the so-called judicial application of law. My intention is to attempt to present the process of operative interpretation of vague legal terms and general clauses as a model for balancing the rules of interpretation, considered as an essential aspect of judicial discretion in the so-called broad terms.[1]

5.1. The concept of judicial discretion

Judicial discretion can be encountered in all cases when the judge does not approach the process of law application in a strictly formalized manner. In these cases, the judge does not face the task of undertaking a simple, rational subsumption but is entitled to balance between a greater number of alternatives; that is, he or she must settle the case up to the point. He or she can then adjudicate between two contradictory decisions (e.g. granting or not granting a permission), or possibly, such a disjunction provides a larger number of feasible solutions. The concept of 'discretion' is also used in the sense of 'evaluation' with regards to evaluative ruling that forms the essence of judicial discretion and the margin of discretion vested in the judge.

[1] The following text was prepared as a part of a research grant financed by National Science Center (Poland), No. DEC-2012/05/B/HS5/01111. I touch upon the problem of judicial discretion in more detail in the monograph *Dyskrecjonalność sędziowska. Studium teoretycznoprawne* [*Judicial Discretion. Jurisprudential Study*] (2004). For the sake of clarity of the considerations presented in this article, I do not address the different perspectives of judicial discretion. In particular I depart from a narrow understanding of discretion as adopted in the cited monograph, limited to determining legal consequences, which does not mean that I modify the previously adopted assumption, as I only adapt them to the problems at issue.

Bartosz Wojciechowski, *Balancing interpretation rules as the element of judicial discretion* In: *Language and Legal Interpretation in International Law*. Edited by: Anne Lise Kjær and Joanna Lam, Oxford University Press. © Oxford University Press 2022. DOI: 10.1093/oso/9780190855208.003.0006

Modern Anglo-Saxon literature devoted to the issue of 'judicial discretion' emphasizes that this problem should be discussed in a broader context that takes into consideration semantic and epistemic aspects.[2] Problems such as knowledge about social phenomena, the status of social ontology, and the interrelations between law and language can then be taken into consideration.

From this point of view, the scope of judicial discretion extends to both the horizontal and the vertical sphere of judicial activity. This scope includes not only the various fields of legal norms, which provide the judge with adjudicating discretion, but also varying degrees of legal qualification required to handle each individual case. Judicial discretion refers to the thinking process, the assessment of facts, interpretation of legal norms, determination of their mutual interrelations, and at times the lawmaking process. It applies to all forms of judicial freedom, regardless of whether its origins can be traced to statutory authorization or whether it is viewed as a result of being merged by the judiciary in '*praeter* or *contra legem*' when adjudicating an individual case that has not been adequately defined in the statute with clarity.

The issue of judicial discretion in its broad sense is typically associated with vague legal concepts and general clauses. The need to use vague concepts in legal texts implies that the legislator—due to the necessity of making law at times for the distant future—must oscillate between the Scylla of legal certainty and the Charybdis of its flexibility. Vague legal concepts appear in all areas of law. 'A vague term' is understood as a term whose content and scope is uncertain since it does not directly or exhaustively determine all the elements of the hypothesis and disposition, as opposed to a specific concept whose hypothesis and disposition exhaustively and reliably determine all the elements of the current state of facts.[3] As the analysis of the

[2] See D. Galligan, *Discretionary Powers: A Legal Study of Official Discretion* (1986); M. I. Vila, *Facing Judicial Discretion: Legal Knowledge and Right Answers Revisited* (2000), 14ff; O. Wiklund, ed. *Judicial Discretion in European Perspective* (2003); J. Andreoni and R. D. Madoff, 'The Role of Judicial Discretion in Dispute Settlement', Boston College Law School Legal Studies Research Paper, No. 151 (2008).

[3] It has been noted in natural language theory that 'all, virtually all, or some of the words are blurred or that all are determinate in some respects and indeterminate in other respects'. See T. Gizbert-Studnicki, *Wieloznaczność leksykalna w interpretacji prawniczej* [*Lexical Ambiguity in Legal Interpretation*] (1978), 54ff; T. Kubiński, 'Nazwy nieostre [Blurred Concepts]', *Studia Logica*, 8 (1958), 18. See also M. Zieliński, *Wykładnia prawa, Zasady. Reguły. Wskazówki* [*Legal Interpretation. Principles. Rules. Guidelines*] (2002), 163–71. Zieliński states, *inter alia*, that 'indeterminateness' and 'blurriness' are interrelated, yet they apply to different aspects of linguistic features. Accordingly, 'indeterminateness' refers to the meaning of phrases, while 'blurriness' refers to their scope. Zieliński notes that since these two terms are interrelated, blurriness is sometimes treated as 'indeterminateness concerning the scope, differentiated from conceptual indeterminateness'. Such a strict distinction between indeterminate and blurred concepts is not indispensable from the point of view of this paper. Therefore, I apply a broad understanding of vague concepts including blurred concepts. See also M. Zieliński and Z. Radwański, 'Wykładnia prawa cywilnego [Interpretation of Civil Law]', *Studia Prawa Prywatnego*, 1 (2006), 28–29.

structure of concepts demonstrates, each abstract regulation is mostly vague, and therefore requires fulfilment and interpretation. Interpretation and subsumption are also required by 'specified' concepts: that is, concepts which are substantively filled, clear and distinguishable from other norms and legal institutions.

The use of vague, evaluative, and typological concepts in legal texts as well as the use of general clauses is related to 'an increasing scope of the semantic openness of modern legal systems'.[4] An example here is the concept of 'substantial reasons for termination', arousing controversy in the case law and found on the grounds of broadly understood civil and labour laws. An imprecisely worded legal concept determines its interpretation in a whole set of grammatically homogeneous languages. The phrase 'substantial reasons for termination' defines a certain set of grammatically homogeneous languages which nevertheless differ in respect of the meaning of this vague concept (in each language, this concept has a clear, yet different meaning).[5]

Indeterminate legal concepts closely resemble general clauses, to mention only the clauses related to 'the socio—economic purpose of law' and 'the principles of social coexistence' as defined in Article 5 of the Civil Code, which owing to their generality and the basic nature should be taken into account by the courts in the settlement of each individual case. Thus, they make the law application process more flexible than other clauses, in accordance with the assumption that *summum ius summa iniuria*.[6]

Applying the institution of a general clause in a specific legal regulation leads to an increase or even directly to creating freedom in the law application process, by referring to extra-legal elements of the axiological environment. In contrast to blurred names (which refer to the extra-linguistic sphere that results from the nature of the language), general clauses are treated as linguistic phrases with evaluative features, referring to the valuable and generally targeted extra-legal criteria,

[4] L. Morawski, *Główne problemy współczesnej filozofii prawa: Prawo w toku przemian* [*The Main Problems of Contemporary Legal Philosophy: Law in the Progress of Changes*] (2000), 157; M. Paroussis, *Theorie des juristischen Diskurses: eine institutionelle Epistemologie des Rechts* (1995), ch. 4; H. L. A. Hart, *Pojęcie prawa* [*The Concept of Law*] (1998), 171ff. See the Supreme Court of the Republic of Poland resolution of 6 May 1966, case number VI KZP 62/65, OSPiKA 1967: 'Any situation where one can encounter differences of interpretation between the various judicial instances, can be viewed as a symptom of a peculiar absence of the clarity of the text. This ambiguity may be established by means of linguistic properties or it may originate from other sources emerging the need to subject certain provisions to interpretation.'

[5] W. Patryas, *Definiowanie pojęć prawnych* [*Defining Legal Concepts*] (1997), 110.

[6] Cf. the ruling of the Constitutional Court of the Republic of Poland as of 17 October 2000, case number SK 5/99; L. Leszczyński, 'Klauzule generalne uelastyczniają stosowanie prawa' [General Clauses Make Law Application Process More Flexible'], *Rzeczpospolita* (12 April 2001); M. Sala, 'Klauzula generalna zasad współżycia społecznego' [General Clause of Social Coexistence], in J. Stelmach, ed., *Studia z filozofii prawa* (2001), 199–206.

which also simultaneously introduce a certain freedom for the law-applying entity. This freedom consists in determining the content of the clause only at the stage of applying the law, thus referring to habits, individual evaluative opinions, or systemic assessments.[7]

5.2. The role of the different contexts of legal interpretation

The aim of interpretation stage is for the judge to interpret the correct (objective) meaning of the analysed provision, based on linguistic and extra-linguistic competence, regardless of whether it contains vague or entirely clear concepts.[8] In case of practical interpretation, which is most essential from the perspective of the deliberations at issue, the judge, when carrying out the interpretation, seeks to restore the norm in order to obtain the legal basis necessary to settle a given case in the law application process. To achieve such an objective, the judge should apply the relevant rules of interpretation. In particular, he or she should make a choice between the respective rules and refer to those which will more effectively and rationally lead him or her to the unambiguous solution. The findings in the course of an operative (practical) interpretation are binding only in a given adjudicated case.

The order of using the rules of interpretation is, as a rule, established. The first rules of interpretation to be used are linguistic ones. Linguistic rules allow to determine the legal meaning of the interpreted concept (phrase), provided the legislator used a legal definition. In the absence of a legal definition, the interpreter should use the meaning resulting from a binding interpretative adjudication (for example, the one applied in the decisions rendered by the Court of Justice of the European Union). In this context, it is worth noting that the law-applying entity is in a certain 'chain of interpretation', which requires the interpreter to consider all that has already been established in relation to similar cases decided earlier (this is of major importance particularly in the common law system)[9] in the interpretation process.

[7] L. Leszczyński, *Klauzule generalne w stosowaniu prawa* [*General Clauses in Law Application*] (1986), ch. 1; Z. Ziembiński, 'Stan dyskusji nad problematyką klauzul generalnych' [The Discussion on the Issue of General Clauses], *Państwo i Prawo*, 3 (1989), 14ff.

[8] See R. Sarkowicz, 'Autorytet a obiektywna interpretacja tekstu' [Authority and Objective Interpretation of the Text], in M. Skąpska, ed., *Prawo w zmieniającym się społeczeństwie: księga jubileuszowa profesor Marii Boruckiej—Arctowej* (1992), 198. The author notes that lawyers are reluctant to talk about the objective interpretation of the legal text, typically using such terms as an 'accurate', 'reliable', or 'real' meaning. Simultaneously, striving to define a certain 'accurate' meaning of the legal text is dictated by practical reasons rather than being based on the idea of the existence of a mere 'accurate' meaning.

[9] Ronald Dworkin, *Imperium prawa* [*Law's Empire*] (2006), 231ff; Stanley Fish, *Interpretacja, retoryka, polityka. Eseje wybrane* [*Interpretation, Rhetoric, Policy. Selected Essays*] (2007), 228ff.

In our system of law, such an obligation also stems from the postulate of the uniformity of law application. Subsequently, when the earlier rules do not provide a binding decision, the interpreter should rely on legal language presumption. Finally, if this last rule does not bring a conclusive outcome, the interpreter should refer to the meaning which the interpreted concept (phrase) has in the natural language. For this purpose, he or she should use the linguistic register of the national (ethnic) language. It should be simultaneously kept in mind that the choice of a particular meaning among dictionary meanings is manifested by considering the assumptions about the language of legal texts. What is most noteworthy is the linguistic context in which the interpreted concept (phrase) has been used.[10]

Clearly, the meaning of the interpreted legal provision obviously not only on the linguistic context but also on the systemic and functional contexts, which in many cases are subject to dynamic changes. It is based on the assumption that the clarity of the interpreted concept (phrase) may depend on many factors and vary over time.[11] In other words, it will be often or possibly always necessary to reconsider the linguistic meaning by referring it to other contexts, including the intention of the legislator, the earlier decisions, the varied conventions, structures and social practices. Such an approach helps avoid the plea of extreme formalism and semantic approach to law, relying more on the interpretative (argumentative—discursive) approach.[12]

In my view, the possibility of taking into account so many crucial factors in interpretative practice weighs against adopting the principle of *clara sunt interpretanda*,[13] introducing simultaneously a certain margin of the interpretative freedom comprising a broadly understood judicial discretion. Consequently, one can speak here of a peculiar phenomenon of 'balancing' interpretative rules distinguished on an account of the different contexts, namely linguistic, systemic, or functional.[14]

[10] Similarly, Zieliński, *Wykładnia prawa cywilnego*, 304–17; A. Choduń, *Słownictwo tekstów aktów prawnych w zasobie współczesnej polszczyzny* [*The Linguistic Register of Legal Acts in the Resources of Contemporary Polish Language*] (2007), 133.

[11] Cf. E. Łętowska, 'Kilka uwag o praktyce wykładni' [A Few Comments on the Practice of Interpretation], *Kwartalnik Prawa Prywatnego*, 1 (2002), 54; L. Morawski, *Wykładnia w orzecznictwie sądów: Komentarz* [*Interpretation in Case Law: Commentary*] (2002), 64–5.

[12] Dworkin even thinks that legal discourse should not begin with the definition of concepts. According to him, all who claim so are 'victims of the semantic sting'. See Dworkin, *Law's Empire*, 45ff.

[13] For a more in-depth discussion of this issue, see A. Choduń and M. Zieliński, 'Aspekty granic wykładni prawa' [Aspects of the Limits of Legal Interpretation], in W. Niemiec, ed., *Księga Jubileuszowa Profesora Ryszarda Mastalskiego: Stanowienie i stosowanie prawa podatkowego* (2009), 84–95, 86ff. In this work, the authors present an ordered and convincing criticism of the *clara non sunt interpretanda* maxim. Therefore, I refer to the quoted text in this regard, because I fully agree with the arguments presented there, while the topic and the modest frames of the present article do not allow for an in-depth analysis of the problem at issue.

[14] I use the term 'balancing', referring to the concept applied by Robert Alexy (*Abwägungsgesetz*). The conflict of principles in the argumentation process outlines a need to understand both the law-making process as well as its application as a model that balances the relevant principles and objectives.

Applying the principles of systemic or functional interpretation in the event of semantic clarity of the interpreted concept based on the rules of linguistic interpretation is not the duty of the interpreter but only serves the purpose of revising the final outcome. The situation is different when the rules of linguistic interpretation are not sufficient to achieve this 'clarity', because using other rules then becomes necessary. However, in judicial practice, it is the judge who determines whether such a necessity arose due to semantic, syntactic or epistemic uncertainties, and therefore, such a decision can be placed within a broadly understood judicial discretion. Such discretion can be encountered in particular while interpreting indeterminate terms and general clauses.

5.3. The weighing of arguments of civil law

The analysis of judicial discretion in the field of substantive civil law will be carried out based on two civil law institutions which, to my mind, are most representative for the purposes of this article: namely, judicial indexation of monetary benefits (in accordance with Article 358[1] § 3 of the Polish Civil Code—the so-called *ius modificandi*) and the issue of determining the amount of damages in tort (in accordance with Article 445 § 1 of the Civil Code). When discussing these institutions by the judicature or by the doctrine, importance is typically attached to the discretion of a judge rendering decisions in civil cases. The above legal institutions serve as the basis for answering the question of the existence of judicial discretion in balancing the rules of interpretation. It is no coincidence that I refer to examples from the civil law. My intention is to demonstrate that this branch of law, which is relatively fairly conservative and traditional, also encountered a significant change in the paradigm of law application because of the legislative changes that occurred in 1990.[15] The

The object of balancing may be preferences, interests, goods, values, or principles. Balancing principles includes justified determination of the relationship of priority between the conflicting principles. Such a collision of principles or objectives follows from the fact that the various rules cannot be simultaneously satisfied in a complete way in a particular case. The most general rule which applies to the balancing of principles reads as follows: 'The higher the degree of a failure or depletion of the operation of one principle, the greater must be in a given case the importance of the validity of other principles'. R. Alexy, *Theorie der Grundrechte* (1985), 77ff, 146ff; R. Alexy, 'The Weight Formula', in J. Stelmach, B. Brożek, and W. Załuski, eds., *Studies in the Philosophy of Law: Frontiers of the Economic Analysis of Law*, iii (2007), 9–27; N. Jansen, *Die Structur der Gerechtigkeit* (1998), 102ff; J.- R. Sieckmann, 'Zur Begründung von Abwägungsurteilen', *Rechtstheorie*, 26 (1995), 45–69, 47ff. T. Spyra aptly notes in this context that the application of the balancing model to legal interpretation requires taking into account the latter's specificity. For an in-depth discussion of this issue, see *Granice wykładni prawa* [*The Limits of Legal Interpretation*] (2006), 257–265.

[15] For an in-depth discussion, see Zieliński and Radwański, *Wykładnia prawa cywilnego*, 1–39.

phenomenon of approaching more closely the argumentative and discursive model in civil law application can be consequently observed.

Judicial indexation of monetary benefits set forth in Article 358^{1} § 3 of the Civil Code in fact constitutes the exception to the principle of nominalism (Article 358^{1} § 1 of the Civil Code). In the event of a significant change in the purchasing power of currency, it enables the court, after considering the interests of both parties in accordance with the principles of social coexistence, to change the extent or the manner of rendering pecuniary performance. Based on his/her own assessment, the judge first states whether according to the principles of social coexistence and taking into account the interests of the parties, the performance should be modified in a given case. Second, if the answer to the latter question is positive, the court assesses the extent to which the performance can be modified. Determining whether a given obligation should be subject to indexation at all remains unresolved. In order to determine the latter, it is necessary to state that there occurred 'a significant change in the purchasing power of currency after the occurrence of the obligation' which constitutes an objective premise, or—in other words—an event substantive from the perspective of law, which determines the necessity of the court applying this provision.

At this point, the legislator uses the concept of an imprecise semantic scope, and moreover, he or she does not provide any guidance that would allow to classify a certain change as significant. The legislator's decision about the very need for the indexation of monetary benefits is related to the occurrence of certain facts that meet the condition of 'significant changes in the purchasing power of currency'. In my opinion, applying the indexation of monetary benefits by the court remains factual and epistemic in nature, designed to examine whether a significant change occurred in the purchasing power of currency in the individual case. The concept of 'significance' naturally requires interpretation and is without doubt insufficient at this point to refer to the rules of linguistic interpretation. However, it is possibly even more crucial to apply the rules of systemic and functional interpretation.

Jurisprudence and literature demonstrate that the indexation of monetary benefits applied by court, as set forth in Article 358^{1} § 3 of the Civil Code, is an expression of 'the judicial law' for other reasons as well, as there are no guidelines or specific directives which would provide a more precise measure of applying the indexation of monetary benefits by the judge. The choice of such a measure and the manner of applying indexation depend on the discretion of the judge, who takes into account the comprehensive consideration of the circumstances of a given case and the application of general, directional guidance contained in the statute. The court may be guided by various measures such as the prices of basic goods, employee wages, pensions, inflation rates, and foreign currency exchange rates. On determining the interests of the parties, the court is obliged to balance them. This means that the legitimate interests of the plaintiff can and should be taken into account, yet only to the limits of the interference with the legitimate interests of the defendant.[16] We therefore once more face an indeterminate concept, the interpretation of which will give rise to major problems and disputes. In order to appropriately understand the concept of 'legitimate interest', recourse to the rules of linguistic interpretation does not suffice.

Article 358[1] § 3 of the Civil Code provides guidance about the determination of legitimate legal consequences through the obligation to take into account the specific facts and rules of extra-legal norms. This provision authorizes the judge to apply a margin of discretion by ordering simultaneously to take into account a general clause of reference. In this case, the latter institutions are closely related to each other.

The second example suggested by me refers to the act of determining the amount of compensation for damage caused by tort. Article 445 § 1 of the Civil Code provides that the court may award to the injured party 'an appropriate amount' as compensation for the damage suffered. The amount of compensation should be determined by the same criteria as those applied when assessing the compensation for damage to property, and the principle of full compensation is irrelevant here. When assessing the compensation, the judge's discretion is greater than with unquantifiable non-pecuniary damages. It does not however imply complete, unlimited discretion of the judge, since despite the inability to determine the exact amount of compensation, the judge should base his/her decision on objective, verifiable criteria. Many authors opine that it is a positive fact that the provisions of Article 445 § 1 of the Civil Code (and also Article 448 of the Civil Code) do not provide clear guidelines allowing for precise determination of the amount of compensation in individual cases.[17] The clarification of the general guideline of 'a proper amount' was left to the judicature, thus providing an example for a vague legal concept.

The case law formulated various criteria and guidelines in the form of 'factual' directives which the court should take into account when determining the amount of compensation, namely

> all factors affecting the extent of the harm suffered, and in particular the degree and duration of physical and mental suffering (the stay in the

[16] Cf. the statement of reasons of the Supreme Court ruling as of 23 November 1993, case citation III CRN 46/93, OSN 1994, no. 4, item 93.

[17] Cf. A. Szpunar, *Zadośćuczynienie za szkodę niemajątkową* [*Compensation for Non-Pecuniary Damage*] (1999), 180, 182. M. Zirk-Sadowski rightly emphasizes that under the definition of damage to property, the latter cannot be evaluated in terms of money, due to the very essence of non-pecuniary damage. Based on this, he deliberates on 'a contradiction in the views of lawyers, which consists in the simultaneous recognition of unquantifiability of values as well as the need to bring them to a certain common criterion'. See M. Zirk-Sadowski, *Rozumienie ocen w języku prawnym* [*Understanding Assessments in Legal Language*] (1984), 152ff.

hospital, painful medical treatment, performed surgeries, sanatorium treatment), the durability of the effects of tort (disability, disfigurement, helplessness, a sense of uselessness), predictions for the future (improvement or deterioration of health), the age of the injured party (disability is typically perceived as greater harm by a younger person), inability to work in a chosen profession, inability to play sports, undertake creative and artistic work, the loss of the possibility to marry, have children, the loss of social contacts, the loss of the possibility of attractive trips, excursions, visiting theatre, cinema, the beach, etc., as well as the fact of the injured party's contributing to the occurrence or increase of damage. (Article 362 of the Civil Code)[18]

When determining the amount of damages based on the provision of Article 445 of the Civil Code, it is important to take into account 'factual' directives that allow to determine that the said amount is not excessive in relation to the harm suffered and to the current property relations of the society and should therefore be kept within reasonable limits. The judge adopting objective criteria does not imply disregard for the individual situation of both parties, particularly that of the injured party. It only favours the recognition that the amount of compensation is determined not by subjective feelings of the injured party, but rather by the overall circumstances of a given case and their assessment by the judge.

The analysis of the presented examples favours stating that the directives which bind the judge and limit his or her freedom in making a choice of particular legal consequences in civil law influence the content of the final court decision. This true regardless of whether these directives have been expressed directly in the applied provision, or rather in an indirect manner, whether they have been adopted as 'abstract' ones, or whether they refer to a specific case. This is because they are always accessorial to the legal provisions applicable in the decision-making process, in particular by reference to the principles of fairness expressed generally in Article 5 of the Civil Code and also in the provisions of specific parts of the Civil Code.

5.4. The necessity of the balancing of legal rules

With respect to the two institutions mentioned above, it becomes necessary—in addition to the application of the said 'factual' directives—to balance between the various rules of interpretation. It is not possible to correctly apply the quoted provisions and the legal institutions regulated there without due consideration of

[18] G. Bieniek, H. Ciepła, S. Dmowski, J. Gudowski, K. Kołakowski, M. Sychowicz, T. Wiśniewski, and C. Żuławska, *Komentarz do kodeksu cywilnego. Księga Trzecia. Zobowiązania* [*Commentary to the Civil Code. Book Three. Law of Obligations*], i (1996), 369ff.

various rules and forms of arguments. When undertaking the interpretative process concerning the said institutions, it is undoubtedly recommended to refer to the rules of systemic interpretation, particularly those that require taking into account the horizontal consistency of the legal system in relation to legal principles. In particular, the interpretation of the said institutions should take into account the constitutional principles of social justice and equality vis-à-vis law. This is of utmost importance in the context of the phrases 'just interest', 'proper amount', or 'the principles of social coexistence'. When analysing the indexation of monetary benefits undertaken by the court as well as the assessment of the compensation, one needs to take into account the *ratio legis* argument. For this purpose, it becomes necessary to reconstruct the reasons inferred based on the applicable provisions of legal norms and thus to determine the values, principles, or positive objectives that underlie a particular legal norm. It is subsequently determined whether the scope of a specific norm covers the established state of facts. In our situation, for example, we examine whether there occurred a 'substantial change in the purchasing power of currency' and 'whether the injured party may be awarded pecuniary compensation for the harm suffered'. What is important are the functional rules referring to the assumptions about the legislator, cultural conditions, or axiological aspects. It follows, therefore, that it is necessary to confront the linguistic interpretation with the outcome of the systemic interpretation and the functional analysis in order to determine whether exceptional cases which interfere with the linguistic meaning of the legal provision occur.[19]

The starting point in the process of interpretation is always the linguistic layer of the interpreted law, because the use of the rules of sentence structure and the meaning of individual words or phrases, and consequently the application of the rules of semantics and syntax, allow to determine the meaning of the legal text to some extent.

While engaged in the process of legal interpretation, there is clearly a need for referring to the linguistic meaning of the wording or phrases used by the legislator. In certain situations, however, one cannot exclude the possibility of using a different kind of interpretation, which should be treated as an exception to the rule. The lexical understanding of respective legislative phrases in the process of interpreting the legal provisions can be departed from only when it is justified by compelling reasons, namely:

[19] Zieliński and Radwański, *Wykładnia prawa cywilnego*, 29–31. The authors present here the position of the Supreme Court which expressed that the following view: 'one cannot depart from the linguistic meaning of interpretation, although the provision is clear and obvious, if it leads to grossly unfair or irrational consequences, when especially important legal, social, economic or moral reasons weigh in favour of it'. Supreme Court resolution as of 25 April 2003, case citation III CZP 8/03, OSN 2004, no. 1, item 1.

- the need to respect the fundamental constitutional principles, including those containing guarantees to satisfy certain personal rights to the recipient of statutory norms;
- taking account of significant changes in economic relations which occurred after the entry into force of the interpreted provisions;
- the need to eliminate the discrepancy between the content of the interpreted provision and other laws of the same rank which govern the same issues and are related to the same group of recipients;
- the need to ensure compatibility of the norms of the Polish law with the EU law (or, more broadly, international law), as well as the compatibility of hierarchically lower norms with hierarchically higher norms;
- inability to explain the content of the legal norm using the linguistic interpretation or the situation when this interpretation leads to ambiguous results which cannot be reconciled with the assumption of the legislator's rationality; and
- the need to take into account the specific context of the normative statement and its relations with other elements of the legal framework (systemic interpretation).[20]

In this context, it is worth remembering that interpretation queries cannot be associated merely with a simple difference of certain aspects of the results of teleological or functional interpretation in relation to linguistic-systemic interpretation. Such a discrepancy can indeed be often encountered in practice, but it does not generally lead to negating the pattern of behaviour built on the basis of linguistic and systemic rules, particularly if the absence of rational justification cannot be attributed to the application of the linguistic rules and their results. Significant interpretative doubts arise, first, when linguistic and systemic rules placed at the same level of the process of interpretation result in equally acceptable and justifiable results of interpretation which are substantially different and opposing. Second, these doubts arise when the teleological–functional and axiological verification refers to such important objectives, effects or social values prevailing in the results of linguistic–systemic interpretation that the failure to take them into account would violate the rule of law. These relations would further need to be imposed on certain elements of the state of facts that would justify such an adjustment.

On the other hand, however, one needs to consider the existence of the limit of permissible modifications of the content of the legal norm (particularly classified as the norms of public law) in the process of applying law by the administrative court. An interpretation whose results would be utterly contrary to the literal wording of the analysed provision is considered unacceptable. Interpretative rules, different

[20] The Administrative Supreme Court of the Republic of Poland resolution as of 4 December 2012, case citation II FPS 3/12.

from linguistic rules, cannot provide the basis for such interference in the content of the provisions, which could be qualified as norm-making activity, not covered, after all, by the cognition of courts. In its 24 January 1999 decision (case number Ts 124/98), the Constitutional Court of the Republic of Poland noted that none of the forms of the interpretation and legal reasoning can change the obvious wording of the legal provision. In another decision (dated 26 March 1996, case number W.12/95, OTK ZU 1996/2/16), the Constitutional Court stated that the purpose of interpretation is not to create norms or to modify them, but to determine the content of the norms expressed in the analysed provisions.

If, therefore, in the process of subsumption—that is, in the course of relating a specific state of facts to the content of the statutory norm determined in the course of linguistic interpretation—the court believes that circumstances favour using other instruments of interpretation, but also simultaneously finds that their application would lead to attributing the norm with completely different content (because, for example, the compliance with the constitutional principles requires so), the Constitutional Court should be addressed, pursuant to Article 193 of the Polish Constitution, with a legal query about the conformity of the normative act with the Constitution, ratified international agreements or statute.

The rules and principles that the judge should take into account are most often evaluative in nature and are formulated in an abstract manner, allowing the inclusion of all potential situations and indicating, in a very general manner, the recommended choice. The directives and rules thus formulated can be then treated as rules of reference.[21]

J. Wróblewski notes that under such directives of the choice of consequences one should choose a settlement which is 'fair', 'good', 'corresponding to the principles of morality', or which remains 'in accordance with the rules of natural law', thus referring to extra-legal values. The author notes that in a situation requiring such discrete decision making, one should indicate the two following points of view: legal—descriptive and theoretical.[22] From a legal point of view, one cannot talk about limiting the judge's discretion because it remains beyond the scope in which certain legal provisions govern the said choice by definition. However, from a descriptive and theoretical point of view, it should be stated that the judge's discretion is limited to the extent to which the judge feels bound by the prevailing ideology and to the extent to which this ideology provides him/her with certain directives. Descriptive and theoretical point of view requires substantiation of the legal consequences of one's choice based on instrumentally or thetically relativized assessment.

[21] Wróblewski, *The Judicial Application of Law* (Springer, Dordrecht, 1992), 245ff.

[22] J. Wróblewski, *The Judicial Application of Law* (Springer, Dordrecht, 1992), 231ff.

The judge should always choose such a solution that will respect the claim to the accuracy, fairness, justice, and justifiability of the final decisions. The court, issuing in such cases the decision based on the premises of fairness or common sense, finds its justification in the general legal principles contained in the constitution or in the *ratio legis* argumentation. The judge's decision should be legally linked to avoid the objection of the wilfulness of action. The judge must also have regard to the already developed case law (the so-called prognostic motivation). The fact that during adjudication, the judge takes into consideration the views previously expressed in the literature or case law (*ratio decidendi* of the decision), arising in connection with adjudicating similar cases, will weigh in favour of unifying the jurisprudence by adopting the same or similar rules and guidelines of interpretation.

This inherently involves a change in the paradigm of judicial law application, namely the transition from the syllogistic model to an argumentative-discursive one.[23] In the latter model, the process of judicial law application is not so much of decision-making nature as Dworkin's assessment within which the judge has to be socially aware and truly participating in the legal culture.[24] Law application does not therefore imply a mere and simple subsumption, but requires referring to a variety of legal topoi and argumentative rules, including the rules of interpretation. This allows preservation of the said flexibility of law and takes into account the demand of responsiveness to the changing reality of law application.

References

Alexy, R., *Theorie der Grundrechte* (Baden-Baden, 1985).

Alexy, R., 'The Weight Formula', in J. Stelmach, B. Brożek, and W. Załuski, eds., *Studies in the Philosophy of Law: Frontiers of the Economic Analysis of Law*, vol. 3 (Kraków, 2007), 9–27.

Andreoni, J. and R. D. Madoff, 'The Role of Judicial Discretion in Dispute Settlement', Boston College Law School Legal Studies Research Paper, No. 151 (2008).

Bieniek, G., H. Ciepła, S. Dmowski, J. Gudowski, K. Kołakowski, M. Sychowicz, T. Wiśniewski, and C. Żuławska, *Komentarz do kodeksu cywilnego. Księga Trzecia: Zobowiązania* [*Commentary to the Civil Code. Book Three: Law of Obligations*] (Warsaw, 1996), vol. I.

Choduń, A., *Słownictwo tekstów aktów prawnych w zasobie współczesnej polszczyzny* [*The Linguistic Register of Legal Acts in the Resources of Contemporary Polish Language*] (Warsaw, 2007).

Choduń, A. and M. Zieliński, 'Aspekty granic wykładni prawa' [Aspects of the Limits of Legal Interpretation], in W. Niemiec, ed., *Księga Jubileuszowa Profesora Ryszarda Mastalskiego: Stanowienie i stosowanie prawa podatkowego* (Wrocław, 2009), 84–95.

Dworkin, Ronald, *Imperium prawa* [*Law's Empire*] (Warsaw, 2006).

Fish, Stanley, *Interpretacja, retoryka, polityka. Eseje wybrane* [*Interpretation, Rhetoric, Policy. Selected Essays*] (Kraków, 2007).

Galligan, D., *Discretionary Powers: A Legal Study of Official Discretion* (Oxford, 1986).

[23] Morawski, *Główne problemy współczesnej filozofii prawa*, 151.

[24] For an in-depth discussion, see M. Zirk-Sadowski, *Prawo a uczestniczenie w kulturze* [*Law vis-à-vis Participating in Culture*] (1998).

Gizbert-Studnicki, T., *Wieloznaczność leksykalna w interpretacji prawniczej [Lexical Ambiguity in Legal Interpretation]* (Kraków, 1978).
Hart, H. L. A., *Pojęcie prawa* [*The Concept of Law*] (Warsaw, 1998).
Jansen, N., *Die Structur der Gerechtigkeit* (Baden-Baden, 1998).
Kubiński, T., 'Nazwy nieostre' [Blurred Concepts], *Studia Logica*, 8 (1958), 18.
Leszczyński, L., 'Klauzule generalne uelastyczniają stosowanie prawa' [General Clauses Make Law Application Process More Flexible], *Rzeczpospolita* (12 April 2001).
Leszczyński, L., *Klauzule generalne w stosowaniu prawa* [*General Clauses in Law Application*] (Lublin, 1986).
Łętowska, E., 'Kilka uwag o praktyce wykładni' [A Few Comments on the Practice of Interpretation], *Kwartalnik Prawa Prywatnego*, 1 (2002), 54.
Morawski, L., *Główne problemy współczesnej filozofii prawa. Prawo w toku przemian* [*The Main Problems of Contemporary Legal Philosophy. Law in the Progress of Changes*] (Warsaw, 2000).
Morawski, L., *Wykładnia w orzecznictwie sądów: Komentarz [Interpretation in Case Law: Commentary]* (Toruń, 2002).
Paroussis, M., *Theorie des juristischen Diskurses: eine institutionelle Epistemologie des Rechts* (Berlin, 1995).
Patryas, W., *Definiowanie pojęć prawnych* [*Defining Legal Concepts*] (Poznań, 1997).
Sala, M., 'Klauzula generalna zasad współżycia społecznego' [General Clause of Social Coexistence], in J. Stelmach, ed., *Studia z filozofii prawa [Studies in the Philosophy of Law]* (Kraków, 2001), 199–206.
Sarkowicz, R., 'Autorytet a obiektywna interpretacja tekstu' [Authority and Objective Interpretation of the Text], in M. Skąpska, ed., *Prawo w zmieniającym się społeczeństwie: księga jubileuszowa profesor Marii Boruckiej—Arctowej [Law in a Changing Society: Professor Maria Borucka—Arctowa Jubilee Book]* (Kraków, 1992), 1–27.
Sieckmann, J.-R., 'Zur Begründung von Abwägungsurteilen', *Rechtstheorie*, 26 (1995), 45–69.
Spyra, T. *Granice wykładni prawa [The Limits of Legal Interpretation]* (Kraków, 2006).
Szpunar, A., *Zadośćuczynienie za szkodę niemajątkową [Compensation for Non-Pecuniary Damage]* (Bydgoszcz, 1999).
Vila, M. I., *Facing Judicial Discretion. Legal Knowledge and Right Answers Revisited* (Dordrecht, Boston, MA, and London, 2000).
Wiklund, O., ed., *Judicial Discretion in European Perspective* (Stockholm, 2003).
Wróblewski J., *The Judicial Application of Law* (Dordrecht, 1992).
Zieliński, M., *Wykładnia prawa. Zasady. Reguły. Wskazówki* [*Legal Interpretation. Principles. Rules. Guidelines*] (Warsaw, 2002).
Zieliński, M. and Z. Radwański, 'Wykładnia prawa cywilnego' [Interpretation of Civil Law], *Studia Prawa Prywatnego*, 1 (2006), 365–73
Ziembiński, Z., *Stan dyskusji nad problematyką klauzul generalnych [The Discussion on the Issue of General Clauses], Państwo i Prawo*, 3 (1989), 14ff.
Zirk-Sadowski, M., *Prawo a uczestniczenie w kulturze [Law vis-à-vis Participating in Culture]* (Łódź, 1998).
Zirk-Sadowski, M., *Rozumienie ocen w języku prawnym [Understanding Assessments in Legal Language]* (Łódź, 1984).

6

Interpretation of international treaties and the role of Articles 31 and 32 of the Vienna Convention on the Law of Treaties

A Wittgensteinian perspective

JAROSLAV VĚTROVSKÝ

6.1. Introduction

The word 'interpretation' has commonly been employed in many contexts. Whether we talk about philosophy, law, art, or other fields of human activity, references to interpretation generally form an integral part of our vocabulary. Nevertheless, the way we use the word is not uniform, and the meaning of the concept that the word stands for is far from clear. When interpretation is required in a particular case or the concept is considered on an abstract level, such questions as what interpretation is and what an interpreter typically does when they interpret arise and, at first glance, seem legitimate. My intention, however, is to argue that these and similar questions blur rather than guide any serious attempt at investigating what interpretation means. Interpretation is a heterogeneous concept. That is to say, even if we focus on a specific kind of interpretation, including, for example, the judicial interpretation of international treaties, the activities covered by the term 'interpretation' are not identical, despite the obvious fact that in our language the same word is used for all of them.

The arguments I will put forward largely rest on the late philosophy of language of Ludwig Wittgenstein.[1] The point is not, however, to conceive the following lines as a description of what Wittgenstein would have written about the problem

[1] Ludwig Wittgenstein, *Philosophical Investigations*, trans. G. E. M. Anscombe, P. M. S. Hacker, and J. Schulte (4th edn, 2009).

Jaroslav Větrovský, *Interpretation of international treaties and the role of Articles 31 and 32 of the Vienna Convention on the Law of Treaties* In: *Language and Legal Interpretation in International Law*. Edited by: Anne Lise Kjær and Joanna Lam, Oxford University Press. © Oxford University Press 2022. DOI: 10.1093/oso/9780190855208.003.0007

of interpretation of international treaties if he had dealt with the topic. Nor am I seeking to misuse the authority of Ludwig Wittgenstein for making my arguments persuasive, which otherwise they would not be.[2] Instead, my intention is to outline a series of considerations which obviously draw inspiration from Wittgenstein's late work, but shall be considered as autonomous arguments providing, I hope, a convincing alternative to the current international law discourse about what interpretation means and what function it actually fulfils.

6.2. Defining interpretation and Wittgenstein's concept of family resemblances

Stating definitions is a traditional legal technique aimed at dispelling doubts about the meaning of equivocal terms. Legal definitions are sometimes embedded directly in a normative text in which an equivocal term occurs. In most cases, however, a binding definition of legal terms is missing and the task of formulating one falls to legal doctrine and international bodies, especially the courts. This holds also true for the word 'interpretation'. One of the early attempts to formulate a judicial definition of the term 'interpretation' was already undertaken by the Permanent Court of International Justice. Asked to construe one of its previous judgments, the Court stated that 'the expression "to construe"[3] must be understood as signifying to give a precise definition of the meaning and scope which the Court intended to give to the judgment in question'.[4] A similar definition was subsequently formulated by the International Court of Justice, according to which 'to obtain an interpretation of the judgment . . . signifies . . . to obtain clarification of the meaning and the scope of what the Court has decided'.[5] Both judicial definitions of interpretation found acceptance, to a certain extent, also in the international law doctrine, and have regularly been employed in the context of international treaties.[6]

From Wittgenstein's point of view, however, the idea that we can explain the meaning of the word 'interpretation' by means of its definition—that is, by providing necessary and sufficient conditions for the use of the term—is fallacious. Wittgenstein puts forward several arguments why explanation through definitions

[2] Cf. Brian Bix, 'Cautions and Caveats for the Application of Wittgenstein to Legal Theory', in J. K. Campbell, M. O'Rourke, and D. Shier, eds., *Law and Social Justice* (2005), 218–19.

[3] 'Interpréter' in the French version of the Statute (Art. 60).

[4] *Interpretation of Judgments Nos. 7 and 8 (The Chorzów Factory)*, Collection of Judgments, Series A, No. 13, p. 10.

[5] *Request for Interpretation of the Judgement of November 20th, 1950, in the Asylum Case (Colombia v. Peru)*, I.C.J. Reports (1950), 402.

[6] Ulf Linderfalk, *On the Interpretation of Treaties: The Modern International Law as Expressed in the 1969 Vienna Convention on the Law of Treaties* (2007), 10; Allain Pellet, Patrick Daillier, and Mathias Forteau, *Droit International Public* (2009), 276.

cannot succeed, but probably the most important one relates to his conviction that the meaning of a word typically depends on how this word is used in a concrete instance of communication. This idea is fundamental to Wittgenstein's late philosophy and constantly appears throughout his writings stemming from this period. According to Wittgenstein, language has no single function. It is, for example, quite different if we use language to give orders, describe an object, report an event, or tell a joke.[7] To better explain this phenomenon, Wittgenstein introduces the concept of language-games,[8] for, as he wrote, using language in different contexts is like playing games with different rules:

> Imagine a language-game in which A asks, and B reports, the number of slabs or blocks in a pile, or the colours and shapes of the building stones that are stacked in such-and-such a place. —Such a report might run: 'Five slabs.' Now what is the difference between the report or assertion 'Five slabs' and the order 'Five slabs!'? —Well, it is the part which uttering these words plays in the language-game.[9]

Thus, according to Wittgenstein, the meaning of words is not fixed, but depends on the way the words are used and on circumstances in which they are used. A thing has a name only within a particular game, not outside the game or independently of it.[10] Wittgenstein, therefore, opposes the idea developed by Hart,[11] and also expanded within the international law doctrine, that words (and rules they express) always have some semantic core of certainty, '[a]s if the meaning were an aura the word brings along with it and retains in every kind of use'.[12] Moreover, unlike Hart, Wittgenstein does not relate the changing meaning of words exclusively to the vagueness of terms or open-textured character of language, although he does not deny that this can also be a relevant reason in many instances. Yet, as he argues, even if we use a word where no borderline cases exist (like 'number')[13] or we connect the use of the word to some of its paradigmatic examples, the meaning of the word changes depending on the context (i.e. on the language-game) in which it is used. The expression 'Five slabs!' would not become much clearer even if we eliminated all the controversies about what a slab is.

[7] Wittgenstein, *Philosophical Investigations*, para. 23.

[8] Ibid., para. 7.

[9] Ibid., para. 21.

[10] Ibid., para. 49.

[11] H. L. A. Hart, *The Concept of Law* (1994), 128–9.

[12] Wittgenstein, *Philosophical Investigations*, para. 117. See also Anat Biletzki and Anat Matar, 'Ludwig Wittgenstein', in E. N. Zalta, ed. *The Stanford Encyclopedia of Philosophy* (2014), http://plato.stanford.edu/archives/spr2014/entries/wittgenstein/.

[13] Wittgenstein, *Philosophical Investigations*, para. 68.

It seems, therefore, that to formulate a general definition of a word by providing the necessary and sufficient conditions for its use amounts to a Sisyphean task. If we accept that the meaning of a word is always context-dependent, then, obviously, the validity of its definition is also always relative. Such a definition may apply to one case, but not necessarily to other cases in which the word is normally employed. This is not to say, however, that no definition of a word or concept can ever be formulated. As Wittgenstein pointed out, we can indeed give some rigid semantic boundaries to a concept, that is, we can define it and use the word standing for the concept in that meaning.[14] However, such a definition would only be 'a definition of a particular kind', reflecting only one specific meaning that the word bears within a particular language-game.[15] This is, for example, how the Vienna Convention on the Law of Treaties defines the concept of a treaty 'for the purposes' of the said Convention.[16] However, we can also use the word in a way 'that the extension of the concept is *not* closed by [any] boundary'.[17] And this is how we generally use the word 'interpretation'.

The language-games in which the word 'interpretation' commonly appears are manifold. We talk about interpretation when we describe some process—for example, what the courts do when they deal with a text of a treaty—but also when we describe the result of this process.[18] Moreover, if we use the term 'interpretation' in the former sense, it is obviously quite different whether we talk about the interpretation of a particular human activity, natural phenomena (e.g. clouds in the sky), or a text of an international treaty. The nature of our activity is different in each of these cases. Even a child is capable of interpreting what clouds in the sky mean; on the other hand, it would be absurd to ask small children to interpret, for instance, the provisions of the UN Charter.

The meaning of the word 'interpretation' also varies in the very context of law depending on the language-game that we play with it. For example, a group of students is preparing for an exam and tries to learn what the content of a particular legal provision is. They read the text of the provision and in accordance with their actual knowledge seek to determine its meaning. I think that in this case we can say, without any doubt, that the students are *interpreting* the provision, and, by 'interpreting the provision', we mean that they undertake some intellectual operation aiming at finding out what the provision assumes. The following day, they come to an exam where the teacher shows them the text of the same provision and asks them to interpret it. The students obey and repeat what they learnt at home.

[14] Ibid., para. 68.

[15] David G. Stern, *Wittgenstein's Philosophical Investigations: An Introduction* (2006), 114.

[16] Art. 2(1) of the Vienna Convention on the Law of Treaties.

[17] Wittgenstein, *Philosophical Investigations*, para. 68.

[18] Jean-Marc Sorel and Valerie Bore-Eveno, 'Article 31', in O. Corten and P. Klein, eds., *The Vienna Conventions on the Law of Treaties: A Commentary* (2011), 807.

Again, they *interpret* the provision. Nevertheless, this time the interpretation does not consist in finding out what the provision means (they already know it!), but in explaining its content to the teacher. The language-game we play with the word 'interpretation' has changed. While in the former case, the term relates to the process of discovering and learning the meaning, in the latter case, it refers to an external activity consisting of pronouncing the meaning and stating the reasons for its justification.

To sum up, interpretation is a heterogeneous concept covering a wide range of distinct activities. Therefore, paraphrasing Wittgenstein, instead of pointing out something common to all that we call interpretation, it is better to say that these activities have no one thing in common in virtue of which we use the same word for all—but there are many different kinds of *affinity* between them. And it is precisely on account of this affinity, or these affinities, that we call them 'interpretation'.[19] Wittgenstein compares the affinities interconnecting different meanings of the same word to the similarities between family members. For, as he argues, 'the various resemblances between members of a family—build, features, colour of eyes, gait, temperament, and so on and so forth—overlap and criss-cross in the same way'. He thus calls these affinities the 'family resemblances':

> Consider, for example, the activities that we call 'games'. I mean board-games, card-games, ball-games, athletic games, and so on. What is common to them all?—Don't say: 'They must have something in common, or they would not be called "games" '—but look and see whether there is anything common to all.—For if you look at them, you won't see something that is common to all, but similarities, affinities, and a whole series of them at that. To repeat: don't think, but look!—Look, for example, at board-games, with their various affinities. Now pass to card-games; here you find many correspondences with the first group, but many common features drop out, and others appear. When we pass next to ball-games, much that is common is retained, but much is lost. . . . And we can go through the many, many other groups of games in the same way, can see how similarities crop up and disappear. And the upshot of these considerations is: we see a complicated network of similarities overlapping and criss-crossing: similarities in the large and in the small.[20]

Therefore, the different instances of interpretation form a family as do the 'games', Wittgenstein's favourite example. In both cases, we may argue that although the characteristics of different uses of terms may overlap in one way or another, there

[19] Wittgenstein, *Philosophical Investigations*, para. 65.

[20] Ibid., para. 66.

is no one thing common to all of them, or, at least, there is no one thing common to all of them *on account of which* we use for them the same word.[21] Interpretation may amount to the process of discovering or learning the meaning, yet it may also amount to the process of explanation or justification. In some cases, the ability to interpret requires a certain dose of previous knowledge; in others, it is rather a matter of imagination. Sometimes the process of interpretation is conscious, sometimes it is unconscious.[22] In short, despite their manifold semantic affinities, different uses of the word 'interpretation' obviously do not have common essence or shared properties which would enable us to formulate their definition. This is undoubtedly the main conclusion in which the application of Wittgenstein's concept of family resemblances results. As different commentators have pointed out, by introducing the concept of family resemblances, Wittgenstein definitely rejects the idea that 'there must be something common to everything that falls under a given concept';[23] that is, 'a Socratic approach to language and concepts, on which it is always legitimate to ask questions such as "What is language?" or "What is a game?" and to look for an answer that provides a definition in terms of necessary and sufficient conditions'.[24]

Absence of common definitional features and the corresponding impossibility of formulating a definition does not, however, imply that the use of the word 'interpretation' is not circumscribed by any rule so that we can call 'interpretation' whatever we want. All that could be claimed in this regard is that the use of the word 'interpretation' is not circumscribed by rules *in every respect*. However, as Wittgenstein pointed out, such a characteristic of words has never prevented us from using them without facing problems in communication and fearing that other people will not understand what we are trying to say.[25] A parallel with the concept of a game is again helpful:

> For how is the concept of a game bounded? What still counts as a game, and what no longer does? Can you say where the boundaries are? No. You can draw some, for there aren't any drawn yet. (But this never bothered you before when you used the word 'game'.)
>
> 'But then the use of the word is unregulated—the "game" we play with it is unregulated.'—It is not everywhere bounded by rules; but no more are

[21] Gordon P. Baker and Peter M. S. Hacker: *An Analytical Commentary on the Philosophical Investigations*, i, *Wittgenstein: Understanding and Meaning, Part 2: Exegesis* (2005), 153.

[22] 'The assertion that a "plain" text does not require interpretation is not only incorrect, it is also dangerous, because it masks an unconscious act of interpretation'. Aharon Barak: *Purposive Interpretation in Law*, tr. S. Bashi (2005), 13.

[23] Baker and Hacker, *Wittgenstein: Understanding and Meaning, Part 2*, 146.

[24] Stern, *Wittgenstein's Philosophical Investigations*, 110.

[25] Ibid., 114 and 116.

> there any rules for how high one may throw the ball in tennis, or how hard, yet tennis is a game for all that, and has rules too.[26]

We may, therefore, conclude that our inability to state a convincing definition of what 'interpretation' means, that is the inability to provide a list of necessary and sufficient conditions under which the term is to be used, is not the result of our ignorance.[27] It does not stem from our insufficient intellectual capacity, but from the very fact that no such thing as necessary and sufficient conditions under which the term might be employed exists.[28] The meanings of words change, they depend on a language-game we play with them, and so it is with their definitions. It follows that the inability to formulate a definition of a word has also no bearing on our ability to understand that word. As Wittgenstein cogently suggests, if we make a statement 'the ground was quite covered with plants', nobody will assume that we do not know what a plant is until we can give a precise definition of the word 'plant'.[29]

6.3. Interpretation neither discovers nor creates the meaning of a rule

A brief survey regarding the practice of international tribunals and the international law doctrine reveals that the word 'interpretation' has typically been employed in two ways. One approach—also called 'conservative'[30]—attempts to describe interpretation as an activity whereby an interpreter seeks to *discover* a meaning given to the text of a treaty by the state parties.[31] The meaning of a rule, its proponents claim, is not developed during the process of interpretation, but exists already at the very moment of the enactment of the rule. Its scope is circumscribed by the intention of states which an interpreter is bound to respect and which represents a paramount standard distinguishing, in case of a dispute, a correct application of a rule from an incorrect one. Hence, the meaning of a rule is what was meant by state parties to be

[26] Wittgenstein, *Philosophical Investigations*, para. 68.

[27] Cf. Robert Kolb, *Interprétation et création du droit international* (2006), 25.

[28] Wittgenstein, *Philosophical Investigations*, para. 69: "We don't know the boundaries because none have been drawn."

[29] Ibid., para. 70.

[30] Rudolf Bernhardt. Evolutive Treaty Interpretation, Especially of the European Convention on Human Rights', *German Yearbook of International Law*, 42 (1999), 16.

[31] Hersch Lauterpacht, 'Restrictive Interpretation and the Principle of Effectiveness in the Interpretation of Treaties', *British Yearbook of International Law*, 26 (1949), 55; Gerald Fitzmaurice, 'The Law and Procedure of the International Court of Justice 1951–4: Treaty Interpretation and Other Treaty Points', *British Yearbook of International Law*, 33 (1957), 204.

this rule and the task of interpreters is nothing more (but also nothing less) than 'to arrive at the intention of the parties *ex signis maxime probabilibus*'.[32]

The conservative approach, however, has been subjected to severe criticism. One of the most important issues raised by the international law doctrine probably was how to proceed in order to discover what the intention of states was in respect of a concrete legal provision. The traditional answer based on recourse to *travaux préparatoires* has gradually been held unsatisfactory. It was objected, in particular, that preparatory works, consisting mainly of unilateral statements and declarations of the delegates of states, could possibly be deemed to reflect the individual intention of the involved state parties, but not their common intention, which is, however, the sole object of interpretation.[33]

Moreover, recourse to the intention of states might be regarded as suitable only if we are ready to accept, as Hart put it, that the world can be characterized 'by a finite number of features and these together with all the modes in which they could combine [are] known to us'.[34] However, this world is plainly not our world. No legislator, including states themselves, is capable of anticipating all the possible combinations of circumstances which the future will bring and, therefore, having a clear intention to regulate them.[35] Yet if Hart's thesis is correct, and there is no reason to assume the contrary, the following problem arises: how is it logically and practically possible to interpret and apply a norm in such unenvisaged cases if the task of an interpreter is limited to 'arriving at the intention of the parties'?

A similar concern is also at the centre of Wittgenstein's philosophical considerations. His primary solicitude is, however, not whether and how it is possible to discover the intention of a legislator, but rather how such an intention can form the content of a rule and determine its correct application. In particular, Wittgenstein refutes the idea—which is at the base of the conservative approach—that intention is 'a special mental act' accompanying the enactment of a given rule and, consequently, that to understand a rule and to apply it correctly amounts to knowing what this mental act has consisted of.[36] To better explain this point, he introduces an example of a pupil asked by his teacher to write a numerical series in accordance with the rule '+ 2':

[32] Hersch Lauterpacht, 'Some Observations on Preparatory Work in the Interpretation of Treaties', *Harvard Law Review*, 48 (1935), 571.

[33] Ibid., 582: "What one party understood by the treaty is of little importance if the other party disagreed with that interpretation'. See also Hans Kelsen, *The Law of the United Nations* (2000), xiv.

[34] Hart, *The Concept of Law*, 128.

[35] Ibid.

[36] '[A]s if that interior act of meaning will bridge the apparent gap between the rule . . . and the acts that accord with it'. Gordon P. Baker and Peter M. S. Hacker, *An Analytical Commentary on the Philosophical Investigations*, ii, *Wittgenstein: Rules, Grammar and Necessity* (2009), 71–72.

> Let's suppose we have done exercises, and tested his understanding up to 1,000. Then we get the pupil to continue one series (say '+ 2') beyond 1,000—and he writes 1000, 1004, 1008, 1012. We say to him, 'Look what you're doing!'—He doesn't understand. We say, 'You should have added two: look how you began the series!'—He answers, 'Yes, isn't it right? I thought that was how I had to do it.' . . . In such a case, we might perhaps say: this person finds it natural, once given our explanations, to understand our order as we would understand the order 'Add 2 up to 1,000, 4 up to 2,000, 6 up to 3,000, and so on'.[37]

Structurally the same problem occurs when the conservative approach to interpretation is at stake. As in Wittgenstein's example, it amounts to a disagreement about how to decide, in a particular case, whether or not a rule was applied correctly or, more fundamentally, what constitutes the standard according to which a correct application of a rule can be distinguished from an incorrect one. The answer that Wittgenstein suggests through his interlocutor, and that proponents of the conservative approach constantly advance, is that '[t]he right step is the one that is in accordance with the order – as it was *meant*'.[38] Nevertheless, unsatisfied with such an explanation Wittgenstein immediately replies:

> So when you gave the order '+ 2', you meant that he was to write 1,002 after 1,000—and did you then also mean that he should write 1,868 after 1,866, and 100,036 after 100,034, and so on—an infinite number of such sentences?[39]

This is, of course, absurd. Just as one cannot *grasp* the whole use of a word at a stroke when one hears it,[40] one can obviously not *mean* all significations of a word when one writes it, or of a rule when one enacts it. If states reach agreement on a specific rule and include the rule in a treaty, they arguably have in mind a large number of implications the rule will produce, but they do not have them all in mind. For example, when states enacted a rule prohibiting torture and included it in the European Convention on Human Rights, they probably meant some particular forms of mistreatment falling under that prohibition, but arguably they did not mean other forms which existed at the relevant time or, *a fortiori*, have been developed subsequently.

Having accepted the argument, Wittgenstein's interlocutor put forward another explanation: when the teacher gave the order '+2', they probably did not have in

[37] Wittgenstein, *Philosophical Investigations*, para. 185.
[38] Ibid., para. 186.
[39] Ibid.
[40] Ibid., para. 197.

mind all implications the rule could subsequently have, but they 'already knew' at that time that the pupil should write '1,002' after '1,000' or '1,868' after '1,866'.[41] Nevertheless, Wittgenstein did not find this second explanation satisfactory either:

> Your 'I already knew at the time . . .' amounts to something like: 'If I had then been asked what number he should write after 1,000, I would have replied "1,002"'. And that I don't doubt. This is an assumption of much the same sort as 'If he had fallen into the water then, I would have jumped in after him'.[42]

In both cases, however, it remains decisive that nobody fell in the water, so the speaker did not jump in, and nobody asked the teacher which number they would write after '1,000', so the teacher did not think about the case and had no intention about what its solution would be. In other words, the teacher's intention of how to apply the rule '+2' after '1,000' cannot be established because, as a matter of fact, there was no intention in this respect at all. There was only a potential answer that the teacher would have formulated if they had been asked to do so. However, a potential answer on a hypothetical question can evidently not serve as a reliable standard of correctness. Rather, as Baker and Hacker pointed out, 'a merely potential yardstick (what I *would* have said if . . .) is no yardstick at all'.[43] It follows that the conservative approach treating interpretation as a matter of discovering the intention of states can be regarded as justified only in a limited number of cases in which the evidence confirms that a particular intention really existed and, in addition, the court sought to reveal it. Yet the conservative notion of interpretation does certainly not constitute a general explanation of what interpretation, as carried out by international courts, means.

Different authors have, therefore, come up with an alternative solution of what interpretation is. For them, the process of interpretation should not be conceived as a matter of discovering a meaning, but rather as an attribution of a meaning to the text of a treaty by its interpreter. It was in particular Humphrey Waldock, the fourth Special Rapporteur of the International Law Commission on the law of treaties, who advanced this approach during the process of drafting the Vienna Convention on the Law of Treaties. Relying namely on the 1935 Harvard Draft Codification of International Law, Waldock emphasized that

> [t]he process of interpretation, rightly conceived, cannot be regarded as a mere mechanical one of drawing inevitable meanings from the words in a

41 Ibid., para. 187.

42 Ibid.

43 Baker and Hacker, *Wittgenstein: Rules, Grammar and Necessity*, 76.

> text, or of searching for and discovering some pre-existing specific intention of the parties with respect to every situation arising under a treaty… In most instances interpretation involves *giving* a meaning to a text….[44]

It is, therefore, not the intention of state parties reflected either in *travaux préparatoires* or in the words of the text themselves that in Waldock's view determines what the text of a treaty means. Words are the symbols which do not have any specific meaning per se. It is the task of an interpreter to attribute one to them, and this is precisely what characterizes the process of interpretation thus becoming the meaning-creating activity.

From Wittgenstein's perspective, however, neither should this second approach be considered correct. According to Wittgenstein, it is a grammatical truth that describing interpretation as a process of attributing a meaning to rules amounts to accepting that how one interprets a rule is also what the rule requires.[45] However, it is in the nature of rules that they can be variously interpreted; they can be interpreted correctly, but also incorrectly. For instance, a pupil supposed to apply the rule '+2' may interpret it as an obligation to write '1,002' after '1,000', but also as an obligation to write '1,004'. Hence, in Wittgenstein's words, 'every interpretation hangs in the air together with what it interprets, and cannot give it any support'.[46] Whether the pupil applied the rule in one way or another, in both cases we can say, 'he applied the rule *as he had interpreted it*'.[47]

That there is some paradox contained in this statement is, however, evident. A rule, once identified with its interpretation, would be deprived of its normative effect and become powerless. For if a *rule* that one has to follow is assimilated to the written expression of a rule as being interpreted, then the rule in question is not able to provide any guideline or standard allowing one to decide which interpretation of the rule is correct and which is not. Every interpretation could be regarded as expressing the rule, and every act could be considered to be in accordance with the rule as it was interpreted. As a result, the very concepts of 'rule' and 'rule-following' would lose their significance:

> This was our paradox: no course of action could be determined by a rule, because every course of action can be brought into accord with the rule. [But] if every course of action can be brought into accord with the rule, then it can also be brought into conflict with it. And so there would be neither accord nor conflict here.[48]

[44] Humphrey Waldock, 'Third Report on the Law of Treaties', *Yearbook of the International Law* Commission, 2 (1964), 53.

[45] See Baker and Hacker, *Wittgenstein: Understanding and Meaning, Part 2*, 93.

[46] Wittgenstein, *Philosophical Investigations*, para. 198.

[47] Baker and Hacker, *Wittgenstein: Rules, Grammar and Necessity*, 117.

[48] Wittgenstein, *Philosophical Investigations*, para. 201.

In sum, conceiving of interpretation as a meaning-creating activity does not provide a general explanation of what interpretation means either. This does not imply, however, that no situation exists in which one can indeed say that a certain meaning was *attributed* to an interpreted object. This is the case, for example, when one interprets clouds in the sky. Nevertheless, to talk about interpretation of clouds and interpretation of (legal) rules is to play a different language-game with the word 'interpretation' in each instance. If someone interprets clouds in the sky, then nobody seeks to evaluate the compliance of the attributed meaning with a particular standard of correctness. In this case, it is possible to claim that how one interprets an object is also what the object means. The contrary is true, however, in the context of rules. For if we argue that rules acquire their meaning only after they have been interpreted, the question of what made an interpreter give just this interpretation to the rule and not another always arises. Baker and Hacker rightly emphasized that if the answer is 'the rule itself', its interpretation becomes redundant. On the other hand, if interpretation of a rule is identified with a mere personal conviction of an interpreter about what this interpretation ought to be, then such interpretation is arbitrary.[49] 'To think one is following a rule', Wittgenstein declared, 'is not to follow a rule'.[50]

6.4. The role of interpretation revisited

Wittgenstein's distinction between 'to follow a rule' and 'to think one is following a rule' is essential. Indeed, it is a fundamental point of his late philosophy of language to emphasize an important social aspect inherent in every human action governed by rules, whether this action consists in writing a numerical series or speaking a language.[51] In Wittgenstein's view, it is the very concept of a rule and what counts as following a rule which excludes the possibility that one could 'follow a rule "privately" '[52] or that there could have been 'only one occasion on which only one person followed a rule'.[53] According to Wittgenstein, following a rule is a matter of practice. In other words, one may comply with a rule (i.e. such an act is logically or, in Wittgenstein's words, 'grammatically' possible) only if there are established human practices or regular patterns of behaviour connected to the application of a rule;[54] for it is precisely these practices or behaviour that yield a referential framework allowing one to understand which act is in accordance with a rule and which is not:

[49] Baker and Hacker, *Wittgenstein: Rules, Grammar and Necessity*, 119.
[50] Wittgenstein, *Philosophical Investigations*, para. 202.
[51] Ibid., para. 43.
[52] Ibid., para. 202.
[53] Ibid., para. 199.
[54] Baker and Hacker, *Wittgenstein: Rules, Grammar and Necessity*, 119.

> [W]hat has the expression of a rule—say a signpost—got to do with my actions? What sort of connection obtains here?—Well, this one, for example: I have been trained to react in a particular way to this sign, and now I do so react to it. But with this you have pointed out only a causal connection; only explained how it has come about that we now go by the signpost; not what this following-the-sign really consists in. Not so; I have further indicated that a person goes by a signpost only in so far as there is an established usage, a custom. . . . That's why 'following a rule' is a practice.[55]

Nevertheless, the practice to which Wittgenstein refers is not to be understood as a social practice in the sense that one is following a rule correctly only if one acts in accordance with a practice shared within a community of rule-followers.[56] While Wittgenstein had no doubt that only '[s]hared human behaviour is the system of reference' by means of which one can understand what it is to follow a rule and what it is to go against it,[57] he did not suggest that the meaning of a rule is given by some quantifiable community consensus about what this rule requires.[58] For example, an expulsion of suspect terrorists to a country in which they risk being tortured would not conform to Article 3 of the European Convention on Human Rights merely by virtue of the fact that a group of rule-followers (i.e. the contracting states), and possibly even the majority of them, regularly and consciously do so.[59] And, vice versa, the rule prohibiting torture under Article 3 of the European Convention would not be what it is, if sending a terrorist to a torturing country would not be regarded as in breach of that article.

Hence, in Wittgenstein's understanding the meaning of a rule is not something distinct from the rule itself—'[t]he money and the cow one can buy with it'.[60] Rules and their meanings, Wittgenstein argued, are not separate entities. They are grammatically related in the sense that there is an internal relationship between a rule on one hand and what counts as following this rule on the other hand. It follows that unlike the international law doctrine, Wittgenstein does not try to explain how a rule can determine what accords with it by reference to some 'mediating entities',[61] such as the intention of rule-makers, community consensus, process of

[55] Wittgenstein, *Philosophical Investigations*, paras. 198 and 202.

[56] Such an interpretation of Wittgenstein's *Philosophical Investigations* is most often connected to Saul A. Kripke, *Wittgenstein on Rules and Private Language* (1982).

[57] Wittgenstein, *Philosophical Investigations*, para. 206. See also para. 54.

[58] ' "So you are saying that human agreement decides what is true and what is false?"—What is true or false is what human beings say; and it is in their language that human beings agree. This is agreement not in opinions, but rather in form of life.' Wittgenstein, *Philosophical Investigations*, para. 241.

[59] See, for example, *Mamatkulov and Askarov v. Turkey*, judgment of 4 February 2005; *Abdelhedi v. Italy*, judgment of 23 March 2009; *Labsi v. Slovakia*, judgment of 15 May 2012; and many others.

[60] Wittgenstein, *Philosophical Investigations*, para. 120.

[61] Baker and Hacker, *Wittgenstein: Rules, Grammar and Necessity*, 87.

interpretation, and so on. Following a rule is a matter of practice. There is no gap separating a rule from what accords with it, and, consequently, there is no need to employ elements which are external to a rule (intention, consensus, interpretation) in order to bridge the gap.[62] The meaning of a rule is its use in practice, and it is exhibited, as Wittgenstein pointed out, 'from case to case of [its] application in what we call "following the rule" and "going against it"'.[63]

As to the role that interpretation plays in this process, Wittgenstein suggests that 'one should speak of interpretation only when one expression of a rule is substituted for another'.[64] Such an explanation of what interpretation means is not, of course, intended to be general, and Wittgenstein would probably be the last person to deny that the word 'interpretation' may also have other meanings depending on the language-game we play with it. Nevertheless, his description of interpretation in terms of a substitution of words in which a rule is formulated seems particularly well suited to explaining what interpretation means in the context of international treaties as applied by international courts. For if we look at the courts' interpretive practice, all we can see—as external observers—is that judges substitute one expression of a rule, contained in a treaty, for another, contained in the reasoning of their judgments.

Such a substitution of one text for another is evidently powerless to attribute a meaning to an interpreted rule or to discover it. Instead, the purpose of the substitution is to *explain* how judges *understand* the rule and, if such an understanding is correct, how the rule ought to be followed.[65] To put it simply, if judges want the right-holders to understand a rule, they have to explain it. And the only tool they have at their disposal is to substitute the original expression of a rule with another linguistic expression or series of expressions (i.e. with its interpretations) consisting of common patterns of legal reasoning, such as analogies, arguments of logic, references to previous case law, and so on.

[62] Ibid., 95.

[63] Wittgenstein, *Philosophical Investigations*, para. 201. For example: 'If a rule reads "No castling through check", then "my not castling through check" describes an act that accords with this rule, and "my castling through check" an act that contravenes it. More generally, it is a grammatical truth that an F's V-ing in circumstances C is an act that accords with the rule that Fs should V in C. Like the relation between a true proposition and the fact that makes it true, the relation between a rule and an act in accordance with it is internal. This rule would not be the rule that it is, nor would this act be the act that it is, if this act did not count as being in accord with this rule.' Baker and Hacker, *Wittgenstein: Rules, Grammar and Necessity*, 87.

[64] Wittgenstein, *Philosophical Investigations*, para. 201.

[65] Gordon P. Baker and Peter M. S. Hacker, *An Analytical Commentary on the Philosophical Investigations*, i, *Wittgenstein: Understanding and Meaning, Part 1: Essays* (2005), 35. See also Denis Patterson, 'Wittgenstein on Understanding and Interpretation', *Philosophical Investigations*, 29 (2006), 130.

Furthermore, interpretation provides the right-holders (or other interested persons) with a *double normative standard* allowing them to determine whether or not a rule has been followed in a particular instance of its application. That is to say, first, interpretation of a rule enables the right-holders to evaluate whether judges themselves understood the rule correctly.[66] For example, if a judge decides that the prohibition of torture under Article 3 of the European Convention forbids electroshock and explains that (i.e. interprets a rule in a way that) the prohibition of torture applies to every act the name of which starts with a vowel, then obviously one may infer that the judge does not understand the rule, although he or she accidentally arrives at the same conclusion to which the correct application of a rule would lead. Second, interpretation provides a standard against which it is possible to assess how a rule shall be—now and henceforth—applied.[67] For example, if a judge interprets the prohibition of torture as forbidding all acts causing serious physical or mental hardship, including electroshock, and such an interpretation is not manifestly erroneous, then every abstention from acts causing serious physical or mental hardship will be, from now on, considered as what counts as following the rule, and, vice versa, every act causing serious physical or mental hardship will be considered as in breach of it.

One may add that conceiving of interpretation as a matter of explanation also requires the reassessment of the function that the so-called rules of interpretation, as stated in Articles 31 and 32 of the Vienna Convention on the Law of Treaties, fulfil in this process. According to the prevailing view among international legal scholars, the goal of the interpretive rules is to provide guidelines allowing an interpreter to discover or to attribute the correct meaning of/to a treaty rule they ought to apply. However, as was already emphasized, interpretation neither discovers nor creates the meaning of rules, and, consequently, neither do the rules of interpretation. Their function is different. Given that they form part of the motivation of judgments, the courts and tribunals use them to explain the meaning of rules they apply and to convince the relevant audience about the correctness of such explanations. As a result, analogically to the process of interpretation itself, Articles 31 and 32 of the Vienna Convention, and the rules of interpretation they express, fulfil both a descriptive and a normative function. That is to say, they first play a part in explaining what the meaning of an interpreted rule is and, second, enable each participant in the legal discourse to assess whether judges understood the rule correctly and, if so, how the rule ought to be applied to future cases.

[66] Baker and Hacker, *Wittgenstein: Understanding and Meaning, Part 1*, 32–33.

[67] Ibid., 35.

6.5. Conclusion

The word 'interpretation' has commonly been used to denote many similar but different activities, such as discovering the meaning, attributing the meaning, clarifying the meaning, choosing between meanings, and so on. Accordingly, to call something 'interpretation' does not disclose anything about the nature of the activity and does not require the activity to be executed in a specific way. As Wittgenstein pointed out, 'with the mere naming of a thing, nothing has yet been done'.[68] Moreover, it should be noticed that the very process of arriving at a conclusion about the meaning of terms or legal rules amounts to a mental activity which can probably be scrutinized using the methods elaborated in psychology, but not using the methods developed in legal science. Information about whether someone determined the meaning of a rule by means of searching for the intention of its authors or created it, or whether the process of interpretation was guided by rules or by the intuition of an interpreter, is always of an introspective character and cannot be verified in an intersubjective way.[69]

The question therefore is: how can we best explain what the courts do when they interpret a treaty? Wittgenstein's methodological advice would probably be '[d]on't think but look!'[70] And the only evidence one may look into is usually a judgment of the court and its written reasoning consisting of a number of linguistic expressions which together represent *the* interpretation of an applied rule. Hence, inasmuch as the judicial interpretation of international treaties is concerned, Wittgenstein's suggestion that 'one should speak of interpretation only when one expression of a rule is substituted for another' is particularly appropriate.[71] Yet substituting one expression for another is obviously powerless both to discover the meaning of a rule and to create it. Accordingly, interpretation does not determine meanings. Rather, its purpose is to explain what the meaning of a rule, as applied by the court, is and to provide a normative framework allowing each participant in the legal discourse to assess whether the court understood the rule correctly and, if so, how the rule ought to be applied to future cases.

References

Baker, Gordon P., and Peter M. S. Hacker, *An Analytical Commentary on the Philosophical Investigations*, i, *Wittgenstein: Understanding and Meaning, Part 1: Essays* (2nd edn, Oxford, 2005).

[68] Wittgenstein, *Philosophical Investigations*, para. 49.

[69] Jerzy Wróblewski, 'L'interprétation en droit: théorie et idéologie', *Archives de Philosophie du Droit*, 17 (1972), 55.

[70] Wittgenstein, *Philosophical Investigations*, para. 66.

[71] Wittgenstein, *Philosophical Investigations*, para. 201.

Baker, Gordon P., and Peter M. S. Hacker, *An Analytical Commentary on the Philosophical Investigations*, i, *Wittgenstein: Understanding and Meaning, Part 2: Exegesis* (2nd edn, Oxford, 2005).

Baker, Gordon P., and Peter M. S. Hacker, *An Analytical Commentary on the Philosophical Investigations*, ii, Wittgenstein: Rules, Grammar and Necessity (2nd edn, Oxford, 2009).

Barak, Aharon, *Purposive Interpretation in Law*, trans. S. Bashi (Princeton, NJ, 2005).

Bernhardt, Rudolf, 'Evolutive Treaty Interpretation, Especially of the European Convention on Human Rights', *German Yearbook of International Law*, 42 (1999), 11–25.

Biletzki, Anat and Anat Matar, 'Ludwig Wittgenstein', in E. N. Zalta, ed., *The Stanford Encyclopedia of Philosophy* (spring 2014 edn), http://plato.stanford.edu/archives/spr2014/entries/wittgenstein/.

Bix, Brian, 'Cautions and Caveats for the Application of Wittgenstein to Legal Theory', in J. K. Campbell, M. O'Rourke, and D. Shier, eds., *Law and Social Justice* (Cambridge, MA, 2005), 217–29.

Fitzmaurice, Gerald, 'The Law and Procedure of the International Court of Justice 1951–4: Treaty Interpretation and Other Treaty Points', *British Yearbook of International Law*, 33 (1957), 203–93.

Hart, H. L. A., *The Concept of Law* (2nd edn, Oxford, 1994).

Kelsen, Hans: *The Law of the United Nations* (New Jersey, 2000).

Kolb, Robert, *Interprétation et création du droit international* (Brussels, 2006).

Kripke, Saul A., *Wittgenstein on Rules and Private Language* (1982).

Lauterpacht, Hersch, 'Restrictive Interpretation and the Principle of Effectiveness in the Interpretation of Treaties', *British Yearbook of International Law*, 26 (1949), 48–85.

Lauterpacht, Hersch, 'Some Observations on Preparatory Work in the Interpretation of Treaties', *Harvard Law Review*, 48 (1935), 549–91.

Linderfalk, Ulf, *On the Interpretation of Treaties: The Modern International Law as Expressed in the 1969 Vienna Convention on the Law of Treaties* (Dordrecht, 2007).

Patterson, Denis, 'Wittgenstein on Understanding and Interpretation', *Philosophical Investigations*, 29 (2006), 129–39.

Pellet, Allain, Patrick Daillier, and Mathias Forteau, *Droit International Public* (8th edn, Paris, 2009).

Sorel, Jean-Marc, and Valerie Bore-Eveno, 'Article 31', in O. Corten and P. Klein, eds., The Vienna Conventions on the Law of Treaties: A Commentary (Oxford, 2011), 804–37.

Stern, David G. *Wittgenstein's Philosophical Investigations: An Introduction* (Cambridge, 2006).

Waldock, Humphrey, 'Third Report on the Law of Treaties', *Yearbook of the International Law Commission*, 2 (1964), 5–65.

Wittgenstein, Ludwig, *Philosophical Investigations*, trans. G. E. M. Anscombe, P. M. S. Hacker, and J. Schulte (4th edn, Oxford, 2009).

Wróblewski, Jerzy, 'L'interprétation en droit: théorie et idéologie', *Archives de Philosophie du Droit*, 17 (1972), 51–69.

PART II

LANGUAGE AND TRANSLATION IN THE INTERPRETATION OF INTERNATIONAL LAW

7

Interpreting multilingual laws

Some costs and benefits

LAWRENCE M. SOLAN

7.1. Introduction

To a continent with a long history of warfare, the European Union (EU) has brought a long period of peace among its members, with no serious threat of war on the horizon. Much of what this chapter says can be applied to other multilingual legal regimes as well. However, both because of the difficult times, and the interesting cases that necessarily arise when a single legal system operates in twenty-four equally authoritative language versions, it will focus principally on Europe.[1]

How has the EU accomplished these important achievements, which have earned it a Nobel Prize?[2] Europe has gone to great lengths to create a supranational legal system despite there being no common language of law that everyone understands. This structure creates a strange contradiction: the difficulty in communication that comes from an autonomous supranational legal system in which every law is written in twenty-four different versions, many of which are not widely understood outside of a single country, is not an unintended consequence of a system that is otherwise functioning smoothly. Rather, it is an important element of the system's design. Simultaneous recognition of the autonomy of European law and the cultural and linguistic autonomy of the member states is precisely what has enabled the EU to attract members and to keep them. Thus, all laws enacted by the EU are promulgated in all twenty-four official languages and each version stands as equally authoritative

[1] This work was supported by a summer research grant from Brooklyn Law School. I wish to express my gratitude to Anne Lise Kjær for comments on an earlier draft, and to Aleksandra Matulewska for valuable discussion.

[2] In 2012, the EU was awarded the Nobel Peace Prize 'for over six decades [having] contributed to the advancement of peace and reconciliation, democracy and human rights in Europe', http://www.nobelprize.org/nobel_prizes/peace/laureates/2012/.

Lawrence M. Solan, *Interpreting multilingual laws* In: *Language and Legal Interpretation in International Law*. Edited by: Anne Lise Kjær and Joanna Lam, Oxford University Press. © Oxford University Press 2022.
DOI: 10.1093/oso/9780190855208.003.0008

as the other twenty-three. Frequently quoted is the 1982 decision of the European Court of Justice (as it was then called) in the *CILFIT* case:

> It must be borne in mind that community legislation is drafted in several languages and that the different language versions are all equally authentic. An interpretation of a provision of community law thus involves a comparison of the different language versions.[3]

Now more than thirty years old, *CILFIT* remains controversial, both for its political statement about the relationship between the Court of Justice of the EU (CJEU) and the member states,[4] and the consequences of its linguistic mandate, which would seem impossible to follow literally with the EU now having twenty-seven members and twenty-four official languages.[5]

This chapter discusses some of the many costs and benefits of this system. The costs are fairly clear. First, the EU structure enables conflicts among various versions that have nothing to do with the case at hand to have legal influence over disputes in which each side regards the language version on which that side relies as authoritative. This creates rule of law issues because the parties in a dispute may be 'blindsided' by interpretations that they would have no reason to have considered. Second, and most obviously, it costs a lot to translate laws into twenty-four versions that are as equivalent as the translators can make them. The EU now budgets 330 million Euros annually for translation services, and even with the use of cost-saving technology, predictions are that this sum will rise before it falls.[6] And third, even a perfunctory reading of the literature on legal translation demonstrates that the expectation of true equivalence is a fantasy.

These costs of multilingualism are real, especially the rule of law issues. Yet the interpretive methods of the CJEU produce results that most often seem fair when there appears to be a conflict among the various language versions. The Court typically examines multiple versions of the law, and then triangulates in an effort to extract the meaning that the Court concludes best reflects the intent of the enacting

[3] Case 283/81 Srl CILFIT and Lanificio di Gavardo SpA v. Ministry of Health [1982] ECR 3415. para. 18.

[4] Hjalte Rasmussen, 'The European Court's Acte clair Strategy in C.I L.F.I.T. Or: Acte clair, of Course! But What Does It Mean?', *European Law Review*, 9 (1984), 242–59.

[5] See Geert Van Calster, 'The EU's Tower of Babel: The Interpretation by the European Court of Justice of Equally Authentic Texts Drafted in more than One Official Language', *Yearbook of European Law*, 17 (1997), 363–93; Anne Lise Kjær, 'Nonsense: The CILFIT Criteria Revisited from the Perspective of Legal Linguistics', in Henning Koch, et al. eds., *Europe. The New Legal Realism: Essays in Honour of Hjalte Rasmussen* (2010), 297–316.

[6] http://ec.europa.eu/dgs/translation/faq/index_en.htm.

legislature. I have elsewhere[7] called this method *Augustinian Interpretation* after the method employed by St Augustine in late antiquity to interpret the Scriptures. It is sometimes (misleadingly) referred to in EU law as *the literal* method, in that a look at various language versions without much further inquiry suffices.

The Augustinian method most often coincides with investigating the purpose of the law using other legal tools. Generally, if most of the language versions are in accord, it is because they are all trying to express identical or at least very similar thoughts. When there is either significant divergence among the various versions, or the purpose of the law appears clear in any event, the court defaults to the traditional teleological approach and advances the purpose of the law, consistent with the most common method of interpretation in civil law legal systems.[8]

In this chapter I will argue that this method is largely successful, and explore what it is about the human language faculty that makes it successful. Somewhat ironically, the absence of a single text protects interpretation against judicial reliance on linguistic accidence. By permitting the interpreter to consider more data points, the system *increases* the likelihood of interpretation faithful to the goals of the legislature, as the system, by adding new members and new languages, *decreases* the mutual comprehensibility of the law throughout the EU. It is the irony of developing a text-oriented system of interpretation in a system that has no single text that brings success to the interpretation of laws by European courts.

This chapter looks at three different scenarios: cases in which multilingual drafting successfully disambiguates those language versions that would permit multiple interpretations; cases in which outlying versions are rejected as inconsistent with the will of the legislature; and cases in which the versions are not in accord, and the court must rely on other methods, such as discerning the purpose behind the law, to come to a single legal interpretation. In discussing each of these scenarios, I compare the CJEU's method with that of the US Supreme Court in cases that raise relatively similar interpretive issues. In all three scenarios, examining versions of the law written in different languages provides opportunities for more refined inquiry into how well competing interpretations reflect the legislative will further, or at least better further, the purpose behind the law. Before that, though, let us turn to some of the difficulties caused by this expensive and cumbersome system.

[7] Lawrence M. Solan, 'The Interpretation of Multilingual Statutes by the European Court of Justice', *Brooklyn Journal of International Law*, 34 (2009), 277–301.

[8] Cornelis J. W. Baaij, 'Fifty Years of Multilingual Interpretation in the European Union', in Peter M. Tiersma and Lawrence M. Solan, eds., *The Oxford Handbook of Language and Law* (2012), 217–31.

7.2. Some costs of multilingual legislation

7.2.1. Inadequate notice

In a famous 1931 US Supreme Court decision, *McBoyle v. United* States,[9] Justice Oliver Wendell Holmes, writing for a unanimous court, held that an airplane is not a vehicle. A law made it a crime to transport stolen vehicles across state lines. McBoyle had flown a stolen plane from one state to another. The law defined vehicle as follows: 'The term "motor vehicle" shall include an automobile, automobile truck, automobile wagon, motor cycle, or any other self-propelled vehicle not designed for running on rails'. The Court held that the legislature that wrote this definition in 1919—before there was a commercial airline industry—could not have intended it to include airplanes. Recognizing that the decision might sound silly to some because McBoyle, like anyone else, must have known that it is illegal to steal an airplane and fly it to a different state, Holmes concluded:

> Although it is not likely that a criminal will carefully consider the text of the law before he murders or steals, it is reasonable that a fair warning should be given to the world, in language that the common world will understand, of what the law intends to do if a certain line is passed. To make the warning fair, so far as possible, the line should be clear. When a rule of conduct is laid down in words that evoke in the common mind only the picture of vehicles moving on land, the statute should not be extended to aircraft simply because it may seem to us that a similar policy applies, or upon the speculation that, if the legislature had thought of it, very likely broader words would have been used.[10]

Given that the law is a social instrument enforceable by coercion or even physical punishment, it always matters that those made subject to the law can understand it, whether they go to the trouble of learning it or not. It is this accessibility that gives the coercive power of the law its legitimacy.

Multilingual legislation adds a layer of potential uncertainty that Holmes did not need to contend with in *McBoyle*. Consider *E.C. Commission v. Italy*,[11] decided by the European Court of Justice. An EU directive requires member states to exempt from VAT (value-added taxation) 'the provision of medical care in the exercise of medical and paramedical professions'. The Italian law implementing this directive was worded in such a way as to allow for the exemption of veterinarians. But this

[9] 283 US 25 (1931).

[10] 261 US at 27.

[11] Case 122/87, *E.C. Comm'n v. Italy*, 1988 E.C.R. 2685.

version was an outlier.[12] Other language versions made it clear that the directive was intended to apply only to doctors that treat people. Using the Augustinian method, the Court held that the directive does not apply to veterinary services.

I have no complaint about the decision or the method by which it was reached. But the losing party in that case surely had a legitimate complaint. As others have pointed outby Leung (2012) and Baaij (2012b),[13] there is a serious notice issue when an individual sensibly believes that the laws have been complied with, only to find that a version of the law that the person could not possibly understand is inconsistent with the one in that person's own language, but more loyal to the intent of the legislature that drafted the law. It is difficult to deny that one cost of a multilingual legal order is that economic actors, in addition to taking market risks, are compelled to take language risks. Not only must they comply with the law of the member state in which they operate, and with the law of the EU as stated in it directives and other legal enactments, but they must take a chance that the version of the directive upon which they rely will be deemed to be in error.

As the Court of Justice repeats formulaically:

> According to settled case-law, the need for a uniform interpretation of European Union acts makes it impossible, in case of doubt, for the text of a provision to be considered in isolation but requires, on the contrary, that it should be interpreted and applied in the light of the versions existing in the other official languages.[14]

The underlying principle is that EU law is not derivative of the law of any individual member, but is rather itself an autonomous body of law.[15]

Consequently, when there appears to be a difference in how different language versions would apply in a particular case, the court considers various versions in an effort to search for the interpretation that would best promote the purpose underlying the directive. That inquiry may result in the court's accepting one or the other interpretations offered by the parties in the case at hand, or in neither, if the court

[12] The Italian version read in relevant part: 'le prestazioni mediche effecttuate nell'esercizio delle professioni mediche e paramediche quali sono definiti dagli Stati membri interessati'.

[13] Janny Leung, 'Statutory Interpretation in Multilingual Jurisdictions: Typology and Trends', *Journal of Multilingual and Mulicultural Development*, 33/5 (2012), 481–95; Cornelis J. W. Baaij, 'The Significance of Legal Translation for Legal Harmonization', in Cornelis J. W. Baaij, ed., *The Role of Legal Translation in Legal Harmonization* (2012), Ch. 1.

[14] Ahmed Abdelaziz Ezz v. Council of the European Union, Case T-256/11 (CJEU 2014).

[15] See, e.g., Anne Lise Kjær, 'Theoretical Aspects of Legal Translation in the EU: The Paradoxical Relationship between Language, Translation and the Autonomy of EU Law', in Susan Šarčević, ed., *Language and Culture in EU Law: Multidisciplinary Perspectives* (2015), 91–107; Barbara Pozzo, 'Comparative Law and the New Frontiers of Legal Translation', in Susan Šarčević, ed., *Language and Culture in EU Law: Multidisciplinary Perspectives* (2015), 73–87.

concludes that another version, or some hybrid of language versions, better furthers the statutory goals.

I have argued elsewhere[16] and argue again here that the inquiry into the various language versions actually improves statutory interpretation in that it reduces the opportunity for parties to take advantage of linguistic accident to persuade a court to accept an interpretation that is linguistically available, but contrary to the law's intended purpose. This enhanced fidelity to the legislative mission is a great benefit of multilingual systems. Nonetheless, it is important to recognize that Leung and Baaij are right in their criticism of multilingual regimes. Fair notice, the very basic rule of law value espoused by Oliver Wendell Holmes in *McBoyle*, is compromised when the citizenry is subject to laws that they cannot understand because they do not speak the language. This happens whenever a legal system relies on two or more versions of the law as equally authoritative, as in the EU, but also in the national laws of many countries, including Canada, Switzerland, Belgium, and Hong Kong.

7.2.2. The impossibility of achieving equivalence among different language versions of the same law

As the literature on legal translation expands, it is worth noting that just about every commentator has something to say about the failures of legal translation.[17] Leung refers to the notion of linguistic equivalence as a legal fiction, which, when combined with the principle of equal authenticity adhered to by the EU and other multilingual legal regimes, creates expectations of success in translation that can never be met.[18] The problems lie not only in nuanced differences that exist between languages in the concepts expressed generally (see Quine 1960), but also in the fact that many (but not all) multilingual legal systems are multijural in addition to being multilingual. Ruth Sullivan, a leading scholar on statutory interpretation in Canada,

[16] Solan, 'The Interpretation of Multilingual Statutes'.

[17] See, e.g., Janet Ainsworth, 'Lost in Translation? Linguistic Diversity and the Elusive Quest for Plain Meaning in Law', in Le Cheng, Kui King, and Anne Wagner, eds., *The Ashgate Handbook of Legal Translation* (2014), 43–55; Anne Lise Kjær, 'Legal Translation in the European Union: A Research Field in Need of a New Approach', in Krzysztof Kredens and Stanislaw Gozdz-Roszkowski, eds., *Language and the Law: International Outlooks* (2007); Anne Lise Kjær, 'Theoretical Aspects of Legal Translation in the EU: The Paradoxical Relationship between Language, Translation and the Autonomy of EU Law', in Susan Šarčević, ed., *Language and Culture in EU Law: Multidisciplinary Perspectives* (2015), 91–107; Baaij, 'Fifty Years of Multilingual Interpretation in the European Union'; Baaij, 'The Significance of Legal Translation for Legal Harmonization'; and Susan Šarčević, 'Legal Translation: Possible, but not Perfect', in Peter M. Tiersma and Lawrence M. Solan, eds., *The Oxford Handbook of Language and Law* (2012), 187–99.

[18] Janny H. C. Leung, 'Translation Equivalence as Legal Fiction', in Le Cheng, Kui King, and Anne Wagner, eds., *The Ashgate Handbook of Legal Translation* (2014), 57–69.

discusses this issue in detail.[19] In addition to dealing with conventional problems of translation, the legal system must also take account of the fact that French-speaking Quebec operates within a Civil Law framework, while most of the rest of Canada operates within a common law framework. Louis Beaudoin, a Canadian legal translator, discusses difficulties that the combination of bilingualism and bijuralism causes.[20] Many have remarked similarly about European law, which not only must contend with the civil law/common law conceptual gap, but also with differences from country to country in the meanings of terms within the civil law framework.[21]

These points are very well established, and I need not elaborate on them in detail here. One distinction, however, is worth noting. Much of the concern, as expressed by translators, by legal theorists, and by the European Commission itself, involves the inconsistent use of legal terminology. For example, Matulewska advocates for an approach to translation in which the translator focuses on the purpose for which the translation will be used in order to reduce the volume of pernicious non-equivalences.[22] Trevor Hartley illustrates the point by discussing uncertainty in determining whether a directive regulating consumer contracts applies to the sale of land as well as the sale of goods.[23] The English 'goods' does not include land, the French 'biens' does. Oliver Brand, a German legal scholar, puts it well:

> Each national legal system uses terminology that does not necessarily correspond with the legal languages of other countries. Therefore, a literal translation of a given legal term into another language may not exactly express the same concept. This might have doctrinal reasons. Possession, for example, in some jurisdictions requires a will to possess (*animus domandi*), in others not. Similarly, the concepts of property titles, of mortgages or the concepts of impossibility vary to such an extent in different legal systems that a literal translation is misleading at best.[24]

[19] Ruth Sullivan, 'The Challenges of Interpreting Multilingual, Multijural Legislation', *Brooklyn Journal of International Law*, 29 (2004), 985–1066.

[20] Louis Beaudoin, 'Legal Translation in Canada: The Genius of Legal Language(s)', in Frances Olsen, Alexander Lorz, and Dieter Stein, eds., *Translation Issues in Language and Law* (2009), 136–44.

[21] See, e.g., Baaij, 'The Significance of Legal Translation for Legal Harmonization'; and Pozzo, 'Comparative Law and the New Frontiers of Legal Translation', for discussion of the problem of multijuralism in Europe.

[22] Aleksandra Matulewska, *Legilinguistic Translatology: A Parametric Approach to Legal Translation* (2013).

[23] Trevor C. Hartley, 'Five Forms of Uncertainty in European Community Law', *Cambridge Law Journal*, 55 (1996), 265–88.

[24] Oliver Brand, 'Language as a Barrier to Comparative Law', in Frances Olsen, Alexander Lorz, and Dieter Stein, eds., *Translation Issues in Language and Law* (2009), 22.

Efforts are made to avoid drafting statutory language that has technical meaning in one or more legal systems, opting instead for descriptions of factual or legal situations that carry with them less legal baggage. Indeed, these situations are nightmarish for translators, and the literature in which they complain of the problem and seek solutions is well-motivated.[25]

While these issues are vitally important to the establishment of a multilingual legal order, the problem is sufficiently salient that the European legal community is surely on notice of them. There appears to be consensus that the understanding of a legal concept should not conform, without further argumentation, to its meaning in one legal system, at the exclusion of competing systems. Thus, it should not be entirely surprising that despite the focus on these problems with legal terminology, many, if not most, of the cases that reach the CJEU really are not about legal terminology understood differently from one legal system to another because of differences in the legal systems of individual nations. Rather, they are instances of syntactic ambiguity and the vagueness of everyday words, and technical non-legal vocabulary.[26] It is on those cases that I focus in this chapter.

7.3. Why multilingual legal interpretation works so well

In this section, I offer an explanation for why multilingual legal systems seem to work, and why they seem to work even better when there are more than two languages. The core of my argument is that multiplying language versions tends to reduce opportunities for parties to take advantage of linguistic accidence, resulting from what Bernard Williams has called 'fetishizing assertion'.[27] All languages are subject to various species of linguistic indeterminacy, whether in the form of vagueness, ambiguity, referential uncertainty, or simply the use of terms so general that their application is not understood uniformly.[28] When language bearing these

[25] See, e.g., Jan Engberg, 'Autonomous EU Concepts? Fact or Fiction', in Susan Šarčević, ed., *Language and Culture in EU Law: Multidisciplinary Perspectives* (2015), 91–107; and Kjær, 'Theoretical Aspects of Legal Translation in the EU' for discussion of the range of solutions considered.

[26] For examples, see Cornelis J. W. Baaij, *Legal Integration and Language Diversity: Rethinking EU Lawmaking* (Oxford University Press, 2018), 162; Baaij, 'Fifty Years of Multilingual Interpretation in the European Union'; and Solan, 'The Interpretation of Multilingual Statutes by the European Court of Justice'.

[27] Bernard Williams, *Truth and Truthfulness* (2002), 100–10.

[28] For discussion of the differences between vagueness and ambiguity in legal settings, see Ralf Poscher, 'Ambiguity and Vagueness in Legal Interpretation', in Peter M. Tiersma and Lawrence M. Solan, eds., *Oxford Handbook of Language and Law* (2012), 128–44; and Antonin Scalia and Bryan A. Garner, *Reading Law: The Interpretation of Legal Texts* (2012). For a general taxonomy of uncertainty in the meanings of words, see Steven Weschsler, *Word Meaning and Syntax: Approaches to the Interface* (2015).

uncertainties occurs in laws (or contracts and other authoritative or instrumental legal texts), they require construction. Lawyers attempt to take advantage of such ambiguity in order to argue for whichever interpretation best suits their clients. Judges, in turn, recognizing their obligation to be faithful to the language that the legislature used, but having choices among the legitimate interpretations of the language, have opportunities to interpret laws in ways that coincide with their personal values while not—at least as a formal matter—usurping the prerogative of the legislature to make the laws.

Construing the law in a manner consistent with its purpose is one way of resolving ambiguity in a manner not dependent upon the judge's own values. However, it is not always the case that one interpretation will further a statute's goals while the other undermines them, and it is not always easy to articulate a statute's goals at the level of detail that a particular case demands, especially when the law is complex and serves a regulatory function. Purposive analysis, then, can never be a complete substitute for linguistic analysis.

In *On Christian Doctrine*, Augustine proposed a solution for the problem of confronting in the scriptures expressions with which the reader is unfamiliar:

> For either a word or an idiom, of which the reader is ignorant, brings him to a stop. Now if these belong to foreign tongues, we must either make inquiry about them from men who speak those tongues, or if we have leisure we must learn the tongues ourselves, or we must consult and compare several translators.[29]

It is the comparison of translations that Augustine and the CJEU share methodologically.

What we now know about language informs us that Augustine's solution makes sense. First, we know that some vocabulary differs subtly from one language to another, and these differences affect perception. Not only does Russian have two words for what we call 'blue' in English (light blue and dark blue), but in colour discrimination tasks, Russian speakers perform differently from English speakers.[30] When a legal system communicates in more than one language, a survey of various language versions will tend to show consensus, to identify a language as an outlier, or to demonstrate that there is no consensus among the languages with respect to the interpretive task at hand, triggering additional inquiry into the law's purpose and the legislature's intent. Disparate meanings are likely to occur especially when multilingual legal systems use technical legal terms that have particular, but

[29] Augustine, Book II, Chapter 14, Paragraph 21.

[30] Phillip Wolff, and Kevin J. Holmes, 'Linguistic Relativity', *Wiley Interdisciplinary Reviews: Cognitive Psychology*, 2 (2011), 253–65.

differing, understandings in the different languages and legal systems. The very fact that there is confusion among the various language versions is strong indication that the court should not resort to the term's meaning in a single legal system, as such a move would elevate that legal system over all others. The CJEU is well aware of this issue and has repeated many times the need to develop a system of European legal concepts, not reliant on the national concepts of any individual country.[31]

Moreover, people react similarly to exposure to the same concept with the same prototype. While there may be debate about whether 'medical personnel' includes veterinarians, there is no doubt that the term includes cardiologists who treat people. To take Fodor's term,[32] we 'lock on' to concepts similar to one another upon exposure to prototypical examples of the concept. The result is that most cases—those that involve the very set of circumstances that the law was written to address—present no more of a problem in multilingual systems than they do in monolingual ones.

Most legal cases that deal with word meaning and make their way all the way to the CJEU, however, are not about the prototype. Rather, they are about events that are unusual enough that they arguably fit within the statutory vocabulary, but then again, they arguably do not fit within the statutory vocabulary. The British psychologist James Hampton and his colleagues have demonstrated in a series of experiments that consensus about category membership degrades as we stray further from the prototypical case.[33] The problem is that in resolving borderline cases, people do not always turn to the same features. Take the case of lying. When a speaker says something that is literally true but intended to deceive, some turn to the speaker's deceptive intent, while others rely on the fact that the statement was literally true. Thus, there is disagreement about whether to call such a statement a lie.[34] Here again, multilingual legislation helps to flag the fact that the language of the law is not as clear as it might seem, triggering inquiry into the law's teleology.

What all of this contributes is a reduction in the opportunity to rely on linguistic accidence, or, returning to Bernard William's expression, to fetishize assertion. The proliferation of language versions is likely to reveal the fact that there was no legislative consensus revealed in the language with respect to the law's application to non-prototypical events. It is a maxim of all legal systems that laws must be construed in

[31] See Engberg, 'Autonomous EU Concepts?'; Kjær, 'Legal Translation in the European Union'; and Kjær, 'Theoretical Aspects of Legal Translation in the EU' for discussion of such efforts.

[32] Jerry A. Fodor, *Concepts: Where Cognitive Science Went Wrong* (1998).

[33] James A. Hampton, Zachary Estes, and Sabrina Simmons, 'Metamorphosis: Essence, Appearance, and Behavior in the Categorization of Natural Kinds', *Memory & Cognition*, 35 (2007), 1785–1800.

[34] Linda Coleman, and Paul Kay, 'Prototype Semantics: The English Word *Lie*', *Language*, 57 (1971), 26–44.

context. However, when the language appears plain on the surface, the contextual nature of the interpretation may remain opaque to the decision maker.

7.4. Improving statutory interpretation by reducing mutual understanding

Here we look at three scenarios: cases involving syntactic ambiguity, cases in which certain meanings are considered outliers, and cases in which the Augustinian method does not work, and the court must turn to teleology. In each instance, I compare a multilingual case from the EU to a monolingual one from the United States.

7.4.1. Syntactic ambiguity: Comparing EU and US methods

When it comes to syntactic ambiguity, multilingual legislation has a positive, disambiguating effect, a fact that has been recognized by commentators.[35] As Baaij observes, a great many cases before the CJEU concern syntactic ambiguity.[36] The problem is that languages differ with respect to where these ambiguities occur. Thus, a provision may be clear in one language but ambiguous in another. As we will see, examination of numerous versions can root out cases in which a linguistic accident produces a possible reading at odds with the intended scope of the law.

Consider *Case Brought by X*,[37] decided by the CJEU in 2013. A woman in the Netherlands said that she had never received a notice imposing a fine for a traffic violation because the notices had been sent to the wrong address. To prove this, she asked the local municipality to send her what records they had of her address during the relevant time period. The municipality responded by sending her a transcript with the relevant information, and charged her 12.80 Euros as a processing fee, which is allowed under Dutch law.

Directive 95/46 of the European Commission guarantees to European citizens the right to their own personal information maintained by the government. The English version says:

> Member States shall guarantee every data subject the right to obtain [information about the person making the request that is held by the government] from the controller:
>
> (a) without constraint at reasonable intervals and without excessive delay or expense.

[35] See discussion in van Calster, 'The EU's Tower of Babel'.

[36] Baaij, 'Fifty Years of Multilingual Interpretation in the European Union'.

[37] Case C-486/12, 2013 ECJ EUR-Lex LEXIS 3964.

The English version is ambiguous (as is the Dutch version in exactly the same way).[38] It can be understood in either of the following ways, quoting from the decision (Paragraph 11), which accurately describes the ambiguity:

> the communication of personal data must take place without excessive delay or excessive expense, or
>
> the communication of personal data must take place without excessive delay and without expense.

Now compare this version to the Spanish version: 'sin retrasos ni gastos excesivos' (*without delays nor expenses excessive*). Spanish and many other languages place an adjective after the noun it modifies. In the Spanish version, 'excesivos; must modify 'gastos' (expenses), but optionally modifies the whole expression, which would also include 'retrasos' (delays). The English and Spanish versions, then, are both ambiguous, between 'excessive' modifying the entire expression, or only the noun that is adjacent to the adjective. But the versions differ as to which noun is adjacent to the adjective.

The Court looked at a variety of language versions and noted that some were like Dutch in that either both nouns or only 'delay' is modified by 'excessive' (English and Swedish), while others, including French, Spanish, Danish, and German, permit 'excessive' to modify either both nouns or only 'delay'. Seeing nothing in the legislative history to suggest that the EC intended to disallow any fee whatsoever, the Court ruled in favour of the government, permitting the 12.80 Euros to be assessed.

By employing the Augustinian approach, the Court reduced the opportunism that the Dutch version allowed. The complaining party indeed relied on a legitimate reading of the directive. However, her reading was not the reading that the legislature intended. Examining the other versions made it clear which reading of the syntactically ambiguous Dutch version should be given weight. This is the benefit of Augustinian interpretation.

The problem of adequate notice is quite clear in this case. As Leung points out, parties not conversant in multiple languages may not be on adequate notice of their rights and obligations.[39] Moreover, there is a certain amount of luck involved in these cases. If the complaining party had been a native speaker of Spanish, there would, presumably, have been no case in the first place. It must be kept in mind that the price of faithful interpretation in multilingual legal systems is paid by the losing party in the case being decided. She had no practical means of determining in advance that she had misconstrued the law.

[38] The Dutch version is: 'bovenmatige vertraging of kosten'.

[39] Leung 'Statutory Interpretation in Multilingual Jurisdictions'.

Yet the benefits of this approach to interpretation are great. To show how valuable the Augustinian interpretation is in cases of syntactic ambiguity, let us look at a monolingual case from the United States in which precisely the same linguistic issue was in play. The case, *California v. Brown*,[40] involved the death penalty. The jurors, who sentenced Brown to death for a murder he had committed, were instructed that they:

> must not be swayed by mere sentiment, conjecture, sympathy, passion, prejudice, public opinion or public feeling.

Jurors should not be swayed by prejudice, public opinion or passion at all, and any instruction that suggests they are legitimate factors for jurors to consider would be deemed unconstitutional. Here, again, the question was whether an adjective ('mere') modifies only the noun adjacent to it ('sentiment'), or the entire noun phrase, which would include 'prejudice'. In contrast, jurors may, in deciding on the death penalty, take into account sympathy for the defendant.

By a five-to-four majority, the Supreme Court upheld Brown's death sentence. Writing for the majority, Chief Justice Rehnquist chose the reading in which 'mere' modifies all of the nouns. This reading solves the interpretive problem with 'sympathy'. The instruction does not prohibit the jurors from considering sympathy, only from considering sympathy as the exclusive consideration. This reading, though, necessarily imposes the same reading on the illegal considerations, including 'prejudice'. It is just as unconstitutional to consider any prejudice as it is to consider 'mere' prejudice.

The dissenting opinion, written by Justice Brennan, pointed out this inconsistency. Brennan chose the reading in which 'mere' modifies only 'sentiment', the noun adjacent to it. If that is the case, the law is unconstitutional for banning 'sympathy' as a consideration. Brennan had the better of the argument. It is unlikely that a court instructing a jury in a death penalty case would have intended the jury to take prejudice or public opinion into account as long as it was not mere prejudice or mere public opinion. Rather, the court would have intended to instruct the jury that these are not factors to be taken into account in making a decision.

Just like *The Case Brought by X*, the US Supreme Court case was about an ambiguity in the scope of adjectives. But the US case did not have Augustinian interpretation available to it. As those familiar with the US court would recognize, the five justices voting in favour of affirming the death sentence were the more conservative ones, and the four voting to reverse it were the more liberal ones. It is inconceivable that one's preference for broad or narrow adjectival scope is a function of one's

[40] 479 US 538 (1987). I discuss this case in more detail in Solan, *The Language of Judges* (1993), 55–61.

political commitments to the death penalty. It is very difficult to avoid the conclusion that the personal values of the judges infiltrated the US opinion, and did so less, if at all, in the CJEU opinion that dealt with the same ambiguity.

My argument in this regard is not that US judges are affected by their personal values while the CJEU judges are not. For example, Rasmussen argues convincingly that the *CILFIT* decision, which established a great deal of the CJEU's interpretive methodology was more about entrenching European federalism than it was about interpretation.[41] By the same token, the Augustinian methodology that this chapter applauds is by no means applied uniformly by the Court, and it would be fantasy to assume that it ever looks at all twenty-four language versions in a single case.[42] Rather, the point made here is that the very existence of multiple language versions imposes constraints on interpretation beyond the constraints present in monolingual systems. These constraints do not entirely eliminate judicial opportunism, but they certainly reduce it.

One can also point out many differences in the roles and appointment processes that distinguish between these courts. Nonetheless, methods of legal interpretation that reduce uncertainty and make it less possible to rely on linguistic accidence to further a judge's own values are prized in all legal systems. This has been a virtual mantra of US Justice Antonin Scalia.[43] Multilingual legislation, combined with the use of the Augustinian method of interpretation, reduces the opportunity for personal values to replace analysis based on shared legal values.

The *Case Brought by X* also illustrates a very important aspect of Augustinian Interpretation, which has caused some controversy. The method should not result in a contest with the interpretation that follows from the most language versions winning, say by a score of 14–10. A quantitative approach makes sense when the issue is the identification of an outlier. For the most part, however, the examination of multiple versions of the law should not be a mechanical process. The flexibility, though, comes with a price, as Baaij observes.[44] The price is that one cannot tell in advance what the court will do with information about the distribution of versions of the law. The court sometimes goes with the majority, sometimes goes

[41] Hjalte Rasmussen, 'The European Court's Acte clair Strategy in C.I L.F.I.T. Or: Acte clair, of Course! But What Does It Mean?', *European Law Review*, 9 (1984), 242–59. See also Mattias Derlén, 'In Defence of (Limited) Multilingualism: Problems and Possibilities of the Multilingual Interpretation of European Union National Courts', in Anne Lise Kjær and Silvia Adamo, eds., *Linguistic Diversity and European Democracy* (2011), 143–66.

[42] See Trevor C. Hartley, 'Five Forms of Uncertainty in European Community Law', *Cambridge Law Journal*, 55 (1996), 265–88; Derlén, 'In Defence of (Limited) Multilingualism', 150–1, Anne Lise Kjær, 'Nonsense: The CILFIT Criteria Revisited from the Perspective of Legal Linguistics', in Henning Koch, et al. eds., *Europe. The New Legal Realism: Essays in Honour of Hjalte Rasmussen* (2010), 297–316; Baaij, 'The Significance of Legal Translation for Legal Harmonization'.

[43] See Scalia and Garner, *Reading Law*.

[44] Baaij, 'Fifty Years of Multilingual Interpretation in the European Union'.

with a minority, and sometimes seems to pay no attention at all to the distribution after announcing it.

Furthermore, teleology would not have been good enough in this case. Twelve Euros is not a lot of money. It would be perfectly reasonable to have inferred, other things being equal, that the EC intended to make the information at issue in the case available to individuals without charge. The purpose of the directive—to make the information available quickly and affordably—would be furthered by either interpretation, and even more so by requiring that the information be given without charge to the recipient. Thus, the ultimate decision came not from a statistical exercise, nor from an independent analysis of the directive's purpose. Rather, it was an argument based on an inference about the intent of the EC in enacting the directive. That intent, in turn, was inferred from the relationship between the different language versions, taken as a whole.

7.4.2. Eliminating outliers

In monolingual legal systems questions arise as to whether a reading of a law that is within its permitted interpretations but outside the core, or prototypical meaning, should be recognized as coming within the statute. The classic case from US law is *Church of the Holy Trinity v. United States*,[45] decided in 1892. A New York church had paid to bring its new minister to New York from London by ship. A law in effect at the time prohibited the payment of transportation for anyone coming to the United States 'to perform service or labor of any kind'. Although a lower court had fined the church for violating the statute, the Supreme Court ruled unanimously that while the case came within the letter of the law, 'yet not within the statute, because not within its spirit, nor within the intention of its makers'.[46] The case continues to draw controversy.[47] Regardless, the Court's sense that the word 'labour' in this context was most likely to apply to physical work, even though at the margins it can be used to describe intellectual activity, has intuitive appeal.

Contemporary American judges refer to the 'ordinary meaning rule' and the 'whole act rule' in deciding such cases.[48] One must read statutes in the context of the law taken as a whole. In addition, there is a presumption that the legislature uses words in their 'ordinary sense', making it legitimate for courts to ignore meanings

[45] 143 US 457 (1892).

[46] Ibid., 459.

[47] See Adrian Vermeule, *Judging Under Uncertainty: An Institutional Theory of Legal Interpretation* (2006).

[48] See, for discussion, Scalia and Garner, Reading Law; William N. Eskridge, Jr, *Interpreting Law: A Primer on How to Read Statutes and the Constitution* (2016).

remote from the prototypical understanding of the language.[49] Both of these are familiar principles in European jurisprudence as well.

Problems arise when judges favour one interpretation over another by designating a reading as an outlier when it is not, or when the history underlying the law shows that a minority interpretation was clearly intended. Consider a much more recent case decided by the US Supreme Court: *Ledbetter v. Goodyear Tire & Rubber Co.*[50] Ledbetter claimed that she had been discriminated against based on her sex. The law set a time limit of 180 days to bring such a 'discrimination' claim. Ledbetter claimed that she was entitled to damages for the most recent 180 days of her receiving a lower salary even though the discrimination had been going on for some time.

The Supreme Court, in a five-to-four decision ruled in favour of the employer, Goodyear. The argument was largely linguistic: More often than not, we use the word 'discriminate' in an active sense, rather than as a reflection of a continuing practice. Whether or not this is an accurate description of the word's usage (it was not supported by empirical evidence), the interpretation overrode the statute's purpose, which was to provide a remedy to employees who were paid less because of their race, sex, national origin, or religious identity. Surely the legislature did not intend for employers to have the right to announce, as blatantly as they wished, 'now that six months have passed I'm free to continue paying you less because you are a woman, and there is nothing you can do about it', a point raised in Justice Ginsburg's strong dissenting opinion. Soon after the decision, the Congress overrode the decision by clarifying the law.[51]

Thus, monolingual legal systems leave room for making arguments about which meanings are 'ordinary' and which meanings are outlying, based on subtle linguistic nuance that may undermine the purpose of the statute. That is far more difficult to do in the teeth of a multilingual system in which the very existence of multiple versions (putting aside single outliers) makes it necessary to investigate what the statute was attempting to accomplish, and to resolve the differences in light of this investigation. Sometimes what is an outlier in one language may be totally unacceptable in others, making the decision easier for the court. That is what happened in *E.C. Commission v. Italy* (the veterinarian case).

Problems do arise in multilingual systems when the court must decide how much disagreement there must be to deem an interpretation outlying. Consider the *Codan*[52] case, which involved taxation on shares of stock not listed on exchanges. The German and Danish versions said one thing, the Greek, Spanish, French, Italian, Dutch, Portuguese and English versions, another (Paragraph 23). The Court sided

[49] See Solan 2010; Brian G. Slocum, *Ordinary Meaning: A Theory of the Most Fundamental Principle of Legal Interpretation* (2015).

[50] 550 US 618 (2007).

[51] 42 USC § 2000e-(2)(a)(1) (2006).

[52] *Skatteministeriet v. Aktieselskabet Forsikringsselskabet Codan*, Case C-236/97 [1998] ECR I-8679.

with the 'great majority' of language versions (Paragraph 29), holding both that the majority seemed to better serve the purpose of the directive, and that uniformity of interpretation was an important value of European law.

Despite the decision's language, it is not generally the Court's practice to count the versions in each interpretation and to rule in favour of the majority, unless it appears that one of the interpretations is sufficiently outside the mainstream that it is probably in error. This is really what Augustine had in mind when he advocated for placing translations side by side. Exactly where to draw the line as to what counts as an outlier and what is part of a minority position that should be given more weight is not clear, though. Moreover, any attempt to draw a specific line could only be arbitrary.[53]

7.4.3. Resorting to the purpose when the language versions are not in accord

Sometimes Augustinian interpretation fails to yield an answer. Consider in this regard *EMU Tabac*,[54] decided by the CJEU in 1998. I simplify the facts here for exposition. The EU permits members to charge excise tax on imported tobacco. However, there are exceptions to the excise tax. There is no excise tax when a private individual buys tobacco in one member state and transports it to another when that tobacco is intended for personal consumption. What happens when a private individual appoints the seller of tobacco from another country as his agent for transporting the tobacco from the seller's country to the buyer's? Should the tax be paid in the buyer's country, or is transportation by an agent of the actual consumer good enough? That was the question when a seller of tobacco from Luxembourg was appointed the transportation agent of a consumer of the tobacco in the United Kingdom.

Most of the language versions are silent on the issue, but two are not: the Danish and Greek versions. The petitioners in the case asked the court to ignore these two versions as outliers inconsistent with the other versions, and representing two countries with only a small percentage of the EU population. Instead, the court was asked to apply a canon of civil law states that the act of an agent with authority is

[53] See Kjær 'Nonsense'.

[54] The Queen *ex parte* EMU Tabac SARL, Case C-296/95 [1998] ECR I-1605. There are many such cases. I illustrate the point with a single example only because of limitations on space. See Baaij, 'Fifty Years of Multilingual Interpretation in the European Union'; Baaij, 'Legal Integration and Linguistic Diversity'; Ainsworth, 'Lost in Translation'; Jan Engberg, 'Statutory Texts as Instances of Language(s): Consequences and Limitations on Interpretation', *Brooklyn Journal of International Law*, 29 (2004), 1135–66; Lawrence M. Solan, 'The Interpretation of Multilingual Statutes by the European Court of Justice', *Brooklyn Journal of International Law*, 34 (2009), 277–301 for other cases illustrating this point.

regarded as the act of the principal. But the court refused to do so (Paragraphs 34–37). This argument is problematic. For one thing, the versions are only inconsistent if one construes the silence of the majority of versions as defaulting to the civil law canon. However, a tenet of EU law is that it is autonomous and separate from the notational law of particular members. For another, the various language versions of a directive are each deemed to be authoritative and equal. Thus, there is no legal basis for shunting any of them aside without first determining why they differ from the other versions and whether they better reflect the views of the EC.

The Court determined that, contrary to the argument made by EMU Tabac and the other petitioners, EU directives typically do not apply to agents appointed by those parties specified in the directive unless the directive specifically says so. The Greek and Danish versions were not inconsistent with the others, but rather specified the more likely intent of the EC in greater detail. The excise tax in the United Kingdom was due. Baaij observes that many decisions of the CJEU have this structure: a rejection of the comparison of language versions in favour of a teleological approach when the language versions do not yield a clear result.[55]

Compare the CJEU approach to the approach taken by the US Supreme Court in *West Virginia University Hospitals, Inc. v. Casey*.[56] A law calls for a party who successfully brings a civil rights case against a state to recover 'a reasonable attorney's fee' as part of the costs of the law suit. The case, which comes within the statute, was about costs for treating indigent people from a different state. The hospital won its case and was trying to collect the attorney's fees it had paid. A large part of the cost of the litigation was for money paid to expert medical economists and other such experts. Pennsylvania (Casey was its governor), the losing state, argued that the payment of expert fees is not actually an 'attorney's fee' because it is not for services provided by the lawyers.

The expression in question is ambiguous. Possessives like 'attorney's' in English do not specify the relationship between the possessive and the noun that follows. 'Mary's house' can refer to the house Mary designed, lives in as a rental unit, owns, or any other relevant relationship. Similarly, 'attorney's fees' can mean fees paid to the attorney, or fees charged by the attorney specifically for the attorney's own, personal services. Yet the Court disallowed the expert fees in part because the expression 'attorney's fee' is unambiguous.[57] There were certainly plausible arguments for each side in this case. But plain language should not have been one of them.

One cannot say whether, had this statute been drafted in many languages, the temptation to claim that the language was plain would have disappeared, or at least have been diminished to a point beneath its having plausibility. Nonetheless, the

[55] Baaij, 'Fifty Years of Multilingual Interpretation in the European Union'.

[56] 499 US 83 (1991).

[57] Ibid.

case illustrates the temptation to use plain language as a basis for decision making, whether the language is plain or not. The teleological cases of the CJEU illustrate how, at least in some cases, multilingual legislation reduces the opportunities to impose false arguments as to clarity and forces additional analysis.

7.5. Conclusion

I have argued here that multilingual legislation has its costs: it is expensive and it results in decisions that parties could not have possibly anticipated. However, it also has its benefits: it creates far less opportunity for linguistic opportunism, the taking advantage of linguistic accidence to undermine the purpose behind a law. Note that this method requires not only that there be more than one language, but that there be more than two. When there are only two versions, it is impossible to identify outliers, an inquiry at the heart of Augustine's interpretive methodology. Thus, the bilingualism of legal systems such as Canada's and Hong Kong's reduce the opportunity for judicial mischief in some instances, but create it in others.

Whether these benefits are worth all the expense and trouble that such a complex legal order requires is a matter of balancing them against the costs. But the gains are clear, and countries within the EU have stopped going to war and compete favourably much of the time in worldwide economic markets. At least with respect to legal interpretation, the CJEU's interpretive methods seem to work fairly well as designed.

References

Ainsworth, Janet, 'Lost in Translation? Linguistic Diversity and the Elusive Quest for Plain Meaning in Law', in Le Cheng, Kui King, and Anne Wagner, eds., *The Ashgate Handbook of Legal Translation* (Farnham, 2014), 43–55.

Augustine, *On Christian Doctrine*. Available at: http://faculty.georgetown.edu/jod/augustine/ddc2.html.

Baaij, Cornelis J. W., 'Fifty Years of Multilingual Interpretation in the European Union', in Peter M. Tiersma and Lawrence M. Solan, eds., *The Oxford Handbook of Language and Law* (Oxford, 2012), 217–31.

Baaij, Cornelis J. W., 'The Significance of Legal Translation for Legal Harmonization', in Cornelis J. W. Baaij, ed., *The Role of Legal Translation in Legal Harmonization* (Alphen aan den Rijn, 2012) Ch. 1.

Baaij, Cornelis J. W., *Legal Integration and Language Diversity: Rethinking EU Lawmaking* (Oxford, 2018).

Beaudoin, Louis, 'Legal Translation in Canada: The Genius of Legal Language(s)', in Frances Olsen, Alexander Lorz, and Dieter Stein, eds., *Translation Issues in Language and Law* (Basingstoke, 2009), 136–44.

Brand, Oliver, 'Language as a Barrier to Comparative Law', in Frances Olsen, Alexander Lorz, and Dieter Stein, eds., *Translation Issues in Language and Law* (Basingstoke, 2009), 18–34.

Coleman, Linda and Paul Kay, 'Prototype Semantics: The English Word *Lie*', *Language*, 57 (1971), 26–44.

Derlén, Mattias, 'In Defence of (Limited) Multilingualism: Problems and Possibilities of the Multilingual Interpretation of European Union National Courts', in Anne Lise Kjær and Silvia Adamo, eds., *Linguistic Diversity and European Democracy* (Farnham, 2011), 143–66.

Engberg, Jan, 'Statutory Texts as Instances of Language(s): Consequences and Limitations on Interpretation', *Brooklyn Journal of International Law*, 29 (2004), 1135–66.

Engberg, Jan, 'Autonomous EU Concepts? Fact or Fiction', in Susan Šarčević, ed., *Language and Culture in EU Law: Multidisciplinary Perspectives* (Farnham, 2015), 91–107.

Eskridge William N., Jr, *Interpreting Law: A Primer on How to Read Statutes and the Constitution* (St Paul, MN, 2016).

Fodor, Jerry A., *Concepts: Where Cognitive Science Went Wrong* (Oxford, 1998).

Hampton, James A., Zachary Estes, and Sabrina Simmons, 'Metamorphosis: Essence, Appearance, and Behavior in the Categorization of Natural Kinds', *Memory & Cognition*, 35 (2007), 1785–1800.

Hartley, Trevor C., 'Five Forms of Uncertainty in European Community Law', *Cambridge Law Journal*, 55 (1996), 265–88.

Kjær, Anne Lise, 'Legal Translation in the European Union: A Research Field in Need of a New Approach', in Krzysztof Kredens and Stanislaw Gozdz-Roszkowski, eds., *Language and the Law: International Outlooks* (Frankfurt am Main, 2007), 69–95.

Kjær, Anne Lise, 'Nonsense: The CILFIT Criteria Revisited from the Perspective of Legal Linguistics', in Henning Koch, et al. eds., *Europe. The New Legal Realism: Essays in Honour of Hjalte Rasmussen* (Copenhagen, 2010), 297–316.

Kjær, Anne Lise, 'Theoretical Aspects of Legal Translation in the EU: The Paradoxical Relationship between Language, Translation and the Autonomy of EU Law', in Susan Šarčević, ed., *Language and Culture in EU Law: Multidisciplinary Perspectives* (Farnham, 2015), 91–107.

Leung, Janny, 'Statutory Interpretation in Multilingual Jurisdictions: Typology and Trends', *Journal of Multilingual and Multicultural Development*, 33/5 (2012), 1–15.

Leung, Janny H. C., 'Translation Equivalence as Legal Fiction', in Le Cheng, Kui King, and Anne Wagner, eds., *The Ashgate Handbook of Legal Translation* (Farnham, 2014), 57–69.

Matulewska, Aleksandra, *Legilinguistic Translatology: A Parametric Approach to Legal Translation* (Bern, 2013).

Poscher, Ralf, 'Ambiguity and Vagueness in Legal Interpretation', in Peter M. Tiersma and Lawrence M. Solan, eds., *Oxford Handbook of Language and Law* (Oxford, 2012), 128–44.

Pozzo, Barbara, 'Comparative Law and the New Frontiers of Legal Translation', in Susan Šarčević, ed., *Language and Culture in EU Law: Multidisciplinary Perspectives* (Farnham, 2015), 73–87.

Quine, Willard Van Orman, *Word and Object* (Cambridge, MA, 1960).

Rasmussen, Hjalte, 'The European Court's Acte clair Strategy in C.I L.F.I.T. Or: Acte clair, of Course! But What Does It Mean?', *European Law Review*, 9 (1984), 242–59.

Šarčević, Susan, 'Legal Translation: Possible, but not Perfect', in Peter M. Tiersma and Lawrence M. Solan, eds., *The Oxford Handbook of Language and Law* (Oxford, 2012), 187–99.

Scalia, Antonin and Bryan A. Garner, *Reading Law: The Interpretation of Legal Texts* (Minneapolis, 2012).

Slocum, Brian G., *Ordinary Meaning: A Theory of the Most Fundamental Principle of Legal Interpretation* (Chicago, 2015).

Solan, Lawrence M., *The Language of Judges* (Chicago, 1993).

Solan, Lawrence M., 'The Interpretation of Multilingual Statutes by the European Court of Justice', *Brooklyn Journal of International Law*, 34 (2009), 277–301.

Solan, Lawrence M., *The Language of Statutes: Laws and Their Interpretation* (Chicago, 2010).

Sullivan, Ruth, 'The Challenges of Interpreting Multilingual, Multijural Legislation', *Brooklyn Journal of International Law*, 29 (2004), 985–1066.

Van Calster, Geert, 'The EU's Tower of Babel: The Interpretation by the European Court of Justice of Equally Authentic Texts Drafted in more than One Official Language', *Yearbook of European Law*, 17 (1997), 363–93.

Vermeule, Adrian, *Judging Under Uncertainty: An Institutional Theory of Legal Interpretation* (Cambridge, MA, 2006).

Weschsler, Steven, *Word Meaning and Syntax: Approaches to the Interface* (Oxford, 2015).

Williams, Bernard, *Truth and Truthfulness* (Princeton, NJ, 2002).

Wolff, Phillip and Kevin J. Holmes, 'Linguistic Relativity', *Wiley Interdisciplinary Reviews: Cognitive Psychology*, 2 (2011), 253–65.

8

On the conceptualization of meaning in legal interpretation

MARTINA BAJČIĆ

8.1. Introduction

On Urban Dictionary.com,[1] a popular website on language usage, the word 'truth' has forty-three definitions. In law, by contrast, the word 'truth' has a far more restrictive interpretation. For example, in defamation law, which aims to protect the reputations of persons and corporations, the truth is an effective defence to a defamation charge. In other words, the truth of a statement protects the defendant from liability. Therefore, in such cases, courts interpret 'truth' according to its specific legal meaning irrespective of plain meanings in general language usage.

Similarly, courts such as the Court of Justice of the European Union and the European Court of Human Rights often use the teleological or purposive method of interpretation, which goes beyond the wording of a provision and gives more weight to the extralinguistic factors such as purpose and context. Such interpretation underlines the conceptual autonomy that is instrumental for the uniform application of a law in multinational and multilingual legal orders. At the same time, the teleological method of interpretation emphasizes the importance of the extralinguistic context for determining the meaning of a concept. This lies at the heart of the cognitive approach to terminology in which concepts are best understood and described as part of a wider conceptual structure.

Against this background, I argue that an interdisciplinary approach based on state-of-the-art linguistic theories sheds new light on legal interpretation, thus warranting the application of principles of terminology studies to the field of law. It is to be noted that my perspective is purely linguistic, while the proposals made are based on terminology studies. The first section of this chapter addresses the

[1] http://www.urbandictionary.com/define.php?term=truth, accessed 10 September 2014.

Martina Bajčić, *On the conceptualization of meaning in legal interpretation* In: *Language and Legal Interpretation in International Law*. Edited by: Anne Lise Kjær and Joanna Lam, Oxford University Press. © Oxford University Press 2022.
DOI: 10.1093/oso/9780190855208.003.0009

commonalities of terminology and legal interpretation. Since courts often grapple with the meaning of concepts, from a terminological perspective, it is interesting to explore just how courts resolve the task of unravelling meaning. My starting presumption is that terminology studies can prove useful in this respect and provide more clarity to the mysterious ways in which courts do things with words. The second section briefly maps out the discipline of terminology, outlining areas of interest for legal interpretation. The third section exemplifies legal interpretation by analysing selected case law to clarify terminological implications of courts' interpretative methods and case-law reasoning. Finally, the fourth section reflects on the similarities between the terminological and the legal approach to the meaning of concepts. It is hoped that this chapter will provide some initial thoughts on how legal interpretation could benefit from terminology studies.

As a linguistic discipline, terminology studies can offer relevant knowledge about language, especially regarding concepts and terms that can be of use in the field of law.[2] Terminology studies and legal interpretation share many things in common and addressing these enables us to look beyond the traditional legal perspective on interpretation. Among these commonalities is the question of the meaning of concepts which is central to legal interpretation. Therefore, the discipline of terminology can enhance understanding of legal interpretation. By drawing on actual legal cases, I will demonstrate how terminology studies can advance research into legal interpretation. This chapter also takes a more careful look at legal interpretation in multilingual legal orders, such as the European legal environment, bearing in mind that uniform application of multilingual law is instrumental for achieving legal certainty. As Kjær and Adamo notice,[3] natural languages cannot by their nature be absolute copies of each other. Divergences among different language versions of legislation are thus inevitable and call for autonomous interpretation, namely one that is linked neither to a particular language version nor to national laws of the member states of the European Union (EU). Instead, this method of interpretation relies on the concept and often involves a teleological quest for meaning which goes beyond the text, i.e. the wording and considers the purpose and context of a legal provision in question. This 'context and purpose mantra', as Derlén[4] terms it, can be compared

[2] Unfortunately, much relevant knowledge about language, cognition, and communication remains within the confines of the academic disciplines of linguistics and communication studies and is seldom utilized in related disciplines, such as law, sociology, or political science; Anne Lise Kjær and S. Adamo, 'Linguistic Diversity and European Democracy: Introduction and Overview', in Anne Lise Kjær and S. Adamo, eds., *Linguistic Diversity and European Democracy* (2011), 3. Others have noted too that linguistic knowledge can be very useful in understanding aspects of the legal system; see L. M. Solan and P. M. Tiersma, *Speaking of Crime. The Language of Criminal Justice* (2011), 26.

[3] Kjær and Adamo, 'Linguistic Diversity and European Democracy', 7.

[4] M. Derlén, 'In Defence of (Limited) Multilingualism: Problems and Possibilities of the Multilingual Interpretation of European Union Law in National Courts', in Kjær and Adamo, *Linguistic Diversity and European Democracy*, 158.

to a cognitive terminological approach to meaning. In fact, framing legal interpretation in cognitive terminology can direct the 'context and purpose mantra' in a more focused way.

The word 'truth' can have as many as forty-three definitions in general language usage, as opposed to its more restrictive meaning in the legal domain. In defamation law, for instance, *truth* is an effective defence to a defamation charge.[5] This precise legal meaning seems to contradict the general language usage of the word. Dictionaries record wide and variable usage, whereas law strives for a clear expression and exact reasoning. However, we will try to demonstrate that the tensions between specialized and general language do not always reflect the reality. As a matter of fact, courts are sometimes faced with the task of determining the meaning of an ambiguous phrase. As Solan and Tiersma point out,[6] courts understand that context is important in determining meaning. Especially in case of ambiguities, context enables us to infer which of the possible meanings of a word is intended. Legal terms too can be interpreted differently in different legal contexts. For instance, while the term warranty means 'an express or implied promise that something in furtherance of the contract is guaranteed by one of the contracting parties' within the law of contracts, its meaning differs in the context of insurance or property law.[7]

This example shows that although legal language, as a specialized sublanguage, strives for precision, it is by no means free of ambiguities and vagueness. Because of this, courts are sometimes called upon to determine the meaning of concepts. On one occasion the US Supreme Court had to determine whether a tomato is a fruit or vegetable. After having consulted both dictionaries and experts, the court decided tomatoes are vegetables, backing its conclusion with the argument that we eat them as vegetables, usually in a side dish, and not as a dessert (which is how we eat fruits).[8] What is striking about this rather simple explanation is that is seems to follow the cognitive perception of meaning. The meaning rests on our individual, cultural, and social experience. What is important is this conceptual meaning, or knowledge of

[5] As settled case law illustrates: *Vachet v. Central Newspapers, Inc.*, 816 F.2d 313, 316 (7th Cir. 1987), *Guccione v. Hustler Magazine, Inc.*, 800 F.2d 298, 301 (2d Cir. 1986 (substantial truth suffices to defeat a charge of libel). For a more in-depth discussion of this question see Meiring de Villiers: *Substantial truth in Defamation Law*. 32 American J. of Trial Advocacy 91 (Summer 2008).

[6] Solan and Tiersma, *Speaking of Crime*, 23.

[7] *Black's Law Dictionary*, Eighth Edition, Thomson West. p. 1618.

[8] 'Botanically speaking, tomatoes are the fruit of a vine, just as are cucumbers, squashes, beans, and peas. But in the common language of the people, whether sellers or consumers of provisions, all these are vegetables which are grown in kitchen gardens, and which, whether eaten cooked or raw, are, like potatoes, carrots, parsnips, turnips, beets, cauliflower, cabbage, celery, and lettuce, usually served at dinner in, with, or after the soup, fish, or meats which constitute the principal part of the repast, and not, like fruits generally, as dessert' (*Nix v. Hedden*, 149 U.S. 304 (1893). The Court seems to acknowledge the fact that it is the real usage of words that gives them meaning, whereas dictionaries merely log that use.

the world that influences the conceptualization process, that is, the way in which we understand concepts. Hence, neither meaning nor language is regarded as an isolated autonomous phenomenon. Similarly, opponents of a plain meaning rule in law argue that plain meaning rests on the erroneous assumption that words have a fixed meaning. Justice Holmes stated: '[a] word is not a crystal, transparent and unchanged, it is the skin of a living thought and may vary greatly in color and content according to the circumstances and the time in which it is used'.[9] In other instances, courts had to interpret the meaning of nude dancing against the notion of free speech (*Erie v. Pap's A.M.*),[10] and money in terms of the First Amendment right to free association (*McCutcheon v. Federal Election Commission*).[11] From a terminological perspective, it is interesting to explore how the court determines the meaning of concepts in such cases. With this in mind, the following section clarifies basic principles of terminology studies.

8.2. Terminology studies: There is no knowledge without terminology

Before exploring terminological avenues that may be useful for legal interpretation, we must first consider the different meanings of the term *terminology*. In the framework of this chapter, the terms *terminology studies* or *terminology* refer to a linguistic discipline that studies terms, concepts, and the conceptual structure of a field. Preference is given to the term *terminology studies* since *terminology* refers not only to a study of terms and concepts but also to the structured set of terms in a particular field. The term *terminology studies* appears more suitable considering that several different theoretical approaches to terminology have been developed over the years.

Given the purpose of this chapter, different theoretical approaches to terminology will not be analysed in detail. Instead, attention is focused on those areas and

[9] *Towne v. Eisner*, 245 U.S. 418, 425 (1918). In addition to the plain meaning rule, statutory interpretation methods of US courts include: plain meaning and legislative history, the social purpose rule, the context of statutory language, presumptions about the use of language, external influences of statutory interpretation, and other less traditional approaches to statutory interpretation. For more information, see W. Burnham, *Introduction to the Law and Legal System of the United States* (4th edn, 2006), 54–63.

[10] *Erie v. Pap's A.M.*, 529 U.S. 277, 2000.

[11] In *McCutcheon v. Federal Election Commission*, 572 US Supreme Court, 2014, the US Supreme Court lifted restrictions, that is, aggregate limits on political contributions, allowing donors to give as much money to as many political candidates, parties, and committees as they like. Aggregate limits on donations, which had been in place since 1974, were designed to fight corruption and prevent wealthy donors from having more influence on federal elections. See Martina Bajčić, *New Insights into the Semantics of Legal Concepts and the Legal Dictionary* (2017), 72.

approaches that may prove useful for legal interpretation. It is instructive to note that terminology theories are, as a rule, either prescriptive or descriptive. The first theoretical proposal, General Theory of Terminology (GTT),[12] is prescriptive. This discipline was developed with the view of standardization, believing that standardized term usage would facilitate specialized communication and knowledge transfer. This was important because with the expansion of specialized languages and the development of the internet, experts began to lose control over their vocabularies. In response to the internet-spurred information explosion, terminology studies were developed. As the field matured, different approaches surfaced. Modern terminology theories that arose in reaction to GTT were descriptive and pursued goals other than standardization (e.g. creating translation tools, databases, etc.). Today, there is an increasing tendency to infiltrate premises from cognitive linguistics[13] to terminology. Though the development of cognitive science has a universal appeal and is finding application in different scientific fields, its application to linguistics has been particularly productive. What can be dubbed as the cognitive shift in linguistics builds on the Whorfian interrelatedness of language and thought.[14] Within terminology studies, it accentuates the importance of the conceptual structure and extralinguistic context for the terminological description of meaning.

In this context, it is fitting to mention the application of terminology studies to other scientific disciplines. Terminology forms a part of every discipline, although its principles and methods are employed to a different extent and with varying success. Its application manifests itself not just in the use of field-specific terms, but also in different conceptual structures built up by different terminologies (i.e. sets of specialized terms). Differences among conceptual structures are best explained by the fact that knowledge is framed idiosyncratically in different disciplines. We are responsive to how information is framed, as spin doctors and marketing experts are aware. In this respect, terminology can be deployed as a persuasive device to achieve one's objectives. Similarly, terminology is of significance for companies and organizations which must manage their knowledge, name new products, and protect their corporate identity.[15]

[12] Eugen Wüster, the father of terminology science, used the term *Allgemeine Terminologielehre*, which was the title of his seminal work: *Die allgemeine Termniologielehre—Ein Grenzgebiet zwischen Sprachwissenschaft, Logik, Ontologie, Informatik und den Sachwissenschaften* (1974). His followers introduced the terms *General Theory of Terminology* and *Traditional Terminology Theory*.

[13] For an overview of cognitive linguistics, see W. Croft and D. A. Cruse, *Cognitive Linguistics* (2004).

[14] J. B. Carroll, ed., *Language, Thought, and Reality: Selected Writings of Benjamin Lee Whorf* (1956).

[15] For more information on knowledge management, see Blanca Najera Villar and Diana Brändle, 'There Is No Knowledge without Terminology: Key Factors for Organisational Learning', *Systems, Software and Services Process Improvement Communications in Computer and Information Science*, 301 (2012), 300–9.

Another important feature of terminology studies is the distinction made between term and concept, which has bearing on legal interpretation, especially in multilingual contexts. In the simplest terms, this distinction can be explained by the fact that there are concepts without corresponding terms, while there are no terms without a corresponding concept. Terms can be described as linguistic units which denote concepts that in turn convey conceptual meaning within specialized domains.[16] Generally, terminology work is assumed to start from the concept (onomasiological approach). Nevertheless, modern terminology theories, such as Sociocognitive Terminology,[17] advocate a semasiological approach which starts from the term. Under this approach, the terminological description of a domain proceeds from the linguistic denotation in the text, as opposed to the onomasiological approach. This differentiation is important in the context of multilingual EU law. To achieve uniform application of EU law, it is necessary to assume that all twenty-four equally authentic EU languages denote one and the same EU concept; namely a concept with an autonomous meaning delimited under EU law. Yet, as linguists, we are aware of the contradiction pervading this assumption. As legal translation is inherently imperfect,[18] it is impossible that twenty-four different language versions always convey the same meaning and refer to one concept. For this reason, the Court of Justice of the European Union (CJEU), as 'the lord of the words' must reconcile the divergences between language versions by means of the teleological autonomous interpretation. As will be illustrated, this method of interpretation emphasizes the importance of the concept which brings us back to the onomasiological approach. Therefore, the claim of one EU concept and twenty-four different terms does not disregard the fact that there might be differences between language versions. However, those differences are restricted to the terminological level, not to the conceptual level. In this sense, preference should be given to an onomasiological approach to the terminological description of EU law, bearing in mind that there is no universal theory of terminology that would be applicable to every domain. Instead, the specific features of a domain determine which terminology theory is most suitable for its description. With respect to the legal domain, we depart from the assumption that most legal concepts are not fixed, but represent open-ended flexible categories that can be compared to prototype structures with more or less central members.[19] Furthermore, it is assumed that a concept is fully realized and understood only within its conceptual structure, which underlines the

[16] P. Faber , ed., *A Cognitive Linguistics View of Terminology and Specialized Language* (2012), 11.

[17] R. Temmerman, *Towards New Ways of Terminology Description: The Sociocognitive Approach* (2000).

[18] S. Šarčević, 'Legal Translation and Legal Certainty/Uncertainty: From the DCFR to the CESL', in B. Pasa and L. Morra, eds., *Translating the DCFR and Drafting the CESL: A Pragmatic Perspective* (2014), 47.

[19] Bajčić, *New Insights*, 158.

importance of extralinguistic knowledge. Considering these assumptions, we advocate the application of a cognitive terminological approach[20] to legal interpretation.

The following section examines not only how courts interpret the meaning of concepts, but also to what extent they deploy methods that are compatible with the principles underpinning the cognitive terminological approach.

8.3. Legal interpretation: Adjudicating language

This section attempts to answer the question of how courts do things with words. Courts of common law systems and supranational courts often interpret the meaning of a concept by not just relying on the wording of a provision or a statute. Instead, they give more weight to extralinguistic factors (such as the purpose and the context). Two legal cases illustrate courts' interpretative practices. The first case was brought before the U.S. International Trade Court and the second before the CJEU. By examining the interpretation methods of courts from different legal systems, we can make more general conclusions concerning the application of terminology studies to interpretation. Likewise, analysing cases of such courts is interesting from the linguistic perspective, because last-instance courts (such as the CJEU, US Supreme Court, and appellate courts) must detail reasons for their decisions in written opinions. These rationales provide fruitful ground for our terminological analysis. In addition, they have multiple judges and the case is decided by a majority vote, which means there may be dissenting and concurring opinions.[21] Further, supranational and international courts not only interpret rules dynamically, paying little attention to the wording of legislative texts, but also often establish autonomous concepts.[22]

8.3.1. The 'X-Men' Quandary: *Toy Biz, Inc. v. US*

The facts of the case were as follows: Toy Biz, Inc. imported playthings, i.e. action figures from various Marvel Comics series, from China.[23] Under the then valid Harmonized Tariff Schedule of the United States (HTSUS) of 1989, US Customs Service classified the imported items as 'dolls representing only human beings and

[20] This term was first used in my publication 'Towards a Terminological Approach to Translating European Contract Law', in B. Pasa and L. Morra, eds., *Pragmatic Issues in Legal Translation: From the Different Language Versions of the DCFR to the CESL Proposal* (2014), which presented the advantages of a cognitive terminological approach to translation of European contract law.

[21] Burnham, *Introduction to the Law and Legal System of the United States*, 64.

[22] Anne Lise Kjær, 'New Challenges to the Theory of Legal Translation: Transnational Legal Communication and the Autonomization of International Law', *The Translator*, 4 July 2014.

[23] *Toy Biz, Inc. v. US* 248 F.Supp.2d 1234 (Ct. Int'l Trade 2003). Imported items included the 'X-Men', 'Spider-Man', the 'Fantastic Four', and 'Jumpsie'. This case is discussed in Bajčić, *New Insights*, 74–6.

parts and accessories thereof' dutiable at 12 per cent *ad valorem*, meaning Toy Biz, Inc. had to pay a 12 per cent tax. The company was not happy with this decision and contended the items should be classified as 'toys representing animals or other non-human creatures (e.g. robots and monsters) and parts and accessories thereof', which were taxed at 6.8 per cent. The case was brought before the US Court of International Trade. The task of the court could be described as a linguistic challenge because it had to ascertain which meaning the words 'representing' and 'only' was intended in the phrase 'dolls representing only human beings' (heading 9502 of the HTSUS).

As stated in *Pillowtex Corp. v. United States*,[24] a court may use various aids in construing the statute and disclosing legislative intent if the statutory language of a tariff classification is ambiguous.[25] Such various aids include lexicographic and scientific authorities, dictionaries, and other reliable information.[26] A court may also rely upon its own understanding of a term in question.[27] From the perspective of terminology studies, it is interesting to examine the Court's rationale of its interpretation. Rather than just referring to dictionary definitions or expert opinions, the Court resorts to extralinguistic knowledge to determine the meaning of a concept.

While the Court agreed with Toy Biz, Inc., that 'only' means exclusively in keeping with the Oxford English Dictionary (OED) definition, it wrestled with the meaning of 'represent'. Does 'represent' mean 'resemble', or 'embody', or something else? According to the OED, 'to resemble' is only one of the possible meanings of 'to represent'. The Court said one cannot read the 'dolls' provision as meaning exclusively 'dolls resembling human beings', since, if 'to represent' in 'dolls representing only human beings' meant exclusively 'to resemble', a toy that merely resembled a human being would be classified under both the 'dolls' and 'other toys' provisions, thus leading to ambiguity and in turn legal uncertainty.[28]

[24] *Pillowtex Corp. V. United States*, 171 F.3d 1370, 1373 (Fed.Cir. 1999). Whereas it is 'a general rule of statutory construction, that where Congress has clearly stated its intent in language of the statute, a court should not inquire further into the meaning of the statute' (*Bauerhin Techs. Ltd. P'ship v. United States*, 110 F 3.3d 774, 776 (Fed. Cir. 1997). This reasoning is consistent with the Plain Meaning Rule (see Burnham, *Introduction to the Law and Legal System of the United States*, 54–5).

[25] Bajčić, *New Insights*, 75.

[26] *JVC Co. of Am., Div. Of US JVC Corp. v. United States*, 234 F.3d 1352 (Fed. Cir. 2000).

[27] Burnham, *Introduction to the Law and Legal System of the United States*, 54: 'If pressed to give an overall generalization about statutory interpretation in the United States, one could say that courts in the United States generally believe they should interpret the language of a statute in such a way as to give effect to the purpose the legislature sought to accomplish, keeping in mind that ordinarily the best evidence of purpose is the text of the statute'. Yet, as Burnham notes, many approaches ignore or run counter to this goal.

[28] Other toys include toys representing animals or non-human creatures (e.g. robots and monsters). It is interesting to note that the casual observer test was applied to determine whether something can be classified as a doll or a toy. In other words, it should be clear for a casual observer whether something is a doll or a toy.

Assuming that 'represent' means more than just 'resemble' and in keeping with the HTSUS scheme and intent, the Court argued that to be classified as a 'doll', a toy needs to be an 'embodiment' of a human being. Departing from the above HTSUS regulation and the OED definition, the Court found these action figures do not represent human beings, but should be classified as toys representing animals or non-human creatures (for example, robots and monsters) and parts and accessories thereof (HTSUS subheading 9503.49.00). This decision was substantiated with three arguments.

First, most of the figures in question exhibit at least one non-human characteristic, such as claws or robotic eyes, and therefore do not match the OED definition in which dolls represent only human beings. Second, the Court points to the fact that these Marvel characters are known in popular culture as 'mutants' who use their extraordinary and unnatural physical and psychic powers on the side of good or evil. Insofar, they do not represent humans only.[29] The Court's third argument is that the 'X-Men' figures are marketed and packaged as 'mutants' or people born with 'x-tra' power.[30] The court is making the point that the 'X-Men' are conceptualized and known to their fans as mutants, not as human beings. The last two arguments underline the importance of the wider conceptual structure for the understanding of a concept. By recognizing the importance of popular culture as a factor in identifying certain figures as non-humans, the Court in effect addresses the question of conceptualization, whether wantonly or inadvertently, which lies at the heart of the cognitive terminological approach.[31] The Court extrapolates the context in its widest extralinguistic sense as an aid to understanding meaning.[32]

It is interesting to note that the different tariffs for dolls and toys were abolished after this case.

[29] The Court gives the examples of 'Storm', a tall and thin figure with white hair and dark skin, who has a lightning bolt as an accessory and can summon storms; and of 'Pyro', who has the mutant ability to control and shape flames.

[30] In its judgment, the Court refers to the story told on the back of the packaging for the duo 'Professor X vs. Magneto': Both Professor Charles Xavier and his friend Magnus agreed that an upsurge in mutant activity had begun—what they could not agree on is how mutants and normal humans could co-exist. Believing that mutants must rule, Magnus became Magneto, the evil master of magnetism. To combat him, the telepathic Professor X formed the X-Men, a group that would represent his dream of human–mutant cooperation.

[31] Bajčić, *New Insights*, 76.

[32] Justice Crennan of the High Court of Australia made an excellent point in this respect that even an understanding of the *zeitgeist* may rationally assist in understanding the meaning of a statute. In this sense, the context may among other things include history, time, or place. S. Crennan, 'Statutes and the Contemporary Search for Meaning', Statute Society Paper, London, 1 February 2010, p. 3, available at: http://www.hcourt.gov.au/assets/publications/speeches/current-justices/crennanj/crennanj1feb10.pdf.

8.3.2. When is a Hospital an Undertaking: *Henning Veedfald v. Århus Amtskommune*

The facts of this case[33] were the following. The plaintiff, Mr Veedfald, was to undergo a kidney transplant in a publicly funded Danish hospital. The kidney was donated by the plaintiff's brother. After having been removed, the kidney was prepared for transplantation by flushing it with perfusion fluid designed for that purpose. During the flushing process, a kidney artery became blocked, making the kidney unusable for transplantation. The basic fluid and additional liquids used for the flushing were manufactured in the laboratories of the dispensary of another hospital. The defendant, Århus Amtskommune, was the owner of the two hospitals and the dispensary. Relying on the Product Liability Directive 85/374,[34] under the Danish Act[35], Mr Veedfald sued the hospital for damages. The hospital argued there is no liability for a defective product because the perfusion fluid was not 'put into circulation', which is required under Article 7(a) of the Directive. The hospital argued that it was only brought from one medical sphere into another. Furthermore, since the hospital is entirely publicly funded it cannot be asserted that the perfusion fluid was manufactured for economic purposes. After the regional court dismissed the claim, the plaintiff appealed to the Supreme Court which turned to the CJEU for a preliminary ruling.[36]

From our terminological perspective, the meanings of the two concepts, 'put into circulation' and 'economic activity', seem to be instrumental in resolving this case. Accordingly, the first two questions referred to the CJEU concerned the meaning of these concepts, and the last three concerned 'damage' caused by death or by personal injury. We only focus on the CJEU's interpretation of the first two concepts as they are central to determining whether the hospital acted as an undertaking, in that it, under the given circumstances, acted as an entity carrying out economic activity. Unlike in the previous case in which 'toys' and 'dolls' had been defined but their definitions questioned, neither 'put into circulation' nor 'economic activity' is defined by the Product Liability Directive. It is important to note that 'undertaking' is also not defined in the Treaty but has been interpreted widely by the CJEU.[37] In

[33] *Henning Veedfald v. Århus Amtskommune* C-2013/99, judgment of 10 May 2001.

[34] Council Directive of 25 July 1985 on the approximation of laws, regulations, and administrative provisions of the Member States concerning liability for defective products (85/374/EEC), OJ L 210, 7.8.1985, p. 29; amended by Directive 1999/34/EC of the European Parliament and of the Council of 10 May 1999, OJ L 141, 4.6.1999, p. 20.

[35] Law No. 371 on Product Liability of 7 June 1989.

[36] Reference for a preliminary ruling is a procedure exercised before the CJEU, enabling national courts to question the CJEU on the interpretation or validity of European law by virtue of Art. 267 TFEU.

[37] For instance, in *Höfner and Elser v. Macrotron GmbH* C-41/90 (23/04/1991) ECR I-1979 the ECJ held that the concept of an undertaking encompasses every entity engaged in an economic activity, regardless of the legal status of the entity or the way in which it is financed.

such cases, it is up to the CJEU to interpret the meaning of concepts 'in accordance with the purpose and aim pursued by the Directive',[38] as so often articulated in CJEU's settled case law. The CJEU attempts to delimit the meaning of a concept under EU law independently of the meanings attributed to the concept under national laws of the member states. The CJEU's interpretation is autonomous and often teleological (dependent upon purpose and context of a legal provision).

In response to the first question posed to the CJEU—'Whether Article 7(a) of the Directive is to be interpreted as meaning that a defective product is not *put into circulation* when the manufacturer of the product makes it and uses it in the course of providing a specific medical service, consisting in preparing a human organ for transplantation' (emphasis added)—it found that the facts of the present case allow for the perfusion fluid to be considered as 'put into circulation'.[39] The CJEU does not stick to Aristotelian categories in which membership is unambiguous and fixed[40] and do not reflect the fuzzy nature of legal concepts open to interpretation. Instead, the CJEU's interpretative method seems to follow the pattern of prototype-like category,[41] when a concept is considered to be more or less a member of a category, allowing for a more realistic description of vague legal concepts.

Courts must constantly redefine concepts to meet the needs of regulating the changing social and economic circumstances. As Solan observes, 'Strange things happen in this world, and legislatures cannot possibly predict each one of them'.[42] The social and technological progress significantly alters the legal reality, thus requiring legal norms and concepts to be redefined. The advantage of the prototype approach is that it allows for flexibility and adaptability, enabling new members to be added to the category. The CJEU proceeds in a similar manner in its interpretation of the meaning of 'economic activity' or 'product'. Departing from the best example of this category, that is, its prototype member, it examines whether a less central member may also be subsumed in the category. In other words, it examines if 'perfusion fluid' can be a 'product', and if publicly funded hospitals are engaged in 'economic activity'. The CJEU concluded that the perfusion fluid was put into

[38] Para 14 of the judgment.

[39] Para 17: 'As regards the Amtskommune's argument that the product was never put into circulation since it never left the medical "sphere of control" of the dispensary which made the fluid and the hospital where it was used, such circumstances are not decisive where, as in the present case, the use of the product is characterized by the fact that the person for whom it is intended must bring himself within that sphere of control'.

[40] Aristotle first proposed the checklist approach to semantic categories, claiming that every semantic category consisted of a set of defining features.

[41] E. Rosch, 'Cognitive Representations of Semantic Categories', *Journal of Experimental Psychology: General*, 104 (1975), 192–233.

[42] L. M. Solan, *Statutory Interpretation in the EU: The Augustinian Approach*, Brooklyn Law School, Legal Studies Paper No. 78 (2007), available at: http://papers.ssrn.com/sol3/papers.cfm?abstract_id=998167.

circulation and the hospital activity may be deemed as an economic activity.[43] According to the Court's interpretation, Article 7(c) of Directive 85/374's exemption from liability where an activity has no economic or business purpose does not extend to the case of a defective product, manufactured and used in the course of a specific medical service and financed entirely from public funds and for which the patient is not required to pay any consideration.[44]

Several observations can be made based on the CJEU's approach that have terminological relevance. First, in the absence of statutory definitions, vague legal concepts are interpreted autonomously on a case-to-case basis. Second, the CJEU proceeds from the concept, and not the term, as its linguistic denotation. By doing so it avoids favouring one language version over the other. Third, in demarcating the meaning of a concept under EU law, the CJEU considers factors that can be described as extralinguistic, such as the legislative purpose and the wider context. In terms of cognitive terminology, legal concepts are thus perceived as parts of wider conceptual structures in which they realize their full meaning. Whether a hospital performs an economic activity and acts as an undertaking depends on the factual background of each case. While some legal scholars emphasize that the CJEU's approach leads to inconsistent case law which is detrimental for legal certainty,[45] at the

[43] Although elsewhere the CJEU concluded differently. Interesting cases in this respect are *Poucet v. Assurances Generales de France and Pistre* C-159/91 in which the Court found social insurance providers are not undertakings and C-160/91(17/02/1993); *FENIN v. Commission* c-205/03 (1s1/07/2006) ECR I-6295, in which management bodies of the Spanish national health system were not considered undertakings as they fulfilled not an economic, but a social purpose.

[44] Paras 21–22: 'As to that point, the fact that products are manufactured for a specific medical service for which the patient does not pay directly but which is financed from public funds maintained out of taxpayers' contributions cannot detract from the economic and business character of that manufacture. The activity in question is not a charitable one which could therefore be covered by the exemption from liability provided for in Article 7(c) of the Directive. Besides, the Amtskommune itself admitted at the hearing that, in similar circumstances, a private hospital would undoubtedly be liable for the defectiveness of the product pursuant to the provisions of the Directive.

The answer to be given to the second question must therefore be that Article 7(c) of the Directive is to be interpreted as meaning that the exemption from liability where an activity has no economic or business purpose does not extend to the case of a defective product which has been manufactured and used in the course of a specific medical service which is financed entirely from public funds and for which the patient is not required to pay any consideration'.

With respect to damages, the Court found plaintiff is entitled to damages that are to be awarded by the national court. Para 33: 'It follows that the national court is required, under the Directive, to examine under which head the circumstances of the case are to be categorized, namely whether the case concerns damage covered either by point (a) or by point (b) of the first paragraph of Article 9 or non-material damage which may possibly be covered by national law. The national court may, however, not decline to award any damages at all under the Directive on the ground that, where the other conditions of liability are fulfilled, the damage incurred is not such as to fall under any of the foregoing heads.'

[45] See, generally, A. Martinović, 'Europäisierung der nationalen Gesundheitssysteme: Zwischen Solidarität, Binnenmarkt und Wettbewerb—kroatische Erwartungen, Erfahrungen und Perspektiven', PhD thesis, Karl Franzens University Graz, 2014.

same time its approach underscores the importance of the extralinguistic context for the interpretation of a concept's meaning.

These two cases provide important illustrations of how courts determine the meaning of concepts and allow us to explain the terminological implications. In both, the courts adhered to the perception of meaning not as a fixed autonomous entity, but as a dynamic process which involves conceptual knowledge, that is, knowledge of the world. Therefore, the application of terminology studies can provide a better understanding of legal interpretation which is important considering that courts create and develop law.

8.4. Concluding thoughts

My aim was to offer some initial thoughts on the application of terminology studies in the legal field. By analysing selected case law from a terminological perspective, I have singled out commonalities between terminology studies and legal interpretation to show that a cognitive terminological approach may advance research into legal interpretation and contribute to a better understanding. In proof of this proposition, I pointed to the role of the context and legislative purpose in interpreting the meaning of concepts from a cognitive terminological perspective. The example of action figures testifies to the importance of conceptual structure for the meaning of a concept, which hinges on the cognitive terminological understanding that no concept can be studied or defined in isolation. However, concepts should be defined within their specific domains and contexts in which they are used, applied, and interpreted. A concept-centric approach can be especially advantageous in multilingual legal environments. Applying an onomasiological approach in the EU context implies that there is only one European concept which the Court must interpret, despite twenty-four equally authentic language versions. In case of doubt as to the meaning of a single language version, a reference to the concept itself will lessen differences between language versions.

For all the foregoing reasons, the described terminological approach enables a better understanding of the meaning of concepts and in turn of legal interpretation of concepts. This is especially true of vague legal concepts. As the examples illustrate, the cognitive terminological approach provides a suitable platform for delimiting the meaning of concepts and explains the somewhat mysterious ways in which courts do things with words.

References

Bajčić, Martina, *New Insights into the Semantics of Legal Concepts and the Legal Dictionary* (Amsterdam, 2017).

Bajčić, Martina, 'Towards a Terminological Approach to Translating European Contract Law', in B. Pasa and L. Morra, eds., Pragmatic Issues in Legal Translation: From the Different Language Versions of the DCFR to the CESL Proposal (Munich, 2014), 125–47.

Burnham, William, *Introduction to the Law and Legal System of the United States* (4th edn, St Paul, 2006).

Carroll, John B., ed., *Language, Thought, and Reality: Selected Writings of Benjamin Lee Whorf* (Cambridge, MA, 1956).

Crennan, Susan, 'Statutes and the Contemporary Search for Meaning', Statute Society Paper, London, 1 February 2010, available at: http://www.hcourt.gov.au/assets/publications/speeches/current-justices/crennanj/crennanj1feb10.pdf.

Croft, William and D. Alan Cruse, *Cognitive Linguistics* (Cambridge, 2004).

Derlén, Mattias, 'In Defence of (Limited) Multilingualism: Problems and Possibilities of the Multilingual Interpretation of European Union Law in National Courts', in Anne Lise Kjær, and S. Adamo, eds., *Linguistic Diversity and European Democracy* (Aldershot, 2011), 143–67.

Faber, Pamela, ed., *A Cognitive Linguistics View of Terminology and Specialized Language* (Boston, MA, 2012).

Kjær, Anne Lise and Silvia Adamo, eds., 'Linguistic Diversity and European Democracy: Introduction and Overview', in *Linguistic Diversity and European Democracy* (Aldershot, 2011), 1–15.

Martinović, Adrijana, 'Europäisierung der nationalen Gesundheitssysteme: Zwischen Solidarität, Binnenmarkt und Wettbewerb—kroatische Erwartungen, Erfahrungen und Perspektiven', PhD thesis, Karl Franzens University Graz (2014).

Najera Villar, Blanca and Diana Brändle, 'There Is No Knowledge without Terminology: Key Factors for Organisational Learning', *Systems, Software and Services Process Improvement Communications in Computer and Information Science*, 301 (2012), 300–9.

Rosch, E., 'Cognitive Representations of Semantic Categories', *Journal of Experimental Psychology: General*, 104 (1975), 192–233.

Šarčević, Susan, 2014. 'Legal Translation and Legal Certainty/Uncertainty: From the DCFR to the CESL', in B. Pasa and L. Morra, eds., *Translating the DCFR and Drafting the CESL: A Pragmatic Perspective* (Munich, 2014), 47–70.

Solan, Lawrance M., 'Statutory Interpretation in the EU: The Augustinian Approach', Brooklyn Law School, Legal Studies Paper No. 78 (2007). Available at: http://papers.ssrn.com/sol3/papers.cfm?abstract_id=998167.

Solan, Lawrence M. and Tiersma, Peter M., *Speaking of Crime. The Language of Criminal Justice.* (Chicago, 2011).

Temmerman, Rita, *Towards New Ways of Terminology Description: The Sociocognitive Approach* (Amsterdam, 2000).

9

Multilingual interpretation by the CJEU in the Area of Freedom, Security, and Justice

LUCIE PACHO ALJANATI

9.1. Introduction

9.1.1. Definition of the problem and object of study

The fact that EU law addresses not only Member States but also individuals justifies the rendering of EU legislation in all official languages. From a linguistic perspective, the production of multilingual EU law is not based on co-drafting in the usual sense of the term, but on translation.[1] However, from a legal perspective, such drafts are not translations; they are all authentic language versions (Article 55 TEU), which cannot be considered individually but instead must be considered as part of the same legal instrument.[2] In addition, Article 4 of Regulation No 1 states that texts are 'drafted' in all official languages.

As a result, the CJEU has stated that in cases of doubt, a provision of EU law must be interpreted and applied in light of the versions existing in other languages.[3] However, the obligatory character of comparison is very controversial.[4] Does the

[1] For a discussion about drafting or translation, see Agnieszka Doczekalska, 'Drafting or Translation-Production or Multilingual Legal Texts', in Frances Olsen, R. Alexander Lorz, and Dieter Stein, eds., *Translation Issues in Language and Law* (2009), 116–35.

[2] Gilbert Lautissier, 'La législation de l'Union européenne-une règle unique en vingt-trois langues', in Marie Cornu and Michel Moreau, ed., *Traduction du droit et droit de la traduction* (2011), 89–105.

[3] *Sociale Verzekeringsbank v. Van Der Vecht,* Case 19/67, EU:C:1967:49.

[4] See, for instance, Joxerramon Bengoetxea, 'Multilingual and Multicultural Legal Reasoning: The European Court of Justice', in Anne Lise Kjær and Silvia Adamo, eds., *Linguistic Diversity and European Democracy* (2011), 97–122; Michal Bobek, 'The Multilingualism of the European Union Law in the National Courts: Beyond the Textbooks', in Anne Lise Kjær and Silvia Adamo, eds., *Linguistic Diversity and European Democracy* (Farnham, 2011), 123–42; Mattias Derlén, 'In Defence of (Limited) Multilingualism: Problems and Possibilities of the Multilingual Interpretation of European

Lucie Pacho Aljanati, *Multilingual interpretation by the CJEU in the Area of Freedom, Security, and Justice* In: *Language and Legal Interpretation in International Law.* Edited by: Anne Lise Kjær and Joanna Lam, Oxford University Press. DOI: 10.1093/oso/9780190855208.003.0010

comparison of language versions always occur or only 'in cases of doubt'? The case law is not very clear. In certain cases, the CJEU uses the expression 'in cases of doubt', but in other cases it takes comparison for granted. For instance, in *Kraaijeveld*,[5] the Court did not mention 'in cases of doubt' and stated that 'interpretation of a provision of Community law involves a comparison of the language versions'. In *Ferriere*,[6] the Court affirmed that all language versions had to be consulted even if the version at hand was clear and unambiguous in isolation.

What is clear is that genuine comparison of all language versions is difficult or impossible to carry out on a systematic basis, particularly for national courts.[7] However, it is worth exploring whether comparison of different language versions is a valuable tool or an 'unnecessary detour'[8]—in other words, whether comparison contributes added value to interpretation or whether the Court simply compares because it is, in principle, a prerequisite for interpretation.[9]

This study observes the linguistic comparative activity of the Court in the Area of Freedom, Security and Justice (AFSJ), an area associated with a high level of vulnerability for the individuals affected by these policies.[10] This area deals with highly sensitive matters and touches upon personal freedom, fundamental rights, and the core of State autonomy.[11] From the Treaty of Maastricht to Lisbon, via Amsterdam, there were different stages on the path towards the full inclusion of the AFSJ in the EU competences.[12]

Union Law in National Courts', in Anne Lise Kjær and Silvia Adamo, eds., *Linguistic Diversity and European Democracy* (2011), 143–66; Christopher Kuner, 'The Interpretation of Multilingual Treaties: Comparison of Texts Versus Presumption of Similar Meaning', *International and Comparative Law Quarterly*, 40 (1991), 953–64; and Lawrence Solan, 'The Interpretation of Multilingual Statutes by the European Court of Justice', *Brooklyn Journal of International Law*, 34 (2009), 277–301.

[5] *Aannemersbedrijf P.K. Kraaijeveld BV e.a. v. Gedeputeerde Staten van Zuid-Holland*, Case 72/95, EU:C:1996:404, para. 25.

[6] Case 219/95 *P Ferriere Nord v. Commission* [1997] ECR I-4411, para. 15.

[7] Mattias Derlén, *Multilingual Interpretation of European Union Law* (2009); Michal Bobek, 'On the Application of European Law in (Not Only) the Courts of the New Member States: "Don't Do as I Say"?', *Cambridge Yearbook of European Legal Studies*, 1/10 (2007), 1–34; Bengoetxea, 'Multilingual and Multicultural Legal Reasoning'.

[8] Derlén, 'In Defence of (Limited) Multilingualism'.

[9] Elina Paunio, *Legal Certainty in Multilingual EU Law: Language, Discourse and Reasoning at the European Court of Justice* (2013); Bengoetxea, 'Multilingual and Multicultural Legal Reasoning'.

[10] Sergio Carrera, Marie de Somer, and Bilyana Petkova, *The Court of Justice of the European Union as a Fundamental Rights Tribunal: Challenges for the Effective Delivery of Fundamental Rights in the Area of Freedom, Security and Justice* (2012).

[11] Alicia Hinarejos, *Judicial Control in the European Union* (2009).

[12] Koen Lenaerts, 'The Contribution of the European Court of Justice to the Area of Freedom, Security and Justice', *International and Comparative Law Quarterly*, 59 (2010), 255–301.

Still, as to police and judicial cooperation in criminal matters, transitional provisions provide that the full jurisdiction will not apply until five years after the Treaty of Lisbon is entered into force.[13] This is very relevant for this study because no cases have been found in police and judicial cooperation in criminal matters. When the transitional provisions cease to apply, cases in these areas will probably begin to appear.

9.1.2. Objectives

The objective of this study is twofold. First, it aims to study the purpose of comparison: to what extent has comparison been used to reconcile diverging language versions or as a tool to support an interpretation when no divergences are present? Second, it aims to analyse how the CJEU constructs meaning, particularly in managing the interplay between EU law and national law.

The perspective used for this analysis is that of a legal translator concerned with the impact translation has on the production and application of multilingual EU legislation.

9.2. Methodology

The corpus is composed of judgments obtained from the CVRIA database. The covered period is through 31 April 2014. No start date has been used in the search because, as explained above, this area was recently created. In CVRIA, we selected the 'subject-matter' of asylum policy, border checks, immigration policy, judicial cooperation in civil matters, judicial cooperation in criminal matters, and police cooperation. We limited the search to these fields and do not analyse any cases classified under 'Justice and Home Affairs'. This study focuses only on this small portion of the vast case law.

In order to see whether the CJEU utilized comparison, we constructed a search using the following keywords in the field *Text* in CVRIA: *language versions*.

We started by analysing the purpose of comparison in quantitative terms and then proceed to a more detailed analysis of some cases. We only described the most representative of divergences; for the rest, we simply provided a summary of the

[13] These transitional provisions are set out in Article 10 of Protocol No 36, which provides that, as a transitional measure, the powers of the Court of Justice are to remain the same with respect to acts in the field of police cooperation and judicial cooperation in criminal matters that were adopted prior to the entry into force of the Treaty of Lisbon. Then, from 2015 onwards, the jurisdiction of the Court of Justice will expand to give preliminary rulings and will no longer be subject to a declaration by each Member State recognizing that jurisdiction and specifying the national courts that may request a preliminary ruling.

main points. We observed the method of interpretation and, in cases of linguistic divergence, the type of problem (grammatical/syntactical, conceptual, or consistency). We limited the languages used for comparison to English, German, French, and Spanish, because these are our working languages.

As to the methods of interpretation, we found many different classifications in the literature,[14] but they can be classified broadly into the following categories: literal interpretation (which includes comparing different language versions), teleological interpretation (which consists of analysing the purpose of the rules), and systematic interpretation (which consists of taking into account the context of the provision, that is, not only the text, but also the general scheme of which it is a part). As this chapter does not aim to undertake a descriptive study of the methods, we will limit our discussion to our examples.

9.3. Multilingual interpretation

When the Court resorts to comparison of the different language versions, some authors talk about 'multilingual interpretation';[15] others refer to 'comparative linguistic construction'.[16] Bengoetxea refers to 'multilingual judicial reasoning', but explains that it cannot be reduced to simple comparison:

> It is more than mere comparison of language versions although it cannot possibly neglect or elude comparison. It would involve deploying all

[14] Although it is not an exhaustive list on the matter, see Albertina Albors Llorens, 'The European Court of Justice, More Than a Teleological Court', *Cambridge Yearbook of European Legal Studies*, 2 (1999), 373–98; Cornelis J. W. Baaij, 'Fifty Years of Multilingual Interpretation in the European Union', in Peter M. Tiersma and Lawrence M. Solan, eds., *The Oxford Handbook of Language and Law* (2012), 217–31; Joxerramon Bengoetxea, *The Legal Reasoning of the European Court of Justice* (1993); Anna Bredimas, *Methods of Interpretation and Community Law* (1978); Derlén, *Multilingual Interpretation of European Union Law*; Giulio Itzcovich, 'The Interpretation of Community Law by the European Court of Justice', *German Law Journal*, 10 (2009), 534–59; H. Kutscher, *Methods of Interpretation as Seen by a Judge at the Court of Justice* (1976); Paunio, *Legal Certainty in Multilingual EU Law*; Pierre Pescatore, 'Interprétation des lois et conventions plurilingues dans la Communauté européenne', *Les Cahiers de Droit*, 25 (1984), 989–1010; Suvi Sankari, *European Court of Justice Legal Reasoning in Context* (2013); and Isabel Schübel-Pfister, *Sprache und Gemeinschaftsrecht: die Auslegung der mehrsprachig verbindlichen Rechtstexte durch den Europäischen Gerichtshof* (2004).

[15] Derlén, *Multilingual Interpretation of European Union Law*; Baaij, 'Fifty Years of Multilingual Interpretation in the European Union'; Susan Šarčević, 'Multilingual Lawmaking and Legal (Un) Certainty in the European Union', *International Journal of Law, Language and Discourse*, 3 (2013), 1–29.

[16] Barbara Nita and Andrzej Swiatlowski, 'Linguistic Pluralism and Interpretation of European Law in the Third Pillar, Discussed with Reference to the Example of Article 54 of the Convention Implementing the Schengen Agreement', in Joanna Jemielniak and Przemyslaw Miklaszewicz, eds., *Interpretation of Law in the Global World: From Particularism to a Universal Approach* (2010), 231–50.

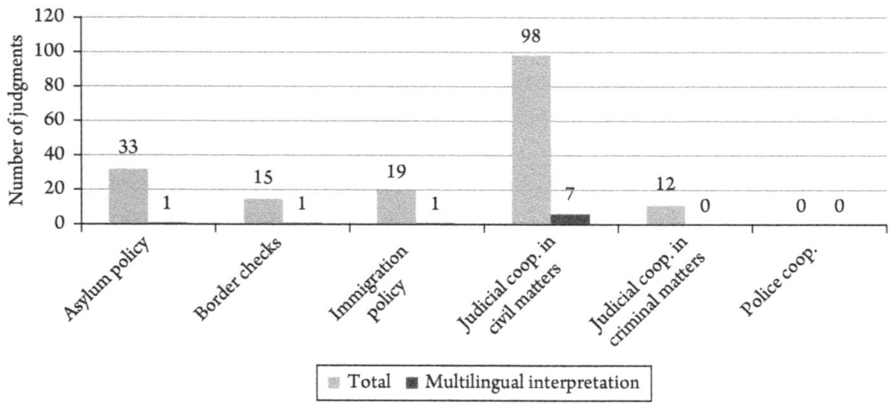

Figure 9.1 Multilingual interpretation per policy

> linguistic techniques or skills and interpretation methods to all language versions and being aware, when drafting the terms of its own reasoning, of how such terms would be translated into the other official languages so that the message is clearly understood and, as the case might be, any possible ambiguity is properly preserved.[17]

As can be seen in Figure 9.1, from a total of 177 judgements in the selected policies, ten cases have used comparison—that is, only 5.64 per cent of the cases.

The cases that involve comparison are as follows.

The use of comparison of the different language versions to reconcile diverging texts is normally included in the category of 'literal method'[18] or 'semiotic or linguistic arguments'.[19] Solan calls it the 'Augustinian approach', whose goal is to determine the intended scope of the statute.[20] Using comparison, the CJEU can reveal a divergence and harmonize texts to find the intended meaning common to all language versions. However, resorting to linguistic comparison does not mean that the method of interpretation is simply 'literal'. The CJEU rarely relies solely

[17] Bengoetxea, 'Multilingual and Multicultural Legal Reasoning'.

[18] Cornelis J. W. Baaij, 'Translation in EU Legislative Procedure: A Receiver-Oriented Approach', in Simone Davide Giannoni and Celina Frade, eds., *Linguistic Insights 121: Researching Language and the Law* (2010), 263–73.

[19] Bengoetxea, *The Legal Reasoning of the European Court of Justice*; Joxerramon Bengoetxea, Neil MacCormick, and Leonor Moral Soriano, 'Integration and Integrity in the Legal Reasoning of the European Court of Justice', in Gráinne de Burca and J. H. H. Weiler, eds., *The European Court of Justice* (2001), 43–85; Paunio, *Legal Certainty in Multilingual EU Law*.

[20] Lawrence M. Solan, 'Statutory Interpretation in the EU: The Augustinian Approach', in Frances Olsen, R. Alexander Lorz, and Dieter Stein, eds., *Translation Issues in Language and Law* (2009), 35–54.

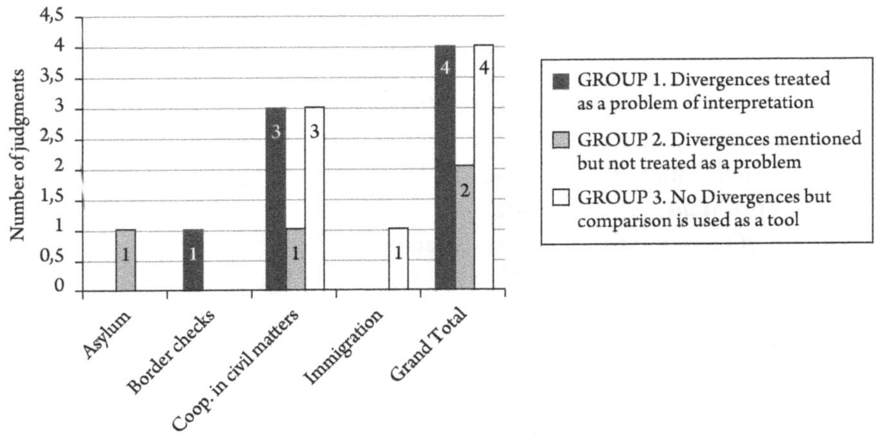

Figure 9.2 Purpose of comparison

on linguistic arguments;[21] mostly it compares and then moves on to teleological or systematic interpretation.[22]

9.4. Purpose of comparison

The cases are divided into three groups, as shown in Figure 9.2. In Group 1, there are cases in which comparison has helped reveal a divergence that poses interpretation problems. The CJEU analyses the divergence and treats it as a problem of interpretation. In Group 2, there are cases of unproblematic divergences; that is, the CJEU admits there is some divergence but it is irrelevant and it is not analysed as a problem as such. In Group 3, there are no divergences, but comparison is used as a tool to support an interpretation or to confirm that the various language versions converge in meaning. Sometimes there are 'borderline' cases and sorting judgments into groups can prove difficult. However, this attempt at systematization may offer an overview of the CJEU's practice of comparison in the chosen area.

Due to length limitations, it is not possible to describe all cases. For this reason, we have selected one case from each policy area (asylum, border checks, cooperation in civil matters, and immigration).

[21] Sieglinde E. Pommer, 'Interpreting Multilingual EU Law: What Role for Legal Translation?', *European Review of Private Law*, 5–6 (2012), 1241–54; Paunio, *Legal Certainty in Multilingual EU Law*.

[22] See Paunio, *Legal Certainty in Multilingual EU Law*, for a discussion of the overlap between systematic, contextual, and teleological arguments.

9.4.1. Group 1: Divergences treated as a problem of interpretation

9.4.1.1. C-412/10 Homawoo

Policy: Cooperation in civil matters
Type of problem: lack of consistency
Method of interpretation: literal + teleological (legal certainty)
Instrument: Regulation (EC) No 864/2007 of the European Parliament and of the Council of 11 July 2007 on the law applicable to non-contractual obligations ('Rome II')

This reference for a preliminary ruling was made in proceedings between Mr Homawoo, who was domiciled in the United Kingdom and the victim of a road traffic accident during a stay in France, and GMF Assurances SA ('GMF'), an insurance company incorporated and established in France.[23]

On 29 August 2007, during a stay in France, Mr Homawoo was involved in a road traffic accident caused by a vehicle being driven by a person insured by GMF.[24] On 8 January 2009, Mr Homawoo brought proceedings for personal injury and indirect damages against GMF before the High Court of Justice.[25]

The applicant in the main proceedings claimed that English law governed the assessment of damages as the *lex fori*, according to the conflict-of-law rules applicable to the dispute in the main proceedings. However, GMF, whilst not disputing that the applicant's claim for compensation was well founded, claimed, however, that French law should govern the assessment of those damages, in accordance with the conflict-of-law rules set forth in the Regulation.[26]

The dispute was whether Regulation No 864/2007 could be applied. Article 32 of that Regulation, entitled 'Date of application', provided that the Regulation was applicable from 11 January 2009. However, the date of entry into force was different. The Regulation had been published in the Official Journal on 31 July 2007, and as no date of entry into force had been established, it entered into force on 20 August 2007, on the twentieth day after its publication, per Article 267 TFEU. In other words, the Regulation had one date for entry into force (20 August 2007) and another date of application (11 January 2009).

The CJEU acknowledged there was a divergence in some of the language versions of Article 32:

[23] *Deo Antoine Homawoo v. GMF Assurances SA*, C-412/10, EU :C :2011 :747.
[24] Ibid., para. 14.
[25] Ibid., para. 15.
[26] Ibid., para. 17.

> Admittedly, three language versions of the title of Article 32 of the Regulation ('Inwerkingtreding', 'Data intrării în vigoare' and 'Entrada en vigor') refer to the term 'Entry into force'. However, even in those three versions, the content of the article refers to 11 January 2009 as being the date set of application of the Regulation.[27]

Article 32 (emphasis added):

DE	EN	ES	FR
Zeitpunkt des Beginns der *Anwendung*	**Date of** *application*	*Entrada en vigor*	**Date d'***application*
Diese Verordnung *gilt* ab dem 11. Januar 2009, mit Ausnahme des Artikels 29, der ab dem 11. Juli 2008 gilt.	This Regulation *shall apply* from 11 January 2009, except for Article 29, which shall apply from 11 July 2008.	El presente Reglamento *se aplicará* a partir del 11 de enero de 2009, excepto por lo que respecta al artículo 29, que se aplicará a partir del 11 de julio de 2008.	Le présent règlement *est applicable* à partir du 11 janvier 2009, à l'exception de l'article 29, lequel est applicable à partir du 11 juillet 2008.

It is clear that the Spanish version, for instance, states *entrada en vigor* when it could have indicated *fecha de aplicación*. The differentiation between *date of entry into force* and *date of application* was intended:

> It is open to the legislature to separate the date for the entry into force from that of the application of the act that it adopts, by delaying the second in relation to the first. Such a procedure may in particular, once the act has entered into force and is therefore part of the legal order of the European Union, enable the Member States or European Union institutions to perform, on the basis of that act, the prior obligations which are necessary for its subsequent full application to all persons concerned.[28]

[27] Ibid., para. 27.
[28] Ibid., para. 24.

Therefore, from the date of entry into force, the Regulation imposes certain obligations on Member States and on the Commission, but this does not mean that judges must apply it to the cases that took place immediately after the Regulation entered into force because the actual date of application was later.

In *Homawoo*, the CJEU invoked legal certainty and the principle of uniform interpretation:

> Such an interpretation is the only one which ensures, in accordance with recitals 6, 13, 14 and 16 of the Regulation, the full attainment of the Regulation's objectives, that is to say the predictability of the outcome of litigation, legal certainty as to the law applicable and the uniform application of that regulation in all the Member States.[29]

The CJEU finally ruled that the Regulation applied only to events giving rise to damage occurring after 11 January 2009. Neither the date on which the proceedings were brought nor the date on which the national court determined the applicable law, therefore, had any bearing on determining the scope *ratione temporis* of the Regulation.[30]

To conclude, in *Homawoo* the divergence appeared at a later stage; that is, the reference for preliminary ruling was not posed because of a divergence, but rather the divergence appeared later when interpreting the scope of the provision. Despite the fact that the main problem of interpretation revolved around this divergence, the CJEU does not seem to treat it as a problem of consistency, nor as a translation error. *Homawoo* could also be considered a case in Group 2 because the divergence seems unproblematic for the Court. However, in our opinion, it is a flagrant divergence that could have been avoided if translators had respected the difference between *date of entry into force* and *date of application*.

9.4.1.2. C-261/08 & C-348/08 **Zurita García**

Policy: Border checks
Type of problem: grammatical, use of future tense
Method of interpretation: literal + real intention of the author and the aim he seeks to achieve
Instrument: Regulation No 562/2006 establishing a Community Code on the rules governing the movement of persons across borders (Schengen Borders Code).

[29] Ibid., para. 34.
[30] Ibid., para. 37.

In *Zurita García,* [31] the references for preliminary ruling occurred in the course of two actions brought by Bolivian nationals relating to orders of expulsion from Spanish territory. More precisely, the competent authorities ordered their expulsion, either on the ground that they had not obtained an extension of their permission to stay or residence permit, or on the ground that the validity of those documents had expired more than three months earlier and they had not sought to have them renewed. That penalty was accompanied with a prohibition of entry to the Schengen area for a period of five years.[32]

Ms García and Mr Cabrera challenged this decision, arguing that the administration had not applied the principle of proportionality when assessing the circumstances of the case, and did not give reasons for replacing a fine (a sanction that was also possible under EU law) with expulsion.[33]

The referring court had doubts as to the interpretation of Article 11 of Regulation No 562/2006. It was unclear whether Member States had to adopt a decision to expel a person who no longer fulfilled the conditions to reside in a country.

The European Commission noted a discrepancy between the wording of the Spanish language version of Article 11(3) of Regulation No 562/2006 and other language versions.[34] The CJEU then affirmed that there was a divergence and treated it as a problem of interpretation.

Article 11(3) of Regulation No 562/2006 (emphasis added):

DE	EN	ES	FR
Wird die Annahme nach Absatz 1 nicht widerlegt, so *können* die zuständigen Behörden den Drittstaatsangehörigen aus dem Hoheitsgebiet der betreffenden Mitgliedstaaten ausweisen.	Should the presumption referred to in paragraph 1 not be rebutted, the third-country national *may* be expelled by the competent authorities from the territory of the Member States concerned.	De no refutarse la presunción a que se refiere el apartado 1, el nacional del tercer país *será expulsado* por las autoridades competentes del territorio del Estado miembro de que se trate.	Dans le cas où la présomption visée au paragraphe 1 ne seraitpasrenversée, les autorités compétentes *peuvent* expulser le ressortissant du pays tiers du territoire de l'État membre concerné.

[31] Joined cases *María Julia Zurita García,* C-261/08, and *Aurelio Choque Cabrera v. Delegado del Gobierno en la Región de Murcia,* C-348/08, EU:C:2009:648.

[32] Ibid., paras. 24–5.

[33] Ibid., para. 26.

[34] Ibid., para. 52.

The Spanish language version used the future verb tense and imposed an obligation, inasmuch as it provided that the competent authorities of the Member State had to expel a third-country national from the territory of that Member State if the presumption was not rebutted. By contrast, in all of the other language versions, expulsion appeared optional for those authorities (*können, may, peuvent*).

The CJEU referred to settled case law and highlighted the need for uniform application and interpretation of EU law. As a first argument, it referred to the real intention of the author and the aim it seeks to achieve, particularly in the light of the versions in all languages.[35]

Immediately after that, the Court reminded that 'the wording used in one language version of a Community provision cannot serve as the sole basis for the interpretation of that provision, or be made to override the other language versions in that regard' because this approach would be incompatible with the requirement of uniform application of Community law.[36]

However, the problem is that knowing the real intention of the author is not always obvious. In this case, the Court seems to arrive at its conclusion by comparing the different language versions and ruling out the language version that differs from the other versions (emphasis added):

> In the present cases, as the Spanish-language version of Article 11(3) of Regulation No 562/2006 is the only one which diverges from the wording of the other language versions, it must be concluded that *the real intention of the legislature* was not to impose an obligation on the Member States concerned to expel, from their territory, third-country nationals in the event that they have not succeeded in rebutting the presumption referred to in Article 11(1), but to grant those Member States the option of so doing.[37]

As Van Calster claims, 'the intention of the author is a good help for the judge confronted with differences or incompatibilities between the various language versions'. However, he recognizes that it is a vague principle and it is not always easy to use. For this reason, he considers it a general principle rather than a practical guideline to solve the problem of divergences.[38] The intention of the author's argument needs to be supported by other methods of interpretation.[39]

[35] Ibid., para. 54.

[36] Ibid., para. 55.

[37] Ibid., para. 56.

[38] Geert Van Calster, 'The EU's Tower of Babel: The Interpretation by the European Court of Justice of Equally Authentic Texts Drafted in More than One Official Language', *Yearbook of European Law*, 17 (1997), 363–93.

[39] For further discussion on the use of intention in interpretation, see Joseph Raz, 'Intention in Interpretation', in Robert Peter George, ed., *The Autonomy of Law: Essays on Legal Positivism* (1999), 249–86.

This argument is also called 'genetic argument', 'historical argument', or 'psychological argument',[40] and it can fall under different classifications. Kutscher,[41] for instance, includes it in the 'subjective historical method' and provides *Stauder*[42] as an example of the use of this argument. Itzcovich considers that it may fall under two categories: literal (linguistic) or systematic (systemic):

> This interpretative directive may be ranked among the linguistic criteria as well as among the systemic criteria: it is a linguistic criteria if we maintain that the meaning of a (normative) statement is influenced by the intentions of the speaker (the legislator); it is a systemic criteria if we hold, as it seems preferable to do, that the relevance of the speaker's (the legislator's) intentions depends upon a choice of the addressee (the interpreter), or that it depends upon a context which is external to the communication (such as a certain legal culture), which may be more or less favourable to this kind of considerations.[43]

Depending on what we take into account, the argument of the intention of the author can fall into one category or another, or it can be 'transcategorical' as MacCormick and Summers put it.[44] The subjective historical method might apply if it is necessary to go back in time to discover the intention of the author at the time the instrument was adopted. But the CJEU often expresses the argument in the following terms: *the real intention of the author and the aim he seeks to achieve.* Therefore, this argument could be considered a kind of teleological argument, meaning the purpose or aim of the legislature.

In any case, as Kutscher claims, this interpretative criterion, although it is not at all alien to the case law of the Court, plays a marginal role within its legal reasoning.[45] A search in the CVRIA database using keywords such as 'intention and the aim or the real intention' actually confirms the marginal role of this criterion; the number of judgments that employ this argument is small.

To summarize, in *Zurita García* the divergence also appeared later, but the European Commission first identified it and then the CJEU confirmed it. This divergence fits the classification as a problem of interpretation and we consider that it could have been avoided. Translators need to know by which grammatical and

[40] Itzcovich, 'The Interpretation of Community Law by the European Court of Justice'.

[41] Kutscher, *Methods of Interpretation.*

[42] *Stauder,* Case 29/69, EU:C:1969:57.

[43] Itzcovich, 'The Interpretation of Community Law by the European Court of Justice'.

[44] Neil MacCormick, and Robert S. Summers, 'Interpretation and Justification', in Neil MacCormick and Robert S. Summers, ed., *Interpreting Statutes: A Comparative Study* (1991), 511–44.

[45] Kutscher, *Methods of Interpretation.*

syntactical means obligation is expressed. The Joint Practical Guide,[46] for example, provides some guidelines in this respect:

2.3.1. The choice of verb and tense varies between different types of act and the different languages, and also between the recitals and the enacting terms (see Guidelines 10 and 12).
2.3.2. In the enacting terms of binding acts, French uses the present tense, whilst English generally uses the auxiliary 'shall'. In both languages, the use of the future tense should be avoided wherever possible.

As Šarčević suggests, like drafters of legislation, translators should be able to analyse and formulate the legal rules laid down in various types of provisions.[47]

Due to space limitations, we will present only the summary of two additional cases. C-144/10 BVG:[48]

Policy: Cooperation in civil matters
Type of problem: grammatical/syntactical - *in the matter of* v. *as their object or subject-matter*
Method of interpretation: literal + systematic (purpose and general scheme)
Instrument: Council Regulation (EC) No 44/2001 of 22 December 2000 on jurisdiction and the recognition and enforcement of judgments in civil and commercial matters ('Brussels I')

And C-347/08 Vorarlberger Gebietskrankenkasse:[49]

Policy: Cooperation in civil matters
Type of problem: scope of concept. *victim* versus *injured party*
Method of interpretation: literal + systematic (purpose and general scheme)
Instrument: Council Regulation (EC) No 44/2001 of 22 December 2000 on jurisdiction and the recognition and enforcement of judgments in civil and commercial matters ('Brussels I')

[46] Joint practical guide of the European Parliament, the Council and the Commission for persons involved in the drafting of legislation within the Community institutions.

[47] Susan Šarčević, 'Translation Procedures for Legal Translators', in Susan Šarčević, ed., *Legal Translation: Preparation for the Accession to the European Union* (2001), 75–109.

[48] *Berliner Verkehrsbetriebe (BVG), Anstalt des offentlichen Rechts v. JPMorgan Chase Bank NA, Frankfurt Branch,* C-144/10, EU:C:2011:300.

[49] *Vorarlberger Gebietskrankenkasse v. WGV-Schwäbische Allgemeine Versicherungs AG,* C-347/08, EU:C:2009:561.

9.4.2. Group 2: Divergences mentioned but not treated as a problem

9.4.2.1. C-245/11 K.

Policy: Asylum
Type of problem: Indeterminacy in law (*person concerned, the other*) + scope of concept (*family member*)
Method of interpretation: literal + teleological ('humanitarian' purpose of the Regulation)
Instrument: Regulation (EC) No 343/2003 of 18 February 2003 establishing the criteria and mechanisms for determining the Member State responsible for examining an asylum application lodged in one of the Member States by a third-country national.

This case[50] concerned K., a national of a third country who entered Poland irregularly and in March 2008 made her first application for asylum there.[51] Without awaiting the conclusion of the examination of that application for asylum, she subsequently left Poland and entered Austria irregularly, where she rejoined one of her adult sons who already held refugee status there, along with his spouse and their three minor children.[52] In April 2008, K. lodged a second application for asylum in Austria, but it was rejected on the ground that the Republic of Poland was the Member State responsible for examining the application for asylum.[53]

The Asylgerichtshof (Austria) proved that K's daughter-in-law was dependent on K because the daughter-in-law had a newborn baby and suffered from a serious illness and handicap following a serious and traumatic occurrence that had taken place in a third country.[54]

It was necessary to establish whether Article 15(2) of Regulation No 343/2003 could be applied in a situation of dependency, such as that at issue in the main proceedings, where it was not the asylum seeker herself who was dependent on the assistance of the member of the family present in a Member State, but rather the family who was dependent on the assistance of the asylum seeker.

In *K.*, there are two remarkable points. First, the Court recognizes the indeterminate character of the provision. Article 15(2) of Regulation No 343/2003 (that introduces a 'Humanitarian Clause') uses indeterminate wording and the CJEU

[50] *K v. Bundesasylamt*, C245/11, EU:C:2012:685.

[51] Ibid., para. 13.

[52] Ibid., para. 14.

[53] Ibid., para. 15.

[54] Ibid., para. 16.

states that it does not refer expressly to the situation of an asylum seeker who is dependent on the assistance of another person:

> In cases in which *the person concerned* is dependent on the assistance of *the other* on account of pregnancy or a new-born child, serious illness, severe handicap or old age, Member States shall normally keep or bring together the asylum seeker with *another relative* present in the territory of one of the Member States, provided that family ties existed in the country of origin.

The CJEU explained that with the use of general terms, such as 'the person concerned' or 'the other', the European Union legislature implied that both the concept of 'person concerned' and that of the 'other' can refer to the asylum seeker.[55]

This is an example of a provision that attempts to strike a balance between being determinate and being all-inclusive.[56] In addition, as Conway argues, all law entails some generality; it is not possible to predict every factual scenario to which laws of general applicability may be applied in the future.[57]

Second, the CJEU confirmed that the objective of Article 15 of Regulation No 343/2003 was to allow Member States to bring together 'family members' when necessary based on humanitarian grounds. This objective applies both when it is the asylum seeker who is dependent on a member of his family and, conversely, when a family member is dependent on the assistance of the applicant.[58] Nonetheless, in order to consider the daughter-in-law a 'family member', the Court gave a broad interpretation to the concept:

> Notwithstanding the fact that the definition of 'family members' within the meaning of Article 2(i) of Regulation No 343/2003 does not cover the daughter-in-law or grandchildren of an asylum seeker,

The Court mentioned that the various language versions of Article 15(2) of Regulation No 343/2003 diverged and that some of them, for example the English version, use different and broader wording than used in Article 2(i) of that regulation. However, the CJEU did not analyse this divergence.

As to the responsibility to examine an application for asylum, the CJEU concluded that Article 15(2) of Regulation No 343/2003 must be interpreted to

[55] Ibid., para. 33.

[56] Vijay Bhatia, Jan Engberg, Maurizio Gotti, and Dorothee Heller, 'Introduction', in Vijay Bhatia, Jan Engberg, Maurizio Gotti, and Dorothee Heller, ed., *Linguistic Insights 23: Vagueness in Normative Texts* (2005), 9–23.

[57] Gerard Conway, *The Limits of Legal Reasoning and the European Court of Justice* (2012).

[58] *K v. Bundesasylamt*, C245/11, EU:C:2012:685, para. 36.

mean that a Member State not previously responsible for examining an application for asylum pursuant to the criteria laid down in Chapter III of that regulation becomes responsible.[59]

In summary, comparison confirmed that a broad interpretation was necessary and the CJEU gave priority to the humanitarian purpose of Article 15(2), which delimited the group of family members of the asylum seeker as necessarily wider than that defined by Article 2(i) of that regulation. In this case, the teleological interpretation was beneficial for the individuals. If the CJEU had stuck to a literal interpretation, the Court would not have considered them family members.

Here is a brief summary of the other case in Group 2, C-145/10 *Painer*:[60]

Policy: Cooperation in civil matters
Type of problem: consistency (use of the expression *mise à la disposition du public*)
Method of interpretation: literal + Art. 37 Berne Convention
Instrument: Council Regulation (EC) No 40/94 of 20 December 1993 on the Community trade mark

9.4.3. Group 3: No divergences but comparison is used as a tool

9.4.3.1 C-502/10 Singh

Policy: Immigration
Instrument: Council Directive 2003/109/EC of 25 November 2003 concerning the status of third-country nationals who are long-term residents.
The Court used comparison to claim that literal interpretation was not enough.

In this case, [61] Mr Singh applied for a long-term resident's EC residence permit, but was rejected. This reference for a preliminary ruling concerned the interpretation of Article 3(2)(e) of Council Directive 2003/109/EC:

> reside solely on temporary grounds such as au pair or seasonal worker, or as workers posted by a service provider for the purposes of cross-border

[59] Ibid., para. 54.
[60] *Eva-Maria Painer v. Standard VerlagsGmbH and Others*, C-145/10, EU:C:2011:798.
[61] *Staatssecretaris van Justitie v. Mangat Singh*, C-502/10, EU:C:2012:636.

> provision of services, or as cross-border providers of services or in cases where their residence permit has been formally limited

The question was whether 'residence permit has been formally limited' covered a case different from that of third-country nationals 'who reside solely on temporary grounds'.

When dealing with the question, the CJEU stated that, in a large number of language versions, the literal wording of Article 3(2)(e) of Directive 2003/109 is not unambiguous in meaning. There is no divergence, but after comparing the different languages, the Court admitted it was not possible to determine clearly and at first glance the exact scope of the provision.[62]

From this point onwards, the Court engaged in a teleological and systematic interpretation that was more favourable to Mr Singh, although the CJEU finally left it to the discretion of the national court.

The CJEU claimed that it is not sufficient that a residence permit is formally limited for the purposes of the national law of a Member State for it to be regarded as a 'formally limited residence permit' within the meaning of the Directive.

9.4.4. Independent and autonomous EU concepts

One of the main difficulties in EU law is the constant interplay between EU law and the laws of the Member States. The CJEU stated that, according to the principle of uniform application and the principle of equality, 'the terms of a provision of European Union law which makes no express reference to the law of the Member States for the purpose of determining its meaning and scope must normally be given an independent and uniform interpretation throughout the European Union (Joined Cases C-424/10 and C-425/10 *Ziolkowski and Szeja* [2011] ECR I-0000, paragraph 32 and the case-law cited)'.[63]

The Court affirmed that, for the purpose of application of the directive, those terms had to be regarded as designating an autonomous concept of European Union law that had to be interpreted in a uniform manner throughout the Member States.[64]

9.4.5. Terms not defined in EU law

Immediately after stating that these terms had to be given an independent and autonomous interpretation, the CJEU stated that when terms are not defined in EU law, the context and purpose of the rules need consideration:

[62] Ibid., para. 33.
[63] Ibid., para. 42.
[64] Ibid., para. 43.

> In this respect, it must be borne in mind that the meaning and scope of terms for which European Union law provides no definition must be determined by considering, inter alia, the context in which they occur and the purposes of the rules of which they form part (see, inter alia, Case C-336/03 *easyCar* [2005] ECR I-1947, paragraph 21; Case C-549/07 *Wallentin-Hermann* [2008] ECR I-11061, paragraph 17; Case C-151/09 *UGT-FSP* [2010] ECR I-7591, paragraph 39; and Case C-34/10 *Brüstle* [2011] ECR I-0000, paragraph 31).[65]

Therefore, it ruled that a formally limited residence permit within the meaning of national law 'cannot be classified as a formally limited residence permit within the meaning of Article 3(2)(e) of Directive 2003/109', because otherwise 'the achievement of the objectives pursued by the directive would be jeopardised' and, therefore, 'would be deprived of its effectiveness' (see, to this effect, *Commission v. Netherlands*, para. 65 and the case-law cited).[66]

After all of the analysis, the CJEU stated that it was for the national court to ascertain, in light of all of the circumstances, whether the case of Mr Singh fell within the interpretation given by the CJEU.[67]

In summary, in *Singh* there is no divergence between the language versions; the wording is ambiguous in general. Comparison is used to show that a literal interpretation is not enough; it is necessary to engage in a teleological-systematic interpretation. Moreover, it is apparent from the final conclusion that the CJEU strikes a balance between its power to interpret EU law and the level of discretion left to the Member States under EU law.[68]

The other cases included in Group 3, only summarized here due to space restrictions, are C-251/12 *Van Buggenhout and Van de Mierop*:[69]

Policy: Cooperation in civil matters
Instrument: Council Regulation (EC) No 1346/2000 of 29 May 2000 on insolvency proceedings.
Comparison used to confirm all language versions converge in meaning.

[65] Ibid., para. 44.

[66] Ibid., para. 51.

[67] Ibid., para. 54.

[68] For further discussion on the level of discretion of Member States and the enhancement of the legislation, see Joxerramon Bengoetxea, Neil MacCormick, and Leonor Moral Soriano, 'Integration and Integrity in the Legal Reasoning of the European Court of Justice', in Gráinne de Burca and J. H. H. Weiler, eds., *The European Court of Justice* (2001), 43–85.

[69] *Christian Van Buggenhout and Ilse Van de Mierop v. Banque Internationale à Luxembourg SA*, C-251/12, EU:C:2013:566.

C-92/12 PPU *C*:[70]

Policy: Cooperation in civil matters
Instrument: Council Regulation (EC) No 2201/2003 of 27 November 2003 concerning jurisdiction and the recognition and enforcement of judgments in matrimonial matters and the matters of parental responsibility.
Comparison used to confirm all language versions converge in meaning.

And C-235/09 *DHL Express*:[71]

Policy: Cooperation in civil matters
Instrument: Council Regulation (EC) No 40/94 of 20 December 1993 on the Community trademark.
Comparison used to frame the question posed by the referring court.

9.5. Conclusions

The comparison of different language versions offers an added value to interpretation. As shown in Group 1 and Group 2, it allows the interpreter to unmask discrepancies at a later stage. In other words, after the preliminary ruling was posed, when interpreting the provisions, the CJEU resorted to comparison, which helped uncover the divergences. However, in the Area of Freedom, Security and Justice, the Court used comparison in only 5.64 per cent of the cases, which shows that linguistic comparison is not carried out on a systematic basis.

In Group 1, the CJEU dealt with some divergences that, in our opinion, could have been avoided. For example, in *Homawoo*, the divergences were because of lack of consistency (*date of entry into force* versus *date of application*); in *BVG*, they were grammatical and syntactical (*in the matter of* versus as the *object*); and in *Zurita García*, they were grammatical (the use of future tense). Some other conceptual divergences, like in the case of *Vorarlberger*, may be more difficult to avoid.

In Group 2, the CJEU mentioned some divergences but did not analyse them as a problem of interpretation. In the case of *K*., for example, the Court seemed to give priority to the humanitarian purpose of the Regulation.

[70] *Health Service Executive v. S.C. and A.C.*, C-92/12 PPU, EU:C:2012:255.
[71] *DHL Express France SAS v. Chronopost SA*, C-235/09, EU:C:2011:238.

In Group 3, there are no divergences but the CJEU resorted to comparison for different reasons:

a) to confirm all language versions' convergence on one meaning (*Van Buggenhout and Van de Mierop* and *C.*);
b) to claim the literal meaning is not unambiguous and it is necessary to proceed with a teleological-systematic interpretation (*Singh*); and
c) to frame the question posed in the preliminary observations (*DHL Express*).

Moreover, the requirement of comparison is quite controversial because it implies that individuals cannot rely on a single language version, which is contrary to the principle of legal certainty.[72] On the other hand, comparison can also be beneficial for individuals. For example, in *Zurita García*, comparison actually helped the Bolivian nationals. Thanks to the clarifying effect of comparison, the Court ruled that where a third-country national is unlawfully present in the territory of a Member State because he or she does not fulfil, or no longer fulfils, the conditions of duration of stay applicable there, that Member State is not obliged to adopt a decision to expel that person.

Finally, regarding the way in which the CJEU constructs meaning, in *Singh*, the CJEU reminded that for the purposes of applying the directive, terms have to be regarded as designating autonomous concepts of European Union law that must be interpreted in a uniform manner throughout the Member States.[73] This indicates that the EU has its own conceptual framework of reference.

In *K.*, the Court gave a broad interpretation to 'family members'. Although the term was defined in Article 2(i) of that Regulation, the Court decided that, considering the humanitarian purpose of the Regulation, it was necessary to interpret Article 15(2) more broadly to include daughter-in-law within the scope of the provision. The CJEU has shown that terms acquire their meaning only through their application and interpretation.[74] The examples analysed prove that meaning is dynamic and created in context.[75]

[72] Paunio, *Legal Certainty in Multilingual EU Law*.

[73] *Staatssecretaris van Justitie v. Mangat Singh*, EU:C:2012:636, para. 43.

[74] Similarly, following Luhmann's standpoint, Kjær mentions that legal concepts are generated through the process of legal argumentation; Anne Lise Kjær, 'A Common Legal Language in Europe?', in *Epistemology and Methodology of Comparative Law* (2004), 377–98.

[75] For this notion, see Kjær, 'A Common Legal Language in Europe?'; Anne Wagner, 'Semiotic Analysis of the Multistage Dynamic at the Core of Indeterminacy in Legal Language', in Vijay Bhatia, Jan Engberg, Maurizio Gotti, and Dorothee Heller, eds., *Linguistic Insights 23: Vagueness in Normative Texts* (2005), 173–99; and, on the weak language theory, Ralph Christensen, and Michael Sokolowski, 'Wie normativ ist Sprache? Der Richter zwischen Sprechautomat und Sprachgesetzgeber', in Ulrike Haß-Zumkehr, ed., *Sprache und Recht* (2002), 64–79; Jan Engberg, 'Legal Meaning Assumptions: What Are the Consequences for Legal Interpretation and Legal Translation?',

Table 9.1 **Cases of multilingual interpretation**

Policy	*Case*	*Date of delivery*
Asylum policy	C-245/11 K.	6 December 2012
Border checks	C-261/08 *Zurita García*	22 October 2009
Immigration policy	C-502/10 *Singh*	18 October 2012
Judicial cooperation in civil matters	C-251/12 *Van Buggenhout and Van de Mierop*	19 September 2013
	C-92/12 PPU C.	26 April 2012
	C-145/10 *Painer*	1 December 2011
	C-412/10 *Homawoo*	17 November 2011
	C-144/10 *BVG*	12 May 2011
	C-235/09 *DHL Express*	12 April 2011
	C-347/08 *Vorarlberger Gebietskrankenkasse*	17 September 2009

References

Albors Llorens, Albertina, 'The European Court of Justice, More Than a Teleological Court', *Cambridge Yearbook of European Legal Studies*, 2 (1999), 373–98.

Baaij, Cornelis J. W., 'Fifty Years of Multilingual Interpretation in the European Union', in Peter M. Tiersma and Lawrence M. Solan, eds., *The Oxford Handbook of Language and Law* (Oxford, 2012), 217–31.

Baaij, Cornelis J. W., 'Translation in EU Legislative Procedure: A Receiver-Oriented Approach', in Simone Davide Giannoni and Celina Frade, eds., *Linguistic Insights 121: Researching Language and the Law* (Bern, 2010), 263–73.

Bhatia, Vijay, Jan Engberg, Maurizio Gotti, and Dorothee Heller, 'Introduction', in Vijay Bhatia, Jan Engberg, Maurizio Gotti, and Dorothee Heller, eds., *Linguistic Insights 23: Vagueness in Normative Texts* (Bern, 2005), 9–23.

Bengoetxea, Joxerramon, 'Multilingual and Multicultural Legal Reasoning: The European Court of Justice', in Anne Lise Kjær and Silvia Adamo, eds., *Linguistic Diversity and European Democracy* (Farnham, 2011), 97–122.

Bengoetxea, Joxerramon, *The Legal Reasoning of the European Court of Justice* (Oxford, 1993).

Bengoetxea, Joxerramon, Neil MacCormick, and Leonor Moral Soriano, 'Integration and Integrity in the Legal Reasoning of the European Court of Justice', in Gráinne de Burca and J. H. H. Weiler, eds., *The European Court of Justice* (Oxford, 2001), 43–85.

Bobek, Michal, 'On the Application of European Law in (Not Only) the Courts of the New Member States: "Don't Do as I Say"?', *Cambridge Yearbook of European Legal Studies*, 1/10 (2007), 1–34.

International Journal for the Semiotics of Law, 15 (2002), 375–88; and Jan Engberg, 'Statutory Texts as Instances of Language(s): Consequences and Limitations on Interpretation', *Brooklyn Journal of International Law*, 1 (2004), 1136–66.

Bobek, Michal, 'The Multilingualism of the European Union Law in the National Courts: Beyond the Textbooks', in Anne Lise Kjær and Silvia Adamo, eds., *Linguistic Diversity and European Democracy* (Farnham, 2011), 123–42.

Bredimas, Anna, *Methods of Interpretation and Community Law* (Amsterdam, 1978).

Carrera, Sergio, Marie de Somer, and Bilyana Petkova, *The Court of Justice of the European Union as a Fundamental Rights Tribunal: Challenges for the Effective Delivery of Fundamental Rights in the Area of Freedom, Security and Justice* (Brussels, 2012).

Christensen, Ralph and Michael Sokolowski, 'Wie normativ ist Sprache? Der Richter zwischen Sprechautomat und Sprachgesetzgeber', in Ulrike Haß-Zumkehr, ed., *Sprache und Recht* (Berlin, 2002), 64–79.

Conway, Gerard, *The Limits of Legal Reasoning and the European Court of Justice* (New York, 2012).

Derlén, Mattias, *Multilingual Interpretation of European Union Law* (Alphen aan den Rijn, 2009).

Derlén, Mattias, 'In Defence of (Limited) Multilingualism: Problems and Possibilities of the Multilingual Interpretation of European Union Law in National Courts', in Anne Lise Kjær and Silvia Adamo, eds., *Linguistic Diversity and European Democracy* (Farnham, 2011), 143–66.

Doczekalska, Agnieszka, 'Drafting or Translation-Production or Multilingual Legal Texts', in Frances Olsen, R. Alexander Lorz, and Dieter Stein, eds., *Translation Issues in Language and Law* (Basingstoke, 2009), 116–35.

Engberg, Jan, 'Legal Meaning Assumptions: What Are the Consequences for Legal Interpretation and Legal Translation?', *International Journal for the Semiotics of Law*, 15 (2002), 375–88.

Engberg, Jan, 'Statutory Texts as Instances of Language(s): Consequences and Limitations on Interpretation', *Brooklyn Journal of International Law*, 1 (2004), 1136–66.

Hinarejos, Alicia, *Judicial Control in the European Union* (Oxford, 2009).

Itzcovich, Giulio, 'The Interpretation of Community Law by the European Court of Justice', *German Law Journal*, 10 (2009), 534–59.

Kjær, Anne Lise, 'A Common Legal Language in Europe?', in *Epistemology and Methodology of Comparative Law* (Portland, 2004), 377–98.

Kuner, Christopher, 'The Interpretation of Multilingual Treaties: Comparison of Texts Versus Presumption of Similar Meaning', *International and Comparative Law Quarterly*, 40 (1991), 953–64.

Kutscher, H., *Methods of Interpretation as Seen by a Judge at the Court of Justice* (Luxembourg, 1976).

Lautissier, Gilbert, 'La législation de l'Union européenne-une règle unique en vingt-trois langues', in Marie Cornu and Michel Moreau, ed., *Traduction du droit et droit de la traduction* (Paris, 2011), 89–105.

Lenaerts, Koen, 'The Contribution of the European Court of Justice to the Area of Freedom, Security and Justice', *International and Comparative Law Quarterly*, 59 (2010), 255–301.

MacCormick, Neil and Robert S. Summers, 'Interpretation and Justification', in Neil MacCormick and Robert S. Summers, eds., *Interpreting Statutes: A Comparative Study* (Aldershot, 1991), 511–44.

Nita, Barbara and Andrzej Swiatlowski, 'Linguistic Pluralism and Interpretation of European Law in the Third Pillar, Discussed with Reference to the Example of Article 54 of the Convention Implementing the Schengen Agreement', in Joanna Jemielniak and Przemyslaw Miklaszewicz, eds., *Interpretation of Law in the Global World: From Particularism to a Universal Approach* (Heidelberg, 2010), 231–50.

Paunio, Elina, *Legal Certainty in Multilingual EU Law: Language, Discourse and Reasoning at the European Court of Justice* (Farnham, 2013).

Pescatore, Pierre, 'Interprétation des lois et conventions plurilingues dans la Communauté européenne', *Les Cahiers de Droit*, 25 (1984), 989–1010.

Pommer, Sieglinde E., 'Interpreting Multilingual EU Law: What Role for Legal Translation?', *European Review of Private Law*, 5–6 (2012), 1241–54.

Raz, Joseph, 'Intention in Interpretation', in Robert Peter George, ed., *The Autonomy of Law: Essays on Legal Positivism* (Oxford, 1999), 249–86.

Sankari, Suvi, *European Court of Justice Legal Reasoning in Context* (Groningen, 2013).

Šarčević, Susan, 'Multilingual Lawmaking and Legal (Un)Certainty in the European Union', *International Journal of Law, Language and Discourse*, 3 (2013), 1–29.

Šarčević, Susan, 'Translation Procedures for Legal Translators', in Susan Šarčević, ed., *Legal Translation: Preparation for the Accession to the European Union* (Rijeka, 2001), 75–109.

Schübel-Pfister, Isabel, *Sprache und Gemeinschaftsrecht: die Auslegung der mehrsprachig verbindlichen Rechtstexte durch den Europäischen Gerichtshof* (Berlin, 2004).

Solan, Lawrence, 'The Interpretation of Multilingual Statutes by the European Court of Justice', *Brooklyn Journal of International Law*, 34 (2009), 277–301.

Solan, Lawrence M., 'Statutory Interpretation in the EU: The Augustinian Approach', in Frances Olsen, R. Alexander Lorz, and Dieter Stein, eds., *Translation Issues in Language and Law* (Basingstoke, 2009), 35–54.

Van Calster, Geert, 'The EU's Tower of Babel: The Interpretation by the European Court of Justice of Equally Authentic Texts Drafted in More than One Official Language', *Yearbook of European Law*, 17 (1997), 363–93.

Wagner, Anne, 'Semiotic Analysis of the Multistage Dynamic at the Core of Indeterminacy in Legal Language', in Vijay Bhatia, Jan Engberg, Maurizio Gotti, and Dorothee Heller, eds., *Linguistic Insights 23: Vagueness in Normative Texts* (Bern, 2005), 173–99.

10

Translation of judgments of the European Court of Human Rights into non-official languages

The politics and practice of European multilingualism

ANNE LISE KJÆR

10.1. Introduction

Multilingual law in its most radical form is usually credited to the language regime of EU law. However, if one broadens one's understanding of multilingual law, the legal linguistic landscape of the European Convention on Human Rights and the European Court of Human Rights is even more extreme. Although the Convention text and the judgments of the Court exist only in two official languages (compared with—the impressive—twenty-four official languages of the European Union), the real number of languages involved in the making and shaping of European human rights law is much higher. The domestic legal orders of the forty-seven Member States of the Council of Europe operate in their own national languages when applying and interpreting the Convention and the judgments of the Court. Thus, it can be argued that the actual number of languages of European human rights law is thirty-six rather than only two.[1]

While the language regime of the European Union right from the outset was based on the principle of equal standing of all official languages of the Member States (at the beginning, Dutch, German, French, and Italian), the drafters of the Human Rights Convention and the Rules of Procedure of the European Court of Human Rights seem to have never considered expanding the number of official

[1] Some languages are spoken in more than one Member State, for example, English, French, German, Greek, Italian, Romanian, Spanish, and Turkish; hence the difference in the number of Member States and the number of languages.

Anne Lise Kjær, *Translation of judgments of the European Court of Human Rights into non-official languages* In: *Language and Legal Interpretation in International Law.* Edited by: Anne Lise Kjær and Joanna Lam, Oxford University Press. © Oxford University Press 2022. DOI: 10.1093/oso/9780190855208.003.0011

languages from the traditional two *lingua franca* languages, English and French, to the national languages of the Member States. At first sight, the explanation of this difference seems obvious: the European Union was designed to be a supranational legal system with the competence of passing legislation with direct effect in the Member States, whereas the human rights system was conceived of as a more traditional international system with no supranational power.

In light of this difference it is worth noticing that the need to translate judgments issued by the European Court of Human Rights into the national languages of the Member States has recently been put on the agenda. The Interlaken reform process, leading to the adoption of Protocols 14, 15, and 16 and encompassing so far five Declarations on the continuous functioning and effectiveness of the Court, includes reference to the necessity and desirability that the judgments of the Court be translated into the language of the Member States. For fifty years, the challenges of European multilingualism were addressed neither by the Member States of the Council of Europe, nor by the Court itself. Now, as part of the reform process that began around the turn of the twenty-first century around the turn of the century, translation has become a topic of interest in Strasbourg and among the Member States. Why not before and why now?

In this chapter, I argue that the key answer to these questions is the degree of legitimacy that the Human Rights Court has now compared with the first decades of its existence. Similar to other international courts the ECtHR is increasingly drawing criticism, also in the liberal democracies that established it after World War II.[2] Thus, in order to regain its authority, the Court has responded by endorsing and stressing the necessity of providing translations of its case law into the national languages of the Member States.

Furthermore, I make the case that even if the topic of translation is framed in a discourse of 'access to the Court's case law', the 'effectiveness of the Court system', and ensuring the continued existence of an 'overburdened Court', an underlying narrative is one of promoting national interests of the Member States against the continued Europeanization of human rights protection. This is why, as part of the reform process, the Member States in their Declarations put increasing emphasize on the concepts of 'subsidiarity' and 'margin of appreciation'.

To understand my argument, it is necessary to know the history of the language policy governing the interaction between the Member States and the Convention system. In section 10.2, I first describe the language rules of the Convention and the Court (10.2.1) and then present the drafting history of the Articles on the

[2] See, for example, Øyvind Stiansen and Erik Voeten, 'Backlash and Judicial Restraint: Evidence From the European Court of Human Rights' (17 August 17, 2018), available at: https://ssrn.com/abstract=3166110; and Mikael Rask Madsen, 'The Challenging Authority of the European Court of Human Rights: From Cold War Legal Diplomacy to the Brighton Declaration and Backlash', *Law & Contemporary Problems*, 79 (2016), 141.

implementation of the Convention into the national legal systems (10.2.2). In section 10.3, I further examine the reform process of the Court, the so-called Interlaken process, and trace the development in the reform discourse. In section 10.4, I focus on the role that translation of the Court's case law has played in the reform discourse and comment on the differences between the importance that individual Member States attach to translation of ECHR judgments as a means to effective implementation of the Convention (10.4.1). In section 10.4.2, I comment briefly on recent multilingual initiatives taken by the Court to enhance its accessibility. Finally, in section 10.5, I discuss perspectives in the practice and politics of multilingualism in Europe which my study of the reform process of the human rights system has uncovered.

10.2. Language policy of the European human rights system

10.2.1. Language rules of the European Convention on Human Rights and the European Court of Human Rights

The European Convention on Human Rights exists in two language versions, English and French, which are equally authentic. Moreover, upon adoption of the Convention by the Member States, the states translated the Convention text into their official languages, though for information purposes only. Those translations are available on the Court's web page.[3]

Regarding the judgments passed by the European Court of Human Rights, they are all available in the HUDOC database in both English and French. However, according to the Rules of Procedure of the Court the general rule is that judgments are given in *either* English *or* French, unless the Court decides that they shall be given in both official languages.[4] The Rules further stipulate that judgments selected for publication in the official reports of the Court shall be given in both official languages.[5] In other words, only the most important judgments are published and authoritative in both official languages, whereas judgments of lesser importance are published and authoritative in only one language.[6]

[3] https://www.echr.coe.int/Pages/home.aspx?p=basictexts/convention.

[4] Rule 76, section 1.

[5] Rule 76, section 2.

[6] The Court distinguishes between four importance levels of judgments: key judgments are those that are published in the Case Reports, whereas levels 1 to 3 range from 'high' to 'low' importance. Only key judgments and judgments at importance level 1 are done in both official languages; in terms of numbers that amounts to 1,986 judgments out of a total of 19,201 judgments, or merely 10 per cent of the case law (as of April 2019).

Contrary to the Convention text, until recently the judgments of the Court did not exist in other languages, neither as official texts nor as translations, and translation was not a service provided for, supported, or even mentioned at the European level. As described in the introduction, the lack of translations of ECtHR judgments was highlighted in the Interlaken process as a hindrance to the effective implementation of human rights in the Member States. Today, the HUDOC database is searchable not only in English and French, but also in four other CoE Member States' languages (Russian, Georgian, Turkish, and Spanish). Moreover, translations of a limited number of judgments are available in the HUDOC database in thirty languages of CoE Member States in addition to English and French.

The HUDOC translations are the tangible result of the focus on the accessibility of the ECtHR case law that has been on the agenda since the early beginning of the reform process and culminated in the adoption of the Case-Law Translation Programme in 2010. The reform process and its implications for the language policy of the human rights system are discussed in more detail in sections 10.3 and 10.4. Before we turn to that topic, however, I first consider the debate of the founding fathers on the question of implementation of the Court's case law; it sheds light on the radically different political outlook that existed at that time and, therefore, puts the present debate into perspective. Notably, no mention was made of the necessity of translation.

10.2.2. *Travaux preparatoires* of Article 46 of the European Convention on Human Rights

The creators of the European human rights system did not consider the necessity of translating the Convention text and the judgments of the European Court of Human Rights into the national languages of the Member States. Based on the fact of the multilingual regime set up for the EU system only a few years later, I find it remarkable that the process leading to the adoption of the Convention text and the Rules of Procedure of the European Court of Human Rights did not include any considerations concerning the issue of multilingualism and translation. Of course, the two European legal systems are different, because the EU system introduced legislation which would be adopted at European level, but would have direct effect in the Member States. The human rights system was and is based on a more traditional division of labour between the Member States and the European institutions. However, the lack of attention to the language issue is notable, because the Convention is not a conventional international treaty which governs only interstate relations; in fact, it establishes obligations for states towards individuals and sets up a European system by which individuals can bring cases against their own states. Thus, the importance of the accessibility of the Convention and the Court's decisions for citizens in the CoE Member States was foreseeable already at the time when the system was created.

At the time of drafting the Human Rights Convention, the importance of the national understanding of ECtHR case law was addressed, albeit in a different context. During the preparatory work for Articles 53 and 54 of the European Convention on human rights (which would later become Article 46, sections 1 and 2), they discussed the potential problem that the human rights system would have to rely solely on the willingness of the Member States to implement the Convention and follow the decisions of the Court and would have no enforcement mechanism of its own.[7]

In its present wording, Article 46 reads as follows:

> Article 46
> Binding force and execution of judgments
> 1. The High Contracting Parties undertake to abide by the final judgment of the Court in any case to which they are parties.
> (Former Article 53)
> 2. The final judgment of the Court shall be transmitted to the Committee of Ministers, which shall supervise its execution.
> (Former Article 54)

In the history leading to the final text, the European Movement[8] in July 1949 presented a draft text of the Convention to the Council of Europe. The draft included articles on the functioning of the system and the authority of the Court in the Member States. Compared to the discussions of the reform process of the 2010s, especially Article 11, which did not make it to the final text, is thought provoking. For the human rights system to function at national level, the Member States had to consider how knowledge about the judgments of the Court and statements issued by the Commission[9] was to be communicated to its institutions and the general public.

> Article 11
> Every state, a Party to this Convention, shall by all means available to it, ensure the widest possible publicity for the judgments of the Court, and for any statements published by the Commission.[10]

[7] Preparatory work on Articles 53 and 54 of The European Convention on Human Rights: Information Document prepared by the Registry of the European Court of Human Rights on 28 November 1972.

[8] International Committee of the Movement of European Unity, which was established as a civil society initiative at a Congress at the Hague in May 1948.

[9] The human rights institution, which until its abolition in 1998 filtered cases brought before the Court.

[10] Information document, 2.

The following debate, conducted in the First Sessions of the Consultative Assembly of the Council of Europe (August–September 1949), illustrates the high expectations that the Western leaders had at the time, regarding the role that the general public would play in ensuring the effectiveness of the Court. The fear was that the Court would prove powerless and ineffective because it would rely on the willingness of the states to implement its judgments. The European Movement commented on this fear with the following considerations:

> Governments will be reluctant to be regarded as violators of their people's liberties and will usually prefer to comply with the judgments of the Court, even if they do not always agree with them, rather than face the loss of popularity and electoral support which refusal would probably involve.
>
> . . .
>
> States in which democracy has been completely overthrown and in which absolute dictatorship has been established, admittedly present a much harder problem. However, it must be remembered that it is rare indeed for a democratic country to go over to a totalitarian system in a day. There is almost always a period during which liberty is being progressively curtailed. It is in this transition stage that the publication of the Court's judgments could exercise such an important and perhaps even decisive influence.[11]

The reactions from the national representatives also reveal the degree to which the ideas behind the draft of the convention text were influenced by the values of liberal democracy and the newly gained victory over the Nazi regime. United Kingdom Prime Minister Winston Churchill's words are evidence of the prevailing mindset among Western leaders at that time: 'we hope that a European Court will be set up before which cases of violation of those rights . . . might be brought to justice before the civilised world'. The comment by the Belgian delegate, Mr Fayat, captures the sentiment even more clearly:

> the question of the means of enforcing the judgments appears of only subsidiary importance. Are we not States by right of law? And can it be supposed that States existing by right of law will fail to yield to the authority of a European Court of Justice whose jurisdiction it has deliberately recognised and accepted?[12]

[11] Information document, 2.

[12] Information document, 4.

In the aftermath of World War II, the leaders of the Western European countries were certain that they were 'States by right of law' and that there was no reason to be concerned about their willingness to accept the authority of the European Court. However, as I shall present in the following, during the reform process of the 2000s, the Member States' support and recognition of the Court dwindled. Compared with the discourse of the post-war leaders, the rhetoric used in the reform process of the 2000s was reverted such that implementation today is no longer phrased as a question of Member States acting in accordance with the needs of the Court, but rather the Court acting in accordance with the needs of the Member States.

The topic of translation of the Courts' judgments reflects this turn in the discourse. In the following section, I examine more closely the changes in the overall framing and phrasing of the call for reform of the Convention system with a special view to the focus put on the necessity of translating the ECHR case law and the responsibility for doing and financing translation.

10.3. Reforms of the convention system

In the years following the fall of the Berlin wall in 1989, a number of Eastern European countries became members of the Council of Europe. Consequently, the volume of work for the European Court of Human Rights multiplied. In order to cope with this new situation, the Council of Europe Member States decided to change the Court into a full-time institution and increase its staff considerably, and in May 1994, the Council adopted Protocol No. 11, restructuring the Court. With the reform, the Commission, which had been a filter mechanism with the task of reviewing the incoming applications, was closed down.

However, the Court soon became overburdened again, because the number of applications continued to increase. Therefore, more reforms were necessary that would ensure the longer-time efficiency of the Court.

The International Auditor examining the challenges of the Court said the following regarding this matter:

> It will not be possible endlessly to enhance the Court's human and financial resources on account of both lack of space and budgetary constraints . . . the current system (a single court for 800 million Europeans) has reached its limits and must therefore evolve further and possibly fundamentally.[13]

Among the measures that were suggested in the reform process was re-organizing the relations between the Court and the States Parties to the Convention, including

[13] Audit (2004) 08: Audit Report on The Court's Workload and the Necessary Budgetary Resources 2004–2007.

enhancing the authority of the Court's case law in the Member States, the idea being that the more national authorities and national courts focused on implementing the Human Rights Convention and the judgments of the Court, the more relieved from applications the Court would be. Let us study the wording of the proposals on how to increase the Court's long-term efficiency.

10.3.1. The Early Reform Process

10.3.1.1. The European Ministerial Conference on Human Rights, Rome, 3–4 November 2000

After the Council's adoption of Protocol 11 in May 1994, the European Ministerial Conference on Human Rights meeting in Rome on the 50th anniversary of the Convention in 2000 was the first step undertaken by the Member States and the Court to reform human rights protection in Europe.[14] At the conference, two crucial elements were emphasized: '1. the responsibility of Member States, to ensure constantly that their law and practice conform to the Convention and to execute the judgments of the European Court of Human Rights; and 2. that urgent measures be taken to assist the Court in carrying out its functions, given the ever increasing number of applications.'

The Rome Conference was the first forum in which translation was mentioned; in Resolution 1, 'Institutional and Functional Arrangements for the Protection of Human Rights at National and European Level', the Conference encouraged the Member States to ensure that 'the text of the Convention is translated and widely disseminated to national authorities, notably the courts, and that the developments in the case-law of the Court are sufficiently accessible in the language(s) of the country'. The encouragement is clearly and solely directed to the Member States, whereas the Court's responsibility for dissemination and translation of its case law is not mentioned.

Among the texts adopted by the Committee of Ministers following the Rome Conference 2000 to improve the efficiency of the Convention System are Recommendation CM/Rec(2002)13[15] directed to the Member States, and Resolution CM/Res(2002)58[16] directed to the Court, and both were adopted by

[14] CM(2000)172-Part. I: European Ministerial Conference on Human Rights (Rome, 3–4 November 2000), Report of the Secretary General.

[15] CM/Rec(2002)13: Recommendation of the Committee of Ministers to member states on the publication and dissemination in the member states of the text of the European Convention on Human Rights and the case-law of the European Court of Human Rights (adopted by the Committee of Ministers on 18 December 2002 at its 822nd Session).

[16] CM/Res(2002)58: Resolution of the Committee of Ministers on the publication and dissemination of the case-law of the European Court of Human Rights (adopted by the Committee of Ministers on 18 December 2002 at the 822nd meeting of the Ministers' Deputies).

the Committee of Ministers on 18 December 2002. Both texts address the publication and dissemination of the case-law of the European Court of Human Rights.

The Recommendation, on the one hand, specifies the responsibility of the Member States and states that

> It is important that governments of the member states ...
> ii. ensure that judgments and decisions which constitute relevant case-law developments, or which require special implementation measures on their part as respondent states, are rapidly and widely published, through state or private initiatives, in their entirety or at least in the form of substantial summaries or excerpts (together with appropriate references to the original texts) in the language(s) of the country, in particular in official gazettes, information bulletins from competent ministries, law journals and other media generally used by the legal community, including, where appropriate, the Internet sites;
> ...
> viii. consider the possibility of co-operating, with a view to publishing compilations, in paper or in electronic form, of Court judgments and decisions that are available in non-official languages of the Council of Europe.[17]

The Resolution, on the other hand, considers the responsibility of the Court and highlights the importance for the effective implementation of the Convention at national level that the Court's case law is made easily accessible. Therefore, it 'invites the Court to review its practice as regards the publication and dissemination of its judgments and decisions', stressing, among other things, that it is essential that the judgments and decisions 'are made immediately available in a well-functioning electronic database'.[18]

Thus, the Rome Conference and the follow-up Recommendation and Resolution stipulate the division of labour between the Court and the Member States regarding translation and dissemination of the Court's case law. As I discuss later, some Member States have been reluctant to take on their part of the share, whereas the Court has acted as requested and has stepped in where the Member States have failed to act.

10.3.1.2. The Woolf Report

In the Review of the Working Methods of the European Court of Human Rights of December 2005 which was conducted and authored by Lord Woolf at the request of

[17] Recommendation CM/Rec(2002)13, no. ii and viii.

[18] Resolution Res(2002)58, no. i.

the Secretary General of the Council of Europe and the President of the European Court of Human Rights, Lord Woolf and his team made recommendations as to what could be done in the short term to relieve the Court of the overwhelming caseload.[19] Stating that 'the Court needs to be in a position where it can match input with output', he suggested that the necessary reforms

> be supported by the necessary finance. The Court must be given a lifeline if it is not to be drowned by its own success. It would be tragic if an institution which has played such a critical role in promoting and protecting human rights in each Member State were not rescued. The citizens of Europe are entitled to continue to enjoy its protection.[20]

Lord Woolf did not mention translation into non-official languages as such. He encourages the Court and its Registry to 'devote as little time as possible to questions such as compensation, and to translation work' (p. 18). At the same time he stresses the responsibility of the Member States, indicating that '[t]here should be greater information and education at national level on the jurisdiction and purpose of the Court' (p. 17). The Member States, for their part, should supply the finances necessary to ensure the reform of the human rights system. Financing the reform is a recurrent topic in the political debate, as we shall see in the following.

10.3.1.3. The Report of The Group of Wise Persons

The Report was presented in 2007 by The Group of Wise Persons to the Committee of Ministers and suggested longer-term solutions to the problems addressed by Lord Woolf. [21] Under the heading of 'Enhancing the authority of the Court's case-law in the States Parties"' the following proposals were submitted:

> 71 The Group considers that national judicial and administrative institutions should be able to have access to the case-law of the Court in their respective language. This would assist them in identifying any judgments which might be relevant to deciding the cases before them.
>
> 72 In the Group's view, responsibility for translation, publication and dissemination of case-law lies with the Member States and their competent

[19] The Right Honourable The Lord Woolf, Michael McKenzie CB QC, Peter MacMahon, Dr Colm O'Cinneide, and Laura Clarke, *Review of the Working Methods of the European Court of Human Rights,* December 2005.

[20] Woolf Report, 16, 71.

[21] CM(2006)203, Report of the Group of Wise Persons to the Committee of Ministers, 15 November 2006.

> bodies. Each country should make its own arrangements while taking due account of the importance of these texts.
>
> 73 On the other hand, it is for the Court to decide, as is already the case, which judgments to publish in full (or in summary form, as the case may be, including judgments on the admissibility of applications) and to ensure a structured presentation of these documents. Regular production of handbooks or other summaries in languages other than the Council of Europe official languages, in hard copy and/or in electronic form, might also constitute a useful means of dissemination.[22]

The Wise Persons Report was supported by Amnesty International who, in 2006, issued their response in collaboration with other non-governmental organizations (NGOs).[23] They criticized the Member States for not supplying sufficient funding to the Court and explicitly regretted the fact that not all Member States translated ECtHR judgments into their national languages.

The Court's response to the Report by the Group of Wise Persons also backs up the proposals and highlights a critical additional point, viz. the narrow focus in some states on only those judgments of the Court which concern the particular state in question:

> Some States translate and publish Court judgments in their official journal, but this usually only concerns cases taken against that particular country. Yet the courts in every Contracting State must be aware of both the judgments handed down against that State and the most important judgments of the Strasbourg Court. Although its judgments do not, strictly speaking, have *erga omnes* effect (see Article 46 of the Convention), all States should take due notice of judgments against other States, especially judgments of principle, thereby preempting potential findings of violations against themselves.[24]

In its response the Court also refers to its Grand Chamber judgment in *Scordino v. Italy* in which it finds that 'domestic courts must . . . be able, under domestic law,

[22] Wise Persons' Report, paragraphs 71–73.

[23] NGO Comments on the Group of Wise Persons' Interim Report, July 2006, AI Index: IOR 61/019/2006. NGO Comments on the Group of Wise Persons' Interim Report, July 2006, Amnesty International Index Number: IOR 61/019/2006. The other NGOs were European Human Rights Advocacy Centre (EHRAC), Human Rights Watch, INTERIGHTS, Justice, Liberty, Redress, and The AIRE Centre.

[24] Opinion of the Court on the Wise Persons' Report, as adopted by the Plenary Court on 2 April 2007, section 3, *Enhancing the authority of the Court's case law in the States Parties.*

to apply the European case-law directly and their knowledge of this case-law has to be facilitated by the State in question'.[25]

This is a clear indication of how the Court viewed the issue of dissemination and translation at the beginning of the reform process. In the Memorandum of 3 July of the President of the European Court of Human Rights to the States with a view to preparing the Interlaken Conference, the obligation to 'facilitate knowledge of the case-law' is taken a step further and framed in a language of 'ownership':

> 1. Measures that can be taken immediately without amending the Convention
>
> What is crucial in this context is that the States acquire ownership of the Convention for the benefit of the persons within their jurisdiction. The Convention is now part of the domestic law of the States. Citizens must be able to assert their Convention rights before the national authorities. Beyond the need to establish effective remedies, which must be introduced where they do not exist, States must, with the help of the Council of Europe, take initiatives in the fields of training, translation of Strasbourg judgments, preventive action etc.[26]

The major problem with reaching this aim was (and is) funding. Because many states were unwilling to provide the necessary money for case law translation, the Case Law Translation Programme, which was launched in the following years, was funded by the Court in cooperation with a private actor, the Human Rights Trust Fund (HRTF). In section 10.4, I examine the content and results of this initiative; but first I discuss the Interlaken process and the increasing backlash that the European human rights system has experienced, especially after the 2012 meeting of the Committee of Ministers in Brighton.

10.3.2. The Interlaken Process

While the report of the Group of Wise People concentrated on measures to improve the efficiency of the Court, it is obvious that the measures adopted and recommended by the States' Parties in the series of high-level conferences, beginning in Interlaken in Switzerland in 2010 and therefore termed 'The Interlaken Process', have increasingly had the additional aim of regaining the Member States' power vis-à-vis the Court in Strasbourg. Hence, a close examination of the wording of the declarations and Action Plans issued by the Member States in Interlaken

[25] *Scordino v. Italy* (no. 1) [GC], no. 36813/97, § 239, ECtHR (2006).

[26] Memorandum of 3 July 2009 of the President of the European Court of Human Rights to the States with a View to Preparing the Interlaken Conference, B2, 1.

(2010), Izmir (2011), Brighton (2012), Brussels (2015), and Copenhagen (2018) shows that the discourse has shifted from expressing support to the overburdened Court to addressing concerns about the Court's perceived disrespect of the sovereignty of the Member States. The Court's responses to those declarations exhibit a corresponding attempt at re-legitimizing itself by stressing the need to protect and respect the Member States' legal traditions and national languages while at the same time referring to the Member States' responsibility to secure human rights protection within their domestic legal systems.

10.3.2.1. The Interlaken Declaration 2010

The Interlaken Declaration does not mention translation at all and simply reminds the Member States of their responsibility to 'guarantee the application and implementation of the Convention'.[27]

This absence is not an oversight, but instead the first indication of the reluctance that the Member States have exhibited in relation to translation of the Court's case law. This becomes even clearer at the Izmir Conference held the following year.

10.3.2.2. The Izmir Declaration 2011

Under the heading of 'Implementation of the Convention at National Level' the Izmir Declaration[28] first refers to the need that 'programmes for professional training of judges, prosecutors and other law-enforcement officials as well as members of security forces contain adequate information regarding the well-established case-law of the Court concerning their respective professional fields' (1c); next it encourages Member States to 'consider contributing to translation into their national language the Practical Guide on Admissibility Criteria prepared by the Registry of the Court' (1d); and finally it encourages Member States to 'consider contributing to the Human Rights Trust Fund' (1e).

Compared with the Wise Persons' Report and the Court's response to that report, the importance of translation of the Court's case law is clearly downplayed. The Member States are asked to 'consider contributing' to the translation of the Practical Guide to Admissibility Criteria. Notably, there is no call on them to do so, the responsibility is placed with the Court. For the first time, the Izmir Declaration refers to the Human Rights Trust Fund.[29] The HRTF's purpose is 'to provide funding

[27] High Level Conference on the Future of the European Court of Human Rights, 19 February 2010, Interlaken Declaration, B.4.

[28] High Level Conference on the Future of the European Court of Human Rights, 26–27 April 2011, Izmir Declaration.

[29] The HTRF was established in March 2008 by Norway, the Council of Europe and the CEB—the Council of Europe Development Bank—and later joined by Germany, the Netherlands, Finland, Switzerland, and the United Kingdom.

for states' efforts to meet their commitments under the European Convention on Human Rights and other Council of Europe human rights standards'.[30] In section 10.4, I describe how the HRTF has contributed heavily to the translation task which the Court by itself cannot finance and which Member States have been reluctant to take upon themselves.

10.3.2.3. The Brighton Declaration 2012

The High-Level Conference held in Brighton, United Kingdom, in 2012[31] sets a new direction in the reform process. Until Brighton, the centre of attention was the Court and what Member States could and should do to help the Court manage the case overload. In Brighton, the Governments of the Member States reversed the attention.

The Preliminary Opinion of the Court in preparation for the Brighton Conference indicates this change in the balance of power between the Court and the Member States. Thus, the Court almost submissively reports in paragraph 17 that

> 17. Responding directly to Interlaken and Izmir the Court has also made a considerable effort to increase the information available on its procedure and particularly on admissibility conditions. Thus the Court has published a detailed admissibility guide now available in 14 languages, notably thanks to contributions from different States.[32]

Moreover, in in paragraph 26 of the preliminary opinion in preparation for the Brighton Conference the Court

> stresses the importance of the effective implementation by the States of pilot judgments and of giving serious consideration to the implications of judgments against other States. From the Court's point of view it will continue its efforts to ensure better dissemination of the case-law, including in national languages. The Court has set up a judicial training institute after having received financial support from the Human Rights Trust Fund. The programme will start to operate in April this year.[33]

[30] https://www.coe.int/en/web/programmes/human-rights-trust-fund.

[31] High-Level Conference on the Future of the European Court of Human Rights, on 19 and 20 April 2012, Brighton Declaration.

[32] Preliminary opinion of the Court in preparation for the Brighton Conference, adopted by the Plenary Court on 20 February 2012, paragraph 17.

[33] Preliminary opinion of the Court in preparation for the Brighton Conference, adopted by the Plenary Court on 20 February 2012, paragraph 26.

In direct response to the Member States' reluctance to take over the responsibility to translate the Court's case law, the Court acts and promises to 'continue its efforts to ensure better dissemination of the case-law, including in national languages' (paragraph 26).

The tangible evidence of the shift in power is the adoption of Protocol 15 in 2013, which was a follow-up to the Brighton Declaration's paragraph 12 b.

Article 1 of Protocol 15 stipulates that the following new recital shall be added to the Preamble of the European Convention on Human Rights:

> Affirming that the High Contracting Parties, in accordance with the principle of subsidiarity, have the primary responsibility to secure the rights and freedoms defined in this Convention and the Protocols thereto, and that in doing so they enjoy a margin of appreciation, subject to the supervisory jurisdiction of the European Court of Human Rights established by this Convention.[34]

This recital explicitly states that Member States have the primary responsibility of protecting human rights in their countries, and this responsibility has a price: the Court recognizing the supremacy of the nation states. The language of 'authority of the Court' and 'implementation of the Court's case law' has developed into a language of 'subsidiarity' and 'margin of appreciation'.

If one interprets the recommendations in the Brighton Declaration in the light of this shift, including those relating to translation, clearly, the government representatives that convened in Brighton did not consider the translation of the Court's case law a necessary instrument in achieving human rights protection in their countries.

Under the heading of 'Implementation of the Convention at National Level', the Declaration:

> d) Encourages the States Parties, if they have not already done so, to:
> i) Ensure that significant judgments of the Court are translated or summarised into national languages where this is necessary for them to be properly taken into account;

and then repeats the encouragement, already mentioned in the Izmir Declaration in 2011, to

> ii) Translate the Court's Practical Guide on Admissibility Criteria into national languages; and

[34] Article 1, Protocol No. 15 amending the Convention on the Protection of Human Rights and Fundamental Freedoms, Strasbourg, 24.VI.2013.

iii) Consider making additional voluntary contributions to the human rights programmes of the Council of Europe or to the Human Rights Trust Fund.

What is new, is the address directed to the Court, where the Conference

h) Invites the Court to indicate those of its judgments that it would particularly recommend for possible translation into national languages.[35]

Notable in this regard is the weak formulation of the responsibility of both parties: the Court is *invited* to *recommend* judgments for *possible* translation.

In plain language, what is effectively stated in the Declaration is that Member States can choose to translate or summarize significant ECtHR judgments if they consider it necessary. Thus, no commitment to translate is stipulated—just a free choice to translate. Once the focus has shifted to subsidiarity (the Member States role as primary protectors of human rights) and the margin of appreciation (the Court giving Member States more room to interpret the Convention in accordance with the traditions in their respective societies and cultures) the necessity of understanding all the nuances of the Court's case law is not that compelling—so it seems to be stated implicitly the Brighton Declaration.

10.3.2.4. The Brussels Declaration 2015

To prepare for the Brussels Conference in 2015, the conference that followed the Brighton Conference, the Court issued its recommendations.[36]

At this stage, the Case Law Translation Programme (see section 10.4) was approaching the end of its funding, and the Court, therefore, underlined the importance of continuing, and even expanding the translation work beyond that date. Additionally, the Court reminded the Member States that translation of the Court's case law into the national languages 'at the end of the day must be for Member States themselves to ensure'.[37]

The Brussels Declaration is more balanced than the Brighton Declaration, and the Court's recommendation actually seems to have resonated with the Governments, who in the Declaration text 'call upon the States Parties . . . [to] maintain and develop the financial resources that have made it possible for the Council of Europe, since 2010, to translate a large number of judgments into national languages'.[38]

[35] Brighton Declaration, paragraph 9 d and h.

[36] High-Level Conference on the 'Implementation of the European Convention on Human Rights, our shared responsibility', Brussels, 26–27 March 2015.

[37] Contribution of the Court to the Brussels Conference, 26 January 2015, paragraph 7.

[38] Brussels Declaration, No. B 2 g.

It is worth noticing that the Court referred back to the Brussels Declaration and its call for financial resources in its 2018 annual report.

10.3.2.5. The Copenhagen Declaration 2018

The most recent conference in the reform process was held in Copenhagen in 2018.[39] The governments once again failed to make promises relating to their responsibility in terms of translating the Court's case law into the national languages. In the final text, the Member States are unambitiously encouraged to 'continue strengthening the implementation of the Convention' at the national level *inter alia* by

> d) promoting translation of the Court's case law and legal materials into relevant languages, which contributes to a broader understanding of Convention principles and standards.[40]

The perspective on the translation issue offered in the final version of the Copenhagen Declaration is even narrower than that adopted in Brighton in 2012. The phrasing 'promote' translation into 'relevant languages' does not imply any commitment in terms of funding and provides a leeway for individual Member States to conclude that translation into their languages is not relevant.

Remarkably, the draft version prepared by the Danish Government who had the Chairmanship at the time, did not mention translation at all. In other words, the paragraph on translation was added afterwards; the Danish government did not consider the issue of translation to be important at all.[41]

As a matter of fact, the Danish government has not commissioned full translations or summaries of ECtHR case law except for a limited time period between 2011 and 2012. Ending in May 2012, Danish summaries were offered on a monthly basis by the Ministry of Justice and made accessible on their website. The selection included 'relevant judgments' and all judgments and decisions involving Denmark.[42]

In late 2017, the Danish Institute for Human Rights introduced a searchable database with summaries of all judgments and decisions by the European Court of Human Rights and the former European Commission on Human Rights, as well

[39] The High-Level Conference meeting in Copenhagen on 12 and 13 April 2018.

[40] Copenhagen Declaration, paragraph 16 d.

[41] The draft version of the Copenhagen Declaration was heavily criticized by the Court, NGOs, and by other key actors, including lawyers and academics, though for other reasons; see, for example, Joint NGO Response to the Draft Copenhagen Declaration, 13 February 2018; Opinion on the draft Copenhagen Declaration, adopted by the Bureau in light of the discussion in the Plenary Court on 19 February 2018; and Andreas Follesdal and Geir Ulfstein: 'The Draft Copenhagen Declaration: Whose Responsibility and Dialogue?', *EJIL Talk!*, 22 February 2018.

[42] http://www.justitsministeriet.dk/arbejdsomraader/international/menneskerettigheder/den-europaeiske-menneskerettighedsdomstol/praksis.

as statements by the United Nations' Treaty Committees in cases where Denmark is a party.[43] This is a well-functioning publicly accessible database which is regularly updated; however, as was the case with the Ministry of Justice summaries, it focuses narrowly on cases against Denmark, and, thus, it does not fulfill the recommendations put forward by the Committee of Ministers and the ECtHR in the reform process to 'ensure that judgments and decisions which constitute relevant case-law developments . . . are rapidly and widely published . . . in their entirety or at least in the form of substantial summaries or excerpts . . . in the language(s) of the country'.[44]

As apparent in the overview that follows, translations into non-official languages of the Convention system vary considerably by language. One explanation for the variance may be the degree to which the individual Member States consider translation 'necessary' for the dissemination of the Court's case law. The topic of necessity was voiced also in the early phase of the reform process. Thus, the perspective held by Secretary-General of the Committee of Ministers in the introductory report presented prior to the Rome meeting in 2000 probably resonates with that of some of the translation-reluctant Member States: 'It would appear that much more can and should be done at the national level: . . . publication and dissemination of key Strasbourg judgments for the legal community, if necessary in translated form, etc.'[45]

10.4. The Case-Law Translation Programme

The HUDOC database of the European Court of Human Rights contains all the judgments and decisions passed by the Court since the beginning of its existence. They are all published in the two official languages, English and French, however, since the adoption of the Case-Law Translation Programme in 2010 a selection of judgments has been translated into the languages of other Council of Europe Member States and made searchable in the database.

By the end of 2009, at the launch of the programme, the ECtHR made the first 500 translations into non-official languages of some of the Court's key judgments available in the database. The Court aimed 'to make its caselaw more easily accessible to those who are not well-versed in either English or French but who may nevertheless turn to the Court's Internet site for guidance'.[46] The 500 translations were

[43] https://menneskeret.dk/monitorering/afgoerelsesdatabase.

[44] CM/Rec(2002)13, recommendation ii.

[45] European Ministerial Conference on Human Rights and Commemorative Ceremony of the 50th anniversary of the European Convention on Human Rights, Rome, 3–4 November 2000 Part I, Institutional and functional arrangements for the protection of human rights at national and European levels; Introductory report of Mr Walter Schwimmer, Secretary General of the Council of Europe. Council of Europe (June 2002), 32.

[46] Press release 982 (2009) of 21 December 2009, issued by the Registrar of the Court.

'commissioned in the past by the Council of Europe', and further translations were added in 2010 'following copyright waivers by web and other publishers willing to share their materials with visitors to the Court's website'.

Hence, the first translations added to the HUDOC database were not provided by the Member States. Realizing that the Member States did not follow the Committee of Ministers' 2002 Recommendation on national publication and dissemination of the case law of the European Court of Human Rights, the Court volunteered to ensure accessibility of its case law in non-official languages. This volunteering on the part of the Court could be interpreted in terms of effectiveness ('we cannot continue just talking about the need to translate the judgments—we must take action'). However, the Court's initiative might also be an indication of the legitimacy crisis that the Court was facing. Translation of the ECtHR case law was perceived as less important in the Member States than in Strasbourg; consequently, to enhance the authority of its judgments, the Court had to intervene, when the Member States did not act. In the following years, more translation projects were launched as joint ventures of the Court, individual Member States, and private initiatives.

10.4.1. "Bringing the Convention Closer to Home"

In 2012, the Court launched the project 'Bringing Convention Closer to Home' with the financial support from the Human Rights Trust Fund mentioned earlier.

As explained above the HRTF was a private initiative established in 2008 by Norway, the Council of Europe, and the Council of Europe Development Bank. Later, Germany, the Netherlands, Finland, Switzerland, and the United Kingdom also joined.

The 'Bringing Convention Closer to Home' project was the Court's reaction to the reluctance exhibited by Member States to ensure translations into their national languages. The project's aim was 'to translate the Court's key judgments and decisions in order to further disseminate its case-law via HUDOC (the Court's database) and partners at national level'. The judgments and decisions selected were 'recent cases of significant relevance to those Member States where the case-law has not yet been translated'.[47]

However, the Court did not and does not take responsibility for the quality and correctness of the translations. Under the 'Language Filter' of the database, the Court adds a disclaimer, stating that:

> Unless otherwise indicated, translations into non-official languages are not produced by the Registry of the Court and the Registry does not check their accuracy or linguistic quality. These translations are published in

[47] Press release ECHR 288 (2012) of 6 July 2012, issued by the Registrar of the Court.

HUDOC for information purposes only and the Court accepts no responsibility for their quality or content. Multiple translations into the same language of individual judgments or decisions may appear.[48]

A critical component of the translation programme was the four-year project for translating key case-law—mainly the leading cases selected by the Court's Bureau—into twelve target languages spoken in Member States with weak democratic traditions. The Member States in question were Albania, Armenia, Azerbaijan, Bosnia and Herzegovina, Georgia, the Republic of Moldova, Montenegro, Serbia, 'The former Yugoslav Republic of Macedonia' (now North Macedonia), Turkey, and Ukraine, all of which are either former Soviet republics or Balkan countries. Table 10.1 gives an overview of the number of translations into non-official languages that have been provided for inclusion into the HUDOC database.

A closer look at what languages are offered and how many judgments have been translated gives one a significant insight into the politics of multilingualism in European human rights law.[49]

First, the above-mentioned target states of the 'Bringing the Convention Closer to Home' project have obviously benefitted from the translations funded by the HRTF, though some much more than others (notably Turkey, Moldova,[50] and Ukraine).

Second, Russia stands out as being the only Eastern European country that has ensured translation of ECtHR judgments acting on their own cost and initiative. Translations of all judgments in cases against Russia as well as landmark decisions against other countries are provided and financed by the Ministry of Justice of the Russian Federation and disseminated from there to constitutional and supreme courts and competent national authorities.[51]

Third, Germany, Austria,[52] and Spain are the only old CoE and EU Member States that have supplied a substantial amount of translations to the HUDOC database initiative. Fourth, a non-European language, Arabic, is included. Most of the

[48] https://hudoc.echr.coe.int/eng.

[49] Not all languages are commented on; some of the numbers require more research before any conclusions can be drawn.

[50] The official language of Moldova is Romanian.

[51] Information given by Stanislav Kovpak, a representative of the Ministry of Justice of the Russian Federation, at the Round Table: *Implementation of the ECHR in the Domestic Legal Systems: Experience in the Translation and Dissemination of the Judgments of the European Court in a Comparative Perspective*, held at the Court 15 October 2018.

[52] Switzerland and Liechtenstein have also contributed to the German language translations in the database, see N. P. Engel, 'Translation and Dissemination of the Strasbourg Case-law; The German Language Experience', speech held at the Round Table: *Implementation of the ECHR in the Domestic Legal Systems: Experience in the Translation and Dissemination of the Judgments of the European Court in a Comparative Perspective*, 15 October 2018.

Table 10.1. **Overview of translations into non-official languages of ECHR judgments (including judgment summaries)**

31 non-official languages of CoE Member States (grouped according to EU Member State status)					
Old (pre-2004) EU Member States	***New (post-2004) EU Member States***	***Non-EU Balkan countries and former Soviet republics***	***EFTA Member States***	***Non-European countries ('Southern Neighbour-hood')***	***Number of translations available in HUDOC (descending)***
		Turkish			3,546
		Russian			2,610
	Romanian (Romania)	Romanian (Moldova)			2,407
		Ukrainian			1,743
German					1,306
Spanish					1,133
	Czech				1,031
		Georgian			924
	Polish				866
			Icelandic		852
		Macedonian			782
		Albanian			778
		Azerbaijani			744
	Croatian				712
		Armenian			703
	Bulgarian				687
	Slovenian				674
Greek					628
Italian					521
		Serbian			418
	Hungarian				340
		Bosnian			228
Portuguese					148
	Lithuanian				145

(continued)

Table 10.1. **Continued**

31 non-official languages of CoE Member States (grouped according to EU Member State status)					
Old (pre-2004) EU Member States	*New (post-2004) EU Member States*	*Non-EU Balkan countries and former Soviet republics*	*EFTA Member States*	*Non-European countries ('Southern Neighbour-hood')*	*Number of translations available in HUDOC (descending)*
				Arabic	98
	Slovak				85
Swedish					81
		Montenegrin			76
	Estonian				73
Dutch					40
	Latvian				17

Source: The HUDOC database as per 21 October 2021

translations into Arabic were produced as the tangible result of cooperation between the Council of Europe and the European Union which, in 2012, launched a three-year joint programme in response to the Arabic Spring, so-called Strengthening Democratic Reform in the Southern Neighbourhood. The remaining translations were provided by The Arab Center for International Humanitarian Law and Human Rights Education (ACIHL).[53]

Fifth, some Nordic languages are missing, namely Danish, Finnish, and Norwegian, while Iceland and Sweden are represented, Iceland with a considerable number of translations (852) while Sweden has only delivered eighty-one translated judgments. The reasons for the differences are multifaceted; here it suffices to say that this is another indication of the fact that the Nordic legal tradition is not as coherent as some textbooks on comparative law tend to claim.[54]

If one considers the amount of translations or summaries offered by the different Member States (ranging from many thousands to none), a picture emerges suggesting that Member States that support and/or finance translation are generally of three kinds:

[53] ACIHL was established in 2000 by a group of human right activists and legal experts from Arabic countries. The Center specializes in the training, studies, research, translation, documentation, and education of International Humanitarian Law and Human Rights (https://www.acihl.org/home.htm).

[54] See, similarly, Anne Lise Kjær, 'European Legal Concepts in Scandinavian Law and Language', *Nordic Journal of International Law*, 80/3 (2011), 321–49.

1. Member States that support the general idea of judicial supervision of the protection of individuals' constitutional rights (e.g. Germany).
2. Member States with more than one official language, namely states accustomed to multilingualism within the confines of the nation state (e.g. Spain).[55]
3. Member States that are forced by the international community to improve their human rights protection and/or are eager to achieve acknowledgement by the international community and the European Union (e.g. Turkey, Russia, Ukraine).

The 'Bringing the Convention Closer to Home' project formally ended in 2016. In its 2016 Annual Report, the Court estimated that the total funding of the project amounted to EUR 1.6 million, with the HRTF contributing a significant EUR 1,340,000. The Court once again stressed the need for Member States to take on more responsibility to translate its case law into non-official languages, at the same time referring to the budgetary constraints on the Court:

> The translations which the Court commissioned over the duration of this project filled a significant gap. It is clear however that its ordinary budget has never been intended to—nor can it be expected to—sustain the cost of translating, on a more permanent basis, its leading cases into 'non-official' languages. As the Council of Europe member States concluded already at the very first Conference on the future of the Court (at Interlaken), it is first and foremost the responsibility of the State Parties to guarantee the application and implementation of the Convention.[56]

With minor translation projects continuing in 2017 and 2018, and existing translations being added by NGOs and various national sources, the resulting number of translations made available in the HUDOC database is over 26,400 texts in thirty-one languages other than English and French (2018 Report).[57] This amount of generally available judgments has been achieved mostly as a result of the Court's active participation. Thus, in the 2018 Report, the Court summarizes the success of the translation programme by stressing the role that the Court (the Registry) has played, while at the same time reminding the Member States of their responsibility for ensuring the accessibility of translations of its case law:

[55] In the case of Switzerland, Belgium, and Finland, which are also multilingual nation states with more than one official language, translations into all their official languages are ensured because the languages in question are also official languages of other CoE Member States (Italian, French, and German; French and Flemish; Swedish and Finnish).

[56] The European Court of Human Rights, *'Bringing the Convention Closer to Home'. The Court's Case-law Translations Project (2012–2016): Achievements and Remaining Challenges*, February 2017, 3.

[57] The European Court of Human Rights, *Bringing the Convention Home: Case-law Information, Training and Outreach*, January 2019, 6.

> The Registry continued its efforts to improve the accessibility and understanding of the main Convention principles and standards in those member States where neither of the Court's official languages is sufficiently understood. The translations programme has been an important catalyst for setting up a network of partners, ensuring the translation of cases and publications into the non-official languages.
>
> The Registry maintains a standing invitation to States, judicial training centres, associations of legal professionals, non-governmental organisations (NGOs) and other partners to offer, for inclusion in HUDOC, any case-law translations to which they have the rights. The Registry has also launched various case-law translation and dissemination projects that have been funded by means of voluntary contributions from the member States and, in some cases, by the European Union. These will make it possible to significantly increase the volume of material available in Armenian, Ukrainian and Arabic. It should be noted that the 2015 Brussels Declaration called upon States Parties to promote accessibility to the Court's case-law by translating or summarising significant judgments as required, and that improved knowledge of the Convention is key to ensuring that the principle of subsidiarity is fully effective. The Registry also references, on the Court's website, third-party sites hosting translations of the Court's case-law, and welcomes suggestions for the inclusion of further sites.[58]

10.4.2. Other multilingual initiatives

Another aspect of the Court's attempt at making its case law accessible in non-official languages is the introduction of the multilingal user interface of the HUDOC database. Since December 2018 HUDOC's interface has existed in six languages, English, French, Georgian, Russian, Spanish, and Turkish.

A Turkish interface was launched in November 2013; the Russian HUDOC interface was introduced in April 2014, following the success of the Turkish version. Then, in the context of the 40th anniversary of Spain's accession to the Council of Europe in November 2017, a Spanish version of the HUDOC interface was launched. Finally, in the context of the twentieth anniversary of the HUDOC database, the Georgian user interface was launched on 20 December 2018.[59]

In October 2015 the Court launched a multilingual Twitter account (ECHRPublication) reserved for news on case-law publications, translations, and

[58] *Bringing the Convention Home: Case-law Information, Training and Outreach*, January 2019, 6.

[59] Press Release ECHR 444 (2018) of 20 December 2018, issued by the Registry of the Court.

the HUDOC case-law database.[60] Such use of a social media platform for information purposes is a clear indication of the Court's need to legitimate itself in the eyes of the European public in the hope, perhaps, of circumventing the reluctant Member States' governments. Ironically, this reflects the vision of the Founding Fathers: as stated above, the European Movement considered public opinion to be the key to ensuring Member States' compliance with the European Convention on Human Rights:

> Governments will be reluctant to be regarded as violators of their people's liberties and will usually prefer to comply with the judgments of the Court, even if they do not always agree with them, rather than face the loss of popularity and electoral support which refusal would probably involve.[61]

The role that public opinion plays in the legitimation of international courts and the courts attempt at reaching out to the general public through social media has garnered increasing attention in IL/IR scholarship in recent years,[62] but is not further investigated here.

10.5. Translation as legitimation

In this chapter I have shown how translation has played a significant role in the struggle between the European Court of Human Rights and the Member States in the past decade. In the course of the reform process of the European Court of Human Rights, language and the need to translate the Court's case law into the national languages of the Member States were added to the agenda. The chronological survey of the reform documents clearly shows that access to the Court's judgments in non-official languages was increasingly the object of contestation between the Member States and the Court. The Court repeatedly emphasized that translation of judgments must be the responsibility of the Member States while stressing that the Court has got neither the personal nor the economic resources to take on the task of translation itself. However, with the dwindling acceptance of the Court's authority among some Member States, the Court's legitimacy was challenged, and the Court ended up initiating a translation programme anyway with the purpose of 'Bringing the Convention Closer to Home', thus rhetorically framing the translation task as

[60] Press Release, ECHR 297 (2015) of 5 October 2015, issued by the Registrar of the Court.

[61] See the *Travaux preparatoires* of Art. 53 and 54 referenced in section 10.2.2.

[62] See, among other sources, Erik Voeten, 'Public Opinion and the Legitimacy of International Courts', *Theoretical Inquiries in Law*, 14/2 (2013), 411–36; and Daniel Joyce, 'Media Witness: Human Rights in an Age of Digital Media', *Intercultural Human Rights Law Review*, 8 (2013), 231–80.

a matter of national identity.[63] The reform story of the Court therefore underlines what has often been highlighted in theories of language policy in international organizations: that language is and always has been a political, rather than a legal issue.[64]

The multilingual regime of the European Union was differently conceived from that of the human rights system. Right from the beginning, the EU broke with the norm established in international law, namely to use widely applied *lingua francas* as official languages in treaties and judgments of international courts.[65] Instead, the founders of the Union decided to strike a balance between the interests of small and big Member States and in the Council's very first regulation[66] designated languages of all Member States as official EU languages. The EU language regime cannot be assessed solely from the perspective of law: legal certainty, protection of legitimate expectations, and non-discrimination on the basis of language. Both in scholarly literature on the language regime of the EU and in case law of the CJEU, such legal concerns are often mentioned as the reason why citizens in all member states should have access to EU legislation in their own language.[67] However, if the accessibility of EU law in an individual's own language were merely a matter of legal certainty and the protection of legitimate expectations, individuals in the respective Member States should have been allowed to base their interpretation of EU law on their own language version; however, this is not the case. The rule is that all language versions must be respected, and a proper interpretation of EU legislation must, therefore, consider all language versions, so as to ensure uniform interpretation throughout the EU—so the mantra goes.[68]

In the human rights system, language policy and translation were not on the agenda from the outset. However, after the legitimacy crisis, given voice in the Declarations of the Interlaken process, translation became a topic of interest,

[63] For a substantiation of this claim, see the analysis of the language of national identity in Danish legal and media discourse on the impact of European Human Rights in the national legal systems in Anne Lise Kjær and Lene Palsbro, 'National Identity and Law in the Context of European Integration: the Case of Denmark', *Discourse & Society*, 19/5 (2008), 599–627.

[64] See, for example, Peter Krauss and François Grin, eds., *The Politics of Multilingualism, Europeanisation, Globalisation and Linguistic Governance* (Amsterdam, 2018).

[65] For a thorough discussion of the history of multilingualism, see Janny H.C. Leung. *Shallow Equality and Symbolic Jurisprudence in Multilingual Legal Orders* (Oxford, 2019).

[66] EEC Council: Regulation No 1 determining the languages to be used by the European Economic Community, OJ 17, 6 October 1958, 385–86.

[67] For a discussion and further references, see, for example, Cornelis Jaap W. Baaij, *Legal Integration and Language Diversity. Rethinking Translation in EU Lawmaking* (Oxford, 2018).

[68] See, for example, paragraphs 17–20 of the CILFIT Judgment: *Srl CILFIT v. Ministry of Health* (1982), Case 283/81 on the possibility of *acte clair* in EU law. For a scholarly discussion, see Theodor Schilling, 'Beyond Multilingualism: On Different Approaches to the Handling of Diverging Language Versions of a Community Law', *European Law Journal*, 16/1 (January 2010), 47–66.

discursively constructed as the need to educate State actors on the guiding principles of human rights law, to disseminate knowledge about the European standards of human rights protection, and to ensure proper implementation of ECHR case law: 'Easy access to good quality translations of the case-law of the European Court of Human Rights is essential for the effective implementation of the Convention at national level.' This was highlighted in the Committee of Ministers' Recommendation (2002) before the initiation of the Translation Programme in 2010 and quoted again sixteen years later in the welcoming remarks by Christophe Poirel[69] at the Roundtable on Translation and Dissemination held at the Council of Europe on 17 October 2018.[70]

Along with the principles of subsidiarity and the margin of appreciation, case law translation and dissemination have been presented as effective and adequate tools to ensure the long-term efficiency of the Court. But it is worth highlighting that there are two divergent (but not necessarily competing) rationalities behind the call for translation.

First, there is the idea that translation is necessary due to lack of foreign language skills in some Member States. By helping those Member States, where neither of the Court's official languages is sufficiently understood, obtain access to the Court's case law in their own language, the Court ensures that the main Convention principles and standards are properly understood, thus avoiding potential infringements of the Convention.

Second, there is the idea that, when promoting accessibility to the Court's case-law in the languages of the Member States, the Convention is 'brought home' and thus becomes integrated into national law and legal culture, which by some is considered key to ensuring that the principle of subsidiarity becomes fully effective.

The first argument is based on a purely instrumental notion of what language is, whereas the second argument views language as an integral part of national culture. While the arguments are not mutually exclusive, the second argument goes hand in hand with a nationalist outlook on human rights law. In that sense, translation has become a matter of debate and controversy between supporters and opponents of the European level of human rights protection.

However, the positions in the debate are not as clear as might be assumed. Thus, on one hand the Russian Ministry of Justice at its own cost and acting on its own initiative translates all ECHR judgments against Russia and landmark judgments against other countries; on the other hand, Denmark, despite being one of the original signatory states, issued a draft of the Copenhagen Declaration in which no mention of translation is made, despite being the most nationalist, pro-subsidiarity

[69] Director of Human Rights, Directorate General Human Rights and Rule of Law.

[70] Round Table: *Implementation of the ECHR in the Domestic Legal Systems: Experience in the Translation and Dissemination of the Judgments of the European Court in a Comparative Perspective.*

declaration formulated in the history of European human rights protection. This is notable because an expectation could be that access to the Convention in one's own language would be high on the agenda among politicians sceptical of the Europeanization of human rights protection. The most likely explanation for Denmark not acknowledging the translation task is that the Danish government is of the impression that Danish lawyers, judges, and other relevant actors are sufficiently competent in the official languages of the Court for them to apply the Court's case law when relevant.[71]

10.6. Conclusion

As I have argued for in this chapter, multilingualism in international organizations is much more than a question of law and legal culture. In fact, the choice of language policy and considerations regarding translations into the national languages of the Member States of international organizations are indicators of the institutional balance that exists at any given time in the history of the institution and of broader socio-political trends. In times when the authority of international institutions is challenged by their constituencies, one way of meeting the challenge is to provide measures that ensure accessibility and dissemination, and acknowledge differences and diversity. In this light, translation strategies must be understood as much more than the legal-linguistic tools that one as a translator can choose to transfer the meaning of legal concepts belonging to one legal system to the language and conceptual world of another legal system. Translation strategies are also a matter of answering questions as to when to translate, what to translate, and under what circumstances.

References

Primary sources

JUDGMENTS

Scordino v. Italy (no. 1) [GC], App no 36813/97, 29 March 2006.

Srl CILFIT v. Ministry of Health [1982], ECLI:EU:C:1982:335.

RULES

EEC Council: Regulation No 1 determining the languages to be used by the European Economic Community, Official Journal 17, 6 October 1958.

[71] As shown in Anne Lise Kjær, 'European Legal Concepts in Scandinavian Law and Language', *Nordic Journal of International Law*, 80/3 (2011), 321–49, this is not always the case.

Protocol No. 15 amending the Convention on the Protection of Human Rights and Fundamental Freedoms, Strasbourg, 24 June 2013.
Rules of Procedure of the Court, 18 October 2021 (latest edition).
The Convention for the Protection of Human Rights and Fundamental Freedoms (the European Convention on Human Rights), No. 005, opened for signature in Rome on 4 November 1950 and entered into force on 3 September 1953.

REPORTS AND RESOLUTIONS

Audit (2004) 08: Audit Report on The Court's Workload and the Necessary Budgetary Resources 2004–2007.
CM(2000)172-Part. I: European Ministerial Conference on Human Rights (Rome, 3–4 November 2000), Report of the Secretary General.
CM/Rec(2002)13: Recommendation of the Committee of Ministers to member states on the publication and dissemination in the member states of the text of the European Convention on Human Rights and the case-law of the European Court of Human Rights (adopted by the Committee of Ministers on 18 December 2002 at its 822nd Session).
CM/Res(2002)58: Resolution of the Committee of Ministers on the publication and dissemination of the case-law of the European Court of Human Rights (adopted by the Committee of Ministers on 18 December 2002 at the 822nd meeting of the Ministers' Deputies).
CM(2006)203, Report of the Group of Wise Persons to the Committee of Ministers, 15 November 2006.
Contribution of the Court to the Brussels Conference, 26 January 2015.
European Ministerial Conference on Human Rights and Commemorative Ceremony of the 50th anniversary of the European Convention on Human Rights, Rome, 3–4 November 2000.
High Level Conference on the Future of the European Court of Human Rights, 19 February 2010, Interlaken Declaration.
High Level Conference on the Future of the European Court of Human Rights, 26–27 April 2011, Izmir Declaration
High-Level Conference on the Future of the European Court of Human Rights, on 19 and 20 April 2012, Brighton Declaration.
High-Level Conference on the 'Implementation of the European Convention on Human Rights, our shared responsibility', 26–27 March 2015, Brussels Declaration.
High-Level Conference, 12 and 13 April 2018, Copenhagen Declaration.
Introductory report of Mr Walter Schwimmer, Secretary General of the Council of Europe. Council of Europe, June 2002.
Joint NGO Response to the Draft Copenhagen Declaration, 13 February 2018.
Memorandum of 3 July 2009 of the President of the European Court of Human Rights to the States with a View to Preparing the Interlaken Conference.
Opinion of the Court on the Wise Persons' Report, as adopted by the Plenary Court on 2 April 2007.
Opinion on the draft Copenhagen Declaration, adopted by the Bureau in light of the discussion in the Plenary Court on 19 February 2018.
NGO Comments on the Group of Wise Persons' Interim Report, July 2006, Amnesty International Index Number: IOR 61/019/2006.
Preliminary opinion of the Court in preparation for the Brighton Conference, adopted by the Plenary Court on 20 February 2012.
Preparatory work on Articles 53 and 54 of The European Convention on Human Rights: Information Document prepared by the Registry of the European Court of Human Rights, 28 November 1972.
The Right Honourable The Lord Woolf, Michael McKenzie CB QC, Peter MacMahon, Dr Colm O'Cinneide, and Laura Clarke, *Review of the Working Methods of the European Court of Human Rights*, December 2005.

The European Court of Human Rights, *'Bringing the Convention Closer to Home'. The Court's Case-law Translations Project (2012–2016): Achievements and Remaining Challenges,* February 2017.
The European Court of Human Rights, *Bringing the Convention Home. Case-law Information, Training and Outreach,* January 2019.

PRESS RELEASES

Press release ECHR 982 (2009) of 21 December 2009, issued by the Registrar of the Court.
Press release ECHR 288 (2012) of 6 July 2012, issued by the Registrar of the Court.
Press Release ECHR 444 (2018) of 20 December 2018, issued by the Registry of the Court.
Press Release, ECHR 297 (2015) of 5 October 2015, issued by the Registrar of the Court.

Secondary sources

Baaij, Cornelis Jaap W., *Legal Integration and Language Diversity. Rethinking Translation in EU Lawmasking* (Oxford, 2018).
Brandeis Institute for International Judges, 'Language and International Courts', *International Justice: Past, Precence and Future.* (2009), 19–25.
Dothan, Shai, 'How International Courts Enhance Their Legitimacy', *Theoretical Inquiries in Law,* 14/2 (2013), 455–78.
Dörr, Oliver, 'European Convention on Human Rights', in Stephanie Schmal and Martin Breuer, eds., *The Council of Europe: its Laws and Policies* (Oxford, 2017), 465–506.
Engel, N. P., 'Translation and Dissemination of the Strasbourg Case-Law; The German Language Experience', speech held at the Round Table: *Implementation of the ECHR in the Domestic Legal Systems: Experience in the Translation and Dissemination of the Judgments of the European Court in a Comparative Perspective,* 15 October 2018.
Follesdal, Andreas and Geir Ulfstein, 'The Draft Copenhagen Declaration: Whose Responsibility and Dialogue?', *EJIL Talk!* (22 February 2018).
Harmsen, Robert, 'The Reform of the Convention System: Institutional Restructuring and the (Geo-)Politics of Human Rights', in Jonas Christoffersen and Mikael Rask Madsen, eds., *The European Court of Human Rights between Law and Politics* (Oxford, 2011), 119–43.
Joyce, Daniel, 'Media Witness: Human Rights in an Age of Digital Media', *Intercultural Human Rights Law Review,* 8 (2013), 231–80.
Kjær, Anne Lise, 'European Legal Concepts in Scandinavian Law and Language', *Nordic Journal of International Law,* 80/3 (2011), 321–49.
Kjær, Anne Lise, and Lene Palsbro, 'National Identity and Law in the Context of European Integration: the Case of Denmark', *Discourse & Society,* 19/5 (2008), 599–627.
Kovpak, Stanislav, Speech held at the Round Table: *Implementation of the ECHR in the Domestic Legal Systems: Experience in the Translation and Dissemination of the Judgments of the European Court in a Comparative Perspective,* 15 October 2018.
Krauss, Peter and François Grin, eds., *The Politics of Multilingualism, Europeanisation, Globalisation and Linguistic Governance* (Amsterdam, 2018).
Leung, Janny H. C., *Shallow Equality and Symbolic Jurisprudence in Multilingual Legal Orders* (Oxford, 2019).
Madsen, Mikael Rask, 'The Challenging Authority of the European Court of Human Rights: From Cold War Legal Diplomacy to the Brighton Declaration and Backlash', *Law & Contemporary Problems,* 79 (2016), 141–78.
Madsen, Mikael Rask, Paula Cebulak, and Micha Wiebusch, 'Backlash against International Courts: Explaining the Forms and Patterns of Resistance to International Courts', *International Journal of Law in Context,* 14 (2018), 197–220.
Mahoney, Paul, 'New Challenges for the European Court of Human Rights Resulting from the Expanding Case Load and Membership', *Penn State International Law Review,* 21/1 (2002), 101–14.

Mowbray, Alastair, 'Crisis Measures of Institutional Reform for the European Court of Human Rights', *Human Rights Law Review*, 9/4 (2009), 647–56.

Poirel, Christophe, 'Access to the Translated Court's Case-Law as an Essential Element for Successful Implementation of the ECHR at the National Level', welcoming remarks at the Round Table: *Implementation of the ECHR in the Domestic Legal Systems: Experience in the Translation and Dissemination of the Judgments of the European Court in a Comparative Perspective*, 15 October 2018.

Schilling, Theodor, 'Beyond Multilingualism: On Different Approaches to the Handling of Diverging Language Versions of a Community Law', *European Law Journal*, 16/1 (January 2010), 47–66.

Stiansen, Øyvind and Erik Voeten, 'Backlash and Judicial Restraint: Evidence from the European Court of Human Rights' 17 August2018. Available at: https://ssrn.com/abstract=3166110.

Voeten, Erik, 'Public Opinion and the Legitimacy of International Courts', *Theoretical Inquiries in Law*, 14/2 (2013), 411–36.

PART III

INTERPRETATION IN SPECIAL AREAS OF INTERNATIONAL LAW

1. Trade, Investment and Commercial Law

11

Fundamental values being introduced into the treaty interpretation process under the WTO beyond semantic finding of conveyed meaning

CHANG-FA LO

11.1. Introduction

This chapter will argue that treaty interpretation, similar to other legal interpretation, is not merely a semantic finding of the meaning supposedly conveyed by the interpreted term in a treaty. Treaty interpretation should go beyond the semantic analysis (i.e. the analysis of linguistic and logical meaning) of an interpreted term. When encountering the selection of different ordinary meanings, different contexts, and different objects-and-purposes, a treaty interpreter will have to consider certain fundamental values to help conduct his/her interpretation. Appropriate application of various methods of treaty interpretation are the way to help consider these values.

As a general principle, treaty interpretation is an essential element in the operation of a treaty. It ensures that a treaty will properly work and its parties will faithfully perform their treaty obligations. Like other legal interpretation (i.e. the interpretation of a law or regulation), the process of treaty interpretation must be of high extent of objectiveness and the outcome must be of high level of predictability.

Although there are various treaty interpretation methods to help achieve the highest objectiveness and predictability, the achievement is not a one hundred per cent guarantee. This is because treaty interpretation is not a mechanical procedure to include inputs, processes, and outputs so as to produce a mechanically consistent and standardized result.

A treaty interpreter always faces the need to evaluate certain elements and select certain approaches to discharge his/her duties. He or she constantly has to compare different ordinary meanings, to decide the scope of context for the interpreted

Chang-fa Lo, *Fundamental values being introduced into the treaty interpretation process under the WTO beyond semantic finding of conveyed meaning* In: *Language and Legal Interpretation in International Law*. Edited by: Anne Lise Kjær and Joanna Lam, Oxford University Press. DOI: 10.1093/oso/9780190855208.003.0012 provision, and to consider the reliance on the object-and-purpose of the interpreted treaty. Since a treaty interpreter will have to make decisions in the selection of the 'most appropriate ordinary meaning' of a treaty term, the 'most relevant context' of it, and the 'most appropriate object-and-purpose' of the interpreted treaty, the values or positions regarding the subject matter held by the interpreter will definitely play a key role in the process.

From this perspective, treaty interpretation is not merely a linguistic issue. It goes beyond the semiotic finding of a meaning conveyed by the text. It is apparently unavoidable to introduce certain values into the process. Hence it is of high importance to ensure that the introduction of certain basic human values into the process of treaty interpretation will be made in a consistent, systematic, and transparent manner so that the result of treaty interpretation will still be in conformity with the requirements of objectiveness and predictability.

The agreements under the World Trade Organization (WTO) form the most comprehensive set of rules addressing various aspects of trade issues. Some basic human values are either included in the relevant agreements or affecting some of these agreements. Hence, the WTO agreements are a good source for finding certain basic human values embedded in or relevant to these agreements. These values can be introduced into the process of treaty interpretation in an objective and predictable way.

In the following discussions, the basic/fundamental human values are categorized into internal/external values and domestic/universal values to help conceptualize the issues. The ways of introducing these values through treaty interpretation are also suggested in connection with the relevant values.

11.2. Examples of human values and the methods of treaty interpretation to introduce such values

11.2.1. The overall scope of fundamental human values

There are various values that the people across the human society or the people in a specific society firmly believe. Nevertheless, not all of the values have the same role to play in treaty interpretation. For instance, pluralism could be an important value of a specific group of people in their culture, their society, and their political beliefs. However, the value of pluralism is not a factor that can be introduced to help interpret a trade agreement.

A value must be a deeply held belief and the highest priority of the international society so that it can be considered as a fundamental universal value to be introduced into the process of treaty interpretation. A value must also be a profoundly held belief and the highest priority of a domestic society in order to be considered as a fundamental domestic/local value affecting treaty interpretation.

No matter whether values are universal or domestic, legal systems at the local and international levels will have to be operated in a way to respect and support them.

Examples of inherent fundamental values include the protection of human life and health and the respect of the human dignity. Examples of fundamental human values, which are recognized and protected by various international human rights treaties, include the right to self-determination, to liberty, to due process of law, to freedom of movement, to freedom of thought, to freedom of religion, to freedom of expression, to peaceable assembly, and to freedom of association. These rights are specified in the International Covenant on Civil and Political Rights and the International Covenant on Economic, Social, and Cultural Rights. These human rights are the core human values that should be respected both in the context of the relevant human rights treaties, and in the context of other treaties (such as the WTO agreements).

11.2.2. The dichotomy of internal and external values and the ways of introducing the values into a treaty's operation

Here I use the terms 'internal values' and 'external values' to refer to the distinction between the values which are explicitly provided in a relevant treaty and those which are not explicitly incorporated in the relevant treaty but are relevant to the interpretation of such treaty.

The WTO is a very good example to show that some fundamental values were seriously considered during the negotiations and were incorporated into the texts of various trade agreements. The following are the examples of such internal values.

Under the General Agreement on Tariffs and Trade (GATT), WTO Members are required not to adopt measures to discriminate goods from other WTO Members, not to impose tariffs that exceed the bound rates, and not to impose quantitative restrictions on imported and exported products. However, GATT has a number of exceptions to such general principles. One of the exceptions is provided in GATT Article XX(b), which states that a measure which is necessary to protect human life and health can be adopted even it violates other GATT obligations. Article XIV(b) of the General Agreement on Trade in Services (GATS) has a similar provision. These exceptions are in line with the idea of human life being the highest value of human beings. Human health is also one of the core human values of highest importance. The Constitution of the World Health Organization (WHO) states very clearly in its Preamble and in Article 1 that '[t]he enjoyment of the highest attainable standard of health is one of the fundamental rights of every human being' and that the objective of the WHO shall be 'the attainment by all peoples of the highest possible level of health'. Since human life and health are the important basis to exempt the specified measures from the GATT and GATS general obligations, they are actually given priority over trade obligations. GATT Article XX and GATS Article

XIV show that trade rules should pay the high respect to the fundamental values of human life and health protection.

The Appellate Body of the WTO also specifically recognizes in its report on *European Communities—Measures Affecting Asbestos and Asbestos-Containing Products* (*EC—Asbestos*) that human life and health is vital and is of the highest importance,

> the objective pursued by the measure is the preservation of human life and health through the elimination, or reduction, of the well-known, and life-threatening, health risks posed by asbestos fibres. The value pursued is both vital and important in the highest degree.[1]

The texts of GATT Article XX(b) and GATS XIV(b) have already introduced the value of protecting human life and health into the operation of these trade agreements. The Appellate Body emphasizes these values and the justification of such protection by relying on the 'ordinary meaning' of the terms as required by Article 31.1 of the Vienna Convention on the Law of Treaties (VCLT), which reads: 'A treaty shall be interpreted in good faith in accordance with the ordinary meaning to be given to the terms of the treaty in their context and in the light of its object and purpose.'

Another example is in GATT Article XX(a), which provides that the measures necessary to protect public morals are exempt from other GATT obligations. GATS Article XIV(a) also provides that measures necessary to protect public morals or to maintain public order are exempt from other GATS obligations. Hence, public morals and public order are clearly given priority over trade obligations.

The WTO dispute settlement Panel explains the meaning of public morals and public order in its report on *United States—Measures Affecting the Cross-Border Supply of Gambling and Betting Services*[2] (hereafter, *US—Gambling*): 'the term "public morals" denotes *standards of right and wrong* conduct maintained by or on behalf of a community or nation'[3]. According to the Panel, the dictionary definition of the word 'order', read together with GATS footnote 5,[4] suggests that '"public order" refers to the preservation of the fundamental interests of a society, as reflected in public policy and law'. The Panel noted that '[t]hese fundamental interests can relate, *inter alia*, to standards of law, security and morality.'[5]

[1] Appellate Body Report on *EC—Asbestos*, para. 172; emphasis added.

[2] Appellate Body Report, WT/DS285/AB/R (April 7, 2005); Panel Report, WT/DS285/R (November 10, 2004)

[3] Panel Report, WT/DS285/R, para. 6.464; emphasis added.

[4] 'The public order exception may be invoked only where a genuine and sufficiently serious threat is posed to one of the fundamental interests of society.'

[5] Panel Report, WT/DS285/R, para. 6.467; emphasis added.

The texts of GATT Article XX(a) and GATS XIV(b) have already introduced the value of protecting public morals and public order into the operation of these trade agreements. The Panel emphasizes these values and the justification of such protection by relying on the 'ordinary meaning' of the terms (reflected in dictionary) as required by Article 31.1 of the VCLT.

Yet another example is about the protection of exhaustible natural resources/ endangered species. GATT Article XX(g) provides that measures 'relating to the conservation of exhaustible natural resources' (if they are made effective in conjunction with restrictions on domestic production or consumption) are exempt from other GATT obligations. The protection of biodiversity and the preservation of endangered species are very important values not only for specific jurisdictions, but also for the international community.[6] Appropriate efforts can help such protection. Measures recognized by the GATT Article XX(g) can contribute to the protection of endangered species and preservation of biodiversity and enhance such human values. The text of GATT Article XX(g) has already introduced the value of protecting exhaustible natural resources into the operation of this trade agreement.

The protection of sustainability is an example of an internal value under the WTO. 'Sustainable development' is specifically emphasized in the preamble of the Agreement Establishing the WTO: 'their relations [i.e. the relations of the Parties] in the field of trade and economic endeavour should be conducted with a view to . . . expanding the production of and trade in goods and services, while allowing for the optimal use of the world's resources in accordance with the objective of sustainable development'.

Sustainable development means a constrained use of limited resources so that the world's poor and the future generations will be able to meet their needs.[7] The concept of sustainable development is widely recognized as a very important principle to governing economic development and related activities. The protection of sustainability has not achieved the status of an international law principle. However, since it has been explicitly provided in the Agreement Establishing the WTO, it can be considered as a built-in value of the international trade rules and as an important objective of the WTO. The value of protecting sustainability provided in the preamble of this agreement can be introduced into the interpretation of other WTO agreements as an object-and-purpose of the interpreted treaty, or as a context of the interpreted term.

Public health is different from human health in that the former concerns the health of the overall population of a society by preventing diseases, promoting health and prolonging life, whereas the letter concerns the health of individuals (or

[6] http://www.davidsuzuki.org/issues/wildlife-habitat/science/endangered-species-legislation/protecting-biodiversity/.

[7] World Commission on Environment and Development (WCED), *Our Common Future* (1987), 43.

patients).[8] Public health is of pivotal importance in all society. International treaties should also respect its protection. Public health is explicitly incorporated into the text of the Agreement on Trade-Related Aspects of Intellectual Property Rights (TRIPS Agreement). Article 8.1 of the TRIPS Agreement states, 'Members may, in formulating or amending their laws and regulations, adopt measures necessary to protect public health and nutrition . . . , provided that such measures are consistent with the provisions of this Agreement.'

From the perspective that public health is explicitly provided in the text, it is an internal value of the TRIPS Agreement. On the other hand, from the perspective of other WTO agreements, public health is not a built-in value. Nevertheless, it should still be considered an external value due to the high importance of its protection. For other WTO agreements, public health can be introduced into their operation through treaty interpretation methods (such as through identifying the ordinary meaning of certain terms).

There are other values which are not included in the texts of WTO agreements but are relevant to the operation of the WTO. These values can be called 'external values'. The key examples are as follows.

First, the protection of the overall human rights. Human rights and fundamental freedoms are supposed to be respected, promoted, and fulfilled by all states. It would be wrong if the interpretation and application of a WTO provision will result in human rights being infringed or the dignity of the people being disrespected. A very important way of protecting human rights under the WTO is to interpret the textual meaning (i.e. the ordinary meaning) of the term 'public morals' provided in the GATT and in the GATS to include the respect of human rights.

Second, the protection of core labour standards. Core labour standards can be considered the important parts of human rights. However, they can also be treated as a separate group of human values. These standards include the freedom of association (as provided in Conventions 87 and 98), the effective recognition of the right to collective bargaining (as provided in Conventions 87 and 98), the elimination of all forms of forced and compulsory labour (as provided in Conventions 29 and 105), the effective abolition of child labour (as provided in Conventions 138 and 182), and the elimination of discrimination in respect of employment and occupation (as provided in Conventions 100 and 111).[9] Although these minimum standards are not mentioned in the WTO agreements, they also have similar human rights natures and should be considered so important as to be universally accepted. The core labour standards can also be introduced into the GATT and the GATS through interpreting the textual meaning (i.e. the ordinary meaning) of the term

[8] http://www.who.int/trade/glossary/story076/en/.

[9] http://www.cleanclothes.org/issues/faq/ilo.

'public morals' provided in these agreements to include the need of protection of core labour standards.

Third, the protection of minimum animal welfare. The protection of the well-being and the requirement of proper treatment of animals in laboratories, companion animals, farm animals, marine life, and wildlife has been a very important issue at international and regional levels. Animals do not enjoy the same level of protection of fundamental rights as human beings. However, it is still the best of human nature to treat animals in a humane way. The WTO does not explicitly recognize the protection of animal welfare as a fundamental value. However, it is possible that animal welfare can be introduced into the GATT and the GATS through interpreting the textual meaning of the term 'public morals' provided in these agreements to include the protection of animal welfare. This will be further explained below.

11.2.3. The dichotomy of domestic and universal values and the ways of introducing the values into a treaty's operation

Another categorization is the distinction between the domestic/local and universal vales. The need of introducing human values into the operation of a treaty does not limit to the universal values. Even if a value is purely a domestic one, a treaty interpreter should still respect it through relying on certain treaty interpretation methods. The following are the salient examples of domestic values.

First, the protection of public morals and public order is domestic/local value: public morals and public order are important values. However, their content can be understood only in a domestic context. For example, some countries might consider gambling as a lawful activity, whereas other countries could consider gambling as a serious criminal and immoral activity. Hence, although the idea of protecting public morals and maintaining public order is widely recognized (including being recognized in the WTO agreements), the content of public morals and public order is of local nature and does not have to be universally accepted. Such important value has been built into the GATT and the GATS. A treaty interpreter only has to rely on the methods of textual interpretation to ensure the respect of such value.

Second, the protection of animal welfare is also a domestic value. A set of universally accepted standards for treating animals is yet to be developed. However, regionally, there has been Article 13 of the Treaty on the Functioning of the European Union (TFEU), which provides as follows:

> In formulating and implementing the Union's agriculture, fisheries, transport, internal market, research and technological development and space policies, the Union and the Member States shall, since animals are sentient beings, pay full regard to the welfare requirements of animals, while respecting the legislative or administrative provisions and customs of the

> Member States relating in particular to religious rites, cultural traditions and regional heritage.

Hence, for the regional community of the European Union, the protection of animal welfare has become an important value. It is put 'on equal footing with other key principles mentioned in the same title i.e. promote gender equality, guarantee social protection, protect human health, combat discrimination, promote sustainable development, ensure consumer protection, protect personal data' provided in Title II of the TFEU.[10] Such regional value needs to be respected by other countries and international regimes. One way of respecting such value is also through textual interpretation of the ordinary meaning of 'public moral' provided in the GATT and the GATS.

As opposed to domestic values, there are other fundamental values, which are universal and should not be limited to meet an individual country's situation. For instance, human rights and the minimum labour standards are universally accepted as reflected in many treaties. Countries are not supposed to deviate from these standards based on different stages of economic development, different cultural backgrounds, and different social structures. Since they are universal values, they should be respected by all countries. Hence, these values should also be considered as forming the domestic values of 'all jurisdictions'. In this sense, such values can be introduced into the operation of an interpreted treaty (such as the GATT) through various treaty interpretation methods (such as through interpreting the ordinary meaning of the textual wording 'public morals' in GATT Article XX to include the protection of human rights).

11.3. A systemic reliance on the 'internal values' through treaty interpretation methods

Treaty interpretation is guided mainly by Articles 31 and 32 of the above-mentioned VCLT. As quoted above, Article 31.1 requires a treaty to 'be interpreted in good faith in accordance with the ordinary meaning to be given to the terms of the treaty in their context and in the light of its object and purpose'. Article 31.2 provides as follows:

> The context for the purpose of the interpretation of a treaty shall comprise, in addition to the text, including its preamble and annexes: (a) Any agreement relating to the treaty which was made between all the parties in connexion with the conclusion of the treaty; (b) Any instrument which

[10] http://ec.europa.eu/food/animal/welfare/policy/index_en.htm.

> was made by one or more parties in connexion with the conclusion of the treaty and accepted by the other parties as an instrument related to the treaty.

Article 31.3 further clarifies the scope of the 'context' and provides in part that '[t]here shall be taken into account, together with the context: . . . (b) any subsequent practice in the application of the treaty which establishes the agreement of the parties regarding its interpretation'.

The above-mentioned 'internal values' of the WTO are incorporated into the text of its agreements. Depending on the way of incorporating the fundamental values into the treaty, the ordinary meanings of public morals, public order, human life and health, exhaustible natural resources, and sustainable development can be properly expended so as to extend their coverages and to strengthen such values. These values can also be considered as the 'context' to help identify the proper meaning of the interpreted term or as the 'object-and-purpose' to guide the interpretation of a term. For example, the terms 'human life and health' are explicitly included in GATT Article XX and GATS Article XIV as exceptions to other obligations in the agreements assumed by WTO Members and as defences to justify the violation of their obligations. These fundamental values should play the roles that they are instructed by the text of the agreements. Sustainability is included in the preamble of the Agreement Establishing the WTO. The preambular provision of sustainable development, for example, can also serve as an 'object-and-purpose' of all WTO agreements or as the context for the interpretation of other WTO provisions. Public health is explicitly listed in TRIPS Article 8.1. Since Article 8 is entitled 'Principles', the provision of public health in this article can serve as the 'object-and-purpose' of whole provisions of the TRIPS Agreement or the 'context' of the TRIPS provisions other than Article 8.1.

11.4. A systemic reliance on 'external values' through treaty interpretation

If an external value (such as the protection of human rights) is so fundamental and of such high importance for a specific society and its people as a whole, or even for the international society, it is desirable that WTO agreements pay proper respect to them. I argue that, whenever it is permitted by treaty interpretation rules, a treaty interpreter should be expected to choose the interpretation the result of which would lead to providing a higher extent of protection for such fundamental value. This is not to transform the WTO into a human rights organization or any other type of organization. This is merely to have the WTO agreements being interpreted and operated in a 'human values'-friendly manner.

For example, suppose there is a lack of protection of human rights in the exporting country and such human rights violation is directly connected to the production of the goods exported to the importing country. And further suppose that the importation and the use of the goods produced in connection with human rights violation would undermine or adversely affect the moral values in the importing country. It should be made possible, through treaty interpretation, for the importing country to adopt trade measures to protect its moral values concerning the protection of human rights.

The interpretative skills to help protect fundamental external values are the flexible and extended use of the traditional treaty interpretation rules, including the textual interpretation of ordinary meaning, the contextual interpretation (including subsequent practice), and the consideration of object-and-purpose.

For example, it is practically possible to rely on the textual interpretation to incorporate an external value of 'public health' into the ordinary meaning of 'public morals' and 'public order' provided in the GATS. The Appellate Body elaborated the concepts of 'public morals' and 'public order' in its Report on *US—Gambling* and considered that they include organized crime, money laundering, risks to children, fraud, and public health risk (such as pathological gambling).[11] Although the public health provision in TRIPS Article 8.1 cannot be applied to the GATS provisions, the Appellate Body was still able to incorporate the public health concern into the scope of the terms 'public morals' and 'public order' through treaty interpretation.

Another example to show an external value (i.e. the value of 'animal welfare') to be introduced into the GATT through textual interpretation of the ordinary meaning of 'public morals' is found in the Panel Report on *European Communities—Measures Prohibiting the Importation and Marketing of Seal Products* (*EC—Seal Products*).[12] In that case, 'the European Union seeks to address the public moral concerns on seal welfare through the EU Seal Regime'. The Panel confirmed that the EU public concerns on seal welfare were 'of a moral nature within the European Union'.[13] It noted that the 'moral concern with regard to the protection of animals' is regarded as 'a value of high importance in the European Union'. The Panel considered, and the parties did not dispute, that 'the protection of such public moral concerns is indeed an important value or interest'.[14]

Based on similar reason, if a country includes the criteria of human rights or minimum labour standards in its Generalized System of Preferences (GSP) to exclude those countries not meeting these criteria from enjoying its GSP treatment, such discriminatory measures against certain developing countries might be justified under the 'public morals' exception of GATT Article XX(a). The importing country

[11] Appellate Body Report on *US—Gambling*, paras. 278–284.

[12] WT/DS400/R and WT/DS401/R; 25 November 2013.

[13] Panel Report on *EC- Seal Products*, para. 7.631.

[14] Ibid., para. 7.632.

might be able to argue that in its society, there are public moral concerns about human rights and core labour standards. Such public concerns fall within the scope of exception under GATT Article XX(a).

Similarly, it is also feasible to incorporate the concept of 'public health' into the GATT through textual interpretation of the ordinary meaning of 'human life and health': For instance, the Framework Convention on Tobacco Control (FCTC) was created to prioritize the protection of public health and to remove the global concern of tobacco epidemic.[15] The measures required or recommended by the FCTC include the strict control of tobacco supply and demand. These measures are mostly trade related. For instance, the tax measures recommended by the FCTC concern internal taxes, which are governed by GATT Article III. The regulations of tobacco contents, tobacco disclosures, packaging, and labelling recommended by the convention concern internal regulations (which are also governed by GATT Article III) and concern technical barriers to trade (TBT) (which are governed by the WTO's Agreement on Technical Barriers to Trade). The regulations on tobacco advertising, promotion, and sponsorship concern internal regulation, which are also governed by GATT Article III. The FCTC is created to protect public health. However, its ultimate purpose is also to protect human life and health. Hence, the tobacco control measures mentioned above should be considered as falling within the scope of exceptions provided in GATT Article XX(b) and TBT Article 2.2.

An example to show the incorporation of an external value (i.e. 'right to health') into the WTO through the consideration of object-and-purpose is in the preambular statement of the Agreement Establishing the WTO. The first sentence of the Preamble already clearly indicates WTO Members' recognition of their relations in the field of trade and economic endeavour to be conducted 'with a view to raising standards of living, ensuring full employment'. The objective of raising livelihoods coincides with the state's responsibility of 'protecting' and 'fulfilling' human rights so as to ensure that health-related resources, including food and medicines, are available, accessible, and affordable to people. Such an objective could be useful in interpreting the fair or legitimate use of certain intellectual property rights provided in the TRIPS Agreement concerning pharmaceutical products.

It is also possible to incorporate the value of 'right to health' into the WTO through subsequent practice. Article 31.3(b) of the VCLT requires treaty interpreter to take into account, together with the context, 'any subsequent practice in the application of the treaty which establishes the agreement of the parties regarding its interpretation'. In this regard, the Appellate Body states in its Report on *Japan—Alcoholic Beverages* that it must be 'a "concordant, common and consistent" sequence of acts or pronouncements which is sufficient to establish a discernible pattern implying the agreement of the parties [to a treaty] regarding its interpretation'.[16] Take the

[15] See the Preamble of the FCTC.

[16] Appellate Body Report on *Japan—Alcoholic Beverages*, para. 107.

FCTC as an example: The membership of the convention largely overlaps with that of the WTO. The FCTC has established a discernible pattern of prioritizing public health for the disputing Members under the WTO if both of them are also parties to the FCTC. This subsequent practice should be useful in interpreting the possible justification of restrictive measures recommended by the FCTC and adopted for the purpose of controlling tobacco supply and use.

11.5. The relations between semantic analysis and treaty interpretation

It must be emphasized that semantic analysis is still important for treaty interpretation. When engaging in treaty interpretation, an interpreter will have to understand the grammatical and logical structure and the linguistic meaning of a provision. This is a very important method of conducting the textual interpretation for the purpose of identifying the ordinary meaning of the interpreted term.

The reason for this chapter to argue that semantic analysis is not sufficient is that when an interpreter encounters the need to introduce either an internal or external value into the interpretation process or the need to select a value to be incorporated into the operation of a treaty, the semantic analysis does not help.

The relations between semantic analysis and treaty interpretation are twofold. The first aspect for the relation is that semantic analysis and treaty interpretation are mutually supportive. When conducting textual interpretation, an interpreter will have to decide the linguistic meaning of an interpreted term through semantic analysis. However, this is only the first step of treaty interpretation. Whether or not to consider certain human values to decide the ordinary meaning of the textual language is not a matter that can be resolved through semantic analysis. Hence, the second relation between semantic analysis and treaty interpretation is that they merely overlap for a limited extent. Treaty interpretation is not merely semantic analysis. It goes beyond the semantic finding of a conveyed meaning.

A semantic analysis cannot replace the finding of an appropriate 'ordinary meaning' for the interpreted textual wording, especially when certain fundamental values are involved. Neither can a semantic analysis be used to conduct contextual interpretation or to serve as a basis for the consideration of the object-and-purpose of a treaty for the purpose of introducing fundamental values into the operation of a treaty.

11.6. Some concluding remarks

I argue here that there are some fundamental human values that need to be protected by individual countries and the international community. The ways of protecting such values are multiple. One way is to impose a treaty obligation on countries to protect such values. Another way is to allow countries to rely on the protection of such values as the basis to exempt their international obligations.

I take the WTO as an example. Some fundamental values have already been explicitly included in the WTO rules; some others are not explicitly included. If they are not explicitly included, a proper way to respect such human values is to incorporate them into the operation of the WTO through treaty interpretation.

The semantic analysis of treaty language is not sufficient for such purpose. Properly relying on the skills of treaty interpretation (such as the proper used of textual and contextual interpretation and the proper consideration of the object-and-purpose of a treaty) is the way to address the issue. Such treaty interpretation skills are also the proper balance between the need of respecting basic human values on the one hand, and the maintenance of objectivity and predictability of treaty interpretation on the other hand.

The ultimate argument here is that an introduction of external values into treaty interpretation generally or specifically with respect to the WTO is necessary and workable. Such an approach can still be objective and predictable. Treaty interpretation should go beyond the semiotic finding of the meaning of a treaty term.

Reference

World Commission on Environment and Development (WCED), *Our Common Future* (Oxford, 1987).

12

Legal interpretation and adjudicatory activism in international commercial arbitration

JOANNA LAM

12.1. Introduction

The issue of the creative aspects of adjudication has traditionally been perceived as one of the key problems of the theory of legal interpretation. Its analysis, usually undertaken in the context of the interpretive activity of domestic judges, has largely been informed by the determinants and performance of the role of the judge in the context of specific national legal systems.

The term 'adjudicatory activism' is used in this chapter to describe cases in which judges and arbitrators arrive at their decisions by reaching beyond the letter of the applicable law—either within the limits of their discretion or by exceeding them. The author shares the semiotic assumption that every process of legal interpretation is a process of meaning making. The chapter aims to explore those cases in which legal interpretation reaches further, leading to an expression, formulation, and consolidation of formerly unspecified rules. As a consequence, the focus is on the creative aspects of legal interpretation in international commercial arbitration, in particular on those which have developed in a way specific to this form of adjudication.

The structure of the paper reflects those considerations. The theoretical part opens with a presentation of Hugues Rabault's classification of theories of legal interpretation, selected due to their orientation regarding the creative aspects of legal interpretation. Their development is discussed in the context of the common law–civil law divide, the decisive character of which is questioned, particularly in the light of the 'statutorification' of common law. The following analysis thus proposes an alternative typology, based on Eskridge, Frickey, and Garret's concept of dynamic theories of legal interpretation, further supplemented by a category of logocentric

Joanna Lam, *Legal interpretation and adjudicatory activism in international commercial arbitration* In: *Language and Legal Interpretation in International Law*. Edited by: Anne Lise Kjær and Joanna Lam, Oxford University Press. DOI: 10.1093/oso/9780190855208.003.0013

theories. The chapter argues for the applicability of dynamic theories in the field of arbitral decision-making in commercial cases. However, because theories of legal interpretation have primarily been formulated in the context of litigation before the domestic courts and judicial decision-making, further analysis requires a highlighting of the differences between it and arbitral adjudication. The specific conditions of exercising legal interpretation in international commercial arbitration are thus discussed in the subsequent part of the chapter.

This presentation of the particularities of the legal and functional setting of arbitration influencing the processes of legal interpretation is followed by an analysis of three interpretative considerations specific to this method of dispute resolution. *Lex mercatoria*, *amiable composition*, and decision-making based on *ordre public* (in particular *ordre public transnational*) are discussed in turn as particularly interesting examples from the arbitral interpretative repertoire. They have been selected for discussion because their use in arbitration has served as an opening for creative legal interpretation aimed at mitigation or avoidance of overly locally oriented effects of application of the relevant rules of national laws. Their use has also led to far-reaching consequences, including the formulation and consolidation of transnational principles. The outcomes of the application of these considerations in processes of arbitral decision-making and prognostics as to their future significance are then discussed in concluding remarks.

12.2. Creative aspects of adjudication: Theoretical approaches

Theoretical proposals aimed at capturing activist aspects of legal interpretation have, to a large extent, followed the civil law–common law divide in terms of their conceptualizations of legal norms, understanding of the role of an adjudicator, and either the creative or reproducing character of legal interpretation. In particular, the binding character of precedents in common law systems has traditionally been perceived as resulting in a broad scope of judicial activity in formulating, expressing, and explicating the law. In contrast, the origins of the primarily textual orientation of modern continental jurisprudence can be connected with the Montesquieuan theory of separation of powers, distinguishing law making from its application in the processes of administration of justice. The judges are thus, for Montesquieu (in his famous paraphrase of the Bible), 'the mouth that pronounces the words of the law, inanimate beings who can moderate neither its force nor its rigour'.[1]

So understood, legal interpretation is, in an ideal state, a transparent transmission of the meaning inscribed in the letter of the law. According to Hugues

[1] Charles de Secondat Montesquieu et al., *The Spirit of the Laws* (1989), 163.

Rabault, such a concept of the limits of the interpretative powers of the judge can be characterized as exegetic, with the authority of the judge being strictly and completely determined by the statutory law. As Rabault argues, this approach also incorporates a denouncement of judicial discretion, associated with undesirable arbitrariness.[2] He further contrasts the exegetic approach with the free hermeneutical approach. In the latter, the statute does not function as a sole and absolute source of the law but merely as an expression of the already pre-existing rules (derived from social norms, nature, or human rationality). Hence, a judge as an interpreter is obligated to take into account legal doctrine and social norms instead of following blindly the letter of the statute. In Rabault's words, the judges are thus perceived as guarantors of the law, guarding it from the arbitrariness of the legislature. As a consequence, in this approach, the limits of judicial authority are defined primarily by legal doctrine and jurisprudence, which formulate demands for the methodology of interpretation.[3]

Associated with nineteenth-century German historical legal scholars (in particular von Savigny and Puchta), the school of free hermeneutics had consolidated in reaction to the proliferation of the French exegetic school. The concept of *Rechtsfindung* (search for the law) introduced by these thinkers is based on the assumption that the law exists independently from the statute. Unlike in the exegetic approach, where the lawyer focuses completely on the text, a hermeneutical adjudicator is thus interpreting not only the text of a legal instrument but also the world and its phenomena. The cultural and historical context is thus necessary for the exercise of legal interpretation, and the free hermeneutics becomes an ontological hermeneutics. While historically embedded in two different continental legal traditions and models of political power (those of a strongly centralized France and the dispersed German Confederation), the exegetic and hermeneutical approaches are, in their contemporary versions, associated by Rabault with the civil law–common law opposition. He emphasizes the praetorian function of common law jurisprudence, claiming that the law is approached by it not as a text but as a fact—either a social one (a custom) or a judicial one (precedent).

However, this opposition of the two ideal types of interpretation seems largely to ignore the findings of various disciplines, from analytic philosophy to legal semiotics, that emphasize the essentially non-transparent, open character of language and, consequently, the importance of its pragmatic aspect and of the social, as well as cultural, contexts of its use. Furthermore, it has been pointed out that even strictly textualist theories of legal interpretation cannot completely eliminate its creative aspects due to the open character of language, as well as the intention of the

[2] Hugues Rabault, *L'interprétation des normes: l'objectivité de la méthode* (1997), 10.

[3] Ibid.

legislator to leave space for judicial discretion. The results take the form of interpretative choices based on values.[4]

On the other hand, the presumption of broad judicial discretion in common law jurisdictions is counterfactual. As emphasized by Eskridge, Frickey, and Garrett, this popular misconception evaporates very quickly in confrontation with the everyday necessity to apply statutory law, which—as they argue—is currently by far the most widespread and rudimentary form of judicial decision-making in the US context.[5] It results directly from the saturation of the American legal system with legislation, characterized by Guido Calabresi as 'statutorification' and associated by him with US legislative policy at least since the Great Depression and the New Deal.[6] The traditional opposition between the conditions of judicial decision-making in the civil law and common law jurisdictions seems thus to have lost much of its original sharpness.

In this context, a different typology of existing theories may be proposed, inspired by Eskridge, Frickey, and Garret's category of dynamic (non-syllogistic) theories, oriented at the meaning making of legal norms.[7] They can be confronted with logocentric theories,[8] according to which legal interpretation aims at discovering the original meaning of the applicable norm encoded in the (text of the) legal rule. Logocentric theories share a platonic view that the meaning of the statute exists objectively and independently from any interpreter, whose task is only to extract and repeat it. This category is not identical with Rabault's exegetic approaches because logocentric theories may include not only textualist but also intentionalist ones. They also generally presume a specific order and hierarchy of interpretative directives and considerations as steps on the way to the goal (the 'true' meaning of the interpreted rule). By contrast, the dynamic, discursive theories of legal interpretation perceive it as a process of meaning making and thus assume its creative character. They may also accept a conventional or preferred order of interpretative directives[9] (as, for example, in Dworkin's theory of judicial decision-making as a way of finding the best answer[10]). Some of the dynamic theories (such as legal deconstructivism or legal semiotics) may reject such hierarchies, however, and expect verification of acquired interpretative results by the means of further analysis

[4] See, for example, Zygmunt Ziembiński, *Szkice z metodologii szczegółowych nauk prawnych* (1983); Jerzy Wróblewski, 'Pragmatyczna jasność prawa', *Państwo i Prawo*, 4 (1988).

[5] William N. Eskridge et al., *Legislation and Statutory Interpretation* (2000), 2.

[6] Guido Calabresi, *A Common Law for the Age of Statutes* (1982), 44.

[7] Eskridge et al, *Legislation and Statutory Interpretation.*

[8] See Joanna Jemielniak, 'Just Interpretation: The Status of Legal Reasoning in the Continental Legal Tradition', *International Journal for the Semiotics of Law*, 15 (2002), 325–35.

[9] See Robert Alexy et al., *A Theory of Legal Argumentation: The Theory of Rational Discourse as Theory of Legal Justification* (1989).

[10] Ronald Dworkin, *Law's Empire* (1986).

even if satisfactory outcomes have been obtained already in the early phases of the process.

Whereas legal interpretation as an aspect of judicial activity is well described and conceptualized, the transferability of such categories onto legal interpretation in international commercial arbitration seems only partially legitimized. Decision-making in commercial arbitration is largely based on the application of domestic contract law, hence the legal basis for rendered awards may be largely identical with the one used in national litigation in analogous cases. However, as described in detail below, the typical sets of rules applied in the resolution of commercial disputes in arbitration are not limited to the domestic law; hence, the national sets of interpretative directives, created and operating within specific legal systems, are not automatically applicable in arbitration. As the resolved cases are of a private character and domestic law serves as part of the legal basis for awards, there is also no direct analogy with the decision-making of international courts and tribunals, rendering decisions on the grounds of international law only to some extent relevant in commercial arbitration.

Owing to these considerations, and to the traditional orientation of the theory of legal interpretation indicated above, in which the figure of the judge takes the central role, a discussion of the role of an arbitrator, in comparison to that of a judge, is offered in the following subchapter, explaining how the limits of arbitral discretion in legal interpretation are defined largely autonomously by the specific rules of procedure. The discussion also demonstrates how these limits are redefined in comparison with those of domestic judges due to the typically heterogeneous character of legal grounds applicable to the merits of the dispute, as well as the status of arbitrators as outsiders to the applicable norms, enhanced by the fact that, unlike the judges, they do not render decisions in the name of the state.

12.3. Arbitrators and judges: Adjudicatory roles and legal interpretation

In the context of international commercial arbitration, a reformulation of these considerations seems necessary for several reasons. First, many of the systemic limitations to the role of the judge do not bind arbitrators. While rendering awards on the basis of applicable law, they do not act in the name of the state and, unlike judges, do not act 'from within' the legal system, the norms of which they apply. This aspect of arbitral decision-making has sometimes been characterized by the statement that arbitrators have no *lex fori*,[11] analogically to the a-national or

[11] See, for example, Klaus Peter Berger, 'The International Arbitrators' Application of Precedents', *Transnational Dispute Management*, 5 (2008); Simon Greenberg, et al., *International Commercial*

floating[12] status of arbitration. Even if they have been selected because of their expertise in the substantive law they are to apply, they do so as outsiders—and not representatives—of the system. This feature of arbitral interpretation is further augmented by formal limitations introduced by the rules of procedure of some international arbitration centres, preventing the appointment of arbitrators of the same nationality as any of the parties without their specific authorization. These standards serve the purpose of ensuring the neutrality of the tribunal, yet, considering that the law applicable to the merits of the dispute is usually the law of one of the parties, it decreases the probability of arbitral decision-making being performed by a person whose primary legal education was obtained in this jurisdiction. It thus further augments the 'outsider's effect' in legal interpretation.

Second, the main role of an arbitrator has frequently been associated with offering a pragmatic and expeditious resolution of specific disputes by flexible procedural means. It has thus been oriented at *a casu ad casum* dispute settlement rather than at the administration of justice. Furthermore, consistency of case law has been difficult to achieve in the setting of dispersed and competing arbitral fora and the limited publicity of awards. While this strongly historically embedded perception of arbitration as informal, speedy, and flexible mechanism might seem somewhat outdated, particularly in the context of processes of judicialization or proceduralization[13] of arbitration, many of the related reservations remain accurate. In particular, it has been suggested that the appointment of arbitrators by the parties and the well-known status of arbitration as a 'creature of contract'[14] is a direct source of the propensity of tribunals to seek the accommodation of the justified needs of the parties rather than impose solutions upon them. While the theory of the autonomization of arbitration is quickly expanding, and the adoption of quasi-judicial functions is considered one of its symptoms, it is arguably not executed at the expense of the broad limits of arbitral discretion.

Third, the differences between common law and civil law styles of adjudication have, as indicated above, heavily influenced the developments of the theory of legal interpretation due to divergent expectations as to the role of the judge. While also

Arbitration: An Asia-Pacific Perspective (2010), 105; Joanna Jemielniak and Stefanie Pfisterer, 'Iura Novit Arbiter Revisited: Towards a Harmonized Approach?' *Uniform Law Review*, 20 (2015), 56–80.

[12] See, for example, William W. Park, 'The Lex Loci Arbitri and International Commercial Arbitration', *The International and Comparative Law Quarterly*, 32 (1983); Filip De Ly, *International Business Law and Lex Mercatoria* (1992).

[13] Charles Nelson Brower, 'Introduction', in Richard B. Lillich and Charles Nelson Brower eds., *International Arbitration in the 21st Century: Towards 'Judicialization' and Uniformity?: The Twelfth Sokol Colloquium* (1994), ix; Fali S. Nariman, 'The Spirit of Arbitration: The Tenth Annual Goff Lecture', *Arbitration International*, 16 (2000), 261ff.

[14] Michael McIlwrath and John Savage, *International Arbitration and Mediation: A Practical Guide* (2010), 13; Emilia Onyema, *International Commercial Arbitration and the Arbitrator's Contract* (2010), 37.

present in arbitration, these particularities affect the processes of legal interpretation to a different degree than in domestic litigation. Perceived for many decades as a continental European method of commercial dispute resolution, arbitration has been largely defined as an alternative to litigation on the procedural level, in terms of the wide discretion of adjudicators in the selection of processual means, as well as in regard to the determination and application of relevant norms.

It should be noted, however, that in the 1980s and 1990s arbitration had been hit by an 'American wave' of parties, their counsel, and arbitrators. This influx of actors and of cases with a mixed (continental–common law) composition of parties resulted in clashes of competing procedural expectations and in reformulation of the role assumed by an arbitrator. A number of authors[15] have associated this phenomenon with the proceduralization of arbitration as a result of the push for adoption of American standards of the domestic civil process in arbitration. Increased procedural formality and a broader inclusion of oral hearings were indicated as symptoms of this development. However, other commentators argue that the suggested 'Americanization' of arbitration has not taken place. Rather, the global popularity of arbitration and the increased number of complex, high-stakes cases have naturally pushed for development of procedural standards. This development has not taken the form of American style quasi-litigation, however. As Elena V. Helmer remarks, arbitration practice has instead incorporated mechanisms of accommodation of the conflicting demands of parties, leading to a hybrid, compromising 'third way':

> [I]nternational commercial arbitration has not become 'Americanized'; nor has it become 'Civilized.' Arbitration is opting for the middle ground and tends to encompass the best of both legal traditions. . . . There are, and always will be, disputes in which parties lean towards one or the other legal tradition. It can be attributed to the parties' and their attorneys' backgrounds, the bargaining power of one of the parties, the composition of the arbitral tribunal, or some other factors. Strong American influence, as well as strong [c]ontinental influence, on arbitration will continue.[16]

In Helmer's view, a one-sided preference for the American procedural model would indeed be detrimental to the arbitration practice because it would undermine the neutrality of the forum, as well as its attractiveness in comparison to the domestic courts, if arbitration was merely mimicking them:

[15] See Yves Dezalay and Bryant Garth, 'Merchants of Law as Moral Entrepreneurs: Constructing International Justice from the Competition for Transnational Business Disputes', *Law and Society Review*, 29 (1995), 27; Lawrence W. Newman, 'International Arbitration: Unfinished Business', *New York Law Journal*, 4/1 (2001), 3.

[16] Elena V. Helmer, 'International Commercial Arbitration: Americanized, "Civilized," or Harmonized?', *Ohio State Journal on Dispute Resolution*, 19 (2003), 66–67.

> The transnational character of arbitration is one of its principal advantages in comparison to litigation before national courts. If arbitration turns into U.S.-style 'off-shore litigation', the incentive to arbitrate international disputes will diminish or even go away.[17]

The analysis of the consequences of the American wave has gained a new importance, along with recent regional developments in arbitration, in particular with the rise of East Asian arbitration centres.[18] The high popularity of arbitration in this region, combined with the growing commercial exchange with Western partners, naturally leads to the question of the impact of this phenomenon on the global practice of arbitration (in particular in connection with the conciliatory orientation of Chinese arbitration and the popularity of hybrid processes—arb-med and med-arb).[19]

Fourth, a characteristic feature of arbitral decision-making is the heterogeneity of the norms applicable to the merits of the dispute, as well as their diverse (national, transnational, and international) origins and various degrees of binding force. A typical arbitral case is rarely resolved solely on the basis of the rules of a single domestic legal system. As will be discussed in detail, it is a consequence of a number of factors: the basic determination of the applicable law not being limited to national standards; a practice described by Gabrielle Kaufmann-Kohler as an 'inclination to "transnationalise" the rules' of domestic law[20] in connection with the international character of the transaction and through a broad inclusion of comparative analysis into interpretative processes;[21] and the mandatory recourse to modifying interpretative considerations, such as the usages and customs of international trade and public policy. The widely accepted broad scope of arbitral discretion in this

[17] Ibid., 67.

[18] See *International Arbitration Cases Received,* compilation by Hong Kong International Arbitration Centre (HKIAC), http://www.hkiac.org. According to the data on the 2012 caseload (the last year with comprehensive comparative statistics provided), China International Economic and Trade Arbitration Commission (CIETAC) handled 1,060 arbitration cases, HKIAC 456 disputes including 293 arbitrations, and Singapore International Arbitration Centre (SIAC) 235 arbitrations (compared to 759 at International Chamber of Commerce (ICC) and 177 at Stockholm Chamber of Commerce). In 2011 CIETAC handled 1,435 arbitrations; HKIAC 502 dispute resolution matters, including 275 arbitrations; and SIAC 188 arbitrations (compared to 795 at ICC, 224 at London Court of International Arbitration (LCIA) and 199 at SCC). About one third of CIETAC's annual caseload is estimated to be foreign-related; see Chen Yun and Lukas Steinberg, *New CIETAC Rules to Internationalize China Arbitration, July 2012 R&P China Lawyers* (2012).

[19] Kun Fan and Joanna Jemielniak, 'Ethnographic Methods in the Study of Hybrid Processes in Arbitration: The Chinese and Western Perspectives', *European Business Law Review,* 27 (2016), 555–85.

[20] Gabrielle Kaufmann-Kohler, 'Arbitral Precedent: Dream, Necessity or Excuse?', *Arbitration International,* 23 (2007), 364.

[21] Joanna Jemielniak, 'Comparative Analysis as an Autonomization Strategy in International Commercial Arbitration', *International Journal for the Semiotics of Law,* 31 (2018), 155–73.

sphere is particularly visible in regard to the first factor. UNCITRAL Model Law, Article 28(2), provides for the authority of the tribunal in determination of the conflict of laws rules, on the basis of which the ascertaining of the proper substantive law shall be exercised. The current dominant trend is even more far-reaching, however: UNCITRAL Arbitration Rules, Article 35(1), as well as the rules of procedure of a number of leading arbitral institutions, have bestowed tribunals with *voie directe* competence, permitting them the direct determination of the law applicable to the merits of the dispute without an explicit demand for a preceding recourse to private international law rules.[22] The popularity of this solution has also been noted by legal doctrine.[23]

Finally, a characteristic feature of arbitral decision-making is the central role of the interpretation of contracts and of determining the common will of the parties with regard to the international character of the transaction. In practice, these considerations can effectively overshadow the issues of substantive law application. In some cases, the intent of the parties to exclude the influence of domestic laws on their relationship takes the form of self-referencing contracts. Typically combined with arbitration clauses, such provisions have been interpreted as an expression of the will of the parties to avoid unnecessary legal parochialisms on the substantive level, as well as on the procedural level[24] (although it should be noted, after Van den Berg, that these two areas of the parties' contractual freedom shall be treated separately[25]).

For all those reasons, the processes of legal interpretation in international commercial arbitration display a number of openings for adjudicatory activism. The distinctly creative character of legal interpretation is determined by the procedural framework of arbitration, by the core conceptualizations of the role of an arbitrator, and by the heterogeneous character of the typical sets of rules applicable to the merits of the disputes. Vijay K. Bhatia, Christopher Candlin, and Jan Engberg observe that the striving for clarity, precision, and certainty in the application of the law, achieved by the means of legal interpretation and aimed at by national legal systems,

[22] See, for example, American Arbitration Association (AAA) International Arbitration Rules Art. 31.1; HKIAC Administered Arbitration Rules Art. 35.1; ICC Arbitration Rules Art. 21.1; LCIA Rules Art. 22.3; SIAC Rules (2013) Rule 27.1; Arbitration Rules of the Arbitration Institute of the SCC Art. 22.1; Rules of Arbitration of the International Arbitration Centre of the Austrian Federal Economic Chamber (VIAC) Art. 27.2.

[23] See Linda Silberman and Franco Ferrari, 'Getting to the Law Applicable to the Merits in International Arbitration and the Consequences of Getting it Wrong', in F. Ferrari and S. Kroll eds., *Conflict of Laws in International Arbitration* (2010), 320.

[24] See Ana M. López Rodríguez, *Lex Mercatoria and Harmonization of Contract Law in the EU* (2003), 67.

[25] Albert Jan van den Berg, 'Consolidated Commentary on New York Convention (109 I. "Arbitral Award: A-National Award")', *Yearbook of Commercial Arbitration*, 28 (2003), 576.

is frequently challenged in the areas of globalized legal relations. Considering the dilemma of the certainty of legal language, they note that, in such conditions,

> there are several other factors that make this claim somewhat problematic: the legal system, the language, the socio-political and the cultural context within which a specific instance of legal discourse is embedded. One of the main issues arising from this variation is the extent to which the integrity of a specific legal genre is likely to be maintained when it crosses linguistic, socio-political, cultural or legal boundaries in the present-day global business, trade or other professional environment. These issues of diversity in construction and interpretation of legal discourse acquire a more serious importance when we see law losing its jurisdictional character in this rapidly changing corporate world of international trade and commerce.[26]

As a consequence, it is the dynamic, non-linear theories, without the universally shared hierarchy of interpretative directives, that seem particularly adequate for capturing the character of the arbitral processes of legal interpretation.[27] Even without such a hierarchy, however, there are the typical interpretative considerations, addressed by the adjudicators and different from domestic litigation. These inform the processes of legal interpretation in international commercial arbitration; augment its unique character, distinguishing it from litigation; and affect the limits of the creative activity of the arbitrators. In the following sections they are discussed in turn, demonstrating how their use in practice may take the form of adjudicatory activism in arbitration.

12.4. Lex mercatoria

One of the best-known areas of adjudicatory activism, leading to the expression and explication of new rules, is the new *lex mercatoria* (merchant law) or autonomous law of international commerce. Characterized as a global law without a state[28] and originally embedded in the usages and customs of cross-border trade, it has been largely developed by means of the arbitral decision-making, discovering, and formulating of *lex mercatoria* principles. As a set of principles created and observed *sua sponte* among private participants, it has also been an object of criticism due to its insufficiently definite content and lack of formally binding power (its status as

[26] V. K. Bhatia, et al., 'Concepts, Contexts and Procedures in Arbitration Discourse', in V. K. Bhatia, et al. eds., *Legal Discourse Across Cultures and Systems* (2008), 9.

[27] Joanna Jemielniak, *Legal Interpretation in International Commercial Arbitration* (2014), 27ff.

[28] Gunther Teubner, ed., *Global Law Without a State* (1997).

law has been challenged from positivistic positions). Moreover, the historical significance of commercial customs as the main source of the *lex mercatoria* has diminished, and harmonized practices of the international business community are achieved instead by contractual means (through model, self-referencing contracts and standard clauses) and arbitral case law.[29]

To a large extent, it was thus the arbitral awards that contributed to the development, consolidation, and increase in the precision of the new merchant law, criticized for its vague and elusive character.[30] The beginnings of this process have been associated with the 1950s and 1960s oil extraction contracts between Western investors and Islamic parties from the countries of the Persian Gulf region. As none of the parties to such transactions were willing to subject the relationship to the law of the co-contractor, these agreements frequently included a reference to shared principles, a common core of legal systems, or suchlike,[31] accompanied by an arbitration clause. The further proliferation of choice of law clauses with a recourse to transnational (instead of domestic) standards accelerated in the 1970s and 1980s and led to an accumulation of arbitral jurisprudence. As observed by Ana López Rodríguez, while lacking formal *stare decisis* status, these awards have directly resulted in an expansion of the *lex mercatoria* as *de facto* precedents, due to their persuasiveness.[32] This has further facilitated the restatement-type codifications of transnational rules of commerce, such as the UNIDROIT Principles of International Commercial Contracts and the CENTRAL Database.

As a consequence, the role of arbitral decision-making in the 'creeping codification' of transnational commercial law (in Klaus Peter Berger's words) has been characterized as decisive.[33] The mandatory regard to the usages and customs of international trade in legal interpretation performed by arbitrators has become common, which is reflected in UNCITRAL Model Law Article 28(4) and UNCITRAL Arbitration Rules Article 35(3), as well as in the rules of procedure of numerous arbitral centres. It functions not only as a standard that guides interpreters in the—still relatively rare—cases in which the *lex mercatoria* has been determined as the primary source of the applicable law, but also as a modifying

[29] Gunther Teubner, 'Global Bukowina: Legal Pluralism in the World Society', in Teubner, ed., *Global Law Without a State*, 15ff.

[30] See Georges Delaume, 'The Proper Law of State Contracts and the Lex Mercatoria: A Reappraisal', *ICSID Review—Foreign Investment Law Journal*, 3 (1988), 79; A. F. M. Maniruzzaman, 'Choice of Law in International Contracts: Some Fundamental Conflict of Laws Issues', *Journal of International Arbitration*, 16 (1999), 151.

[31] See, for example, *Petroleum Development, Ltd v Sheikh of Abu Dhabi* ad hoc award, *International Law Reports*, 18 (1951); *Sapphire International Petroleums v NIOC, International Law Reports*, 35 (1967).

[32] López Rodríguez, *Lex Mercatoria and Harmonization of Contract Law*, 82.

[33] Klaus Peter Berger and Center for Transnational Law, *The Creeping Codification of the New Lex Mercatoria* (2nd edn, 2010), 3.

interpretative directive, effectively 'transnationalizing' the outcomes of interpretation. The standard inclusion of the discussed considerations into processes of legal rendition is combined in arbitration with extensive use of comparative analysis. For Emmanuel Gaillard and other authors, it has served as a basis for a theory in which *lex mercatoria* is in fact not a set of substantive rules but a characteristic method of arbitral decision-making, a specific procedural approach.[34] This approach relies on the purposive use of the comparative method in legal interpretation, the goal of which is the extraction of the most universally accepted rules, which can serve as a ground for the award.[35] It thus draws the legitimization of the process from diverse legal systems, analogically to the early *lex mercatoria* awards in the 'oil cases' of the 1950s–1970s (referring to the 'common core' of different legal orders instead of a specific domestic system) and to the 'comparative snapshots'[36] codification strategy of the UNIDROIT Principles. Such an approach allows for a remarkable margin of discretion in the determination and formulation of relevant rules, at the same time as offering a practical tool to the arbitrators, who are, as Gaillard remarks, always able to find a rule applicable to any claim put forward by the parties.[37]

12.5. Amiable composition

It is also worth noticing—especially in the decades preceding the codifications of the *lex mercatoria*—that an argument often raised by its critics was that *lex mercatoria*-based decision-making is in fact an unauthorized *amiable composition*, performed without the relevant consent of the parties. The latter type of arbitral decision-making (usually translated as 'friendly compromise'[38]) refers to situations in which the parties have empowered an adjudicator to refrain from a strict application of the rules of law; instead, an arbitrator is authorized to resolve the dispute on the basis of principles of fairness and equity. Because *amiable composition* competence is frequently granted together with powers to decide the case *ex aequo et bono*, or on the grounds of equity and conscience, the two concepts are sometimes considered synonymous.[39] However, historically, as defined in French legal doctrine, *amiable composition* is a form of decision-making that is based on rules of law (and not directly on the grounds of equity)—the arbitrators may only abstain from

[34] Emmanuel Gaillard, 'Thirty Years of Lex Mercatoria: Towards the Selective Application of Transnational Rules', *ICSID Review*, 10 (1995), 208–31; Emmanuel Gaillard, 'Transnational Law: A Legal System or a Method of Decision-Making?', *Arbitration International*, 17 (2001); López Rodríguez, *Lex Mercatoria and Harmonization of Contract Law*, 109ff.

[35] Gaillard, 'Thirty Years of Lex Mercatoria'.

[36] Berger and Center for Transnational Law, *The Creeping Codification of the Lex Mercatoria*, 208.

[37] Gaillard, *Transnational Law*, 62 ff.

[38] W. W. Park, 'Arbitration of International Contract Disputes', *Business Law*, 39 (1983), 1785.

[39] M. Rubino-Sammartano, *International Arbitration Law and Practice* (2001), 463.

the application of the rules of law if the results would be inequitable *ex aequo et bono*.[40]

In practice, the parties decide to entitle arbitrators to act as *amiable compositeurs* when they presume that strict application of the letter of the law to the merits of their dispute will result in a decision that would be undesired (for instance, from an economic point of view), inadequate, or unsatisfactory.[41]

Amiable composition is thus a characteristic method of arbitral decision-making, based on the wide discretion of adjudicators and performed upon explicit authorization by the parties.[42] It is a long-established avenue of arbitral activism. However, in the early period of consolidation of the *lex mercatoria*, it was sometimes argued that application of the rules of the latter to the merits of the dispute without a relevant choice of law made by the parties was an abuse of said discretion as *de facto amiable composition* performed without authorization. In *Pabalk Ticaret Limited Sirketi v. Norsolor S.A.*, the ICC arbitrators, unable to establish the parties' intent in regard to substantive applicable law, decided to apply the *lex mercatoria*. The ensuing proceedings before the Austrian courts brought several opinions on this issue. The court of first instance reasoned 'The arbitrators, who were not entitled to act as "amiables compositeurs", did not apply French or Turkish law but, referring to "the principle of good faith which inspires the international *lex mercatoria*" awarded damages on the basis of equity.'[43] This opinion was further upheld by the Vienna Court of Appeal, which argued that application of the *lex mercatoria* (described as 'world law of questionable validity'—'*ein Weltrecht von fraglicher Geltung*'[44]) was a transgression of discretionary powers by the arbitrators. However, the Supreme Court did not find that the arbitrators exceeded their authority.[45]

Subsequent changes in the regulatory framework of arbitration, including the rules of procedure of arbitral institutions, as well as national arbitration laws (and those based on the UNCITRAL Model Law), have led to a recognition of the possibility of applying the rules of law—and not only law—to the merits of the dispute. Such a formulation has been interpreted as officially opening the way to an

[40] R. Briner, *Special Considerations Which May Affect the Procedure (Interim Measures, Amiable Composition, Adaptation of Contracts, Agreed Settlements* (1994), 355.

[41] Jemielniak, *Legal Interpretation in International Commercial Arbitration*, 175.

[42] See, for example, American Arbitration Association (AAA) International Arbitration Rules Art. 31.3; HKIAC Administered Arbitration Rules Art. 35.2; ICC Arbitration Rules Art. 21.3; LCIA Rules Art. 22.4; SIAC Rules (2013) Rule 27.2; Arbitration Rules of the Arbitration Institute of the SCC Art. 22.3; Rules of Arbitration and Conciliation of the Vienna International Arbitral Centre (VIAC) Art. 27.3.

[43] 'Oberster Gerichtshof (Supreme Court), 18 November 1982', in P. Sanders ed., *Yearbook of Commercial Arbitration*, 9 (1984), 159.

[44] Werner Melis, 'Note to the Austrian Supreme Court Decision', in P. Sanders ed., *Yearbook of Commercial Arbitration*, 9 (1984), 160.

[45] Ibid., 160.

application of the *lex mercatoria* without a separate, equity-based authorization by the parties.[46] While the character of the applied standards is different in both types of case, some commentators observe that in practice the difference between the two types of decision-making may be vague:

> Conscientious arbitrators will obviously do their utmost to ensure that their decision is made in accordance with the law governing their contract. Their professional conscience will demand no less; and they will not decide *ex aequo et bono* without the express authorization of the parties. But if the law governing the contract consists of those rules or principles which the arbitrators consider most appropriate, and which may conveniently be labelled as part of the *lex mercatoria*, those arbitrators are in effect free to decide in accordance with what they consider to be just and equitable, whilst purporting to decide in accordance with legal rules.[47]

A distinction between the two types of arbitral decision-making seems to lie in their orientation: either in the discovery and application of pre-existent, external legal standards (in case of the *lex mercatoria*-based adjudication, even in its Gaillardian, functional, comparative version) or in the case-specific dispute resolution based on the arbitrators' sense of equity, allowing for a deviation from the strict application of the rules of law. Especially nowadays, after the body of *lex mercatoria* principles has been expressed and consolidated, both by case law and by codifications, the boundaries between these two mechanisms seem much clearer.

12.6. Public order

Another important area of adjudicatory activism in arbitration is the recourse to public order as an interpretative consideration. While commonly applied as an auxiliary, modifying argument in the processes of legal interpretation (mostly because of recognition and enforcement concerns), public order has also occasionally been used as an autonomous ground for an award. Due to the explicit references to it, arbitral jurisprudence has vitally contributed to the development of the doctrine of international and transnational public order. The key reason for this popularity is the provision of Article V(2)(b) of the New York Convention, which establishes the public policy exception to the recognition and enforcement of an arbitral award.

[46] Alan Redfern and Martin Hunter, *Law and Practice of International Commercial Arbitration* (2004), 118.

[47] Pierre Mayer, 'The UNIDROIT Principles in Contemporary Contract Practice', *ICC Bulletin*, supplement, *UNIDROIT Principles of International Commercial Contracts: Reflections on Their Use in International Arbitration* (2002), 111.

Public order has also served as a ground for the doctrine, pointing to the issuance of an enforceable award as one of the rudimentary duties of an arbitrator (which has been implemented by national arbitration laws, rules of procedure, codes of professional ethics, and arbitral jurisprudence[48]). As a result, arbitrators may seek to satisfy the public policy standards of the seat of arbitration (so as to avoid the award being set aside), as well as those of the anticipated place or places of enforcement—which has been interpreted as a challenge to the neutral, a-national character of arbitration.[49]

These considerations have led some commentators to postulate that only supranational public policy should have an influence on arbitral decision-making in order to avoid fragmentation and the unnecessarily parochial character of case law.[50] Such spontaneous harmonization would undoubtedly face a number of difficulties, though, from the existing national courts' enforcement practice under the New York Convention, through the highly dispersed character of contemporary commercial arbitration, to the issue of the contents of such global public policy. Nevertheless, jurisprudential efforts in this regard can be seen as transgressing the traditional concept of *ordre public international* (as evaluated from within the *domestic* legal systems).[51] Instead, the concepts of 'transnational public policy' and 'transnational public order' have been introduced to characterize fundamental principles common to different national legal systems, or, in Pierre Lalive's words, an osmosis of the genuinely international public policy considerations of different domestic orders.[52] The broad scope of arbitral discretion in ascertaining the contents of *ordre public transnational* (particularly in cases where it would be used to modify the application of substantive law, explicitly made by the parties) has, however, also been an object of reservations, because 'permitting the arbitrators to have regard to transnational principles of public policy introduces an element of discretion which could do much to undermine the certainty which is so essential to international commerce'.[53]

[48] Gunther J. Horvath, 'The Duty of the Tribunal to Render an Enforceable Award', *Journal of International Arbitration*, 18/2 (2001), 135ff.

[49] See N. Voser, 'Mandatory Rules of Law as a Limitation on the Law Applicable in International Commercial Arbitration', *American Review of International Arbitration*, 7 (1996), 335.

[50] Gaillard, *Thirty Years of Lex Mercatoria*, 223.

[51] Pieter Sanders, 'Commentary', in *60 Years of ICC Arbitration: A Look at the Future* (1984); M. Hunter and G.C. e Silva, 'Transnational Public Policy and its Application in Investment Arbitrations', *Journal of World Investment*, 4 (2003), 367.

[52] Pierre Lalive, 'Transnational (or Truly International) Public Policy and International Arbitration', in Pieter Sanders, ed., *Comparative Arbitration Practice and Public Policy in Arbitration*, ICCA Congress Series (1987), 295–6.

[53] M. Pryles, 'Reflections on Transnational Public Policy', *Journal of International Arbitration*, 24 (2007), 6.

In practice, so far, arbitrators in commercial cases (unlike in investment ones) have rarely sought recourse to transnational public order arguments. One such decision, ICC interim award 4695/1984,[54] addressed a case between a Brazilian and an American party, in which the former claimed that the arbitration clause was invalid due to its inconsistency with Article 153.4 of the Brazilian Constitution (establishing the exclusive jurisdiction of the domestic courts, forming a part of the public policy of Brazil and coherent with the country's long-time refusal to accede to the New York Convention). The arbitral tribunal decided that said principle of Brazil's public policy violated transnational public order; hence, giving an effect to it would be an 'extreme and unacceptable proposition, particularly when applied to international commercial contracts', as well as being inconsistent with 'current practice in Brazil'.[55] As a consequence, the tribunal did not apply an explicit provision of constitutional rank and decided that the arbitration clause was valid.

Another case in which the argument of transnational legal order was used to exclude the overly limited effects of the application of national rules was ICC Case No. 8385/1995.[56] The parties (one Belgian, the other American) made an explicit choice of law of the State of New York to govern the merits of their dispute. Nevertheless, the sole arbitrator decided not to apply the provisions of this system (the US Federal Racketeer Influenced and Corrupt Organization Act), which grants a party access to triple damages. The arbitrator argued that because this kind of a punitive remedy is practically unknown in civil law legal systems, awarding it case would violate the principles of legal certainty and good faith:

> [I]n international commerce [it] is very important that legal rules produce foreseeable results, respond to the expectations of the parties and take account of the prevalent usages of the international marketplace. In such context it would be inappropriate to apply rules which solely respond to state interests.[57]

Despite the explicit choice of substantive law made by the parties, the sole arbitrator in this case also sought recourse to *lex mercatoria* principles and reasoned that the case in question posed an 'ideal opportunity' to apply them.[58]

A violation of the *ordre public transnational* was also acknowledged in ICC Award No. 8891/1998[59] as a ground for the annulment of a contract providing for the

[54] Albert Jan van den Berg, ed. 'Interim Award of November 1984 in Case No. 4695', *Yearbook of Commercial Arbitration*, 11 (1986).

[55] Ibid., 156.

[56] ICC Award No. 8385/1995.

[57] López Rodríguez, *Lex Mercatoria and Harmonization of Contract Law*, 127.

[58] ICC Award No. 8385/1995, p. 1066

[59] ICC Award No. 8891/1998.

corruption of officials. Notably, Dominique Hascher, commenting on this award, pointed to the administration of justice—even if it is 'private justice'[60]—as one of the main functions of an arbitral tribunal. Giving force to the contract in question would thus have been a miscarriage of justice. Invoking Pierre Lalive, Hascher remarked that the practice of international arbitration recognizes the existence of transnational public order, rooted in a set of values common to, even if not unanimously shared by, the international community. A recourse to *ordre public transnational* is thus perceived here as an act of exercising adjudicatory discretion, stemming from an autonomous status of arbitration, which is irreducible to a mere legal service of the resolution of isolated controversies. Instead, the concept of international commercial arbitration as a system of administration of justice is implemented, and the interpretative argument of public order serves as a tool to this end.

12.7. Concluding remarks

The existing arbitral case law offers a variety of examples of arbitral decisions exceeding the limits of a mere literal rendition of the rules governing the relationship between parties. As discussed above, this is exercised in a number of ways: from transnationalization of applicable domestic law by means of the extensive use of comparative analysis; through the use of *lex mercatoria* and *ordre public* principles as modificatory arguments, channelling legal interpretation; to clear cases of adjudicatory activism in which relevant rules, serving as the main basis for the award, are expressed and formulated by means of arbitral decision-making. Moreover, even though the majority of cases resolved by international commercial arbitration are based on the application of domestic provisions, such rules serve only exceptionally as the sole legal grounds for the awards and are frequently supplemented by international and transnational norms.

This heterogeneity of sources of the law applicable in international commercial cases supports the transnationalization of legal interpretation in arbitration. Among other factors influencing this process, the international character of the transaction, the combinations of the parties often representing distant legal traditions, and the tendency discussed above of arbitrators to offer hybrid, compromising procedural and substantive solutions in order to accommodate the justified expectations of the parties should be mentioned. Furthermore, arbitrators are bound by *lex fori* (*lex loci arbitri*) only to a limited extent, determined mostly by considerations related to the recognition of an award. This status of formal—and often also actual (when arbitrators are not primarily trained in the law they apply)—outsiders

[60] Dominique Hascher, 'Note to ICC Award No. 8891', *Journal du Droit International*, 1083–5 (2000).

further augments the detachment of conducted interpretation from interpretative directives transferred through legal education within specific legal systems.

All of these factors determine the course of legal interpretation in international commercial arbitration as a dynamic process, conducted without a fixed hierarchy of directives and including a number of characteristic creative components and mechanisms. While in cases of *amiable composition*, arbitrators are explicitly empowered to abandon the relevant substantive law rules in favour of fairness and equity principles, application of the *lex mercatoria* usually takes the form of a supplementary and corrective argument, and rarely constitutes the sole grounds for an award. On the other hand, the grounds of public policy are usually invoked in the domestic context of legal orders interested in the outcomes of arbitration, with regard to the recognition and enforcement of an award. However, in exceptional cases, public order, understood as transnational public order, functions as a 'last resort' interpretative consideration, invoked to modify such results of legal rendition that would openly contradict core values shared by the international community in the sphere of international commerce—with specific instances of such recourse not being free from controversy due to the decidedly activist character of the interpretation applied. Notably, however, the use of *ordre public transnational* arguments has also been characterized as a signal of arbitration assuming the role of a genuine supranational administration of justice. Moreover, as discussed in this chapter, the creative orientation of legal interpretation in arbitration is also present at a procedural level, where arbitrators tend to accommodate the divergent expectations of parties representing different legal traditions. All these diverse interpretative considerations make legal interpretation markedly creative and have been used as instruments of expanding the adjudicatory autonomy of international commercial arbitration.

References

Alexy, Robert et al., *A Theory of Legal Argumentation. The Theory of Rational Discourse as Theory of Legal Justification* (Oxford, 1989).

Berger, Klaus Peter, 'The International Arbitrators' Application of Precedents', *Transnational Dispute Management*, 5 (2008).

Berger, Klaus Peter and Center for Transnational Law, *The Creeping Codification of the New Lex Mercatoria* (2nd edn, Alphen aan den Rijn, 2010).

Bhatia, V. K. et al., 'Concepts, Contexts and Procedures in Arbitration Discourse', in V. K. Bhatia, et al. eds., *Legal Discourse Across Cultures and Systems* (Hong Kong, 2008), 3–31.

Briner, R., '*Special Considerations Which May Affect the Procedure (Interim Measures, Amiable Composition, Adaptation of Contracts, Agreed Settlements)*, in ICCA, Twelfth Int'l Arb. Congress: Proceedings (Alphen aan den Rijn, 1994), 362.

Brower, Charles Nelson, 'Introduction', in Richard B. Lillich and Charles Nelson Brower eds., *International Arbitration in the 21st Century: Towards 'Judicialization' and Uniformity?: The Twelfth Sokol Colloquium* (Irvington, New York, 1994).

Calabresi, Guido, *A Common Law for the Age of Statutes* (Cambridge, MA, 1982).

Delaume, Georges, 'The Proper Law of State Contracts and the Lex Mercatoria: A Reappraisal', *ICSID Review—Foreign Investment Law Journal*, 3 (1988), 79–106.

De Ly, Filip, *International Business Law and Lex Mercatoria* (Bingley, 1992).

Dezalay, Yves and Bryant Garth, 'Merchants of Law as Moral Entrepreneurs: Constructing International Justice from the Competition for Transnational Business Disputes', *Law and Society Review*, 29 (1995), 27–64.

Dworkin, Ronald, *Law's Empire* (Cambridge, MA, 1986).

Eskridge, William N., et al., *Legislation and Statutory Interpretation* (New York, 2000).

Greenberg, Simon, et al., *International Commercial Arbitration: An Asia-Pacific Perspective* (Cambridge, 2010).

Fan, Kun and Joanna Jemielniak, 'Ethnographic Methods in the Study of Hybrid Processes in Arbitration: The Chinese and Western Perspectives', *European Business Law Review*, 27 (2016), 555–85.

Gaillard, Emmanuel, 'Thirty Years of Lex Mercatoria: Towards the Selective Application of Transnational Rules', *ICSID Review*, 10 (1995), 208–31.

Gaillard, Emmanuel, 'Transnational Law: A Legal System or a Method of Decision-Making?', *Arbitration International*, 17 (2001), 59–72.

Hascher, Dominique, 'Note to ICC Award No. 8891', *Journal du Droit International*, 1083 (2000), 1083–5.

Helmer, Elena V., 'International Commercial Arbitration: Americanized, "Civilized," or Harmonized?', *Ohio State Journal on Dispute Resolution*, 19 (2003), 35–67.

Horvath, Gunther J., 'The Duty of the Tribunal to Render an Enforceable Award', *Journal of International Arbitration*, 18/2 (2001), 135–58.

Hunter, M. and G.C. e Silva, 'Transnational Public Policy and its Application in Investment Arbitrations', *Journal of World Investment*, 4 (2003), 367–78.

'Interim Award of November 1984 in Case No. 4695', in Van den Berg, Albert Jan, ed. *Yearbook of Commercial Arbitration*, 11 (1986).

Jemielniak, Joanna, 'Comparative Analysis as an Autonomization Strategy in International Commercial Arbitration', *International Journal for the Semiotics of Law*, 31 (2018), 155–73.

Jemielniak, Joanna, 'Just Interpretation: The Status of Legal Reasoning in the Continental Legal Tradition', *International Journal for the Semiotics of Law*, 15 (2002), 325–35.

Jemielniak, Joanna and Stefanie Pfisterer, 'Iura Novit Arbiter Revisited: Towards a Harmonized Approach?', *Uniform Law Review*, 20 (2015), 56–80.

Kaufmann-Kohler, Gabrielle, 'Arbitral Precedent: Dream, Necessity or Excuse?', *Arbitration International*, 23 (2007), 357–78.

Lalive, Pierre, 'Transnational (or Truly International) Public Policy and International Arbitration', in Pieter Sanders, ed., *Comparative Arbitration Practice and Public Policy in Arbitration*, ICCA Congress Series (Alphen aan den Rijn, 1987).

López Rodríguez, Ana M., *Lex Mercatoria and Harmonization of Contract Law in the EU* (Copenhagen, 2003).

Maniruzzaman, A. F. M., 'Choice of Law in International Contracts: Some Fundamental Conflict of Laws Issues', *Journal of International Arbitration*, 16 (1999), 141–72.

Mayer, Pierre, 'The UNIDROIT Principles in Contemporary Contract Practice', ICC Bulletin, supplement, *UNIDROIT Principles of International Commercial Contracts: Reflections on Their Use in International Arbitration* (Paris, 2002).

McIlwrath, Michael and John Savage, *International Arbitration and Mediation: A Practical Guide* (Alphen aan den Rijn, 2010).

Melis, Werner, 'Note to the Austrian Supreme Court Decision', in P. Sanders ed., *Yearbook of Commercial Arbitration*, 9 (Alphen aan den Rijn, 1984).

Montesquieu, Charles de Secondat, et al., *The Spirit of the Laws* (Cambridge, 1989).

Nariman, Fali S., 'The Spirit of Arbitration: The Tenth Annual Goff Lecture', *Arbitration International*, 16 (2000), 261–78.

Newman, Lawrence W., 'International Arbitration: Unfinished Business', *New York Law Journal*, 4/1 (2001).

'Oberster Gerichtshof (Supreme Court), 18 November 1982', in P. Sanders ed., *Yearbook of Commercial Arbitration*, 9 (Alphen aan den Rijn, 1984).

Onyema, Emilia, *International Commercial Arbitration and the Arbitrator's Contract* (London and New York, 2010).

Park, William W., 'The Lex Loci Arbitri and International Commercial Arbitration', *The International and Comparative Law Quarterly*, 32 (1983), 21–52.

Park, William W., 'Arbitration of International Contract Disputes', *The Business Lawyer*, 39 (1984), 1783–99.

Pryles, M., 'Reflections on Transnational Public Policy', *Journal of International Arbitration*, 24 (2007), 1–8.

Rabault, Hugues, *L'interprétation des normes: l'objectivité de la méthode* (Paris, 1997).

Redfern, Alan and Martin Hunter, *Law and Practice of International Commercial Arbitration* (London, 2004).

Rubino-Sammartano, M., *International Arbitration Law and Practice* (The Hague, Boston, 2001).

Sanders, Pieter, 'Commentary', in 60 Years of ICC Arbitration: A Look at the Future (Paris, 1984).

Silberman, Linda and Franco Ferrari, 'Getting to the Law Applicable to the Merits in International Arbitration and the Consequences of Getting it Wrong', in F. Ferrari and S. Kroll eds., Conflict of Laws in International Arbitration (Munich, 2010).

Teubner, Gunther, ed., *Global Law Without a* State (Aldershot; Brookfield, 1997).

Teubner, Gunther, 'Global Bukowina: Legal Pluralism in the World Society', in Gunther Teubner, ed., *Global Law Without a State* (Aldershot; Brookfield, 1997).

Van den Berg, Albert Jan, 'Consolidated Commentary on New York Convention (109 I. "Arbitral Award: A-National Award")', *Yearbook of Commercial Arbitration*, 28 (2003).

Voser, N., 'Mandatory Rules of Law as a Limitation on the Law Applicable in International Commercial Arbitration', American Review of International Arbitration, 7 (1996), 319–47.

Wróblewski, Jerzy, *Pragmatyczna jasność prawa*, 4 Państwo i Prawo (1988), 3–13.

Ziembiński, Zygmunt, *Szkice z metodologii szczegółowych nauk prawnych* (Warszawa, 1983).

Yun, Chen and Lukas Steinberg, *New CIETAC Rules to Internationalize China Arbitration, July 2012 R&P China Lawyers* (2012).

13

Is a legal implicature only in the eye of the beholder? On the interpretation of the CISG convention

IZABELA SKOCZEŃ

13.1. Introduction

There are two main possibilities of contract interpretation. One can focus either on the bare, literal wording of provisions or on the wording embedded in the pragmatic circumstances of contract formation—the negotiations. The former is referred to as the plain meaning approach or parol evidence rule, while the latter is known as the intentional interpretation. If the approaches clash, it is the intentional approach that, in principle, prevails. Nevertheless, there are exceptions to this rule. These constitute a genuine challenge for any theory of ordinary communication and they will be investigated in this chapter.

13.1.1 The Gricean framework

The backbone of ordinary communication theory was formulated by Paul Grice in 1975, in his article 'Logic and Conversation'. The key observation is that we communicate more than the literal meaning of the words we utter. Consequently, a speaker means more than he actually says. What is not uttered but communicated is referred to as 'conversational implicature'. To decode an implicature, the hearer must carry out some process, either heuristic or quasi-deductive,[1] based on certain assumptions. Moreover, these assumptions must be shared by all parties to the conversation. Grice calls these maxims of conversation. Their content is dependent on the purpose of the communication. Thus, for example, an ordinary chit-chat aimed

[1] The character of these processes is highly controversial.

Izabela Skoczeń, *Is a legal implicature only in the eye of the beholder? On the interpretation of the CISG convention*
In: *Language and Legal Interpretation in International Law*. Edited by: Anne Lise Kjær and Joanna Lam, Oxford University Press.
 DOI: 10.1093/oso/9780190855208.003.0014

at some exchange of information is based on the following maxims of conversation, as defined by Grice:

> QUALITY: Try to make your contribution one that is true.
> 1. Do not say what you believe to be false.
> 2. Do not say that for which you lack evidence.
> QUANTITY:
> 1. Make your contribution as informative as is required
> (for the current purposes of the exchange).
> 2. Do not make your contribution more informative than is required.
> RELATION: Be relevant.
> MANNER: Be perspicuous.
> 1. Avoid obscurity of expression.
> 2. Avoid ambiguity.
> 3. Be brief. (Avoid unnecessary prolixity.)
> 4. Be orderly.[2]

The following example from 'Logic and Conversation' illustrates how the maxims are supposed to work:

(I) A: I am out of petrol.
B: There is a garage round the corner. (Gloss: B would be infringing the maxim 'be relevant' unless he thinks or thinks it possible, that the garage is open and has petrol to sell; so he implicates that the garage is, or at least may be open, etc.)[3]

Furthermore, to make communication successful, and to make the hearer extract the implicature 'the garage is open and has petrol' from (I), all the parties to the linguistic exchange must cooperate. This is labelled the 'cooperative principle' (CP): 'make your conversational contribution such as is required, at the stage at which it occurs, by the accepted purpose or direction of talk exchange in which you are engaged.'[4]

To produce an implicature, three conditions must be fulfilled. Speaker S conversationally implicates q by saying p in context C, if:

(a) S is presumed to observe the relevant conversational maxims in C;

[2] Laurence R. Horn and Gregory Ward, *The Handbook of Pragmatics* (2004), 7.
[3] P. Grice, *Logic and Conversation* (1975), 51.
[4] Ibid., 44.

(b) the assumption that S meant (or intended that) q is required in order to make sense of S's utterance of p in context C, given the conversational maxims that apply;
(c) S believes/assumes that his/her hearers can recognize condition b, and can recognize that S knows that.[5]

The third condition (c) is crucial for the reasoning laid down in this chapter. This is the case for two reasons. First, the speaker must believe that the hearer recognizes that the speaker is implicating something. In addition, it must be possible for the hearer to believe that the speaker knows that the hearer recognizes the implicature. To conclude, the communicative act will be successful if and only if it is possible for the hearer to recognize the speaker's intention.

13.1.2. The Vienna Convention for International Sales of Goods (1980)

The theory sketched above is reflected in the provisions dealing with the interpretation of contracts in the legal instruments of international sales. A perfect example is Article 8 of the Vienna Convention for International Sales of Goods (CISG) of 1980 or the almost identical provisions of chapter 4 of the UNIDROIT Principles of International Commercial Contracts of 2010. They apply only when the wording of contractual clauses is controversial among the parties. Let us take a closer look at the CISG provision:

Article 8:

(1) For the purposes of this Convention statements made by and other conduct of a party are to be interpreted according to his intent where the other party knew or could not have been unaware what that intent was.
(2) If the preceding paragraph is not applicable, statements made by and other conduct of a party are to be interpreted according to the understanding that a reasonable person of the same kind as the other party would have had in the same circumstances.
(3) In determining the intent of a party or the understanding a reasonable person would have had, due consideration is to be given to all relevant circumstances of the case including the negotiations, any practices which the parties have established between themselves, usages and any subsequent conduct of the parties.

[5] A. Marmor, *Philosophy of Law* (2001), 152.

The first subsection of this article states that the subjective intention of a party will be taken into account if the opposing party was aware or could not have been unaware of that intention. Therefore, it is only when the communicative act was fully successful under the circumstances that the subjective understanding of a contractual provision is taken into account. Article 4.2(1) of the UNIDROIT principles has an almost identical wording: 'The statements and other conduct of a party shall be interpreted according to that party's intention if the other party knew or could not have been unaware of that intention.' This is referred to as the subjective test.

Nevertheless, any communication act can fail. Moreover, it is often impossible to prove that the hearer knew of the speaker's intention. For these reasons, subsection (2) of Article 8 CISG was conceived. When the subjective intent has not been successfully conveyed or it is not possible to prove that the hearer knew of the speaker's intention, the provision is interpreted just as it would have been understood by a reasonable person of the same kind as the opposing party and in the same circumstances. In other words, the statement or conduct is understood in the way that any reasonable person standing in the shoes of the other party would have understood it. This is referred to as the 'objective test' and is mirrored by Article 4.1(2) of the UNIDROIT principles.[6]

The definition of circumstances can be found in the last subsection of the discussed provision. Article 8(3) defines the relevant elements of the context in which a statement or conduct is embedded to determine the result of the objective test. These are, respectively, the negotiations, any practices that the parties have established between themselves, usages, and any subsequent conduct of the parties. Article 4.3 of the UNIDROIT principles is almost identical in content. Therefore, the understanding of a reasonable person is a concept rooted in linguistic pragmatics—the study of utterances embedded in context.

In conclusion, the methods of solving interpretational controversies in international legal instruments governing commercial relations are strongly grounded in pragmatic processes analysed by philosophical conceptions created by Paul Grice and his followers. Article 8 of the CISG is underpinned by the very same idea of mutual understanding as the Gricean CP. It is undisputed that the Gricean approach is very convincing when dealing with day-to-day communication. By contrast, what is controversial is its direct application to contract law. Nevertheless, before addressing this controversy, another convergence between the philosophy of language and contract law will be discussed: the occurrence of conversational implicatures.

[6] Martin Schmidt-Kessel, 'Article 8', in Ingeborg Schwenzer, ed., *Schlechtriem and Schwenzer: Commentary on the UN Convention for the International Sale of Goods (CISG)* (2010), 155.

13.2. Implicatures in choice of law clauses encompassing CISG

As noted above, there are two main approaches to contract law interpretation: the plain meaning approach and the intentionalist doctrine. It is possible to detect conversational implicatures in contractual clauses regardless of the approach adopted. Therefore, a brief overview of the plain meaning and intentionalist approaches will be provided, followed by examples of resulting implicatures.

13.2.1. Plain meaning and the parol evidence rule

The basic interpretive approach in contract law is the plain meaning approach. This approach yields an understanding of contractual clauses based on the plain meaning of the words used or based solely on the *wording* of the clause. Any other oral evidence, which could contradict the wording, is barred. Moreover, any recourse to extrinsic evidence is possible only in the case of ambiguity. A similar concept is the parol evidence rule, a doctrine largely applied in the United States of America. The label is deceptive: '[T]he parol evidence rule fits none of the words in its name: it is not limited to parol—that is, oral—testimony, it is not evidentiary, and it is not really a rule.'[7]

In fact, the parol evidence rule forbids interpretation based on factors other than the wording of the contract. It also guarantees a high comfort of certainty and predictability as to the reading of contractual provisions. Nevertheless, it often stands in direct contradiction to another core idea of contract law—the protection of the intention of the parties:

> The parol evidence rule serves a legitimate end. We enter into written contracts to avoid disputes in the future, and if every contract were simply the beginning point in a testimonial battle, we would gain little by writing things down. But the written word is not as infallible a guide as some think, and people often do not read agreements and often do believe themselves protected when they are told 'don't worry about that clause'.[8]

Although Article 8(3) of the CISG excludes the parol evidence rule in interpreting contracts governed by this Convention, the parties can always include

[7] P. Linzer, 'The Comfort of Certainty: Plain Meaning and the Parole Evidence Rule', *Fordham Law Review*, 71/799 (2002), 802.

[8] Ibid., 806.

a merger clause in their agreement.[9] This is a clause that explicitly restates the plain meaning rule and bars any recourse to extra-writing evidence.

13.2.1.1. Choice of law clauses encompassing CISG (self-promoting mechanism)

Pursuant to Article 1(a)[10] of the Convention, the CISG applies by default if two requirements are fulfilled. First, if the contract is concluded between parties that have their places of business in states that are signatories to the Convention. Second, if the concluded contract is a sales contract (the Convention is not excluded by its Article 3).[11]

Article 6[12] of the CISG enables the parties to exclude, explicitly or implicitly, the application of the Convention. As a result, the choice of law clauses must be assessed by the Convention itself. Consequently, several questions arise. What is an explicit exclusion? How is a choice of law clause formulated in order to successfully exclude the CISG? Does a clause referring to the law of a contracting state, such as

(II) This contract is governed by Polish law

exclude the application of the Vienna Convention?

Let us address these questions, first, from the point of view of law and second, from the point of view of the philosophy of language.

From the point of view of law, the answer of both courts and scholars is almost unanimously negative.[13] This is because the principal aim of the CISG is to unify

[9] Ingeborg Schwenzer, *Schlechtriem and Schwenzer: Commentary on the UN Convention on the International Sale of Goods* (2010), 162.

[10] '(1) This Convention applies to contracts of sale of goods between parties whose places of business are in different States:

(a) when the States are Contracting States; or
(b) when the rules of private international law lead to the application of the law of a Contracting State.

(2) The fact that the parties have their places of business in different States is to be disregarded whenever this fact does not appear either from the contract or from any dealings between, or from information disclosed by, the parties at any time before or at the conclusion of the contract.

(3) Neither the nationality of the parties nor the civil or commercial character of the parties or of the contract is to be taken into consideration in determining the application of this Convention.'

[11] '(1) Contracts for the supply of goods to be manufactured or produced are to be considered sales unless the party who orders the goods undertakes to supply a substantial part of the materials necessary for such manufacture or production.

(2) This Convention does not apply to contracts in which the preponderant part of the obligations of the party who furnishes the goods consists in the supply of labour or other services.'

[12] 'The parties may exclude the application of this Convention or, subject to article 12, derogate from or vary the effect of any of its provisions.'

[13] See: Auto case: http://cisgw3.law.pace.edu/cases/060123a3.html; Automobile case: http://cisgw3.law.pace.edu/cases/080331g1.html; Boiler case: http://cisgw3.law.pace.edu/cases/090402a3.html; *Easom automation system v. thyssenkrup fabco corp*: http://cisgw3.law.pace.edu/cases/070928u1.

sales law around the globe. Consequently, the Convention is deemed to have a 'self-promoting mechanism', a presumption of its own application. This political aim is justified by the following line of reasoning. If a state is a signatory to the Convention, then the CISG becomes part of the law of that state. As a consequence, the term 'Polish' encompasses the Vienna Convention. As the court found in the Tantalum powder case, 'The mere resort to national law (here: Austrian law) as in [Buyer]'s standard terms therefore cannot exclude the CISG, where both parties have their places of business in Member States of the Convention.'[14]

A different approach was adopted, for instance, in Russia,[15] where the court made a distinction between the substantive law and the legal system itself. Nevertheless, if a state is a signatory to the Convention, this distinction seems hard to grasp, because the CISG is part of the substantive law of that state. By contrast, in the Viva Vino Import Case,[16] the court found that the existence of a single choice of law clause in a contract (no matter how worded) excludes the Convention. However, were we to follow this line of reasoning, it would lead to the complete annihilation of the application of the Convention around the globe. This is because most contracts concluded worldwide contain a choice of law clause. Consequently, the principle aim of the CISG—the unification of legal systems—would be completely frustrated.[17]

The reasoning sketched above can also be explained from the point of view of the philosophy of language and its tools: the choice of law clause in (II) is considered by both courts and scholars as a sentence giving rise to a conversational implicature in the Gricean sense.[18] What is implicated is the application of the CISG to the contract itself.

html; Fashion textiles case: http://cisgw3.law.pace.edu/cases/900424g1.html; Gasoline and gas oil case: http://cisgw3.law.pace.edu/cases/011022a3.html; Omnibus case: http://cisgw3.law.pace.edu/cases/040421a3.html; F. Enderlein and D. Maskow, *International Sales Law: United Nations Convention on Contracts for the International Sale of Goods Convention on the Limitation Period in the International Sale of Goods* (1992), 48–9; Schwenzer, *Schlechtriem and Schwenzer*, 109; and Ingeborg Schwenzer, P. Hachem, and Ch. Kee, *Global Sales and Contract Law* (2012), 39.

[14] http://cisgw3.law.pace.edu/cases/031217a3.html.

[15] 11 October 2002 Arbitration proceeding 62/2002, http://cisgw3.law.pace.edu/cases/021011r1.html.

[16] *Viva Vino Import v. Farnese Vini*, United States Federal District Court (Pennsylvania), 29 August 2000, http://cisgw3.law.pace.edu/cases/000829u1.html.

[17] *Claudia v. Olivieri Footwear Ltd*, 1998 WL 164824 (SDNY April 7, 1998), at 4.

[18] Philosophers of language are quite unanimous that conversational implicatures are pragmatic occurrences. By contrast, there is heated discussion about the character of the sentence meaning (as opposed to the pragmatic speaker's meaning). There are formal semantic theories that tend to argue that sentences express full or partial propositions, which can be attributed truth or falsity, such as those of E. Borg, H. Cappelen and E. Lepore, or K. Bach and R. Harnish. On the other hand, there are theories such as those of F. Recanati, Ch. Travis, and J. Searle which state that without pragmatic enrichments, a bare sentence meaning does not express any proposition that could be attributed a truth value. Nevertheless, this debate has no influence upon the considerations laid out in this paper,

Let us analyse step-by-step the formation of this implicature. The starting point is a choice of law clause worded as in (II). The issue is the interpretation of the word 'Polish', 'Austrian', 'English', and so on. The dispute started when courts were forced to decide between two lines of argumentation. The first line of argumentation was given by the party for whom the national law, for example Polish (and not the CISG), was more favourable. Therefore, it stated that the literal meaning of adjectives such as 'Polish', 'Austrian', and 'English' cannot designate the Convention. The Oxford Dictionary provides the following definition of the adjective 'Polish': 'Relating to Poland or its people or language'. Consequently, the adjective in the choice of law clause (II) encompasses statutes that are of Polish origin, that is, were drafted in Poland and enacted by the Polish Parliament. Thus, they are national and not international in origin. The opposing party, for whom the CISG was more favourable, argued that Poland had signed the Convention and that its provisions had become part of the country's substantive law. Thus, the term 'Polish' encompasses the CISG. Moreover, the opposing party saw the choice of law clause, knew its wording, and did not object to it during the negotiations.

When faced with such dilemmas, the courts always rule in favour of the Vienna Convention, bearing in mind its aim of unifying the law around the globe. Nevertheless, they cannot change the literal meaning of adjectives such as 'Polish' in dictionaries. Therefore, to justify their decisions, they deploy a line of argumentation based on linguistic pragmatics and conversational implicatures: if the clause (II) is drafted in a context in which

1 Both parties are from different states;
2 Both parties have their places of business in member states of the Convention;
3 The law mentioned in the clause (here, Polish law) is the law of a state that signed the CISG; and
4 The contract is a contract of sale within the meaning of the Convention,

then, in this context, the adjective 'Polish' encompasses the Vienna Convention, regardless of the international provenance of this statute. In other words, in such a context, the sentence (II) implicates conversationally that the Convention applies. This is confirmed by the Gricean Maxim of Quantity for two reasons. First, the maxim requires not making your contribution more informative than required. Stating explicitly that the CISG applies would be superfluous. Second, the maxim requires making the contribution exactly as informative as required. Thus, if the parties had wanted to exclude the Convention, they would have stated it explicitly in the clause (the means of excluding the CISG by the parties are discussed in point ii, below).

considerations that are focused on strong, non-controversial forms of pragmatic inferences; that is, conversational implicatures.

The legal basis for such reasoning is Article 8(2) and the objective test. Thus, in the court's eyes, any reasonable person, when faced with a clause like (II) during such international negotiations, would have understood that the CISG applies. He or she would have grasped the implicature because of the context of the utterance and the need to abide by the Maxim of Quantity.

Despite the fact that such an implicature would probably not be formed in natural language, every court will recognize it and point to the CISG as the applicable law. The court will recognize it even though both parties may have thought that the Polish national law would apply when they approved a choice of law clause, as in (II). Consequently, it is a very convenient political tool to identify implicatures in sentences where there are none in natural language. It is thus an interesting example of how such linguistic tools can be used to achieve certain, I must concede, noble, political goals.

13.2.1.2. Cancellation of the implicature and exclusion of the CISG

Cancellability is an undisputed feature of every conversational implicature. The speaker can always cancel the implicature by stating some additional information, for example:

(III) A: I am out of petrol.
B: There is a garage round the corner, but I doubt that it is open.[19]

In the above example, B has cancelled the implicature that the garage is open and can sell A petrol. This was achieved by the provision of additional information to the sentence that contradicted the initial hypothetical conversational implicature.

Analogously, courts and scholars also acknowledge the possibility of cancelling the implicature created by a choice of law clause (II). This cancellation of the implicated application of the CISG amounts to a successful explicit exclusion of the Convention. This exclusion can be achieved in two ways. First, there is the express opt-out doctrine, which formulates the clause in the following manner:

(IV) This contract is governed by Polish law with the exclusion of the Vienna Convention on the International Sale of Goods.[20]

This is the safest way to preclude the application of the CISG.

Second, it can be done by an express reference to the national sales law of a contracting state:

[19] Marmor, *Philosophy of Law.*

[20] Schwenzer, *Schlechtriem and Schwenzer.*

(V) This contract is governed by the Polish National Sales Act from 2000.[21]

These are the two exclusive methods of cancelling the above-described implicature.

In conclusion, the adoption of the plain meaning doctrine or parol evidence rule in contract law does not mean avoiding the use of linguistic tools such as conversational implicatures. Quite the contrary. Courts and scholars use them willingly, as excellent technical means of backing up their political arguments. The choice of law clauses encompassing CISG are only one particular example of a much broader scheme of linguistic manipulation, a manipulation that is possible because the legal language is deemed different from the natural one. It is a manipulation that allows global goals to be achieved. Let us now turn to the second and alternative way of dealing with contract interpretation: the intentionalist doctrine.

13.2.2. The intentionalist interpretation

Article 4.1(1) of the UNIDROIT principles states the most fundamental idea of contract law: 'A contract shall be interpreted according to the common intention of the Parties.' Thus, it is not only the bare wording of contractual provision that is decisive. Due regard must be given to the parties' intent. Consequently, it is what the parties want and not what they write that is to prevail. This idea is reflected by Article 8 of the CISG, which sets out the subjective and objective test for determining the parties' intentions. Article 8(1) states the condition for taking into account the subjective intention of a party. This condition is that the hearer has recognized or could not have been unaware of the speaker's intention. It thus requires that the communication act performed by the speaker be fully successful. Furthermore, Article 8(2) establishes the objective test, which is employed in cases where the communicative act has failed. As a result, it is the objective understanding of a reasonable person of the same kind as the hearer, standing in her shoes, that prevails. Finally, Article 8(3) lists the elements that are relevant to determining the pragmatic context in which the reasonable hearer from Article 8(2) is situated.

To sum up, there are four possible, hypothetical outcomes, as far as the state of mind of the parties to a contract is concerned:

1 Both parties want the CISG to apply to their contract.
2 Only one party wants the CISG to apply.
   a The other party knows and does not object.
   b The other party does not know.
   c The other party knows and objects.

[21] Fashion textiles case: http://cisgw3.law.pace.edu/cases/900424g1.html.

3 Both parties do not want the CISG to apply.
4 Both parties do not know that the CISG applies to their contract.

The first situation is clear—the Vienna Convention applies. The second situation is more complex. If the party willing to apply the CISG successfully communicates this intention to its contractual partner, and the latter does not object, then pursuant to Article 8(1) CISG, the Convention applies. By contrast, if it does not communicate its will successfully, the CISG might not apply. Furthermore, when it is not clear whether the communication of the intention was successful, the objective test from Article 8(2) must be applied. However, if the party willing to apply the CISG successfully communicates this intention to the other party and the other party objects, then the Convention is not applied. The third possibility in principle results in the exclusion of the Vienna Convention. This exclusion is performed either through a special wording of the choice of law clause, as depicted above, or through an implicit exclusion of the CISG pursuant to its Article 6. The implicit exclusion can be performed through certain acts other than being written in the contract or stated during the negotiations that the CISG is excluded. The fourth situation is the most controversial one. This is because if both parties do not know that the CISG exists and governs their contract by default, they cannot want the Convention to apply to their contract. However, the courts rule that the fact that none of the parties has knowledge of the CISG's existence can constitute neither an explicit nor an implicit exclusion of the CISG.[22] Moreover, the reasoning of the court is sensible, because in order to exclude something, two requirements must be met:

(VI) You must know WHAT you are excluding

and

(VII) You must know THAT you are excluding it.

As a result, in the fourth situation, the parties cannot successfully exclude the CISG. Nevertheless, the situation can easily be reversed: to apply the CISG to a contract, both parties must agree to the Vienna Convention governing their agreement.

[22] Automobile Case: '[A]pplication of the CISG cannot be excluded because both parties solely argued on the basis of German national law in the first instance', and 'It is true that both parties have based their allegations prior to and during the proceedings in the Court of First Instance on the BGB; however, this does not imply a post-contractual exclusion of the CISG. There is no mutual agreement of intent of the parties, as this requires an express declaration of intent in respect to a specific legal consequence. The application of the wrong provisions due to a legal misapprehension does not meet this requirement.'

Consequently, to have the contractual partners agree on a matter, the same two requirements need to be fulfilled. Therefore, it is a necessary condition that both parties know

(VIII) WHAT they are agreeing to

and

(IX) THAT they are agreeing to it.

Thus, while in the fourth situation the parties could not have excluded the Convention, they cannot have agreed to the CISG governing their contract either. Let us attempt to address this paradox.

13.3. Discussion

When both parties are ignorant of the fact that the CISG exists and that their contract is a sales contract within the meaning of the Convention, the CISG should apply on the basis of the plain meaning doctrine or parol evidence rule. Moreover, under this doctrine, even if the same contractual partners include a choice of law clause in their contract, which is worded as clause (II) and are persuaded that this will trigger the application of national non-unified law, the CISG will still apply. However, the CISG contains Article 8, which is viewed by scholars as a rejection of the plain meaning doctrine or parol evidence rule. Consequently, in the case of both parties' ignorance, the paradox stated in section 2.2 of this chapter must be resolved. In the author's view, the courts should rule in favour of the CISG for two solid reasons.

First, the disputed legal act is an international legal instrument aiming at the unification of sales law around the globe. This is confirmed even in the preamble of the CISG, where its drafters explain it thus:

> The State Parties to this Convention, . . . Being of the opinion that the adoption of uniform rules which govern contracts for the international sale of goods and take into account the different social, economic and legal systems would contribute to the removal of legal barriers in international trade and promote the development of international trade, have agreed as follows . . .

Thus, the courts are willing to resolve any doubts in favour of the CISG application.

Second, the law contains rules that are binding upon agents. Even in contract law, the parties' autonomy faces limitations and constraints. The parties cannot act against compulsory provisions of the law that regulates their relations. If a state joins the Convention, the Convention becomes part of the law of this state and binds the agents just as any other piece of legislation. A contrary argument could lead to absurd outcomes. Consider the following example. If two Polish citizens conclude a sales contract in Poland governed by the Polish Civil Code, the contract will be governed by this Code regardless of whether the business partners knew about the existence of the Code and its application to their agreement at the moment of its conclusion. This is because this Code contains provisions that are directly binding upon the parties. In other words, in international trade, the parties are free to choose the law governing their agreement. Nevertheless, if they choose the law of a contracting state, the CISG applies. This is because the CISG is part of the law of that state and contains binding provisions. Therefore, it is sensible to apply the CISG in the fourth situation discussed, of 'ignorant parties'.

However, while the line of thought stated above is perfectly convincing from a legal point of view, it is contrary to the classical Gricean theory. Nevertheless, it might not be contrary to other theories of ordinary human communication. Consider the following example:

> (X) Jack and John are having a conversation at a party. Jack points to a lady standing next to Joe and says to John:
>
> Jack: Joe's wife is very beautiful.
>
> John: She could be slightly thinner though.[23]

Let us assume that the lady at whom Jack is pointing is not Joe's wife but merely Joe's girlfriend. From the point of view of a theory of meaning, Jack expresses a proposition that is false. Nevertheless, from the point of view of a theory of communication, the communicative act is fully successful. Jack has referred to the lady he wanted to refer to. John grasped the intention of referring to that lady and understood that Jack meant that she had the property of being beautiful. Consequently, the fact that both Jack and John are ignorant or mistaken, because the lady was not Joe's wife, has no influence on the success of communication. Jack and John referred to the lady they wanted to refer to, even though they were mistaken about the property of being a wife. Thus, we can refer to people or objects even if we are mistaken about their properties. Moreover, we can refer to sets of objects even when we are mistaken about what elements the set has. For example, we can refer to a collection of books in a library while not knowing what books are parts of it. Analogously, we

[23] A similar example can be found in K. Donellan, 'Reference and Definite Descriptions', *The Philosophical Review*, 77 (1966), 281–304.

can refer to the library of a certain law without knowing that the CISG book is a part of it. This requires an externalist approach to communication.

The 'ignorant parties' situation discussed in this section is an example of successful communication. The contractual partners are ignorant or mistaken as to the application of the CISG. However, they can be in perfect agreement that, for instance, Polish national law will apply to their contract, regardless of their ignorance of the existence of the CISG. As a result, we have a successful communication of intentions. Thus, the classical Gricean approach cannot explain the court's decision to apply the CISG. However, this reasoning can be explained by externalist theories of communication.

To sum up, we have reached a point at which the court's explanation clashes with the classical Gricean one. In other words, the court's explanation given by the plain meaning doctrine contradicts the intentional approach.

13.4. Conclusion

To conclude, the employment of linguistic-theoretical concepts from the philosophy of language in the realm of law can be either extremely helpful or quite harmful. It can be helpful when the technical-linguistic explanation backs up a legal line of reasoning aimed at achieving a broader political goal. This is the case of choice of law clauses referring to the law of a state, such as 'Polish law'. They are regarded as sentences giving rise to a conversational implicature, an implicature whose content is the applicability of the CISG.

The employment of linguistic-theoretical arguments can also be harmful, however, because natural language has quite different aims from those of the goals of legal parlance. Moreover, their employment does not take into account the limitations created by legal provisions to the communicative acts occurring within the realm of law. Consequently, theories dealing with natural language communication cannot be straightforwardly applied to legalese. We need a new, flexible theory of communication, created to address all the challenges posed by modern contract law.[24]

References

Donellan, Keith, 'Reference and Definite Desciptions', *The Philosophical Review*, 77 (1966), 281–304.

Enderlein, Fritz and Dietrich Maskow, *International Sales Law: United Nations Convention on Contracts for the International Sale of Goods Convention on the Limitation Period in the International Sale of Goods* (New York, 1992).

[24] I sketch such a theory in Skoczeń, Izabela 2019. Implicatures within legal language. Berlin: Springer.

Grice, Paul, 'Logic and Conversation', in P. Cole and J. Morgan, eds., *Syntax and Semantics*, iii (New York, 1975), 22–40.

Horn, Laurence R. and Gregory Ward, *The Handbook of Pragmatics* (Oxford, 2004).

Linzer, Peter, 'The Comfort of Certainty: Plain Meaning and the Parole Evidence Rule', *Fordham Law Review*, 71/799 (2002), 799–839.

Marmor, Andrei, *Philosophy of Law* (Princeton, NJ, 2001).

Schmidt-Kessel, Martin, 'Article 8', in Ingeborg Schwenzer, ed., *Schlechtriem and Schwenzer: Commentary on the UN Convention for the International Sale of Goods (CISG)* (3rd edn, Oxford, 2010).

Schwenzer, Ingeborg, *Schlechtriem and Schwenzer: Commentary on the UN Convention on the International Sale of Goods* (3rd edn, Oxford, 2010).

Schwenzer, Ingeborg, Hachem Pascal, and Kee Christopher, *Global Sales and Contract Law* (Oxford, 2012).

14

The vague meaning of the Fair and Equitable Treatment principle in investment arbitration and new generation clarifications

GÜNEŞ ÜNÜVAR

14.1. Introduction

The promotion and protection of foreign investments are traditional, yet prevalent, objectives of international investment agreements (IIAs).[1] To capture these objectives, these agreements usually include obligations for states to extend the treatment they accord to their domestic investors (or favoured third party investors) to foreign investors. They further incorporate an independent obligation of fair treatment, which may require a treatment better than that accorded to domestic investors.[2] Provisions that embody the 'fair and equitable treatment' (FET) principle, what has been called 'the most important standard in investment disputes',[3] work exactly towards that goal. In many IIAs, parties have an obligation to 'ensure fair and equitable treatment to the investments of investors of the other [party]'.[4]

Over the course of the last five decades, states have formulated different ways to include this obligation in their IIAs. Some treaty parties included different qualifiers

[1] This research has been funded by the Carlsberg Foundation (Carlsbergfondet), and conducted under the auspices of iCourts, funded by the Danish National Research Foundation Grant no. DNRF105.

[2] Klein Bronfman, 'Fair and Equitable Treatment: An Evolving Standard', *Max Planck Yearbook of UN Law*, 10 (2006), 611.

[3] Christoph Schreuer, 'Fair and Equitable Treatment in Arbitral Practice', *Journal of World Investment and Trade*, 6/3 (2005), 357–385.

[4] Netherlands—Turkey Bilateral Investment Treaty (1989) Article 3(1).

Güneş Ünüvar, *The vague meaning of the Fair and Equitable Treatment principle in investment arbitration and new generation clarifications* In: *Language and Legal Interpretation in International Law*. Edited by: Anne Lise Kjær and Joanna Lam, Oxford University Press. © Oxford University Press 2022. DOI: 10.1093/oso/9780190855208.003.0015

to their FET provisions so as to prevent any responsibility beyond what is required under 'customary international law',[5] or 'international law'.[6] This variety of FET clauses stems from states' intentions to clarify the extent and scope of their understanding of the standard of treatment accorded to foreign investments. Despite these differences, FET clauses have usually lacked any elaborate description of what kinds of state acts would be deemed 'unfair'.

The puzzle of the content of FET clauses has thus sustained its relevance in the last few decades due to this perpetual lack of specificity and its constant appearance in arbitral claims. The arbitral practice has strived to determine its content over time with a keen regard to rules of interpretation in international law,[7] as well as preceding arbitral decisions and doctrinal arguments. States have not always agreed with what the arbitral tribunals thought the FET to be. Many have revisited their IIAs in order to further elaborate on their meaning of 'fair and equitable', and reshaped (or, depending on their goals and interests, chose not to change) their projected approach to the future IIAs they might sign and, in different ways, addressed the vagueness embedded in the principle.

The state obligation of according FET to foreign investors is a remarkably specific manifestation of a multi-faceted set of semantic, legal, and political ideas on the concept of fairness. From Aristotle to Rawls, fairness and justice have been discussed across a temporal and intellectual expanse.[8] It is evident why the concept of fairness is particularly important to jurists—it sits at the core of countless legal-philosophical inquiries and is bound by the context offered by each legal field from which it stems.

In IIA practice, any perceived difference between the ordinary meanings of the words 'fair' and 'equitable' seems to have little to do with their interpretation. Furthermore, the use of the word 'just' instead of 'fair' probably will not have a profound effect on the interpretation of the FET clause in an IIA.[9] Some scholars further assert that the term 'fair and equitable' and its variables interchangeably aim to attest normativity to a particular sphere of state intervention which remains sub-expropriatory or non-discriminatory.[10] In a sense, this framework collectively determined by different formulations of FET provisions is similar to the Kelsenian approach on general norms as 'frames', which argues that when a judicial decision

[5] United States—Colombia Trade Promotion Agreement (2012) Article 10.5; Canada—Czech Republic Bilateral Investment Treaty (2012) Article 3(1)(a).

[6] France—Ethiopia Bilateral Investment Treaty (2004) Article 3.

[7] Article 31, Vienna Convention on the Law of Treaties (1969).

[8] John Rawls, *A Theory of Justice* (rev. edn, 1999).

[9] Rudolf Dolzer and Christoph Schreuer, *Principles of International Investment Law* (2nd edn, 2012).

[10] Andreas F. Lowenfeld, *International Economic Law* (2nd edn, 2008), 557.

is based on a statute, it represents *one* of those individual norms, rather than *the* individual norm.[11]

However, it is through the analysis of the ordinary meaning of 'fair' that its situational content becomes apparent. The Oxford Dictionary defines 'fair' as '(1) in accordance with rules and standards; legitimate, or (2) just or appropriate in the circumstances'.[12] Other definitions, as referred to by some arbitral tribunals, include 'just', 'even-handed', 'unbiased', [and] 'legitimate'.[13] This chapter, however, will not discuss in depth the independent word meaning of 'fair' and how it differs from others such as 'equitable' or 'just', which would far exceed its intended scope. It will use the abovementioned definitions as the 'ordinary' meaning of the word 'fair'. It will also take into account the arbitral *jurisprudence constante* on FET principle and its constituent elements to better understand its substantive normative transformation.

Another underlying assumption of this chapter is that vagueness and ambiguity are distinct concepts in law and language studies. Poscher associates vagueness with 'borderline cases', defined as 'cases "in which one just does not know whether to apply the expression or withhold it, and one's not knowing is not due to ignorance of the facts" '.[14] Ambiguity is linked with expressions having multiple meanings—as in the word 'fair', which, without an explicit context, can refer to fairness as in a *fair sovereign*, or, say, *fair hair*. This chapter concerns itself with the *vagueness* of what is fair—what gives rise to the controversy at this junction is whether or not certain acts and treatments can be regarded as fair in borderline cases.

In the light of the background above, I will examine the most recent wave of efforts to tackle the vagueness of FET *as a manifestation of fairness*, and a normative legal rule commonly found in IIAs. I will explore what I identify as the latest phase of the decades-long evolution of the principle in international investment arbitration. In section 14.2, I will outline the historical development of the 'fair treatment' of foreign investors and modern FET provisions. In section 14.3, I will explore the cumulative effect of arbitral practice, as well as the initial reactions to the arbitral interpretation and application of FET. In section 14.4, I will analyse the FET clauses contained particularly in the final text of the Comprehensive Economic and Trade

[11] Hans Kelsen, *General Theory of Norms*, tr. Michael Hartney (1991), 366; also generally see Timothy A. O. Endicott, *Vagueness in Law* (2000).

[12] The Oxford Dictionaries, definition of 'fair', available at http://www.oxforddictionaries.com/us/definition/american_english/fair.

[13] *MTD Equity Sdn. Bhd. and MTD Chile S.A. v. Chile* (2004), Award, ARB/01/7, par. 113. The Tribunal, in its FET analysis, cited the Concise Oxford Dictionary to discern the ordinary meaning of 'fair' and 'equitable'. Roland Klager, *'Fair and Equitable Treatment' in International Investment Law* (2011), 41.

[14] Ralf Poscher, 'Ambiguity and Vagueness in Legal Interpretation', in Lawrence Solan and Peter Tiersma, eds., *Oxford Handbook on Language and Law* (2011), 3; also see generally Endicott, *Vagueness in Law*.

Agreement (CETA),[15] the draft text of the Trans-Pacific Partnership (TPP),[16] and the EU negotiation text of the Transatlantic Trade and Investment Partnership (TTIP),[17] in order to highlight the impact of states' past arbitral experience on the construction of these new instruments. In my conclusions, I will argue that explicit clarifications on the subset of FET in IIAs as included in the CETA and TTIP texts would work in favour of encouraging coherent interpretation and a better understanding of this principle, in light of its transformation towards a normative legal rule and the accumulated arbitral experience attesting to this transformation.

14.2. Historical background on fairness and foreigners

14.1. Fairness and protection of foreign investments

Rules and thoughts on fair treatment of foreigners, specifically foreign merchants, go far back in history. In 1157, Henry II issued a charter to the merchants of Cologne, in which he provided that the persons and possessions of the merchants shall be 'in [his] custody and protection' and that they shall be protected 'as if they were [his] men'.[18] A century later, the 1215 Magna Carta read that 'if [our merchants] are safe [in a foreign land], [their merchants] shall be safe in our land'.[19] Five centuries later, in his 1758 treatise T*he Law of Nations*, De Vattel wrote that 'as soon as [the sovereign] admits [foreigners], he engages to protect them as his own subjects, and to afford them perfect security, as far as depends on him'.[20] Twenty years after De Vattel, the US and France signed a Treaty of Amity and Commerce which included a most-favoured-nation clause (Article 2) and a mutual obligation to 'protect and defend' the property owned by the other party.[21]

These few examples illustrate an obligation of a sovereign towards a group, in this case foreign merchants, shaped in accordance with the treatment accorded to another group. Henry II's protection emulates that which he provides to his own subjects. The Magna Carta emphasizes the treatment accorded to domestic

[15] CETA Final Text as of 29 February 2016, available at http://trade.ec.europa.eu/doclib/docs/2016/february/tradoc_154329.pdf.

[16] European Commission TTIP Proposal Draft, available at http://trade.ec.europa.eu/doclib/docs/2015/september/tradoc_153807.pdf.

[17] TPP draft text, available at https://ustr.gov/trade-agreements/free-trade-agreements/trans-pacific-partnership/tpp-full-text.

[18] Kim Keechang, *Aliens in Medieval Law: The Origins of Modern Citizenship* (2001), 27.

[19] 'Magna Carta, 1215', in David C. Douglas and Harry Rothwell, eds., *English Historical Documents Volume III c.1189–1327* (1975), 312.

[20] Emer de Vattel, *Law of Nations*, tr. Joseph Chitty (1834), 104.

[21] Treaty of Amity and Commerce between the United States and France (1778), available at http://avalon.law.yale.edu/18th_century/fr1788-1.asp.

merchants abroad and equilibrates it to that accorded to foreigners, implicitly setting the limits of what would be regarded as just. De Vattel focuses on the protection of aliens in and of themselves: he envisioned foreigners to be granted the same protection accorded to a sovereign's own subjects, yet not greater than that of this 'domestic' threshold. Again, fairness is determined on the basis of the treatment of another group—however this time, the comparative elements are domestic and foreign merchants within the same jurisdiction. The US–France Treaty has an embedded objective of establishing just rules, embodied by, *inter alia,* a rule ensuring the most favourable treatment in commerce and navigation to merchants of both parties. In each example, fair treatment of merchants and their property had been left to the sovereigns' discretion as well as the interactions between the discretion of sovereigns, since unfair treatment accorded by one sovereign would have reciprocal consequences or it would determine whether or not treatment accorded to another group could be deemed as fair. An intrinsic, relative notion of fair treatment is present, similar to the principles of 'national treatment' (NT) and 'most favoured nation' (MFN) in contemporary trade and investment law.

Until the eighteenth century, it was not easy to find explicit references to overarching international legal standards with which all states were to comply, regardless of their domestic rules and practices on fair treatment of aliens. Then, this notion of relative fairness started to converge upon a non-contingent *meta-principle,* usually referred to as the international minimum standard (IMS) on treatment of aliens. The origins and the content of this standard, from its conception until now, have been elusive—Root, in his famous 1910 address to the American Society of International Law, stated that each country 'is bound to give to the nationals of another country in its territory the benefit of the same [laws, administration, protection, and redress]' only if said country conformed with the 'established standard of civilization'. He continued by asserting that '[t]here is a standard of justice, very simple, very fundamental, and of such general acceptance by all civilized countries as to form a part of the international law', yet did not elaborate on the content or the origins of such standard.[22] Borchard, in 1941, wrote about the misconception of such a standard being 'definable'.[23]

The conception of IMS, however, did not lead to the dissipation of other, contingent manifestations of fairness such as NT or MFN; to the contrary, it continued to co-exist, even overlap (yet occasionally conflict) with them.[24] In effect, the assessment of fairness of treatment accorded by a sovereign had become increasingly

[22] Elihu Root, 'The Basis of Protection to Citizens Residing Abroad', *Proceedings of the ASIL and Its Annual Meeting (1907–1917),* 4 (1910), 19–21.

[23] Edwin Borchard, 'Minimum Standard of the Treatment of Aliens', *Michigan Law Review,* 38/4 (1940), 458.

[24] UNCTAD, ed., 'Fair and Equitable Treatment', in *UNCTAD Series on Issues in International Investment Agreements* (1999).

embedded in this standard rather than as a treatment accorded to others. The Calvo Doctrine (refusing international remedies and diplomatic protection to foreigners), which appeared in 1868, is a reactionary development towards the then-emerging IMS, which required a higher level of protection for foreigners than accorded to nationals.[25] Why, then, did this independent standard of treatment to foreigners come about?

The answer lies within the foundations of sovereignty and the systematization of international legal order. Anghie explains the development of international law as an elaborate series of events towards legitimization of colonial exploitation of resource-rich territories.[26] It is argued that the notion of sovereignty is devised to set a (Westphalian) threshold for 'civilization', and therefore, a gateway to legitimate polity (namely, state)[27] and an inter-state endorsement of a particular territory as a fully-fledged subject of the international legal order.[28] Early on, religious endorsement was an essential component of this threshold.[29] The abysmal socio-economic gap between the Western states and their colonies/quasi-colonies[30] was sustained through perpetual debt relations, extensive resource exploitation, and use of force.[31] Other non-European territories which were under European control or influence without formal responsibility (McLean calls this the 'informal empire' from a nineteenth-century British perspective)[32] did not fit into the definition prescribed by the European states. There was little or no notion of an international society in the contemporary sense, nor a compatible notion of common polity.[33]

Historically, the very idea of a foreigner being entitled to higher protection than that accorded to nationals in a particular territory systematically appears within the colonial context and the 'civilized nations' discourse.[34] Later in the nineteenth

[25] Andrew Newcombe and Lluis Paradell, *Law and Practice of Investment Treaties: Standards of Treatment* (2009), 13; Katia Yannaca-Small, *Arbitration Under International Investment Agreements: A Guide to the Key Issues* (2010), 413.

[26] Antony Anghie, *Imperialism, Sovereignty and the Making of International Law* (2007); see also Kate Miles, *The Origins of International Investment Law: Empire, Environment and the Safeguarding of Capital* (2013).

[27] Daniel Philphott, *Revolutions in Sovereignty: How Ideas Shaped Modern International Relations* (2001), 33.

[28] Ibid.

[29] Ibid.

[30] Nico Schrijver, *Sovereignty over Natural Resources: Balancing Rights and Duties* (2008), 173.

[31] Charles Lipson, *Standing Guard: Protecting Foreign Capital in the Nineteenth and Twentieth Centuries* (1985), 148–149.

[32] David McLean, 'Finance and "Informal Empire" before the First World War', *Economic History Review*, 29/2 (1976), 291–305.

[33] Philphott, *Revolutions in Sovereignty*, 20.

[34] Anghie, *Imperialism, Sovereignty and the Making of International Law*; Miles, *The Origins of International Investment Law*.

century, 'national treatment', as the Calvo Doctrine envisaged it, failed to satisfy colonial empires and capital-exporting states due to a lack of sufficient legal and physical protection, rampant corruption, and a lack of adequate governance in those territories.[35] The backdrop of the 'capital-importing and capital-exporting' dichotomy widely used in the international investment law doctrine may be seen as an extension of this colonial reflex. However, with decolonization, subsequent efforts to prohibit the use of force, the pacific settlement of international disputes,[36] and the advent of international human rights especially, after the Second World War,[37] this colonial drive has been curbed as more territories emerged as sovereign states.

In contemporary IIA practice, such protection is not without limits. For instance, a plethora of arbitral awards distinguish between commercial and political risks, and many IIAs do not protect foreign investors against the former.[38] *Barcelona Traction*,[39] an oft-cited ICJ award, reads as follows:

> When a State admits into its territory foreign investments or foreign nationals it is . . . bound to extend to them the protection of the law. However, it does not thereby become an insurer of the part of another State's wealth which these investments represent. Every investment of this kind carries certain risks.[40]

When compared to the earlier examples of the Magna Carta and De Vattel's Law of Nations, the *Barcelona Traction* award builds upon the same foundation, and aims at a fair balance between a sovereign's conduct and its protection of foreign property, despite its relative complexity.

What is deemed to be fair depends on context—it develops over time and adapts to changing circumstances. 'Fair treatment' accorded by a sovereign to

[35] Anghie, *Imperialism, Sovereignty and the Making of International Law*; Miles, *The Origins of International Investment Law*; Miriam Hood, *Gunboat Diplomacy 1895–1905 Great Power Pressure in Venezuela* (1975).

[36] William I. Hull, *The Two Hague Conferences and Their Contributions to International Law* (1970), 267–448.

[37] Paparinskis observes that '[w]ith the human rights arguments being increasingly put forward in different fora after [WW2], a reassessment of the international standard was required not only in philosophical terms but also as a matter of positive law'. Martins Paparinskis, *The International Minimum Standard and Fair and Equitable Treatment* (2013), 74.

[38] The premise that commercial and business risks fall outside the scope of an IIA seems to stem directly from the well-known *Maffezini* Case: *Emilio Augustin Maffezini v. Kingdom of Spain*, ARB/97/7. Political and commercial risk dichotomy has also been acknowledged on an expropriatory level, for instance, *Generation Ukraine, Inc. v. Ukraine*, ICSID Award, no. ARB/00/9, par. 20.30.

[39] *Case Concerning Barcelona Traction, Light, and Power Company, Ltd* [1970] ICJ 1.

[40] Ibid., paras. 33 and 87.

foreigners has been a relative concept. The recurring question of whether or not a situation, measure, or verdict is fair has been answered in accordance with variables such as reciprocity and fairness based on treatment of the sovereign's own subjects. It is no coincidence that the emergence of IMS coincided with the colonial expansion and conception of state sovereignty—a primarily domestic concern in the absence of a systemic international legal order, 'fairness' has been redesigned to fit the international context. IMS stood as the meta-principle that there exists an overarching standard of treatment, inherently bound to be fair, with which all states are expected to comply. This 'frame' conceptualization, however, may have never been clear enough. Jennings, after refusing the a priori deduction of commercial rules and concessions from 'the idea of an international standard',[41] concluded that:

> The international standard thus means little more in practice than the assertion of the primacy of international over municipal law. . . . [T]he time has probably come to concentrate on the development of specific rules of law for particular situations rather than to hark back to an obsolete controversy over the most general of principles.[42]

14.2.2. Fair treatment provisions in early IIAs (1940s—1990s)

Despite the fact that the US Friendship, Commerce, and Navigation treaties which were signed in 1946 contained provisions on treating foreign investment and capital fairly and equitably,[43] the first example of a modern FET obligation is found in the 1948 Havana Charter.[44] Article 11(2)(a)(i) ensures 'just and equitable treatment for the enterprise, skills, capital, arts and technology brought from one Member country to another'.[45] Similarly, the Economic Agreement of Bogota refers to 'equitable treatment' for foreign capital. It further elaborates on what is meant by *equitable* by stating that '[t]he States therefore agree not to take unjustified, unreasonable or discriminatory measures'.[46]

[41] Robert Y. Jennings, 'State Contracts in International Law', *British Yearbook of International Law*, 37/156 (1961), 180–181.

[42] Ibid.

[43] See, for instance, Article XIX of the US–Taiwan Friendship, Commerce, and Navigation Treaty (1946).

[44] Havana Charter for an International Trade Organization (1948).

[45] Ibid., Article 11(2)(a)(i).

[46] Economic Agreement of Bogota (1948), Article 22(3).

In 1949, the International Chamber of Commerce (ICC) published the International Code of Fair Treatment for Foreign Investments.[47] Its Article 2 ensures fair treatment to investments of any kind, made in the territory of another party. Article 3 links fairness to non-discrimination. Article 5 guarantees due process and access to justice 'under the same conditions as nationals'.[48] A well-articulated framework of relative fairness framed in accordance with the treatment offered to nationals is evident. What truly stands out, however, is its Article 5(4):

> Should the nationals of one of the [parties] not enjoy the full benefit of the civil rights generally recognized by the [parties] or by international law, the nationals of the other [parties] shall be entitled to such rights and this protection shall not be denied to them on the ground that a preferential system would thus be established in their favour.

This provision is one of the earliest contemporary provisions in an investment treaty that includes an obligation of fairness attached to a higher, international standard. Its limits are set by the civil rights enjoyed in other parties, as well as international law. 'Rights generally recognized . . . by international law', however, is not articulated in its entirety, despite several discernible elements such as 'non-discrimination', 'due process', and 'access to justice'—all relevant subsets of the contemporary FET principle.

The Abs-Shawcross Draft Convention on Investments Abroad (1959) contains a 'fair and equitable treatment' obligation.[49] It is considered to have had a profound effect on the subsequent IIA practice along with the OECD Draft.[50]

Most treaties signed in the early 1960s associate fair treatment with another relative treatment obligation. In its Article 1, the Switzerland–Tunisia BIT states that foreign investments shall benefit from 'fair and equitable' treatment, and at the least, equal treatment shall be accorded to national investors. One example of a standalone FET provision is Article 1 of the US–Germany Friendship, Commerce, and Navigation Treaty (FCN) of 1956, which states that each 'Party shall at all times accord fair and equitable treatment to the nationals and companies of the other Party, and to their property, enterprises and other interests'. The influence of the Abs-Shawcross Draft is noteworthy.

[47] International Code of Fair Treatment for Foreign Investments (1949).

[48] Ibid., Article 5(2).

[49] See also Georg Schwarzenberger, 'The Abs-Shawcross Draft Convention on Investments Abroad: A Critical Commentary', *Journal of Public Law*, 9 (1960), 147. Article 1 reads: 'Each Party shall at all times ensure fair and equitable treatment to the property of the nationals of the other Parties.'

[50] OECD Draft Convention on the Protection of Foreign Property (1967).

14.3. Thresholds for fairness in contemporary IIAs and case law on FET

The last decade of the twentieth century is regarded as the heyday of IIAs in the aftermath of the collapse of the Soviet Union and the shifting political and economic global climate. Although it is not possible in this chapter to refer to each and every IIA negotiated during the 1990s, there are several outstanding IIAs, NAFTA[51] being one of them, that have had a recognizable impact on how the FET principle has come to be understood in arbitral practice.

The negotiations for the CUSFTA[52] had already been concluded by 1987. The agreement had an investment chapter; however, it contained neither an FET clause or, despite being hailed for having a 'relatively robust' dispute resolution procedure,[53] an investor-state arbitration clause. NAFTA, which came into force in 1994, extended the CUSFTA to Mexico with several alterations. Its Chapter 11 is an elaborate investment protection text with an added clause including a 'Minimum Standard of Treatment'.

NAFTA's Article 1105 is the relevant provision on treatment of foreign investment. The first paragraph states that each party 'shall accord to investments of investors of another Party treatment in accordance with international law, including fair and equitable treatment'.[54] This provision and its application sparked widespread controversy about the content of the minimum standard of treatment and FET particularly in the first half of the 2000s. In *Pope & Talbot v. Canada*,[55] the disputing parties differed in their interpretation of the relationship between IMS and FET. As Canada argued, 'fairness' was included in the prescribed minimum standard, and did not require additional 'fairness elements'. It further argued that the challenged state act needed to be *egregious*; that is, 'a denial of fairness would have to be shocking to be a violation of Article 1105'.[56]

The tribunal, interestingly, referred to Article II.2 of the US Model Investment Treaty of 1987 and its FET clause. After concluding that the NAFTA provision had evolved over time from this particular provision, it analysed the NAFTA provision in accordance with Article II.2, despite the fairly different NAFTA language. The tribunal then contended that 'compliance with the fairness elements must be ascertained free of any threshold that might be applicable to the evaluation of measures under the [IMS]'.[57] Although the tribunal differentiated treatment accorded to foreigners pursuant to a threshold, and treatment accorded without reference to a

[51] The North American Free Trade Agreement (1994).

[52] Canada–United States Free Trade Agreement (1987).

[53] Magnus Blomström and Ari Kokko, 'Regional Integration and Foreign Direct Investment', *World Bank Policy Research Working Paper Series no. 1750* (1997), 20.

[54] NAFTA, Article 1105.

[55] *Pope & Talbot Inc v. Canada* (2001), ad hoc, UNCITRAL Rules.

[56] Ibid., Award on the Merits of Phase 2, para. 109.

[57] Ibid., para. 111.

threshold, it does not elaborate on how the two interpretations might have differed in application.

Shortly after, the trade ministers of the US, Canada, and Mexico (NAFTA Free Trade Commission, FTC) released notes on interpretation to clarify, *inter alia*, the content of Article 1105.[58] The parties anchored the fairness principle to customary international law (CIL) in an attempt to delimit its application beyond what was perceived to be the IMS. The note, as Newcombe argues, 'has not brought any finality to the debate about the meaning of [FET] within the NAFTA since it does not clarify the content of [IMS]'.[59] This lack of clarification can be identified in a number of arbitral awards rendered after the FTC interpretation. The *Mondev v. USA*[60] award, for instance, refers to the evolutionary[61] nature of the IMS.

Arbitral tribunals seem to have an inclination to refer to the *Neer* case[62] while establishing the standard's point of origin.[63] This is clear especially in arbitral awards rendered during the early 2000s. Although *Neer* was a case concerning the murder of a US citizen and not protection of a foreign investment or property, this tendency somehow persists. The US–Mexico General Claims Commission, deciding on the case, stated that 'the treatment of alien, in order to constitute an international delinquency, should amount to an outrage, to bad faith, to wilful neglect of duty, or to an insufficiency of governmental action that every reasonable man would readily recognize its insufficiency'.[64] Similarly, *ELSI*,[65] an ICJ case, is frequently cited for its elaboration on arbitrariness: it is 'not . . . opposed to *a* rule of law, as it is . . . opposed to *the* rule of law . . . It is a wilful disregard of due process of law, an act which shocks, or at least surprises, a sense of judicial propriety'.[66]

Some tribunals managed to articulate a few constituent elements of FET. The *Waste Management v. Mexico*[67] tribunal, referring to a collection of awards,[68] stated that a treatment would violate the FET principle[69] if it was

[58] NAFTA FTC, Notes of Interpretation of Certain Chapter 11 Provisions (31 July 2001), available at http://www.sice.oas.org/tpd/nafta/Commission/CH11understanding_e.asp.

[59] Newcombe and Paradell, *Law and Practice of Investment Treaties*, 274.

[60] *Mondev International Ltd v. United States of America* (2002), ARB(AF)/99/2.

[61] Ibid., para. 123.

[62] *LFH Neer and Pauline Neer (US) v. United Mexican States* [1926], US–Mexico General Claims Commission IV RIAA 60.

[63] For instance, *Glamis Gold, Ltd. v. United States* (2009) Award, ad hoc, UNCITRAL Arbitration Rules.

[64] *LFH Neer and Pauline Neer (US) v. United Mexican States*, para. 556.

[65] *Elettronica Sicula SpA (ELSI) (USA v Italy)* (1989) ICJ Rep 15.

[66] Ibid., para. 128 (emphasis added).

[67] *Waste Management, Inc. v. Mexico* (2004), Award, ARB(AF)/00/3.

[68] *SD Myers v Canada* (2000) Partial Award; *Mondev*; *ADF Group v. USA* (2003) Award, ARB(AF)/00/1; *The Loewen Group, Inc. and Raymond L. Loewen v. USA* (2003) Award, ARB(AF)/98/3.

[69] *Waste Management, Inc. v. Mexico*, para 98. The tribunal interestingly refers to the standard as 'the minimum standard of treatment of fair and equitable treatment'.

> arbitrary, grossly unfair, unjust or idiosyncratic, is discriminatory and exposes the claimant to sectional or racial prejudice, or involves a lack of due process leading to an outcome which offends judicial propriety – as might be the case with a manifest failure of natural justice in judicial proceedings or a complete lack of transparency and candour in an administrative process. In applying the standard it is relevant that the treatment is in breach of representations made by the host State which were reasonably relied on by the claimant.[70]

This articulation attempts to elaborate on what is unfair in accordance with preceding NAFTA awards and the provision pursuant to CIL. However, the question of how it compares to an unqualified provision remains unanswered. In *MTD v. Chile,* the tribunal interpreted an unqualified FET clause found in the Chile–Malaysia BIT.[71] The tribunal described the FET principle as to include 'good faith, due process, [non-discrimination], and proportionality'.[72] When compared to the subset identified in *Waste Management,* it is not granted that the two sets do not contain vague terms easily substitutable with one another—any elaboration is far from guaranteeing a higher, or lower, international protection.

In *Saluka v. Czech Republic,*[73] the respondent Czech Republic argued that the standard in Article 3(1) in fact referred to a minimum standard by citing the *Genin v. Estonia*[74] award and the abovementioned *Neer* case. The respondent argued that the tribunal should address whether or not 'the governmental action in question was wilfully wrong, actually malicious, or so far beyond the pale that it cannot be defended among reasonable members of the international community'.[75]

The tribunal ascertained that the FET principle retained a subjective and general element, yet also contended the existence of 'sufficient legal content to allow the case to be decided on the basis of law'.[76] Of note, the applicable provision was *not* qualified.[77] In light of this fact, *Saluka* argued that 'since [the provision] is not in any way qualified, it should be interpreted broadly'. Again, what is meant by 'broader' interpretation, as opposed to the perceived interpretation of a CIL threshold, is not

70 Ibid.

71 *MTD Equity Sdn. Bhd. and MTD Chile S.A. v. Chile*; Malaysia–Chile Bilateral Investment Treaty (1992).

72 *MTD Equity*, par. 109, citing Opinion of Judge Steven Schwebel, para. 23.

73 *Saluka Investments B.V. v. Czech Republic* (2006), ad hoc, UNCITRAL Rules.

74 *Alex Genin, Eastern Credit Limited, Inc. and A.S. Baltoil v. Republic of Estonia* (2001) Award, ARB/99/2.

75 *Saluka Investments B.V. v. Czech Republic*, para. 290.

76 Ibid., para. 284.

77 Netherlands–Czech Republic BIT (1992) Article 3(1).

explained. Eventually, the tribunal adopted the *Waste Management*[78] formulation, as based on the *qualified* Article 1105 of NAFTA.

Despite the seeming differences in perspectives and interpretations, arguments do not seem to point at any significant differences in application. The nuance between what is arbitrary, grossly unfair, and unjust—or what is wilfully wrong or actually malicious—is not explicitly distinguishable, as both sets of elements will stem from assertions and deductions reflected upon the circumstances of each case by the arbitrators. While the terms may not be synonymous, one could argue that they would not necessarily lead to narrower or broader outcomes. The *Saluka* tribunal adopts the same approach: 'Whatever the merits of this controversy between parties may be, it appears that the difference between the Treaty standard laid . . . and the customary minimum standard . . . may well be more apparent than real.'[79]

Recent tribunals, such as the *RDF v. Guatemala*[80] tribunal interpreting the CAFTA-DR's qualified FET provision,[81] did not base their conclusions on an *opinio juris* analysis[82] and instead referred to the abovementioned *Waste Management* articulation. In the recent *Al Tamimi v. Oman*[83] award, the arbitral tribunal refers to 'a gross or flagrant disregard for the basic principles of fairness, consistency, even-handedness, due process, or natural justice expected by and of all States under customary international law'.[84]

The persistence of the vagueness has been evidently ineffective for the arbitrators in both doctrinal venues. Frank Berman, an investment treaty arbitrator, notes the following:

> about whether the Parties to a particular bilateral investment treaty intended 'fair and equitable treatment' as a reference to the customary law standard, or to mean something else, I find myself wondering . . . how that is going to help me solve the dispute in the case before me: if the treaty

[78] *Waste Management, Inc. v. Mexico*.

[79] *Saluka Investments B.V. v. Czech Republic*, para. 291.

[80] *Railroad Development Corp v. Guatemala* (2012), Award, ARB/07/23.

[81] Article 10.5, Dominican Republic–Central America Free Trade Agreement (CAFTA-DR) (2004).

[82] Matthew Porterfield, 'A Distinction without a Difference? The Interpretation of Fair and Equitable Treatment Under Customary International Law by Investment Tribunals', *Investment Treaty News* (22 March 2013), available at https://www.iisd.org/itn/2013/03/22/a-distinction-without-a-difference-the-interpretation-of-fair-and-equitable-treatment-under-customary-international-law-by-investment-tribunals/.

[83] *Adel A Hamadi Al Tamimi v. Oman* (2015) Award, ARB/11/33. The applicable IIA was the US–Oman FTA (2009), which contains a qualified FET clause.

[84] Ibid., para. 390.

> provision should be understood as referring to customary law, then what **is** the customary law it is referring to? If it is a reference to something else, then what was it the Contracting States wanted to add to (or subtract from?) the customary standard as they understood it?[85]

The use of arbitral awards to demonstrate constituent elements of FET is useful for subsequent arbitral awards and legal scholars. The present chapter does not deny that theoretical differences may exist between autonomous and CIL interpretations of the FET provisions. Instead, the premise is that an autonomous reading of the FET principle by arbitrators, or an interpretation based on the CIL's minimum standard of treatment, does not *necessarily* differ.

Vandevelde argued that 'virtually all of the awards' are uniform, and that attesting autonomy or a CIL link to the FET principle does not matter in practice.[86] He goes on to identify (a) reasonableness, (b) non-discrimination, (c) consistency, (d) transparency, and (e) due process as constituent elements of his unified FET theory. He further loosely utilizes Dworkin's integrity principle[87] to explain the legitimate expectations discourse which has been another firmly established subset of FET found in a remarkable number of awards. Some borderline awards, such as *Tecmed v. Mexico*, go as far as to construct the entire FET analysis on foreign investors' expectations from a state.[88]

Vandevelde's analysis draws a framework for this collective arbitral experience. Given that none of the cases analysed in his work concern the application of a FET provision containing a list of the subset of FET, his conclusion is that arbitrators, even when unguided by the treaty text due to obscure or non-existent references, tend to draw analytical support from preceding arbitral awards. The arbitral experience has reached a degree of substance that now a context-specific and tangible framework is readily available to treaty-makers which can replace the references made to a meta-principle such as IMS. Fairness, an inherently vague concept, may have now found its context-specific meaning within the discipline of international investment law.

What, then, would happen if the treaty text explicitly articulated the (more or less) five principal elements pinpointed by Vandevelde? This chapter argues this is exactly what CETA, and the proposed TTIP text, aim at doing. TPP follows a more

[85] Frank Berman, 'The Interpretation and Application of Fair and Equitable Treatment: An Arbitrator's Perspective', *EJIL: Talk!* (13 August 2013), available at http://www.ejiltalk.org/the-interpretation-and-application-of-fair-and-equitable-treatment-an-arbitrators-perspective/.

[86] Kenneth J. Vandevelde, 'A Unified Theory of Fair and Equitable Treatment', *International Law and Politics*, 43 (2010), 47.

[87] Ronald Dworkin, *Law's Empire* (1986), 176. Dworkin refers to a legislative integrity, which 'asks lawmakers to try to make the total set of laws morally coherent'.

[88] *Tecnicas Medioambientales Tecmed SA v. Mexico* (2003) ARB (AF)/00/2.

traditional trail. I now turn to the new-wave treaties and their response to this seemingly perpetual and universal uncertainty.

14.4. CETA, TTIP, and TPP: Where do they stand?

14.4.1. CETA, and the TTIP investment chapter proposal

CETA. For CETA, besides the final text released in February 2016,[89] and the draft investment chapter of 7 February 2013,[90] there are three important draft texts which reveal the phases of the negotiation process: drafts dated 21 November 2013,[91] April 2014, and 26 September 2014.[92] They demonstrate the positions of the parties on the interpretation and general framework of substantive principles. As for the TTIP, the negotiations remain suspended as of August 2017. While no negotiated text is publicly available, the European Commission published its proposal text.[93]

Article 8.10 of CETA regulates FET under the title 'Treatment of Investors and of Covered Investments'.[94] In the February 2013 draft, the title had clearly been an issue of debate, as Canada had proposed 'Minimum Standard of Treatment', whereas the EU opted for 'Treatment of Investment'.[95] Parties seem to have agreed on the present title between February and November 2013. The first paragraph of the provision states that each party shall accord FET to investors of the other party 'in accordance with paragraphs 2 through 6'.[96] Specifically, paragraph 2 lists a number of important elements to be taken into account:

(a) denial of justice in criminal, civil or administrative proceedings;
(b) fundamental breach of due process, including a fundamental breach of transparency, in judicial and administrative proceedings;
(c) manifest arbitrariness;

[89] CETA Final Text.

[90] Individual provisions of the unpublished February 2013 draft have been analysed in Nathalie Bernasconi-Osterwalder, 'Commentary to the Draft Investment Chapter of the Canada–EU Comprehensive Economic and Trade Agreement (CETA)', International Institute for Sustainable Development Report (May 2013).

[91] European Commission, CETA Draft as of 21 November 2013, in the Note for the Attention of the Trade Policy Committee.

[92] Consolidated CETA Draft Text of 26 September 2014, available at http://www.international.gc.ca/trade-agreements-accords-commerciaux/agr-acc/ceta-aecg/text-texte/toc-tdm.aspx?lang=eng.

[93] European Commission TTIP Proposal Draft.

[94] CETA Final Text, Article 8.10.

[95] Bernasconi-Osterwalder, 'Commentary', 17.

[96] CETA Final Text, Article 8.10 (1).

(d) targeted discrimination on manifestly wrongful grounds, such as gender, race or religious belief;
(e) abusive treatment of investors, such as coercion, duress and harassment; and
(f) a breach of any further elements of the [FET] obligation adopted by the parties in accordance with paragraph 3 of this Article.[97]

Pursuant to paragraph 3, the parties can regularly, or at the request of another party, review the contents of this list. Thus, the final draft provides for an exhaustive, yet expandable list which further includes, under its paragraph 4, consideration of the *specific* representations made to the investor which created a legitimate expectation.[98]

The February 2013 draft reveals that both Canada and the EU initially intended the list above to be non-exhaustive. The EU proposal simply noted that the articulated subset constitutes a FET breach 'notably' and 'not exclusively', and the Canadian proposal stated that the FET obligation 'includes the following treatment that is unacceptable from an international law perspective'. [99] The parties eventually diverted from the non-exhaustive list approach. An early 2013 draft would have undermined the expected outcome of further clarity in arbitral interpretation, given nothing anchored the arbitral discretion to the articulated subset.[100]

TTIP. Although the EU's investment chapter proposal is not a negotiated text (and therefore lacks US input),[101] it is beneficial in two ways: (a) it hints at what the TTIP, assuming the initiative does not fail and its negotiations resume, might eventually look like; and (b) it exposes the input to the CETA text from its respective parties, given striking similarities between Canadian and American treaty practice.

Article 3 of the TTIP proposal is entitled 'Treatment of Investors and of Covered Investments',[102] and is near-identical to the CETA Article 8.10, except for a few differences. For instance, the TTIP proposal adds 'obstacles to effective access to justice' to its Article 3(2)(b) on due process and transparency. In subparagraph (e) of the same article, the TTIP notes 'harassment, coercion, abuse of power or similar bad faith conduct',[103] instead of the CETA's subparagraph (e), which reads '[a]busive treatment of investors, such as coercion, duress and harassment'. The subparagraph (f), as is the case in the CETA text, gives way to parties to modify the list. One apparent difference is that while the CETA Article 8.10 indicates that the

[97] Ibid., Article 8.10 (2).
[98] Ibid., Article 8.10 (4).
[99] Bernasconi-Osterwalder, 'Commentary'.
[100] Ibid.
[101] European Commission TTIP Proposal Draft.
[102] Ibid., Article 3.
[103] Ibid., Article 3(2)(e).

parties may modify the list either regularly or upon the request of one of the parties, the TTIP proposal allows this only upon request.

Why a list? Despite Canada's attempts to include a reference to associate the FET principle with CIL[104] in line with its traditional NAFTA-inspired approach, it appears as though the European option to refer to a better articulated subset has decisively prevailed in the CETA text. Thus, the CETA stands aside not only from the famously vague and concise European style and practice but also from the North American practice as devised primarily after the early 2000s.[105]

The elements listed under paragraph 2 of both documents were not devised from scratch during the course of their respective negotiations. Principles identified over the years by the arbitral tribunals overlap with the subsets identified under Article 8.10 and Article 3. Reasonableness, consistency, non-discrimination, transparency, and due process, as Vandevelde identified them, echo from the lists which include denial of justice, lack of due process and transparency, arbitrariness, discrimination, and abusive treatment.

Although the attempt to define the content of FET has been praised, it has also not gone without criticism. Kriebaum pointed out that the list did not include stability.[106] Although it is not expressly mentioned, stability as a requirement of fair treatment has been invoked within the context of the investor's legitimate expectations over the years. Tribunals have regularly contended that a *stable* framework is considered to be a legitimate expectation as opposed to a framework *standstill*.[107] While the latter indicates a literal halt in policy and legal framework (and is often excluded from the scope of legitimate expectations), the former allows modifications in line with legitimate public purpose goals and could be relevant under the CETA's FET provision. Kriebaum also claims that discrimination based on nationality is excluded;[108] however, this is far from granted in application since the grounds referred to in Article 8.10(2)(d) are not exhaustive.

14.4.2. TPP Draft

The draft of the Trans-Pacific Partnership (TPP) was released in November 2015.[109] Its Article 9.6 prescribes the FET under the title 'Minimum Standard of Treatment'.

[104] Porterfield, 'A Distinction without a Difference?'.

[105] Canadian 2004 Model FIPA; the US 2004 and 2012 Model BITs.

[106] Ursula Kriebaum, 'FET and Expropriation in the (Invisible) EU Model BIT', *Journal of World Investment & Trade*, 15/3–4 (2014), 454–483.

[107] *AES Summit Generation Limited and AES-Tisza Kft v. Hungary* (2010), Award, ARB/07/22, par. 9.3.27; *LG&E Capital Corp and LG&E International Inc. v. Argentina* (2007), ARB/02/1.

[108] Kriebaum, 'FET and Expropriation'.

[109] TPP draft text. Both TTIP and TPP have been shelved in late 2010s.

The first paragraph of the provision includes the overall obligation to accord 'to covered investments treatment in accordance with applicable customary international law principles, including fair and equitable treatment'. By itself, this paragraph retains the abovementioned NAFTA formulation. The second paragraph, 'for greater certainty', notes that '[FET does] not require treatment in addition to or beyond that which is required by [the IMS], and do[es] no[t] create additional substantive rights'. The same paragraph counts several elements of FET: '[FET] includes the obligation not to deny justice in criminal, civil or administrative adjudicatory proceedings in accordance with the principle of due process embodied in the principal legal systems of the world'. Paragraphs 4 and 5 further specify that 'the mere fact' that a party's actions may be inconsistent with an investor's expectations and that 'a subsidy or grant has not been issued, renewed or maintained, or has been modified or reduced . . . does not constitute a breach of [Article 9.6]'.

Although three out of five subparagraphs begin with the phrase 'for greater certainty', the provision clarifies surprisingly little. As argued above, there is strong adjudicatory evidence that the FET–IMS link does not act as a discernible, let alone consistent, threshold. The formulation echoes from the NAFTA formula, and although the parties seem to have intended to clarify its meaning, it simply falls short of its goal. Although 'denial of justice' and 'due process' are mentioned, they are not a part of any exhaustive list. Even the articulated elements have their own vague qualifiers: it is not clear as to what is meant by 'due process embodied in the principal legal systems of the world'.[110]

Subparagraphs 4 and 5 give some, albeit limited, guidance to adjudicators. However, they do not outright exclude certain acts from the scope of this provision. Instead, they simply note that an arbitral tribunal would need to look further than the existence of an inconsistent act contrary to an investor's expectations or the denial of a subsidy or a grant. These acts may still constitute a breach if said acts violate other elements required under the IMS.

14.5. Conclusions

The notion of fairness predates language. It has existed as a subjective concept, and with the advent of civilization it has assumed specific content according to context. With regard to protecting foreigners and their investments, it has retained its contingency throughout history. It has been defined vis-à-vis other principles, subjects, and objects—the determinant was the sovereign, the treatment accorded to others, and so on. Throughout the twentieth century, globalization has exposed further contextual needs to define fairness in previously unknown domains. International

[110] Ibid., Article 9.6(4).

investment law is still a legal field in its infancy, yet it is increasingly more demanding. Decades-old formulations in relation to fair, just, or equitable treatment simply do not suffice to devise a tangible, normative formula.

CETA, the TTIP proposal, and the TPP draft all represent the latest wave of responses to the vagueness of the FET principle, and they all attempt to tackle this perceived problem from different perspectives. It is clear that, despite differences in their drafting, they all aim to clarify and delimit the notion of FET with regard to past arbitral experience, as well as policy considerations such as regulatory authority.

The CETA text and the TTIP proposal limit the vagueness by pushing the so-called borderline cases further away, establishing a relatively discernible list of acts. They aim to achieve this by injecting explicit clarifications and references to a subset facilitated by arbitral tribunals over the years. Earlier criticisms targeted at CETA drafts highlighted the fact that the incorporated list in the FET provision was non-exhaustive; therefore, it bore the risk of falling short of providing a clear-cut framework for FET. The latest draft arguably remedies this risk. A remarkable feature of these draft texts is that there are no references to CIL or international law.

In comparison, the TPP draft, despite its equally lengthy and elaborate provision on the minimum standard of treatment, falls short of any adequate clarification as to its content. While it refers to several elements such as due process and denial of justice, its NAFTA-esque reference to CIL renders the predictability of the content of this provision largely ineffective.

The unreliability of CIL with regard to the content of FET does not stem from the vagueness of commonly identified subcriteria such as 'denial of justice'—instead, it appears to be about what other potentially unanticipated elements may be included by a specific arbitral tribunal in the course of its interpretation and subsequent application of the principle to a particular case. Autonomy, besides implying an unbound analysis of the terminology, means that a tribunal may or may not include CIL elements in its elaborations. Despite the clear 'shift from incomplete to complete contracting' in the CETA and TTIP texts,[111] numerous vague IIAs still exist and it will be a while before they are irrelevant to scholars working in this field, if ever. Should the negotiating parties wish to grant somewhat broader discretion to adjudicators, the so-called 'gold standard'[112] trail would still be open; however,

[111] Filippo Fontanelli and Giuseppe Bianco, 'Converging towards NAFTA: An Analysis of FTA Investment Chapters in the European Union and the United States', *Stanford Journal of International Law*, 50 (2014), 234; for the regulatory implications of this development, see Amalie Tystrup and Güneş Ünüvar, 'A Waiver for Europe? CETA's Trade in Services, and Investment Protection Provisions and Their Legal-Political Implications on Regulatory Competence', in Giovanna Adinolfi, Freya Baetens, Jose Caiado, Angela Lupone, and Anna G. Micara, eds., *International Economic Law: Contemporary Issues* (2017), 41–59.

[112] See generally Nikos Lavranos, 'In Defence of Member States' BITs Gold Standard: The Regulation 1219/2012 Establishing a Transitional Regime for Existing Extra-EU BITs—A Member State's Perspective', *Transnational Dispute Management*, 10/2 (2013), 1–14.

the fact that it does not guarantee one or the other perceived applicatory result remains unaffected. Any negotiating party aiming at further clarity would be advised to abide by this fact. A reference to CIL becomes even less clear when a tribunal accepts its dynamic, evolving, and therefore (at least in part) undetermined content. There may exist a set of more or less determined elements that form CIL (and there is an impressive number of scholarly work arguing that it does)—however, it is extremely difficult and equally crucial to make sure CIL, as of the day of analysis, had not evolve past that point. As Paparinskis points out, since '[s]tate practice [as a constituent element of CIL] based on arguably erroneous premise is just as capable of contributing to customary international law as well-informed practice',[113] the challenge becomes ever clearer as to what extent CIL is accurately determinable in setting these thresholds. It is simply not enough to have *a rough idea* of the content of the qualifier, which is accepted to be bound to evolve.

One way to tackle the unpredictability of the CIL is to articulate its content, and the identified CIL subset has been largely codified under the new wave treaties such as the CETA and the TTIP.[114] If the goal is to attest at least some level of meaningful normativity and certainty to a historically and philosophically subjective scale such as fairness, the qualifier needs to be known, or at least identifiable.

This, however, does not mean that a list, like those included in the CETA and TTIP drafts, solves the riddle definitely. As Ahdar notes, no 'sensible jurist would deny that there is always going to be a certain degree of fuzziness . . . surrounding rules. The modest but valuable aim is surely to keep the penumbra of uncertainty to a minimum'.[115] Under any circumstance, no matter how intricately parties attempt to clarify the content of fairness, the subset will always retain subjective elements and a borderline case will appear. With this in mind, the CETA and TTIP drafts embody the latest links of the transformation of this principle. They include tangible remedies streamlined towards keeping the vagueness to a minimum.

References

Ahdar, Rex, 'Contract Doctrine, Predictability and the Nebulous Exception', *Cambridge Law Journal*, 73/1 (2014), 39–60.

Anghie, Antony, *Imperialism, Sovereignty and the Making of International Law* (Cambridge, 2007).

113 Paparinskis, *The International Minimum Standard and Fair and Equitable Treatment*, 18.

114 Patrick Dumberry, 'Drafting the Fair and Equitable Treatment Standard Clause in the TPP and the RCEP: Lessons Learned from the NAFTA Article 1105 Experience', *Transnational Dispute Management*, 12/1 (2015), 1–28.

115 Rex Ahdar, 'Contract Doctrine, Predictability and the Nebulous Exception', *Cambridge Law Journal*, 73/1 (2014), 54.

Berman, Frank, 'The Interpretation and Application of Fair and Equitable Treatment: An Arbitrator's Perspective', *EJIL: Talk!* (13 August 2013), available at http://www.ejiltalk.org/the-interpretation-and-application-of-fair-and-equitable-treatment-an-arbitrators-perspective/.

Bernasconi-Osterwalder, Nathalie, 'Commentary to the Draft Investment Chapter of the Canada–EU Comprehensive Economic and Trade Agreement (CETA)', International Institute for Sustainable Development Report (May 2013), available at https://www.iisd.org/system/files/publications/commentary_investment_chapter_CETA.pdf.

Blomström, Magnus and Ari Kokko, 'Regional Integration and Foreign Direct Investment: A Conceptual Work and Three Cases', *World Bank Policy Research Working Paper Series No 1750* (April 1997), available at https://documents1.worldbank.org/curated/en/854171468739561862/pdf/multi0page.pdf.

Borchard, Edwin, 'Minimum Standard of the Treatment of Aliens', *Michigan Law Review*, 38/4 (1940), 455–61.

Bronfman, Klein, 'Fair and Equitable Treatment: An Evolving Standard', *Max Planck Yearbook of UN Law*, 10 (2006), 609–80.

Dolzer, Rudolf and Christoph Schreuer, *Principles of International Investment Law* (2nd edn, Oxford, 2012).

Dumberry, Patrick, 'Drafting the Fair and Equitable Treatment Standard Clause in the TPP and the RCEP: Lessons Learned from the NAFTA Article 1105 Experience', *Transnational Dispute Management*, 12/1 (2015).

Dworkin, Ronald, *Law's Empire* (Cambridge, MA, 1986).

Endicott, Timothy A. O., *Vagueness in Law* (Oxford, 2000).

Fontanelli, Filippo and Giuseppe Bianco, 'Converging Towards NAFTA: An Analysis of FTA Investment Chapters in the European Union and the United States', *Stanford Journal of International Law*, 50 (2014), 211–45.

Hood, Miriam, *Gunboat Diplomacy 1895–1905 Great Power Pressure in Venezuela* (1975).

Hull, William I., *The Two Hague Conferences and Their Contributions to International Law* (1970).

Jennings, Robert Y., 'State Contracts in International Law', *British Yearbook of International Law*, 37/156 (1961), 180–81.

Keechang, Kim, *Aliens in Medieval Law: The Origins of Modern Citizenship* (Cambridge, 2001).

Kelsen, Hans, *General Theory of Norms*, tr. Michael Hartney (Oxford, 1991).

Klager, Roland, 'Fair and Equitable Treatment' in International Investment Law (Cambridge, 2011).

Kriebaum, Ursula, 'FET and Expropriation in the (Invisible) EU Model BIT', *Journal of World Investment & Trade*, 15/3–4 (2014), 454–83.

Lavranos, Nikos, 'In Defence of Member States' BITs Gold Standard: The Regulation 1219/2012 Establishing a Transitional Regime for Existing Extra-EU BITs—A Member State's Perspective', *Transnational Dispute Management*, 10/2 (2013).

Lipson, Charles, *Standing Guard: Protecting Foreign Capital in the Nineteenth and Twentieth Centuries* (Berkeley and Los Angeles, 1985).

Lowenfeld, Andreas F., *International Economic Law* (2nd edn, Oxford, 2008).

John, King of England, Stephen Langton, 'Magna Carta, 1215', in David C. Douglas and Harry Rothwell, eds., *English Historical Documents Volume III c.1189–1327* (London, 1975).

McLean, David, 'Finance and "Informal Empire" before the First World War', *Economic History Review*, 29/2 (1976), 291–305.

Miles, Kate, *The Origins of International Investment Law: Empire, Environment and the Safeguarding of Capital* (Cambridge, 2013).

Newcombe, Andrew and Lluis Paradell, *Law and Practice of Investment Treaties: Standards of Treatment* (Alphen aan den Rijn, 2009).

Paparinskis, Martins, *The International Minimum Standard and Fair and Equitable Treatment* (Oxford, 2013).

Philphott, Daniel, *Revolutions in Sovereignty: How Ideas Shaped Modern International Relations* (Princeton, 2001).

Porterfield, Matthew, 'A Distinction without a Difference? The Interpretation of Fair and Equitable Treatment Under Customary International Law by Investment Tribunals', *Investment Treaty News* (22 March 2013), available at https://www.iisd.org/itn/2013/03/22/a-distinction-without-a-difference-the-interpretation-of-fair-and-equitable-treatment-under-customary-international-law-by-investment-tribunals/.

Poscher, Ralf, 'Ambiguity and Vagueness in Legal Interpretation', in Lawrence Solan and Peter Tiersma, eds., *Oxford Handbook on Language and Law* (Oxford, 2012), 128–44.

Rawls, John, *A Theory of Justice* (rev. edn, Oxford, 1999).

Root, Elihu, 'The Basis of Protection to Citizens Residing Abroad', *Proceedings of the ASIL and Its Annual Meeting (1907–1917)*, 4 (1910), 19–21.

Schreuer, Christoph, 'Fair and Equitable Treatment in Arbitral Practice', *Journal of World Investment and Trade*, 6/3 (2005), 357–85.

Schrijver, Nico, *Sovereignty over Natural Resources: Balancing Rights and Duties* (Cambridge, 2008).

Schwarzenberger, Georg, 'The Abs-Shawcross Draft Convention on Investments Abroad: A Critical Commentary', *Journal of Public Law*, 9 (1960), 147–71.

Thystrup, Amalie and Güneş Ünüvar, 'A Waiver for Europe? CETA's Trade in Services, and Investment Protection Provisions and Their Legal-Political Implications on Regulatory Competence', in Giovanna Adinolfi, Freya Baetens, Jose Caiado, Angela Lupone, and Anna G. Micara, eds., *International Economic Law: Contemporary Issues* (2017), 41–59.

UNCTAD, ed., 'Fair and Equitable Treatment', in UNCTAD Series on Issues in International Investment Agreements (1999).

Vandevelde, Kenneth J., 'A Unified Theory of Fair and Equitable Treatment', *International Law and Politics*, 43 (2010), 43–106.

Vattel, Emer de, *Law of Nations*, tr. Joseph Chitty (London, 1834).

Yannaca-Small, Katia, *Arbitration Under International Investment Agreements: A Guide to the Key Issues* (New York, 2010).

2. Human Rights Law and International Criminal Law

15

Interpretative evolution of the norm prohibiting torture and inhuman or degrading treatment under the European Convention

EZGI YILDIZ

Norms are abstract standards that shape actors' expectations and behavior. As powerful as they are as tools of change, these standards are subjected to change themselves. Even those that are highly institutionalized are not set in stone and they may change in light of societal needs. In this chapter, I give an account of interpretive change—one of the ways in which norms may change—by focusing on the norm prohibiting torture and inhuman or degrading treatment under Article 3 of the European Convention on Human Rights (the Convention).[1] This norm embodies one of the core rights of the Convention: namely, freedom from being subject to torture and inhuman or degrading treatment. It is deeply institutionalized and incorporated in all of the domestic legislation of the Member States.[2] Nonetheless, the norm's definition has changed over time. The judgments delivered by the European Commission on Human Rights (the Commission) and the European Court of Human Rights (the Court)—which I refer to as the Strasbourg institutions—have been the vehicles of this transformation. That is, they have channelled the norm's

[1] See also, Natasa Mavronicola, *Torture, Inhumanity and Degradation under Article 3 of the ECHR: Absolute Rights and Absolute Wrongs* (Oxford, UK; New York, NY: Hart Publishing, 2021); Natalie R. Davidson, "Everyday Lawmaking in International Human Rights Law: Insights from the Inclusion of Domestic Violence in the Prohibition of Torture," *Law & Social Inquiry*, June 14, 2021, 1–31.

[2] A prohibition against torture can be found in the domestic systems of all of the Member States to the Convention. For more, see Aisling Reidy, *The Prohibition of Torture: A Guide to the Implementation of Article 3 of the European Convention on Human Rights*, Human Rights Handbooks No.6, Directorate General of Human Rights, Council of Europe (July 2003).

Ezgi Yildiz, *Interpretative evolution of the norm prohibiting torture and inhuman or degrading treatment under the European Convention* In: *Language and Legal Interpretation in International Law*. Edited by: Anne Lise Kjær and Joanna Lam, Oxford University Press. © Oxford University Press 2022. DOI: 10.1093/oso/9780190855208.003.0016

evolution and confirmed that its definition is not 'fixed once and for all'.[3] Therefore, the change analysed here is the norm's interpretative evolution, which has been (re) produced in the jurisprudence of the Strasbourg institutions.

This development has taken place due to the fact that this norm–similar to many other norms in the Convention–is defined 'in sparse and abstract universal terms', and there are no 'objectively valid interpretations of what [it] mean[s] at all relevant times and in all relevant places'.[4] This has reinforced the Strasbourg institutions' key interpretative ethic, namely, the 'living instrument principle', which underscores that the Convention must be interpreted in line with present-day conditions.[5] Following this principle, which aimed at keeping 'the meaning of rights both contemporary and effective', the norm prohibiting torture and inhuman or degrading treatment has been interpreted in an evolutive manner.[6] Consequently, the norm's evolution has taken account of broader social change and the drafters' '*abstract* intention to promote and safeguard human rights in Europe'.[7]

This chapter contextualizes the norm's transformation by embedding it within the broader socio-political context.[8] As the chapter makes clear, legal interpretation does not take place in a void, and there are several influential factors enabling and constraining the Strasbourg institutions' interpretative preferences. I explain how these factors shape this norm's interpretation by looking at the international, institutional, and discursive factors. The aim of this study is to show the trajectory of the norm by contextualizing how the Strasbourg institutions have (re)defined the norm since the Convention system's inception in the 1950s.

The structure of the chapter is as follows. First, I introduce the key concepts. Second, I lay out the framework of analysis, which allows one to trace the evolution of the norm throughout the different phases of the Convention system's lifetime in light of the surrounding international, institutional, and discursive factors. Third, I analyse the change in understanding of the norm against torture and inhuman or degrading treatment by assessing how these factors have shaped the interpretation

[3] Eirik Bjorge, 'The Vienna Rules, Evolutionary Interpretation and the Intention of the Parties', in Andrea Bianchi et al., eds., *Interpretation in International Law* (2015), 191.

[4] Steven Greer, 'The Interpretation of the European Convention on Human Rights: Universal Principle or Margin of Appreciation?', *UCL Human Rights Review*, 3 (2010), 1.

[5] George Letsas, 'Strasbourg's Interpretive Ethic: Lessons for the International Lawyer', *European Journal of International Law*, 21 (2010), 527.

[6] Kanstantsin Dzehtsiarou, 'European Consensus and the Evolutive Interpretation of the European Convention on Human Rights', *German Law Journal*, 12 (2011), 1730.

[7] Eirik Bjorge, *Evolutionary Interpretation of Treaties* (2014), 63.

[8] George Letsas, *A Theory of Interpretation of the European Convention on Human Rights* (2007); George Letsas, 'The ECHR as a Living Instrument: Its Meaning and Legitimacy', in Andreas Føllesdal et al., eds., *Constituting Europe: The European Court of Human Rights in a National, European and Global Context* (2013).

of this norm by reviewing such changes during the period between 1950 and the early 2000s.

The analysis presented here is, therefore, limited to period before the backlash against the European Court of Human Rights became a salient issue in European politics.[9] The so-called backlash period started in the 2010s and shaped the way the European Court has operated since.[10] Covering the period before the backlash politics began reiging over the European human rights system, the chapter seeks to offer insights into what came before backlash and how the norm against torture and inhuman or degrading treatment came to be (re)shaped within the European legal regime.[11]

15.1. Human rights as moving targets: Some definitions

The concept of 'norm' is used to explain different phenomena on different levels. On the one hand, norms refer to social customs or patterns of expected behaviour in a broader sense. On the other hand, they are utilized to talk about rights, rules, or contracts in a more specific sense. Friedrich Kratochwil clarifies this distinction by looking at the formulation and validity claims of norms. The validity of norms could be based on a variety of sources ranging from tacit rules, customs, and social conventions to contracts or treaties. Furthermore, norms could be formulated either explicitly or implicitly.[12] According to Kratochwil, well-codified norms which

[9] Mikael Rask Madsen, "Two-Level Politics and the Backlash against International Courts: Evidence from the Politicisation of the European Court of Human Rights," *The British Journal of Politics and International Relations* 22/4 (November 1, 2020): 728–38; Mikael Rask Madsen, Pola Cebulak, and Micha Wiebusch, "Backlash against International Courts: Explaining the Forms and Patterns of Resistance to International Courts," *International Journal of Law in Context* 14/2 (June 2018): 197–220; Erik Voeten, "Populism and Backlashes against International Courts," *Perspectives on Politics* 18/2 (2020): 407–22.

[10] Laurence R. Helfer and Erik Voeten, "Walking Back Human Rights in Europe?," *European Journal of International Law* 31/3 (December 15, 2020): 797–827; Isabela Garbin Ramanzini and Ezgi Yildiz, "Revamping to Remain Relevant: How Do the European and the Inter-American Human Rights Systems Adapt to Challenges?," *Journal of Human Rights Practice* 12/3 (November 1, 2020): 768–80; Øyvind Stiansen and Erik Voeten, "Backlash and Judicial Restraint: Evidence from the European Court of Human Rights," *International Studies Quarterly* 64/4 (December 7, 2020): 770–84; Basak Cali, "Coping with Crisis: Whither the Variable Geomety in the Jurisprudence of the European Court of Human Rights," *Wisconsin International Law Journal* 35/2 (2018): 237–76.

[11] Ezgi Yildiz, *Between Forbearance and Audacity: How the European Court Redefined the Norm Against Torture and Inhuman or Degrading Treatment* (Cambridge: Cambridge University Press, Forthcoming).

[12] Friedrich Kratochwil, *Rules, Norms, and Decisions:On the Conditions of Practical and Legal Reasoning in International Relations and Domestic Affairs* (1991), 55.

are grounded in contracts or treaties and which require explicit commitment are the clearest norms, whereas norms which entail implicit social rules are the least clear.[13]

The norm against torture and inhuman or degrading treatment, emanating from a treaty and requiring explicit commitment, falls under Kratochwil's 'clearest norms' category. As a codified norm, it has a characteristic of a contractual agreement, namely, it requires explicit commitment and prescribes obligations. Stephen Krasner's definition of norms corresponds to this logic. Krasner identifies norms as 'standards of behaviour defined in terms of rights and obligations'.[14] Kratochwil's and Krasner's definitions of norms help one understand what the norm prohibiting torture and inhuman or degrading treatment under Article 3 of the Convention entail. In so doing, they offer a useful starting point of inquiry.

However, studying norms' interpretive evolution requires a reference to another concept: 'evolution'.[15] I define evolution as the change in the definition of a norm, which is reflected in the scope of the rights and obligations it prescribes. Human rights norms may be moving targets since they change in light of societal needs; yet their trajectory can still be traced by focusing on their transformation of the rights and obligations they entail.[16]

15.2. Framework of analysis

Legal interpretation, which brings out the general normative position systematically endorsed by Strasbourg institutions,[17] has been the driving source of the evolution of norms under the European Convention. However, norms' interpretation must be read in context. For this purpose, I develop an analytical framework that contextualizes legal interpretation in reference to various factors at the international, institutional, and discursive levels.

First, the international level refers to the broader political context within which the Convention system operates. The Convention's lifetime includes historic events such as the creation of post-Second World War institutions, the decolonization movements, the start and end of the Cold War, and the eastward expansion of

[13] Ibid.

[14] Stephen D. Krasner, 'Structural Changes and Regime Consequences: Regimes as Intervening Variables', in Stephen D. Krasner, *International Regimes* (1983), 2.

[15] Ed Bates, *The Evolution of the European Convention on Human Rights: From Its Inception to the Creation of a Permanent Court of Human Rights* (2010); and Jonas Christoffersen and Mikael Rask Madsen, eds., *The European Human Rights Between Law and Politics* (2013).

[16] Ezgi Yildiz, "A Court with Many Faces: Judicial Characters and Modes of Norm Development in the European Court of Human Rights," *European Journal of International Law* 31/1 (August 7, 2020): 73–99.

[17] Letsas, *A Theory of Interpretation of the European Convention on Human Rights*, 511.

the Council of Europe. These events have shaped the design and operation of the Strasbourg institutions to a great extent.

Second, the institutional level concerns the Member States' relation to the Strasbourg institutions. The evolution of the norm against torture and inhuman or degrading treatment must be situated within the institutional evolution of the Convention system. The system has evolved from one with limited autonomy to one with substantial autonomy. The main hurdle affecting this process was the Member States' reluctance to be reviewed by a supranational body, which could potentially infringe on their sovereignty.[18] This fear was more dominant during the drafting of the Convention and the earlier years of the Convention's lifetime. At the time of the Convention's inception, it became clear that the system's autonomy was linked to two conditions: (1) the jurisdiction of the Court, which would subject the Member States to supranational review, and (2) the individual right to petition, which according to opponents could render the Convention system vulnerable to abuse by communist sympathizers or other figures aiming to discredit the West.[19] These clauses were initially optional to appease the Member States that shared such concerns and they remained so until 1998. Hence, when the Member States demonstrated resistance in accepting these clauses, the institutional autonomy of the Convention system was undercut.[20] Accordingly, there is a negative correlation between the Member States' resistance to these conditions and the institutional autonomy of the Convention system. Moreover, as will be explained in the analysis section, the scope of the norm against torture and inhuman or degrading treatment expanded as the system gained more institutional autonomy.

Finally, the discursive level concerns the interpretive community's prevailing view on what torture and inhuman or degrading treatment signify at a particular period in time.[21] This dominant view shapes legal discourse and, ultimately, the way the Strasbourg institutions define torture and inhuman or degrading treatment.

Accordingly, temporality is an important element in this story of change. In order to show how these factors have come into play at different periods of the Convention system, I adopt a rubric of periodization. I draw inspiration from the works of Jonas Christoffersen and Mikael Rask Madsen[22] and Ed Bates[23] in

[18] Ed Bates, 'The Birth of the European Convention on Human Rights', in Christoffersen and Madsen, eds., *The European Court of Human Rights between Law and Politics*, 41.

[19] Bates, *The Evolution of the European Convention on Human Rights*, 96.

[20] Mikael Rask Madsen, 'The Protracted Institutionalization of the Strasbourg Court: From Legal Diplomacy to Integrationist Jurisprudence', in Christoffersen and Madsen, eds., *The European Court of Human Rights between Law and Politics*, 47.

[21] The concept of interpretive community signifies a group of intellectuals sharing 'interpretive strategies not for reading but for writing texts, for constituting their properties'. Stanley Fish, *Is There a Text in this Class* (Cambridge, MA, 1980), 14.

[22] Christoffersen and Madsen, eds., *The European Human Rights between Law and Politics.*

[23] Bates, *The Evolution of the European Convention on Human Rights.*

formulating this. Looking at the period from the drafting of the Convention in 1950 until the early 2000s, I have identified four stages: (1) the genesis of the Convention (1950), (2) the legal diplomacy phase (1950–1974), (3) the progressive court phase (1975–1998), and (4) the new permanent court phase (1998–2010).

	The Phases of the Evolution of the Norm Prohibiting Torture and Inhuman or Degrading Treatment			
Influential Factors	***Genesis 1950***	***Legal Diplomacy 1950–1974***	***Progressive Court 1975–1998***	***New Permanent Court 1998–2010***
Broader Socio-political Context	Post-WWII/ threat of Communist expansion	Cold War/ decolonization	Cold War (Helsinki Final Act)/end of Cold War	Post-Cold War/eastward expansion
Institutional Evolution	Institution-building	Institution is insecure	Institution is less insecure	Institution is secure
Prevailing View on Torture	Principles of Natural law/ 'evil men do evil'	Secular and victim focused understanding/ 'banality of evil'	Secular and victim focused understanding/ absolute ban on torture	Secular and victim focused understanding/ comprehensive definition of torture

The genesis phase corresponds to the drafting of the Convention. The legal diplomacy phase refers to the first fifteen years during which the Commission and the Court carefully balanced administering individual justice with national and geopolitical interests of the Member States. Therefore, they assumed not only a legal, but a diplomatic role. [24] The progressive court phase is the period during which the Court gave several landmark judgements and began to establish its authority. Finally, the Court increased its autonomy during the new permanent Court phase started with the enactment of Protocol 11—which instantiated the Court as a permanent body and secured individuals' direct access to the Court (i.e. the right of individual petition became mandatory)—and it corresponds to the period until 2010.

In the following section, I will explain how the definition of the norm against torture and inhuman or degrading treatment changed in each phase, together with the reconfiguration of various factors at international, institutional, and discursive levels. This will allow me to show that understanding the evolving internal dynamics of the Convention system is crucial to situate and trace the interpretive evolution of the norm.

[24] Madsen, 'The Protracted Institutionalization of the Strasbourg Court', 45.

15.2.1. Episode I: Back to the beginning—A look into the drafting of the Treaty

The provision on torture and inhuman or degrading treatment—which states that '[n]o one shall be subjected to torture or to inhuman or degrading treatment or punishment'—has an open definition. That is to say, it does not list the types of acts falling under it. Therefore, the Convention itself does not offer a clue about what kind of acts the drafters of the Convention had in mind when they formulated this provision. However, looking at the *travaux préparatoires*, one can understand the essence of this provision.[25]

The surrounding broader socio-political context essentially shaped not only the institution-building process, but also the general understanding of what 'torture' or 'inhuman or degrading treatment' meant at the time. One must keep in mind that the memories of the Second World War triggered the creation of the Convention system. One of the main objectives behind drafting the Convention was to ensure that liberal democracies prevailed in Europe, which was under the threat of Communist expansion.[26] The Convention was instituted as a 'type of collective pact against totalitarianism',[27] and drew inspiration from the Universal Declaration of Human Rights.

Although Sir David Patrick Maxwell-Fyfe and Pierre-Henri Teitgen were the 'Convention's two founding fathers',[28] Seymour Cocks from the British delegation, a journalist and a Labour MP from Broxtowe, was one of the most proactive figures when it came to drafting the provision on torture and inhuman or degrading treatment. Finding the text adopted not sufficiently explicit, Cocks proposed a set of amendments expounding on the absolute nature of this prohibition on 7 September 1949.[29]

The next day, Cocks moved his amendment to the Consultative (today Parliamentary) Assembly, where he also delivered a touching speech. He outlined how torture had been perceived during different periods of history. Discussing Athens, where torture was seen as an 'oriental depravity', and the Middle Ages, when torture was a 'common instrument of power and authority', he argued that 'with the development of civilization, torture disappeared' in the West, only to be returned by Nazi Germany.[30] Cocks accounted on some of the atrocities committed by the Nazis:

[25] This observation is only limited to torture, as there was no discussion on inhuman or degrading treatment.

[26] Madsen, 'The Protracted Institutionalization of the Strasbourg Court', 43.

[27] Bates, 'The Birth of the European Convention on Human Rights', 40.

[28] Bates, *The Evolution of the European Convention on Human Rights*, 76.

[29] DH (56) 5, pp. 2–3.

[30] Ibid., 4.

> Cases occurred in Greece during the Nazi invasion of naked girls being placed on electric stoves and burnt in order to make them disclose the whereabouts of their friends. There was the deliberate infliction upon women of the bacteria and loathsome diseases. All kinds of ghastly mutilations were perpetrated upon thousands of men and women. . . .
>
> I say that to take the straight beautiful bodies of men and women and to maim and mutilate them by torture is a crime against high heaven and the holy spirit of man. I say that it is a sin against the *Holy Ghost* for which there is no forgiveness. I declare that it is incompatible with civilization.[31]

Subsequently, Maxwell-Fyfe André Philip and Teitgen took the floor and congratulated Cocks for his moving speech, to which they entirely subscribed.[32] Then the discussions about whether and how to include Cocks's proposal in the draft Convention started. The deciding argument was put forward by Teitgen, who called for an open definition, underlining 'it is dangerous to want to say more, since the effect of the Convention is thereby limited'.[33]

Following the negotiations, Cocks withdrew his amendment, yet he submitted a draft resolution that noted: '[t]he Assembly records its abhorrence at the subjection of any person to any form of mutilation or sterilization or beating'.[34] The representatives of Denmark, Sweden, and Norway were opposed to this, stating that sterilization was legally allowed in their countries. The British delegation also raised an objection by noting that corporal punishment still existed in the UK.[35] These discussions attested that reaching a consensus on the types of acts that should be considered torture was challenging.

Finally, Cocks's suggestions were not included in the draft text. However, his contribution is still highly important in understanding what the drafters had in mind when drafting this prohibition. Seeing that Cocks's sentiments were not challenged, but supported in principle, indicated a form of consensus concerning the dominant understanding of torture. However, one can infer a couple of points from the speech and the proposal made by Cocks, together with the follow-up discussions in relation to the general nature of this prohibition.

First, this prohibition was written in a reactionary manner. The drafters reacted to the atrocities that took place during the Second World War. Their immediate frame of reference was the war crimes of the Third Reich, and their main principle was 'evil is done by evil men', namely the Nazis.

[31] Ibid.

[32] Ibid., 4–7.

[33] Ibid.

[34] Ibid., 9.

[35] Ibid., 11–13.

Second, this reference point influenced the way they described torture. They identified torture as mutilation, beating, sterilization, as well as subjecting an individual to medical experimentation. These acts were, indeed, committed by the Nazis. This is another indication that Nazi war crimes shaped their viewpoint about the scope of this norm at that time.

Third, there was a religious element to their understanding of torture. Torture is a crime against humanity because it is a 'crime against high heaven'.

Fourth, there was an emphasis on maiming and mutilating the victim's body. The torture victim was seen not as 'the subject' but as 'the object' that was destroyed and deformed. This formulation revolved around the sacredness of the human body, which had its roots in the natural law tradition. One of its foundations was the idea that the body and soul are in unity,[36] created in God's own image.[37] Therefore, deforming it would be a crime against God or 'high heaven', which Cocks mentioned in his speech.

Therefore, it is no surprise that Teitgen wrote in his report that the Convention's text was drafted 'in accordance with the principles of natural law, of humanism and of democracy'.[38] Furthermore, the connection between natural law and human rights can be traced in the works of Hersch Lauterpacht, who was the 'leading intellectual force' behind the Universal Declaration and the Convention to a great extent.[39] According to him, natural law, natural rights and human rights are cut from the same cloth, and the moral force of human rights is grounded in their religious foundations.[40] Consequently, this also explains the religious tone observed in the legal discourse that was dominant during this period.

Accordingly, the Genesis of this prohibition was shaped by the memories of Nazi atrocities and the principles of natural law. Additionally, the overarching concern regarding the possible impact of this Convention on sovereignty was influential when drafting this prohibition. As Bates notes, 'the member States to the Council, who determined that any document produced would have to be agreeable to all participating nations, were only prepared to accept a European Human Rights guarantee that had a limited impact on their sovereignty'.[41] Hence, the definition had

[36] Robert Pasnau, *Thomas Aquinas on Human Nature, A Philosophical Study of Summa Theologiae* (2002), 73.

[37] David Boucher, *The Limits of Ethics in International Relations: Natural Law, Natural Rights and Human Rights in Transition* (2009).

[38] Quoted in Bates, *The Evolution of the European Convention on Human Rights*, 63.

[39] J. Harcourt Barrington, who was involved with drafting the version of the Convention authored by the European Movement, acknowledged '[their] debt to [Lauterpacht] because [they] did quite shamelessly borrow many ideas from his draft Convention on the Rights of Man prepared for the International Law Association in 1948. H. Lauterpacht et al., "The Proposed European Court of Human Rights," *Transactions of the Grotius Society* 35 (1949): 25–47.

[40] Hersch Lauterpacht, *An International Bill of Rights of the Man* (1945), 9.

[41] Bates, *The Evolution of the European Convention on Human Rights*, 56.

to be carefully crafted with a view to receive the Member States' blessings. Having the Nazi atrocities as frame of reference, the drafters set the bar high. Having been guided by the condition to avoid any infringements on sovereignty, the drafters chose a parsimonious and open definition.

15.2.2. Episode II: Legal diplomacy phase (1950–1974)

The legal diplomacy phase transpired in the context of the Cold War, during which Europe remained divided between the West and the East. The ideological battle between these blocs extended to human rights, with each side advocating separate classes of rights. While the West championed civil and political rights, which are embodied in the Convention, the East promoted social and economic rights. As Madsen rightly argues, the human rights agenda was more a matter of politics than of law during this period.[42] The decolonization movements in Africa and Asia were other important developments at the time. The controversy of several Member States' engagement in colonial policies continued to overshadow the European human rights regime.[43]

As for institutional dynamics, the distinguishing feature of the period was 'legal diplomacy'.[44] The Convention system was built on three pillars: the Commission, the Court and the Committee of Ministers. The Commission was in charge of the initial filtering of cases. It would receive applications, decide on their admissibility, and write a report with its non-binding opinion. The Court would receive cases only from the Commission or High Contracting parties, and its jurisdiction was extended to interpretation and application of the Convention. The Committee of Ministers was the executive organ of the Council of Europe and it would supervise the execution of judgments.[45] As mentioned earlier, both accepting the jurisdiction of the Court and granting individual right to petition were optional. The Member States' initial reluctance to accept these conditional clauses meant that the essential functions of the Court were subjected to serious limitations. To overcome this, the Strasbourg institutions undertook 'legal diplomacy', providing both legal and extralegal solutions to the disputes at hand in order to build trust in the Convention system and bring major players on board.[46]

[42] Madsen, 'The Protracted Institutionalization of the Strasbourg Court', 48.

[43] Mikael Rask Madsen, 'France, the UK and the "Boomerang" of the Internalization of Human Rights (1945–2000)', in Simon Halliday and Patrick Delbert Schmidt, eds., *Human Rights Brought Home: Socio-legal Perspectives on Human Rights in the National Context* (2004), 57.

[44] Madsen, 'The Protracted Institutionalization of the Strasbourg Court'.

[45] Bates, *The Evolution of the European Convention on Human Rights*, 120–126.

[46] Madsen, 'The Protracted Institutionalization of the Strasbourg Court', 46.

This manoeuvre was much needed, as until 1966 only nine Member States recognized the Court's jurisdiction.[47] The Convention system initially attracted only small European States, with the exception of Germany. When the United Kingdom joined this club in 1966, the tides turned.[48] However, these countries' acceptance of the Court's jurisdiction was not unconditional; it was limited to two to five years on renewable terms. Hence, legal diplomacy was a necessary tool.

At this stage, the Court had a limited role, and the Commission was the driving force of the Convention system during this period.[49] Sir Humphrey Waldock, then President of the Commission, stated that the main function of the Commission was 'to conduct confidential negotiations with the parties and to try and set right unobtrusively any breach of human rights that may have occurred'.[50] Underlining its diplomatic role, he argued that the Commission 'was not primarily established for the purpose of putting states in the dock and registering convictions against them'.[51] Evidently, they could not openly discredit the West at the height of the Cold War. Following this logic, the Commission adopted a stringent approach when it came to deciding on the admissibility of cases and referring them to the Court by the early 1970s.[52]

Among a handful of decisions given during this period, *the Greek Colonels case* was the probably most influential one in shaping the prohibition of torture and inhuman or degrading treatment. This case was brought by Denmark, Sweden, Norway, and the Netherlands against the Greek military junta. It was the first case in which an international tribunal decided that a State had practised torture.[53] Additionally, this case served as the basis for the definition of torture and inhuman or degrading treatment under the United Nation Convention Against Torture.[54]

The Greek Colonels case stands out compared to earlier cases. For example, in *Greece v. the United Kingdom*, a case concerning British counter-insurgency operations in the then British colony of Cyprus, the Commission found no violation under Article 3.[55] Similarly, in *Lawless v. Ireland*, the first case referred to the Court,

[47] Belgium, Denmark, Ireland, Luxembourg, the Netherlands, Norway, Iceland, Germany, and Austria.

[48] Bates, *The Evolution of the European Convention on Human Rights*, 186.

[49] Ibid., 181.

[50] Quoted in ibid., 223.

[51] Ibid.

[52] For example, in 1966, out of 303 applications five were declared admissible, and in 1974, out of 445 applications only six were declared admissible. Ibid., 241–245.

[53] Ibid., 267.

[54] United Nations Voluntary Fund for Victims of Torture, *Interpretation of Torture in the Light of the Practice and Jurisprudence of International Bodies*, available at http://www.ohchr.org/Documents/Issues/Torture/UNVFVT/Interpretation_torture_2011_EN.pdf.

[55] *Greece v. the United Kingdom*, app. no. 176/56, the European Commission of Human Rights (26 September 1958).

the Court did not find a violation in the Irish government's practice of detaining Irish Republican Army (IRA) suspects without trial.[56] In both cases, the Commission and the Court accepted the responding States' derogation claims, which evoked the 'public emergency threatening the life of a nation' argument. Finally, in the *East African Asians case*, which was brought by British protected persons and the citizens of the United Kingdom and Colonies, the applicants complained about the discriminatory legislation and policies of the British government.[57] The Commission found a violation and declared that 'to single out a group of persons for differential treatment on the basis of race might, in certain circumstances, constitute a special form of affront to human dignity'.[58] Interestingly, this case was never referred to the Court, and the Commission report, which was delayed for a long time in the hope of securing a friendly settlement, was never made public.[59]

These cases exemplify various legal diplomacy methods the Strasbourg institutions adopted. *Greece v. the United Kingdom* and *Lawless v. Ireland* revealed that the Commission and the Court were willing to prioritize the Member States' national security interests over the protection of individual rights, in order to mitigate the Member States' resistance. The *East African Asians* case indicated the Strasbourg institutions' reluctance to publicize human rights violations arising from the colonial practices of a Member State. Such extra-legal concerns seem to have influenced legal interpretation and sidelined the development of the prohibition against torture and inhuman or degrading treatment to a certain extent.

The Greek Colonels case, on the other hand, provided a good opportunity to clarify and develop this norm further. However, the special circumstances of this case should be noted. The case concerned the very thing the Convention system was designed to prevent: the emergence of totalitarianism in Europe. This explains the relatively bold attitude taken in this case.[60] However, its conceptual contribution is just as important, because the definition of torture and inhuman or degrading treatment provided in this case is strikingly different from the one observed in the discussions of the Convention's drafters.

The Commission defined this prohibition in three parts: (1) inhuman treatment is 'at least such treatment as deliberately causes severe suffering, mental or physical, which, in the particular situation is unjustifiable', (2) torture is 'inhuman treatment, which has a purpose, such as the obtaining of information or confessions, or the infliction of punishment, and it is generally an aggravated form of inhuman treatment',

[56] *Lawless v. the United Kingdom (No.3)*, app. no. 332/57, ECHR (1 July 1961).

[57] *East African Asians v. the United Kingdom*, the European Commission of Human Rights Report of 14 December 1973, §1.

[58] Ibid. § 207.

[59] Bates, *The Evolution of the European Convention on Human Rights*, 245.

[60] Legal diplomacy was still at play because the Commission's report was sent to the Committee of Ministers with proposals made for the Greek government in the spirit of legal diplomacy. Ibid., 268.

and (3) a treatment is degrading when 'it grossly humiliates [a person] before others or drives him to act against his will or conscience'.[61] As seen, the Commission provided a more precise definition than did the drafters of the Convention.

This new definition relied on a secular understanding that primarily focused on the psychology of victims. It did not include religious references to prohibit torture on moral grounds, and its focus extended beyond a victim's physical integrity. It identified torture by looking at the physical and psychological pain and suffering felt by the victim. That is, the criterion used to establish which acts would fall under this prohibition is how these acts made victims feel. Therefore, it gave more room to a victim's perspective, rendering the victim a 'subject'.

This subjectivist understanding constituted a paradigm shift in portraying the prohibition on torture and inhuman or degrading treatment. It relied on common emotions that make us human, such as empathizing with the pain and suffering of victims when identifying violations. Therefore, in contrast to the natural law tradition that refers to religious morals to establish why certain acts are wrong, this more contemporary understanding relied on empathy and reason to identify torture and inhuman or degrading treatment.

This paradigm shift in conceptualizing torture and inhuman or degrading treatment occurred as a result of several developments that shaped the dominant legal discourse. Primarily, psychology as a discipline matured. Studies conducted by psychologists, such as Milgram's studies of obedience and the Stanford prison experiment, became known and publicly discussed. These experiments not only sparked a greater interest in human psychology, but also confirmed Hannah Arendt's 'banality of evil' thesis.[62] Watching Eichmann's trial in 1961, Arendt argued that what led Eichmann to commit heinous crimes was not his fanaticism or sociopathic tendencies, but his inability to have moral judgement about his job, the routines of which he obsessively followed.[63] Accordingly, anyone had the capacity to do evil. This was the antithesis of the 'evil is done by evil men' thesis dominant in the previous period.

Second, the discipline of psychology started to be closer to that of legal studies. In the 1960s, the psycho-legal field emerged, and experimental methods became available to investigate legal issues.[64]

Third, the field of victimology also emerged during this period with the works of several *émigré* lawyers in the United States who studied Holocaust victims.[65]

[61] 'The Greek Case', *Year Book of European Convention on Human Rights*, 12 (1969), 186.

[62] S. Alexander Haslam and Stephen Reicher, 'Beyond the Banality of Evil: Three Dynamics of an Interactionist Social Psychology of Tyranny', *Personality and Social Psychology Bulletin*, 33 (2007), 616.

[63] Hannah Arendt, *Eichmann in Jerusalem: A Report on the Banality of Evil* (2006).

[64] June Louin Tapp, 'Psychology and the Law: An Overture', *Annual Review of Psychology*, 27 (1976) ; Andreas Kapardis, *Psychology and Law: A Critical Introduction* (2010).

[65] Sandra Walklate, *Imagining the Victim of a Crime* (2007), 2.

Beginning in the 1960s, a victim-focused agenda surfaced, particularly due to media attention that increased the visibility of victims.[66] Consequently, these different elements created the conditions for a change in legal discourse, which led to the reformulation of the prohibition on torture and inhuman or degrading treatment in more secular terms. This discourse has remained dominant until the present time.

15.2.3. Episode III: Progressive court phase (1975–1998)

The beginning of this phase coincided with the Helsinki Accords at the Conference on Security and Cooperation in Europe, where the West met the East. According to Sarah Snyder, the Helsinki Final Act 'spurred the development of a transnational network that significantly contributed to the end of the Cold War'.[67] Although the Final Act was a non-binding declaration of intent, it shaped the relation between the East and the West and gave rise to transnational contacts among NGOs, human rights activists, journalists, and politicians engaging in human rights issues.[68] This incidentally certified the European nations' commitment to human rights and increased human rights awareness both in the East and in the West.

On the institutional evolution front, there was an increasing willingness to accept the optional clauses of the Convention, namely the jurisdiction of the Court and the individual right to petition. As Bates argues, 'there was a sudden revival of interest in the Convention' in the early 1970s.[69] With Italy accepting the optional clauses in 1973 and France ratifying the Convention in 1974, the last remaining obstacles to making the system fully operational disappeared.[70] By 1974, thirteen of eighteen Member States had accepted the optional clauses,[71] which ensured the institutional autonomy of the Convention system and decreased the need for legal diplomacy. As expected, upon solidifying its autonomy, the Court assumed firmer standing,[72] issued several landmark cases, and defined many key Strasbourg concepts.[73] It now could afford to be more progressive.

One of the leading cases of this period was *Ireland v. the United Kingdom*. The case concerned the treatment of detainees linked to the IRA in Northern Ireland. The allegations included five techniques, namely wall-standing, hooding, subjection to noise, deprivation of sleep, and deprivation of food and drink. The Court argued

[66] James Dignan, *Understanding Victims and Restorative Justice* (2005), 14.

[67] Sarah Snyder, *Human Rights Activism and the End of the Cold War: A Transnational History of the Helsinki Network* (2011), 2.

[68] Ibid., 8.

[69] Bates, *The Evolution of the European Convention on Human Rights*, 278.

[70] Madsen, 'The Protracted Institutionalization of the Strasbourg Court', 53.

[71] Bates, *The Evolution of the European Convention on Human Rights*, 283.

[72] Ibid. 343.

[73] Ibid., 327.

that 'the five techniques were applied in combination, with premeditation and for hours at a stretch; they caused, if not actual bodily injury, at least intense physical and mental suffering', thereby constituting inhuman treatment.[74] Additionally, the Court declared them degrading, as these acts generated feelings of fear, anguish, and inferiority in the victims, breaking their physical or moral resistance.[75] With this case, the Court found a violation of this prohibition for the first time, and in so doing, it departed from the drafters' understanding that this prohibition concerned primarily bodily injury.

Another case signifying the changing conceptions was *Tyrer v. the United Kingdom*. This case concerned a fifteen-year-old who had been subjected to corporal punishment. The National Council for Civil Liberties (today Liberty) brought the case to the Commission.[76] This was an early example of civil society participation in human rights litigation, which became a more frequent practice later on. Upon assessing the case, the Court held that the punishment did not cause serious or lasting physical damages, yet it objectified him and impaired his dignity and physical integrity.[77]

Tyrer represents a drastic change in understanding what types of acts were to be covered under this provision. Corporal punishment was a subject of discussion during the drafting of the Convention, and the British delegation raised objections against listing corporal punishment as a prohibited act. In the twenty-eight years after this incident, the Court declared corporal punishment as a violation of Article 3. As seen, human rights abuses raised in these cases were not nearly as grave as was foreseen in the 'original collective pact against totalitarianism'.[78]

As for the legal discourse at the time, it was a continuation of the secular and victim-focused understanding, which emerged in the previous period. The main difference was, however, the emphasis on the absolute nature of this prohibition. As mentioned in the previous section, in *Greece v. the United Kingdom* or *Lawless v. Ireland*, the Commission and the Court admitted the responding States' derogation claims. They did not find a violation, as the measures that gave rise to the complaints were taken in the context of a public emergency. In *Ireland v. the United Kingdom*, the Court did not take this argument into consideration. It underlined that torture and inhuman or degrading treatment was prohibited in absolute terms, and 'there can be no derogation therefrom even in the event of a public emergency threatening the life of the nation'.[79] The Court, with an increasing institutional

[74] *Ireland v. the United Kingdom*, app. no. 5310/71, ECHR (18 January 1978), §167.

[75] Ibid.

[76] However, the Court refused the NCCL's request for an oral submission. Anna Wilkowska-Landowska, '"Friends of the Court": The Role of Human Rights Non-governmental Organisations in the Litigation Proceedings', *Human Rights Law Commentary*, 2 (2006), 106.

[77] *Tyrer v. the United Kingdom*, app. no. 5856/72, ECHR (25 April 1978), §33.

[78] Bates, *The Evolution of the European Convention on Human Rights*, 385.

[79] *Ireland v. the United Kingdom*, §163.

autonomy and progressive spirit, thereby declared that the prohibition of torture and inhuman or degrading treatment was absolute.

15.2.4. Episode IV: New permanent court phase (1998–)

The defining moment of this phase took place towards the end of the previous phase: the end of the Cold War. Reconfiguration of the political landscape created new opportunities and challenges for the Convention system. The system opened its doors to the newly independent Eastern European countries, a development known as 'the eastward expansion'. The first ratification came in 1992 by Hungary. Then others followed suit.

However, this process gained momentum with the war in the former Yugoslavia. Appalled by the outbreak of yet another war in Europe, the Member States of the Council of Europe issued the Vienna Declaration of 9 October 1993. They extended their invitation to the newly independent countries, saying they would be welcomed 'on an equal footing and in permanent structures', and their accession to the Convention system would be 'a central factor in the process of European construction'.[80] This indicated a colossal shift in the objectives of the Convention system, which was created to prevent the emergence of totalitarianism. With the Vienna Declaration, the Council of Europe pledged not only to facilitate a reconstruction of Eastern Europe, but also the transition of these countries to democracy.

By 1998, the number of parties to the Convention rose to forty-one. When Russia, the largest country in Europe, ratified the Convention in 1998, the Convention system significantly broadened its geographical extent. The new members accepted the jurisdiction of the Court and individual right to petition within a short period after ratification.[81] This translated into an increase in the number of applications. The existing structure of the Convention system was not equipped to cope with this change. The solution to this problem was introduced in Protocol 11. With its enactment in 1998, the Commission and the old Court were abolished, and a new Court was instituted as a permanent body. The jurisdiction of the Court and individual right to petition became obligatory. Without any direct interference in its autonomy, the Court now could engage in judicial activism even more.

However, this new situation came with different challenges. The increased number of applications became a concern, which came to be known as the backlog problem. What changed was not merely the number of applications, but also the nature of issues brought before the Court. As Bates rightly points out, until the 1990s, the Court received cases only from the States with long democratic traditions. Thus,

[80] The Council of Europe, Vienna Declaration of 9 October 1993, available at https://wcd.coe.int/ViewDoc.jsp?id=621771.

[81] Bates, *The Evolution of the European Convention on Human Rights*, 447.

the old Court functioned 'as a tool for the fine-tuning of the democratic engine'.[82] After the enlargement, the Court had to take a pedagogical role to cultivate a human rights tradition in newly independent countries.[83] Therefore, the Court coupled its activist intentions with pedagogical purposes when interpreting this provision, especially when it came to countries with poor human rights records.

Kurt v. Turkey was one of the earliest examples in which the Court practised this double approach. In this case, the applicant complained that she had been subjected to inhuman or degrading treatment due to the government's failure to investigate her son's disappearance, and inform her about the fate of her son, among others. Amnesty International intervened in the proceedings by submitting an *amicus curiae* brief. Citing the jurisprudence of the Inter-American Court of Human Rights and the UN Human Rights Committee on this issue, Amnesty argued that disappearance cases concern complex violations, which include the rights of the family who undergo severe mental anguish due to the uncertainty surrounding the fate of their disappeared relatives.[84]

The Court agreed with this view and found that the State's omission—namely, its inability or unwillingness to fulfil its procedural obligation to investigate into the allegations and duly inform the family of the disappeared person—inflicted anguish and distress on the applicant over a prolonged period of time.[85] It was the first case in which the Court found violation under Article 3 arising from the omission of a State. Hence, this case signalled that not only commissions but also omissions might give rise to violations under Article 3. Additionally, it was one of the first cases in which a third party submitted written comments, a practice that would become more common later on.

Furthermore, the case of *Selmouni v. France* signalled another change in the Court's attitude with respect to the interpretation of Article 3. This case was about ill treatment under custody during which the applicant was subjected to a large number of physical blows and insults. The Court established that the treatment was intentional for the purpose of extracting a confession and declared that it amounted to torture.[86] In response to France's claims that similar acts had not been considered as torture in previous case law (referring in particular to *Ireland v. the United Kingdom*), the Court argued that certain acts which had been defined as inhuman or degrading treatment in the past could be defined as torture in the future. Moreover, it underlined the need for increasingly higher standards with respect to the protection of human rights, and 'greater firmness in assessing breaches of the fundamental

[82] Bates, *The Evolution of the European Convention on Human Rights*, 473.

[83] Robert Harmsen, 'The European Convention on Human Rights after Enlargement', *The International Journal of Human Rights*, 5 (2010), 33.

[84] *Kurt v. Turkey*, app. no. 15/1997/799/1002, ECHR (25 May 1998), §68–71.

[85] Ibid., §134.

[86] *Selmouni v. France*, app. no. 25803/94, ECHR (28 July 1999), §98.

values of democratic societies'.[87] Therefore, the Court expressed its willingness to lower thresholds when it came to interpreting the provision in the future.

The essentiality of elevating human rights standards has dominated the Convention system's legal discourse during this period, to which the following observations attest: (1) the scope of Article 3 has expanded, covering violations arising from omissions and emphasizing procedural obligations, as seen in *Kurt v. Turkey*, and (2) the threshold to define acts as torture and inhuman or degrading treatment has been lowered, as seen in *Selmouni v. France*. This approach was shaped by a couple of developments. First, upon certifying its ultimate autonomy, the new Court began to take a more activist stand. Second, the Court assumed a more pedagogical role with the change in the Member State profiles after the eastward expansion, giving more weight to States' procedural obligations to instil the rule of law. Third, the broader political context was suitable for such a change. The Convention system, which was tested against the Cold War bipolarity, was now equipped to work for the (re)construction of new Europe whose founding myth would be human rights.

15.3. Conclusion

In this chapter I have contextualized the interpretative evolution of the norm prohibiting torture and inhuman or degrading treatment, looking at how the broader political context, the Convention system's institutional evolution, and the dominant legal discourse have influenced the interpretation of this prohibition. These factors have shaped the character of the interpretative body and, thereby, its interpretative output. In order to illustrate how these extra-legal factors have guided the interpretative evolution of this norm, I have analysed various phases of the Convention system's lifetime, looking at the period between 1950 and the early 2000s.

The genesis phase was dominated by a reactionary understanding of the prohibition. The drafters of the Convention formulated this prohibition, in light of the principles of natural law, while still reeling from the Nazi atrocities. This early understanding lacked the victims' perspective and relied on religious grounds. During the legal diplomacy phase, a secular and victim-focused understanding emerged. However, this novel approach had to be cautiously balanced with national security interests of the Member States, as the Convention system had limited institutional autonomy. In the progressive court phase, the Convention system strengthened its autonomous standing and national security concerns ceased to be the defining argument. In this period, the absolute nature of the ban on torture was affirmed. Finally, the new permanent court phase was marked by a more dynamic interpretation, as

[87] Ibid., §101.

the new Court assumed a more audacious stand and a pedagogical role. During this phase, the definition of the norm against torture and inhuman or degrading treatment became more comprehensive, especially with the introduction of procedural obligations, and the threshold to identify the acts falling under this prohibition was lowered.

Dynamism has always been the essence of the interpretative logic defining the Convention system, and its inevitable outcome has been the evolution of norms safeguarded under the Convention. This transformation, however, is not simply an outcome of a linear progression of interpretative preferences. Rather, the sophistication of norms protecting human rights is not only a moral and legal matter, but one of political expediency as well.

References

Arendt, Hannah, *Eichmann in Jerusalem: A Report on the Banality of Evil* (New York, 2006).

Bates, Ed, 'The Birth of the European Convention on Human Rights', in Jonas Christoffersen and Mikael Rask Madsen, eds., *The European Court of Human Rights Between Law and Politics*, 17–42 (Oxford, 2013).

Bates, Ed, *The Evolution of the European Convention on Human Rights: From Its Inception to the Creation of a Permanent Court of Human Rights* (Oxford, 2010).

Bjorge, Eirik, 'The Vienna Rules, Evolutionary Interpretation and the Intention of the Parties', in Andrea Bianchi, Daniel Peat and Matthew Windsor eds., *Interpretation in International Law*, 189–204 (New York, 2015).

Boucher, David, *The Limits of Ethics in International Relations: Natural Law, Natural Rights and Human Rights in Transition* (Oxford, 2009).

Cali, Basak, 'Coping with Crisis: Whither the Variable Geomety in the Jurisprudence of the European Court of Human Rights,' *Wisconsin International Law Journal* 35 (2018): 237–76.

Christoffersen, Jonas and Mikael Rask Madsen, eds., *The European Human Rights Between Law and Politics* (Oxford, 2013).

Davidson, Natalie R., 'Everyday Lawmaking in International Human Rights Law: Insights from the Inclusion of Domestic Violence in the Prohibition of Torture,' *Law & Social Inquiry* (2021), doi: https://doi.org/10.1017/lsi.2021.20

Dignan, James, *Understanding Victims and Restorative Justice* (New York, 2005).

Dzehtsiarou, Kanstantsin, 'European Consensus and the Evolutive Interpretation of the European Convention on Human Rights', *German Law Journal*, 12 (2011): 1730–45.

Fish, Stanley, *Is There a Text in this Class* (Cambridge, MA, 1980).

'The Greek Case', *Year Book of European Convention on Human Rights*, 12 (1969).

Greer, Steven, 'The Interpretation of the European Convention on Human Rights: Universal Principle or Margin of Appreciation?', *UCL Human Rights Review*, 3 (2010): 1–13.

Harmsen, Robert, 'The European Convention on Human Rights after Enlargement', *The International Journal of Human Rights*, 5 (2010): 18–43.

Haslam, S. Alexander and Stephen Reicher, 'Beyond the Banality of Evil: Three Dynamics of an Interactionist Social Psychology of Tyranny', *Personality and Social Psychology Bulletin*, 33 (2007): 615–22.

Helfer, Laurence R. and Erik Voeten, 'Walking Back Human Rights in Europe?,' *European Journal of International Law* 31 (2020): 797–827.

Kapardis, Andreas, *Psychology and Law: A Critical Introduction* (New York, 2010).

Krasner, Stephen D., 'Structural Changes and Regime Consequences: Regimes as Intervening Variables', in Stephen D. Krasner, *International Regimes*, 1–22 (New York, 1983).

Kratochwil, Friedrich, *Rules, Norms, and Decisions: On the Conditions of Practical and Legal Reasoning in International Relations and Domestic Affairs* (Cambridge, 1991).

Lauterpacht, Hersch, *An International Bill of Rights of the Man* (New York, 1945).

Lauterpacht, Hersch, J. Harcourt Barrington, Norman Bentwich, W. Harvey Moore, Patrick Spens and Mr. Barrington, 'The Proposed European Court of Human Rights,' *Transactions of the Grotius Society* 35 (1949): 25–47.

Letsas, George, 'The ECHR as a Living Instrument: Its Meaning and Legitimacy', in Andreas Føllesdal, Birgit Peters, Geir Ulfstein eds., *Constituting Europe: The European Court of Human Rights in a National, European and Global Context*, 106–41 (Cambridge, 2013).

Letsas, George, 'Strasbourg's Interpretive Ethic: Lessons for the International Lawyer', *European Journal of International Law*, 21 (2010): 509–41.

Letsas, George, *A Theory of Interpretation of the European Convention on Human Rights* (Oxford, 2007).

Madsen, Mikael Rask, 'France, the UK and the "Boomerang" of the Internalization of Human Rights (1945–2000)', in Simon Halliday and Patrick Delbert Schmidt, eds., *Human Rights Brought Home: Socio-legal Perspectives on Human Rights in the National Context*, 57–86 (Oxford and Portland, OR, 2004).

Madsen, Mikael Rask, Pola Cebulak and Micha Wiebusch, 'Backlash against International Courts: Explaining the Forms and Patterns of Resistance to International Courts,' *International Journal of Law in Context* 14 (2018): 197–220.

Madsen, Mikael Rask, 'The Protracted Institutionalization of the Strasbourg Court: From Legal Diplomacy to Integrationist Jurisprudence', in Jonas Christoffersen and Mikael Rask Madsen, eds., *The European Court of Human Rights between Law and Politics*, 43–60 (Oxford, 2013).

Madsen, Mikael Rask, 'Two-Level Politics and the Backlash against International Courts: Evidence from the Politicisation of the European Court of Human Rights,' *The British Journal of Politics and International Relations* 22 (2020): 728–38.

Mavronicola, Natasa, Torture, *Inhumanity and Degradation under Article 3 of the ECHR: Absolute Rights and Absolute Wrongs* (New York, 2021).

Pasnau, Robert, *Thomas Aquinas on Human Nature, A Philosophical Study of Summa Theologiae* (New York, 2002).

Ramanzini, Isabela Garbin and Ezgi Yildiz, 'Revamping to Remain Relevant: How Do the European and the Inter-American Human Rights Systems Adapt to Challenges?,' *Journal of Human Rights Practice* 12 (2020): 768–80.

Reidy, Aisling, *The Prohibition of Torture: A Guide to the Implementation of Article 3 of the European Convention on Human Rights*, Human Rights Handbooks No.6, Directorate General of Human Rights, Council of Europe (July 2003).

Snyder, Sarah, *Human Rights Activism and the End of the Cold War: A Transnational History of the Helsinki Network* (Cambridge, 2011).

Stiansen, Øyvind and Erik Voeten, 'Backlash and Judicial Restraint: Evidence from the European Court of Human Rights,' *International Studies Quarterly* 64 (2020): 770–84.

Tapp, June Louin, 'Psychology and the Law: An Overture', *Annual Review of Psychology*, 27 (1976): 359–404.

Voeten, Erik, 'Populism and Backlashes against International Courts," *Perspectives on Politics* 18 (2020): 407–22.

Yildiz, Ezgi, 'A Court with Many Faces: Judicial Characters and Modes of Norm Development in the European Court of Human Rights,' *European Journal of International Law* 31 (2020): 73–99.

Yildiz, Ezgi, *Between Forbearance and Audacity: How the European Court Redefined the Norm Against Torture and Inhuman or Degrading Treatment* (Cambridge, Forthcoming).

Walklate, Sandra, *Imagining the Victim of a Crime* (New York, 2007).

Wilkowska-Landowska, Anna, '"Friends of the Court": The Role of Human Rights Non-governmental Organisations in the Litigation Proceedings', *Human Rights Law Commentary*, 2 (2006): 99–119.

16

Crimes against women in armed conflicts

Judicial activism and feminist legal interpretation as key factors in the reconstruction of concepts of international humanitarian law

KAROLINA RISTOVA-AASTERUD

Introduction

The wars in the former Yugoslavia and the civil war in Rwanda in the early 1990s shocked the international community with the widespread use of sexualized violence as a weapon of war, in most cases with women and girls as the main victims. The ironical aspect of this pivotal 'moment of discovery' is that these crimes have existed as long as warfare itself,[1] more so in modern warfare, as shown by the evidence gathered during the post-World War II Nuremberg and Tokyo military tribunals in 1945 and 1946 respectively. Yet the contemporary international humanitarian law (IHL) that governs international and internal armed conflicts with respect to the treatment of categories of members of the armed forces and civilians has long been inadequate regarding crimes against women (CAW). Moreover, there is no formal legal definition for these crimes. The standard understanding in IHL circles is that CAWs are war crimes and crimes against humanity that target women solely based on their sex/gender or that affect women disproportionally. The analytical overview of the statutory developments in contemporary IHL in section 16.1 of this chapter reveals two indicative aspects. First, in stark disproportion to their occurrence in the reality of warfare, CAWs have long been on the margins of IHL because of their ontological status as 'crimes of honour'. Second, a significant ontological shift towards treating CAWs as 'crimes of violence' has happened only in the period between the statutes of the ad hoc criminal tribunals for the former

[1] Theodor Meron, 'Rape as a Crime under International Humanitarian Law', *American Journal of International Law*, 87 (1993), 424–425; Maurice Keen, *The Laws of War in the Late Middle Ages* (1993).

Karolina Ristova-Aasterud, *Crimes against women in armed conflicts* In: *Language and Legal Interpretation in International Law*. Edited by: Anne Lise Kjær and Joanna Lam, Oxford University Press. © Oxford University Press 2022.
DOI: 10.1093/oso/9780190855208.003.0017

Yugoslavia (ICTY) and Rwanda (ICTR) of 1993 and 1994 respectively, and the Statute of the International Criminal Court (ICC) of 1998. This inevitably points towards the judicial interpretation of the ad hoc tribunals, an issue addressed in section 16.2. However, the judicial interpretative approaches can only shed light on how some of these novelties came about in a strictly legal context. They cannot alone reveal the driving force behind the ontological change regarding CAWs. For that purpose, it is necessary to look for the deeper ideological, political, and legal forces that have been in play. As is asserted in section 16.3, those forces are of feminist origin, in other words, the long-standing critical feminist standpoint with respect to the patriarchal character of international law. It is argued that the feminist 'interpretative community' has been formed to advance the cause of CAWs in the prosecutorial agenda and the judicial interpretations of both tribunals, subsequently, in the course of drafting the ICC Statute, turning them into statutory law. It is also suggested that the most specific contribution of the feminist discourse to the legal semiotics of international lawyering is the insistence on (and indeed the achievement of) fair gender representation in the institutional composition of the international criminal courts. Feminism has long advocated this as an important safeguard against interpreting international law through only the lens of the patriarchal 'male norm' of social experiences and practices.

16.1. Key developments in statutory international humanitarian law regarding crimes against women in armed conflicts, from Nuremberg to Rome

16.1.1. The Charters of the Nuremberg (1945) and Tokyo (1946) tribunals

The explicit legal recognition of CAWs in contemporary IHL can be traced back to the two military tribunals established by the Allied powers in the aftermath of World War II. The Charter of the International Military Tribunal at Nuremberg (1945)[2] and the Charter of the International Military Tribunal for the Far East at Tokyo (1946)[3] gave the tribunals jurisdiction to try war crimes, crimes against humanity, and crimes against peace committed by 'the major war criminals of the European Axis' and by the 'war criminals in the Far East'. In their wording and lists of crimes (Article 6 of the Nuremberg Charter and Article 5 of the Tokyo Charter), neither charter contained any reference to 'women' or to 'sexual violence'; not even rape was mentioned. Despite the mounting evidence that CAWs had been committed during the war on a massive scale, both tribunals accepted evidence for CAWs as

[2] 82 UNTS 280.

[3] TIAS 1589.

admissible only for building cases for war crimes and crimes against humanity explicitly listed in the charters.[4] Yet an important precedent had been established in the Tokyo Tribunal's jurisprudence, by treating wartime rape as a war crime, though in conjunction with other crimes ('murder, rape, and other cruelties').[5] This had influenced the subsequent sanctioning of rape as a crime against humanity in Article 2(a) of Control Council Law 10 of 1945 in Germany, which was used as a legal basis for trying suspected war criminals who were not tried at the Nuremberg Tribunal.[6]

16.1.2. Geneva Conventions of 1949 and the two Additional Protocols of 1977

The four Geneva Conventions (GC)[7] and the two Additional Protocols[8] represent the core of the post-World War II codification of IHL, also known as the 'Geneva Regime'. In addition to the declaratory language of Article 12 of the First and Second Geneva Conventions and Article 14 of the Third Geneva Convention that 'women shall be treated with all consideration due to their sex', this codification introduced, for the first time, an explicit criminalization of CAWs in Article 27 of the Fourth Geneva Convention: 'Women shall be especially protected against any attack on their honour, in particular against rape, enforced prostitution, or any form of indecent assault'. In addition, the 'Common Article 3' of all four Geneva Conventions, applicable to armed conflicts of a non-international character, has criminalized 'outrages upon personal dignity, in particular humiliating and degrading treatment' and ever since has been interpreted to cover the crimes included in Article 27.[9] This

[4] For more on this topic, see Patricia Viseur Sellers, 'The Prosecution of Sexual Violence in Conflict: The Importance of Human Rights as Means of Interpretation' (2007), https://www.peacewomen.org/node/89506.

[5] Kelly D. Askin, 'Prosecuting Wartime Rape and other Gender-Related Crimes under International Law: Extraordinary Advances, Enduring Obstacles', *Berkeley Journal of International Law*, 21 (2003), 288–349.

[6] Control Council Law No. 10, Punishment of Persons Guilty of War Crimes, Crimes Against Peace and Against Humanity, 20 December 1945, 3 Official Gazette Control Council for Germany 50–55 (1946).

[7] Geneva Convention for the Amelioration of the Condition of the Wounded and Sick in Armed Forces in the Field, 75 UNTS 31; Geneva Convention for the Amelioration of the Condition of the Wounded, Sick and Shipwrecked Members of the Armed Forces at Sea, 75 UNTS 86; Geneva Convention Relative to the Treatment of Prisoners of War, 75 UNTS 135; Geneva Convention Relative to the Protection of Civilian Persons in Time of War, 75 UNTS 287.

[8] Protocol Additional to the Geneva Conventions of 12 August 1949, and Relating to the Protection of Victims of International Armed Conflict, 1125 UNTS 3; Protocol Additional to the Geneva Conventions of 12 August 1949, and Relating to the Protection of Victims of Non-International Armed Conflicts, 1125 UNTS 609.

[9] See commentaries on articles 3 and 27 of IV GC, ICRC, http://www.icrc.org/applic/ihl/ihl.nsf/Comment.xsp.

criminalization has been transformed into the articles of the Additional Protocols of 1979 (Articles 7 and 4, respectively) and covers CAWs both in international and non-international armed conflicts. However, the Geneva Regime also recognizes a concept of 'grave breaches' consisting of an exclusive list of crimes,[10] for which the state parties have an obligation to pass national legislation, and for which they have universal prosecutorial jurisdiction. Yet none of the recognized CAWs is explicitly included in this list. In other words, the Geneva Regime recognizes a 'hierarchy of crimes', but none of the CAWs is included at the top of that hierarchy.

16.1.3. Statutes of International Criminal Tribunal for the former Yugoslavia of 1993 and International Criminal Tribunal for Rwanda of 1994

When it comes to CAWs, neither statute went beyond the existent Geneva Regime. The Statute of the ICTY that has provided the tribunal with subject-matter jurisdiction over the serious violations of IHL committed in the former Yugoslavia since 1991[11] lists only rape as a crime against humanity in Article 5(g). The Statute of the ICTR, which provided the tribunal with subject-matter jurisdiction over the violations of IHL committed in Rwanda and by Rwandan citizens in the territory of neighbouring states between 1 January and 31 December 1994,[12] did the same in its Article 3(g), while Article 4(e) listed outrages upon personal dignity, in particular humiliating and degrading treatment, rape, enforced prostitution, and indecent assault of any kind as serious violations of Common Article 3. In the case of both tribunals, these crimes have been recognized as crimes against humanity only if committed in the course of an armed conflict, the difference being that, in the case of the ICTY, the jurisdiction covers a wider range of armed conflicts (international and non-international) and crimes against any civilian population (Article 5 of the ICTY Statute), while in the case of the ICTR, the crimes must be committed as part of a widespread and systematic attack against any civilian population on national, political, ethnic, racial, or religious grounds (Article 3 of the ICTR Statute).

16.1.4. Statute of the International Criminal Court of 1998

The establishment of a permanent ICC with statutory jurisdiction over genocide, crimes against humanity, war crimes, and the crime of aggression, complementary

[10] The grave breaches are specified in articles 50, 51, 130, and 147 of the four GCs respectively, and in articles 11 and 85 of the First Protocol. See notes 7 and 8.

[11] Articles 1–5, 32 ILM 1159 (1993).

[12] Articles 1–4, 33 ILM 1598 (1994).

to the national criminal jurisdictions of the state parties,[13] marks a major step forward in statutory IHL. Unlike the ICTY and the ICTR that have been established as UN bodies, their statutes adopted by way of UN resolutions,[14] as well as being mandated to cover armed conflicts in specific countries with limited temporal and territorial jurisdiction, the ICC is a treaty-based court. Its statute is an international treaty among an open-ended number of states, and it came into force only after the required number of states had ratified it in 2002.[15] With respect to CAWs, the overall characteristic of the ICC Statute is that the list of relevant crimes is much more elaborate than ever before in IHL. First, the list of crimes against humanity in Article 7(1)(g) enumerates not only rape and enforced prostitution, but adds sexual slavery, forced pregnancy, enforced sterilization, or 'any other form of sexual violence of comparable gravity'. In Article 7(1)(h), the crime of persecution against 'any identifiable group or collectivity', in addition to political, racial, national, ethnic, and cultural grounds, explicitly includes 'gender' for the first time. Second, this list of crimes is replicated in terms of war crimes in Article 8(2)(xxii). However, again none of them is included in Article 8(1) where the grave breaches of the Geneva Convention are enumerated. Similarly, Article 8(2)(e)(vi) lists as war crimes in non-international armed conflicts the same crimes, but again none of these crimes are included in Article 8(2)(c) that explicitly enumerates the 'serious violations of Article 3 common to Geneva Conventions'. Third, there is an evident legislative effort to provide for legal definitions of all the crimes, distinctly charged with considerations of the cultural differences among state parties, especially about anything that is conceptually connected to sex/gender differentiation. The most notable example is the definition of 'gender' in Article 7(3): 'For the purpose of this Statute, it is understood that the term 'gender' refers to the two sexes, male and female, within the context of society. The term 'gender' does not indicate any meaning different from the above'.[16] The ICC Statute is also accompanied with a document named 'Elements of Crime', which, according to Article 9(1)

[13] Articles 1, 5–8, 2187 UNTS 90.

[14] S.C.Res.827, U.N.Doc.S/RES/827 (25 May 1993) for ICTY, and S.C.Res.955 U.N.Doc.S/RES/955 (8 November 1994).

[15] The Statute was adopted at the UN Diplomatic Conference of Plenipotentiaries on the establishment of an International Criminal Court, held from 15 June to 17 July 1998 in Rome, and entered into force on 1 July 2002 after 60 states had ratified it. As of October 2021, 123 states were treaty parties. Data from http://www.icc-pi.int/en_menus/asp/states.

[16] At the ICC diplomatic conference, mostly Arab countries insisted on defining 'gender' in terms of biological sex, pre-empting any other understanding of sexual identity, as well as any socially construed concept of gender ('women's rights concept') other than the one 'within the context of society'. For more, see Barbara Bedont and Katherine Hall Martinez, 'Ending Impunity for Gender Crimes under International Criminal Court', *The Brown Journal of World Affairs*, 6/1 (1999), 65–85.

of the Statute, should assist the Court in the interpretation and the application of Articles 6, 7, and 8.[17] Adopted in 2000, it defines each crime in the ICC's jurisdiction, in many cases for the first time in the history of IHL, most notably with respect to the crimes of sexual violence.[18] Fourth, the ICC Statute is the first international treaty, indeed, the first international court, to introduce institutional fair gender representation and gender expertise. In Article 36(8)(a)(iii), the Statute insists on 'fair representation of male and female judges', and in Article 44(2) the same consideration applies to the Court's staff.[19] As for the gender expertise, in Article 36(8)(b) the Statute insists that the selection of judges must take into account 'the need to include judges with legal expertise on . . . violence against women', and in Article 44(2) this *mutatis mutandis* applies to the Court's staff. In Article 42(9), the ICC Prosecutor is required to appoint advisers with legal expertise on specific issues, including on 'sexual and gender violence'. Furthermore, as provided in Article 43(6), a 'Victims and Witnesses Unit' is to be set up, and such a unit must include staff 'with expertise in trauma, including trauma related to crimes of sexual violence'. Such protective measures are also provided in Article 68 for the trial proceedings, with special consideration for the 'gender' of the victims and witnesses, in particular when the crime involves 'sexual or gender violence'.[20] Finally, in Article 21(3), in the application and interpretation of the statute's provisions, ICC is bound to be 'consistent with internationally recognized human rights' and with no 'adverse distinction founded on grounds such as gender as defined in article 7'.

16.1.5. The ontological shift regarding CAWs from 'crimes of honour' to 'crimes of violence'

There is no doubt that the ontological concept of CAWs in the Geneva Regime is a concept of 'crimes against honour'. Unlike the other crimes in the Geneva Conventions, none of the CAWs is termed and/or otherwise treated as a crime of violence. This only logically leads to the Geneva Regime's exclusion of CAWs from the 'grave breaches' and 'Common Article 3'. By treating CAWs as crimes of lesser legal gravity in their very ontology, the Geneva Regime contains no prohibitive legal language and no comprehensive list of CAWs in order to meet

[17] Available at the official website of ICC at http://www.icc-cpi.int/nr/rdonlyres/336923d8-a6ad-40ec-ad7b-45bf9de73d56/0/elementsofcrimeseng.pdf.

[18] In ibid., 7(1)(g)-6 and in 8(2)(e)(vi)-6.

[19] After the adoption of the ICC Statute, in 2000, the statutes of the ICTY and ICTR were also amended to include fair gender representation for the *ad litem* judges, but *not* for the permanent judges. See Article 13 S.C.Res.1329, U.N.Doc.S/RES/1329.

[20] These measures are elaborated in ICC *Rules of Procedure and Evidence* (Rules 70, 71, 72, and 88). See http://www.icc-cpi.int/iccdocs/PIDS/legal-texts/RulesProcedureEvidenceEng.pdf.

the variety of atrocities that women commonly suffer during armed conflicts. However, in the early 1990s, the statutes of the ICTY and ICTR, without any prior amendment intervention to the explicit language of the GC, in other words, to the body of law that the tribunals were bound to implement, have initiated an important shift in the ontology of CAWs. In these statutes, the crime of rape was listed as a predicate crime of crimes against humanity, but without the language about 'women's honour', which mysteriously disappeared. In addition, in the ICTR Statute, rape, enforced prostitution, and indecent assault of any kind are listed as violations of Common Article 3. What was implicit in these two statutes has become very explicit in the ICC Statute of 1998. Although they continue to be excluded from the lists of grave breaches and Common Article 3, it is statutorily recognized that they can amount to such qualification. The list of CAWs is more comprehensive than ever before, as well as accompanied by a 'basket clause' ('any other forms of sexual violence of comparable gravity'), to include other crimes (such as forced nudity and sexual mutilation). Most CAWs are covered with gender-neutral language, unless reference to the biological sex (female) is inherently required ('forced pregnancy'), but, at the same time, the new requirements for fair gender representation in the institutional aspects of the Court, as well as those regarding expertise on gender/sexual violence, clearly indicate that the treaty-makers were quite aware that in the reality of warfare most of these crimes would predominantly take the form of CAWs.

16.2. Crimes against women in the jurisprudence of the ad hoc criminal tribunals for the former Yugoslavia and Rwanda: Judicial interpretation in service of gender justice

16.2.1. The pioneering jurisprudence of the ad hoc criminal tribunals regarding CAWs

When the ICTY and ICTR were established in the early 1990s, they had not much to go on, apart from their own statutes, the Geneva Regime, and the jurisprudence of the Nuremberg and Tokyo military tribunals. In terms of contemporary IHL, they were the pioneering judicial bodies, more so when CAWs are concerned, because neither the statutes nor the jurisprudence of the World War II tribunals treated these crimes as a priority. Indeed, they have become the very jurisprudential vehicle for the subsequent ontological shift regarding CAWs from 'crimes of honour' to 'crimes of violence' in the ICC Statute. As the key judicial decisions regarding CAWs are presented, the key point is that such a pioneering jurisprudence could not have been achieved if it had not also been for some pioneering approaches to judicial interpretation by these tribunals.

16.2.2. Defining the crimes of rape and sexual violence

The ICTR first created historical jurisprudence by defining rape and sexual violence[21] in its *Akayesu* judgment[22] of 1998. It was a clear manifestation of judicial activism, as the ICTR itself declared that 'the Chamber must define rape, as there is no commonly accepted definition of this term in international law'.[23] The ICTR qualified its definitional approach as 'conceptual', explaining it by analogy to the Torture Convention, which also does not catalogue any specific acts in its definition of torture, but rather focuses on the conceptual framework of the sanctioned violence.[24] Later, in the *Musema* judgment of 2000, the ICTR added that this approach was preferable because of the 'ongoing evolution of the understanding of rape and the incorporation of this understanding into principles of international law'.[25] The ICTY, instead of following *Akayesu*'s definition, came up with its own definition of rape in its *Furundzija* judgment of 1998.[26] Its definition is the result of a combination of two interpretative approaches: strict construction and teleological. As the ICTY specified, in establishing the elements of a crime, preference must be given to the strict construction of the relevant statutory or customary law. However, if that is not possible, then to arrive at an accurate definition based on the criminal law principle *nullum crimen sine lege stricta,* it is necessary to look for the principles of criminal law common to the world's major legal systems. This is subject to two conditions: first, the international court must engage in a process of identifying the common denominators that they share; and, second, the international court must be mindful of the specificity of international criminal procedure when utilizing notions from national law.[27] If such a path of strict construction is still not helpful, then, as the ICTY declared, turning to the teleological interpretation is quite appropriate. As it was elaborated, the essence of IHL lies in the protection of human dignity of every person, whatever the gender, as that is the very *raison d'être* of this body of law and that is why the Court favoured broadening the definition of rape.[28] This overall interpretative reasoning explains why the ICTY, just like the ICTR, has embarked on construing a definition of rape, previously non-existent in IHL. However, unlike the ICTR's conceptual and evolutionary approach, the ICTY has then opted for a descriptive, mechanical, and gendered definition, which is more in

[21] Rape was defined as 'a physical invasion of a sexual nature, committed on a person under circumstances which are coercive', while sexual violence was defined as 'any act of sexual nature which is committed on a person under circumstances which are coercive'. Ibid., para. 598.

[22] *Prosecutor v. Akayesu,* Case No. ICTR -96-4-T, 2 September 1998.

[23] Ibid., para. 596.

[24] Ibid., para. 597.

[25] *Prosecutor v. Musema,* Case No. ICTR-96-13-T, 27 January 2000, para. 228.

[26] *Prosecutor v. Furundzija,* Case No. IT-95-17/1-T, 10 December 1998, paras. 177 and 178.

[27] Ibid.

[28] Ibid., paras. 183–185.

line with what we find in major national jurisdictions, as well as in line with the strict construction method of interpretation. For a while, the trial chambers of the ICTR had followed *Akayesu*, while those of the ICTY had followed *Furundzija*. When the latter was upheld on an appellate level that is common to both tribunals in the *Kunarac* judgment,[29] it has become binding for both tribunals in accordance with the doctrine of *stare decisis* declared in the *Aleksovski* judgment of 2000.[30] The definition of rape later adopted in the Elements of Crime of the ICC Statute is a mixture between these two definitions.[31]

16.2.3. Rape and sexual violence as predicate crimes of the crime of genocide

The *Akayesu* judgment of the ICTR is also a first instance in which an international criminal tribunal recognizes that rape and other acts of sexual violence may constitute *actus reus* of the crime of genocide, because they may cause 'serious bodily or mental harm to members of the group' if such acts are committed with 'intent to destroy, [in] whole or in part, [a] national, ethnical, racial or religious group'.[32] In this instance, the ICTR has predominantly used the following interpretation methods: (a) systemic interpretation of its own statute, the ICC Statute, GC, and the Genocide Convention of 1949; (b) the original intent method, by relying on the *travaux préparatoires* of the Genocide Convention; (c) the legal-historical approach by reference to historical precedents (Nuremberg and Tokyo judgments); and (d) cross-reference to the jurisprudence of the ICTY.[33]

16.2.4. Rape as war crime of torture

In the *Celebici* judgment of 1998, the ICTY established that rape and other forms of sexual assault can meet the elements of both 'torture' and 'inhumane treatment', thus constituting grave breaches of the Geneva Conventions and war crimes.[34] The ICTY, after expressing its initial awareness that rape was not explicitly included in the grave breaches nor in Common Article 3, declared that it still intended to consider whether this crime could meet the elements of torture as a war crime. In establishing the legal status of both torture and rape under international law, the ICTY first engaged in strict construction of the provisions of various IHL treaties and other international and regional human rights conventions or instruments,

[29] *Prosecutor v. Kunarac et al.*, Case No.: IT-96-23 and IT-96-23/1-A, 12 June 2002.

[30] *Prosecutor v. Aleksovski*, Case No. IT-95-14/1-A, 24 March 2000, paras. 110–114.

[31] 'Elements of Crime', Articles 7(1)(g)-1, 8(2)(b)(xxii)-1, and 8(2)(e)(vi)-1.

[32] *Prosecutor v. Akayesu*, paras. 688 and 731.

[33] Ibid., part 6.

[34] *Prosecutor v. Delalic ('Celebici' Judgment)*, Case No.: IT-96-21-T, 16 November 1998, para. 496.

as well as employing the legal-historical approach to establish historical judicial precedents.[35] However, in establishing whether rape can amount to torture, the ICTY turned to the recent jurisprudence of the ICTR in *Akayesu*, which had already interpreted rape as amounting to torture (as a crime against humanity), as well as the more contemporary decisions of other international and regional juridical or quasi-judicial bodies, such as the Inter-American Commission on Human Rights (*Fernando and Raquel Mejia v. Peru* case of 1996) and the European Court of Human Rights (*Aydin v. Turkey* case of 1997).[36] Moreover, in *Celebici*, the ICTY established that rape can be purposed to discriminate based on sex and, as such, that rape represents a prohibited purpose for the offence of torture.[37] This was achieved solely by relying on a teleological interpretation of the Torture Convention and by elaborating that the 'prohibited purposes listed in the Torture Convention as reflected by international customary law do not constitute an exhaustive list, and should be regarded as merely representative'.[38] What is also outstanding about *Celebici* is that the ICTY used this case to make an extensive elaboration of its approaches to legal interpretation in Part III of the judgment titled 'Applicable Law'. There, the ICTY emphasized that its statute and rules are the synthesis of two dominant legal traditions (common law and civil law systems), which makes it necessary for the judges to consider the interpretative principles, methods, and 'other canons of interpretation' of both these traditions. At the same time, the ICTY indicated that it was very much aware that it is a criminal court and that the principles *nullum crimen sine lege, nullum poena sine lege* and the prohibition against *ex post facto* criminal laws are fundamental principles in the world's major criminal justice systems. The real dilemma, as the ICTY points out, is that 'it is not certain to what extent they have been admitted as part of international legal practice'.[39] By this, the ICTY clearly refers to the different methods of criminalization of conduct: whereas in national legal systems, it is done by legislation which dictates the time when the conduct is prohibited and the content of such prohibition, in the international context that same objective can be attained only through treaties and conventions, or after customary practice and creation of customary law. What the ICTY is basically stating is that the international criminal justice may be operative *ex post facto*, as was the case with the ICTR, or even as the facts are unfolding, as was the case with the ICTY. Having in mind these particularities, the ICTY reasons that the method of strict construction should be prevalent in its legal interpretation, but that it will not be violated by the judges if and when they give the terms their full or alternative

[35] Ibid., paras. 452–477.
[36] Ibid., paras. 478–490.
[37] Ibid., para. 941.
[38] Ibid., paras. 470–471.
[39] Ibid., para. 403.

meaning, if that best effectuates the legislative intent, of course, always construed *contra proferentem*. Thus, the Court gives its strongest 'endorsement' of the teleological method:

> The interpretation of the provisions of the Statute and Rules must, therefore, take into consideration the objects of the Statute and the social and political considerations which gave rise to its creation. The kinds of grave violations of international humanitarian law which were the motivating factors for the establishment of the Tribunal continue to occur in many other parts of the world, and continue to exhibit new forms and permutations. The international community can only come to grips with the hydra-headed elusiveness of human conduct through a reasonable as well as a purposive interpretation of the existing provisions of international customary law.[40]

16.2.5. (Sexual) enslavement as a crime against humanity

The *Kunarac* judgment was the first conviction under IHL for conduct that effectively amounted to what is now defined as a crime of sexual slavery in the ICC Statute, although the ICTY Statute itself, in Article 5(c), explicitly listed only enslavement. The judgment also did not use the term 'sexual slavery', but the defendants were convicted of the crime of enslavement through heavy reliance on facts that included sexual violence against women (rape, enforced prostitution, etc.), and thus through sexual slavery being implicitly construed as a predicate crime of enslavement. Again, given that its statute did not define 'enslavement', the ICTY took it upon itself to 'look to various sources that deal with the same or similar subject matter, including international humanitarian law and human rights law'[41] (notably, the Slavery Convention of 1956), and by implementing the same interpretative methodological approach as in defining rape.

16.2.6. Persecution based on gender as a crime against humanity

As mentioned in section 16.1.4, gender was introduced as an explicit discriminatory ground only with Article 7(1)(h) of the ICC Statute, but this came only as a reflection of the jurisprudence of the ICTY in the *Kvocka* judgment of 2001.[42] In

[40] Ibid., para. 170.

[41] *Prosecutor v. Kunarac et al.*, Case No.: IT-96-23-T and IT-96-23/1-T, 22 February 2001, para 518.

[42] *Prosecutor v. Kvocka et al.*, Case No. IT-98-30/1-T, 2 November 2001.

this case, the ICTY observed that 'rape and other forms of sexual violence were committed only against non-Serb detainees, and that they were committed solely against women, making the crimes discriminatory on multiple levels'.[43] Although in accordance with the letter of the Statute only 'racial' discriminatory grounds could be invoked ('non-Serb detainees'), the ICTY still expressed its view that the persecution took the form of sexual violence and that it was discriminatory 'solely against women'. By this, it clearly suggested that gender could be and should be taken as a discriminatory ground for the purposes of the crime of persecution. What is also particular in this case is the ICTY's dominant reliance on its own and the ICTR's previous jurisprudence.[44]

16.2.7. (Female) judges as gender-sensitive readers of the law

In the *Furundzija* appeals case of 2000,[45] one of the grounds for appeal was that the presiding female judge in the trial of the appellant had an appearance of bias because of her previous engagement as a member of the UN Commission on the Status of Women, as well as because of her personal feminist views and activities on behalf of women's human rights, which it was alleged made her additionally predisposed to promote her agenda in her judicial work regarding rape trials and other sexual violence against women. The Appeals Chamber, after a discussion based on the ICTY's statutory requirements for judicial impartiality, persuasive jurisprudence from the common law, and civil law systems, as well as the extensive jurisprudence on the issue by the European Court of Human Rights, found that the fact that the judge was an advocate of women's human rights should not prevent her from 'sit[ting] on a case and impartially decid[ing] upon issues affecting women', and that her inclination 'being of a general nature, is distinguishable from an inclination to implement those goals and objectives as a judge in a particular case'.[46] Moreover, the judgment emphasized that the ICTY Statute required that, in the selection process of the judges, due account must be taken of their experience in human rights, international law, and criminal law, and, consequently, a judge could not be disqualified 'because of the qualifications he or she possesses which, by their very nature, play an integral role in satisfying the eligibility requirements'.[47]

[43] Ibid., para. 560.
[44] Ibid., paras. 184–205.
[45] *Prosecutor v. Furundzija,* Case No. IT-95-17/1-A, 21 July 2000.
[46] Ibid., para. 200.
[47] Ibid., paras. 204–205.

16.3. The feminist 'interpretative community' as a driving force behind the statutory and jurisprudential advancements regarding crimes against women in armed conflicts

16.3.1. The feminist critical agenda in international law

Prior to any conception of the ICTY, ICTR, or ICC, feminist legal theory has been at the forefront of criticizing international law as gender-biased and androcentric. Feminists have asserted that, despite the formal objectivity and apparent neutrality of its norms, international law makes women either invisible or projected through the patriarchal 'male norm'.[48] Two prevalent reasons have been pointed out for this, the first being the patriarchal nature of the states as main subjects of international law, and the second being international law's embedded public/private dichotomy. States are dominated by male political elites who want to preserve their patriarchal nature, including by reproducing it in the international institutions as their functional extensions. This institutional masculinity logically results in a male-biased normative content to international law. As for the public/private dichotomy, feminists find a deep resonance in how this operates in national legal systems and international law. As national law favours the public sphere of male-dominated power in national politics, while depreciating the private sphere of home and family as the 'rightful domain for women', so does international law by treating the private sphere as an exclusive jurisdiction of the states. In effect, by reproducing this dichotomy, women's interests and problems stay on the margins of both national and international law.[49] Building on this critical standpoint, feminists have started to shape their reformist agenda in international law, openly asserting feminist normativity as its rightful source. IHL and CAWs have become the obvious targets. Armed conflicts belong to the public sphere of both national and international law and involve all the 'sacred cows' of public international law, such as state sovereignty, territorial integrity, and legitimization of the use of force. How CAWs are treated in armed conflicts is also an excellent opportunity to exemplify the operation of the public/private dichotomy, because in all cultures and societies, almost exclusively, armed conflicts are perceived as a masculine activity, and evidently organized and regulated as such. The creation of the ad hoc tribunals had only ignited a process of a more targeted empirical research and theoretical work. The agenda was outlined in some notable

[48] Hilary Charlesworth, Christine Chinkin, and Shelley Wright, 'Feminist Approaches to International Law', *The American Journal of International Law*, 85 (1991), 613–645.

[49] Margareth Etienne, 'Addressing Gender-Based Violence in an International Context', *Harvard Women's Law Journal*, 18 (1995), 139–170.

reports and publications that were aimed at influencing the drafting of statutes of the ad hoc tribunals or, subsequently, its judges.[50] The feminist demands covered three aspects of IHL: substantive, procedural, and institutional. First, with respect to the substantive IHL, feminists demanded (a) an ontological reconstruction of CAWs from 'crimes of honour' to 'crimes of violence', with accompanying changes in the legal language, using not only the language of 'protection', 'respect', and 'consideration', but also the language of 'prohibition' and 'prosecution'; (b) legal qualification of crimes of 'gender violence', instead of 'sexual violence'; (c) introduction of interpretative principles connecting IHL to 'peacetime' human rights law, as well as including a non-discrimination clause, with gender included as an explicit basis; (d) a more comprehensive list of CAWs than the one in the Geneva Regime and adding gender to the crime of persecution; (e) changes in the hierarchy of crimes, in order to include the most serious gender crimes (rape) in the grave breaches and in Common Article 3; and (f) treatment of gender crimes in a 'separate section', not as predicate crimes to war crimes and crimes against humanity. In terms of procedural IHL, feminist proposals aimed at gender-sensitive investigation, prosecution, and trials regarding CAWs; requirements for gender issues expertise; and special protective and supportive measures for victims and witnesses of gender violence. As for the institutional operation of IHL, feminists insisted on clauses for fair gender representation in the composition of international tribunals and courts (prosecutors, judges, and legal staff).

16.3.2. Feminist 'interpretative community' shaping gender justice in international criminal tribunals and courts

If we compare the feminist agenda in IHL to recently introduced legal novelties in this body of international law, we can safely assert that feminism has succeeded in projecting its normativity, its feminist *opinio juris,* onto the contemporary IHL almost in a form of a checklist. Recent testimonial and anecdotal information, as well scholarly research,[51] indicates that very organized activism by a network of feminist lawyers from politics, academia, NGOs, and prosecutorial and judicial circles had directly affected the process of statute drafting, prosecutorial priorities, and judicial

[50] Jennifer Green, Rhonda Copelon, Patrick Cotter, and Beth Stephens, 'Affecting the Rules for the Prosecution of Rape and Other Gender-Based Violence Before the International Criminal Tribunal for the Former Yugoslavia: A Feminist Proposal and Critique', *Hastings Women's Law Journal*, 5 (1994), 171–221; 'No Justice, No Peace Report: Accountability for Rape and Gender-Based Violence in the Former Yugoslavia: Based on a Mission of the Women in the Law Project of the International Human Rights Law Group', *Hastings Women's Law Journal*, 5, 89–128 (1994).

[51] Janet Haley, 'Rape at Rome: Feminist Interventions in the Criminalization of Sex-Related Violence in Positive International Criminal Law', *Michigan Journal of International* Law, 1 (2008), 1–123.

interpretation. As early as the drafting of the ICTY Statute, feminist NGOs, lawyers, and groups submitted to the drafters in the UN circles position papers, draft legislation, written talking points, and reports.[52] Later, within the framework of preparatory committees for ICC and at its Rome Conference, the Women's Caucus for Gender Justice, a coalition of about 200 NGO affiliates, with no fewer than thirty with the word 'women' in their titles, was engaged in submitting restatements of law and legislative proposals, parallel to requesting meetings with the negotiating teams and media time.[53] All this was part of the very intensive lobbying effort, for which they had also built inside alliances within the political circles of state delegations supportive of their agenda,[54] some of which had included renowned feminist lawyers and activists, such as Valerie Oosterveld, who did impressive work in negotiating the ICC Statute's provisions.[55] As early as the first case to be tried before the ICTY, the *Tadic* case,[56] feminists were alert to making sure that CAWs would not be sidelined. They had readily started submitting amicus briefs to the Tribunal, as well as lobbying the prosecutor's office and the judges, especially the female judge in the case.[57] The effectiveness of this *modus operandi* is best exemplified in the *Akayesu* judgment, whereas the groundbreaking development regarding CAWs (as presented in sections 16.2.2 and 16.2.3) is widely credited, including by the Chief Prosecutor of the ICTY and ICTR at the time, Richard Goldstone, to the combined effort of amicus brief intervention (submitted by 80 feminist NGOs); the diligence of female lawyers in the Office of the Prosecutor, notably by Patricia Viseur Sellers;[58] and the only female judge on the ICTR trying the case, Judge Navi

[52] Ibid, 12–13.

[53] Ibid, 21–25.

[54] Ibid, 23–24.

[55] Valerie Oosterveld had served as a legal officer for the Foreign Affairs Department in Canada, focusing on international criminal justice, including gender issues related to the ICTR. As a member of the Canadian delegation, she had been deeply involved in negotiations of the provisions of the ICC Statute regarding sexual slavery and the definition of gender.

[56] *Prosecutor v. Dusko Tadic,* Case No. IT-94-1-A, 15 July 1999.

[57] An amicus brief was submitted by the International Women's Human Rights Law Clinic, the Harvard Human Rights Program, and the Jacob Blaustein Institute, consisting of arguments that the indictment should have included rape and other forms of sexual violence. Subsequently, Judge Odio Benito, the only female judge in the trial panel, questioned the prosecutor on these defalcations, in the aftermath of which the amended indictment followed, including these crimes. Janet Haley, 'Rape at Rome: Feminist Interventions in the Criminalization of Sex-Related Violence in Positive International Criminal Law', *Michigan Journal of International Law,* 1 (2008),14.

[58] Sellers was the first 'Legal Advisor for Gender-Related Crimes', a position instituted in 1995 in the Office of the Prosecutor by the Chief Prosecutor of both the ICTY and ICTR, Richard Goldstone. She has served as principal legal advisor to several of the cases analysed in this chapter, including *Akayesu* and *Kunarac,* as well as a trial attorney in *Furundzija.* She has used her insider legal experience at the ad hoc courts to produce scholarly work on the issues regarding CAWs.

Pillay, who took the initiative to question the witnesses about sexual violence and subsequently insisted that the indictment include charges of sexual violence.[59] The latter's crucial role in this case had only reaffirmed the feminist demand for fair gender representation at the bench and had further motivated them to engage in political lobbying to elect more female judges at the ad hoc tribunals.[60] Finally, the role of the feminist mock tribunals must be mentioned. It is usually neglected in academic acknowledgment, but in hindsight, it can safely be stated that the mock trials played an important role, not only in raising the public awareness about CAWs, and the shameful lack of justice thereof, but also in the formation of the feminist 'interpretative community' and its efforts to restate and develop IHL. Most notable are the mock tribunals during the Vienna Conference on Human Rights of 1993, the Beijing Fourth World Conference on Women of 1995, and the Tokyo Women's International War Crimes Tribunal on Japan's Military Sexual Slavery of 2000.[61]

16.4. Challenges in preserving gender justice before the international and hybrid criminal courts

The creation of the ICTY, ICTR, and ICC undoubtedly represents the most significant turning point in the development of the modern IHL regarding CAWs, the major achievement being that these crimes will no longer go ignored or unpunished by international criminal justice. The legal novelties that have been put in place send a clear message that treating women as 'spoils of war' is no longer acceptable

[59] Richard Goldstone, 'The United Nations' War Crimes Tribunals: An Assessment', *Connecticut Journal of International Law*, 12 (1997), 231.

[60] Nienke Grossman, 'Sex Representation on the Bench and the Legitimacy of International Criminal Courts', *International Criminal Law Review*, 11 (2011), 650.

[61] At the Vienna and Beijing conferences, NGO tribunals were organized to hear testimonies regarding violations of women's human rights, including CAWs, suffered by the 'comfort women' of World War II; Palestinian, Somali, Peruvian, Algerian, and Ugandan women; and women from the conflicts in the former Yugoslavia. The Tokyo Tribunal of 2000 included renowned international legal experts with prosecutorial or adjudication experience from the ICTY and ICTR, such as G. McDonald and P. V. Sellers, acting as judges and chief prosecutors of the former ICTY. All of the proceedings were conducted as in a formal court case. The background of the cases referred to the 'comfort women' system of sexual slavery organized by the Japanese military during World War II, which had victimized many women in Asia, but was totally ignored by the Tokyo Tribunal. See Niamh Reilly, ed., 'Testimonies of the Global Tribunal on Violations of Women's Human Rights at the United Nations World Conference on Human Rights, Vienna, June 1993', July 1994, Center for Women's Global Leadership, available at https://www.cwgl.rutgers.edu/docman/coalition-building-publications/283-demand-accountability/file; Rumi Sakamoto, 'The Women's International War Crimes Tribunal on Japan's Military Sexual Slavery: A Legal and Feminist Approach to the 'Comfort Women' Issue', *New Zealand Journal of Asian Studies*, 3 (2001), 49–58.

in modern warfare, as is indicated with the initial experiences of the ICC, and of the subsequent hybrid courts, such as those established for Kosovo (2000), Sierra Leone (2002), East Timor (2002), Cambodia (2003) and Iraq (2003). However, several challenges remain to be addressed with respect to preserving and developing that legacy.

16.4.1. The remainder of the feminist agenda in IHL

The remainder of the feminist agenda in IHL is as follows: (a) The legal qualification of 'crimes of sexual violence' should be replaced with 'crimes of gender violence' as a more adequate term to enable criminalization of assaults that are not sexualized or inter-connected with the biological meaning of the sexes, but more with the socially construed roles of the biological sexes; (b) CAWs, especially rape, should be explicitly classified in the list of the grave breaches and Common Article 3; and (c) Gender crimes should be treated as freestanding crimes in the subject-matter jurisdiction of international and hybrid criminal courts. This last is all the more important because crimes of this nature tend to happen on the margins of armed conflicts, as isolated incidents, and thus the need to prove the nexus between the armed conflict and CAWs should be loosened. If unchanged, this would remain a serious challenge in prosecution and adjudication processes, effectively contributing to many CAWs remaining unpunished.

16.4.2. Preserving (feminist) judicial interpretations regarding CAWs

The judicial interpretations of the ICTY and ICTR regarding CAWs, as well as their gender-sensitive procedural and institutional novelties, have been almost entirely turned into statutory law with the ICC Statute and its Elements of Crime. Furthermore, there is an explicit obligation for the ICC to make the application and interpretation of the ICC Statute consistent with internationally recognized human rights, as well as non-discriminatory on a gender basis. In certain instances, CAWs are also covered with basket clauses in the ICC Statute, which gives a solid legal basis for recognizing and punishing such new crimes through future judicial interpretations. Framing the legacy into a statutory law is a solid guarantee for the continuing recognition and punishment of CAWs. However, it must be understood that this is up to a degree. There are still certain challenges to preserving these (feminist) judicial interpretations regarding CAWs. For one thing, it is still not clear whether the 'Elements of Crime', as a document, is legally binding or merely advisory for the ICC itself, let alone for any other international or hybrid criminal court.[62] In addition, despite the

[62] Article 9(1) of the ICC Statute stipulates that the Elements of Crime 'shall assist the Court in the interpretation', while Article 21(a) stipulates that the Court 'shall apply' the Elements of Crime.

evident use of judicial cross-fertilization, all international criminal courts so far hold to the position that they are not 'bound by past doctrine', as stated by the ICTY in the *Tadic* judgment,[63] and that 'the Tribunal is not bound by precedents established by other international criminal courts', as stated in the *Kupreskic* judgment of the same court.[64] This indicates that there is no coherent 'theory of precedent' at work with these courts.[65] In this respect, the judicial interpretation by the Special Court of Sierra Leone (SCSL)[66] gives illustrative examples of the challenges ahead, one encouraging, one discouraging. Although 'forced marriage' did not make it explicitly onto the list of CAWs in the ICC Statute, the SCSL, in its *Brima* judgment[67] of 2007, after reviewing the jurisprudence of the ICTY, ICTR, and ICC, has held that forced marriage constitutes a crime against humanity as '[an]other inhumane act' under the SCSL Statute. On the other hand, in the same judgment, the SCSL found it necessary to come up with its own definition of rape, ignoring the definition in the ICC Elements of Crime, and adopting that of the ICTY in *Kunarac*. Then, in its *Sesay* judgment[68] of 2009, the SCSL yet again adopted a new definition of rape, a combination of the ICC and *Kunarac* definitions, which may lead to the conclusion that there still is no uniform definition of rape in international law. These examples of ongoing uncertainty and unpredictability in the judicial interpretations lead us to the conclusion that perhaps the best safeguard now available for preserving and developing the IHL regarding CAWs is again one of the feminist arsenals—fair gender representation at the international and hybrid criminal courts. The experience has demonstrated that international judges are not plain readers of law, but very instrumental in its development, and that the 6.3 per cent and 23.1 per cent of female judges at the ICTY and ICTR respectively have made a crucial impact in developing the CAWs jurisprudence. As of October 2021, out of eighteen judges, nine are female (50 per cent). From a feminist perspective, this offers the promising proposition that the gender-sensitive reading of the IHL would continue and, it is hoped, give an equivalent legal guidance to the other international or hybrid criminal courts.

[63] *Prosecutor v. Dusko Tadic,* Case No. IT-94-1-T, 7 May 1997, para. 654.

[64] *Prosecutor v. Kupreskic,* Case No. IT-95-16-T, 14 January 2000, para. 540.

[65] Aldo Zammit Borda, 'The Direct and Indirect Approaches to Precedent in International Criminal Courts and Tribunals', *Melbourne Journal of International Law,* 14 (2013), 32–33.

[66] SCSL is a hybrid court established in 2002 with an agreement between UN and the Government of Sierra Leone, in order to address serious violence against civilians and UN Peacekeepers during the civil war of 1991–2002.

[67] *Prosecutor v. Brima, Kamara and Kanu,* Case No. SCSL-04-16-T, 20 June 2007, para. 202.

[68] *Prosecutor v. Sesay, Kallon and Gbao,* Case No. SCSL-04-15-T, 25 February 2009, para. 145.

References

Askin, Kelly D., 'Prosecuting Wartime Rape and other Gender-Related Crimes Under International Law: Extraordinary Advances, Enduring Obstacles', *Berkeley Journal of International Law*, 21 (2003), 288–349.

Bedont, Barbara and Katherine Hall Martinez, 'Ending Impunity for Gender Crimes under International Criminal Court', *The Brown Journal of World Affairs*, 6/1 (1999), 65–85.

Borda, Aldo Zammit, 'The Direct and Indirect Approaches to Precedent in International Criminal Courts and Tribunals', *Melbourne Journal of International Law*, 14 (2013), 1–35.

Charlesworth, Hilary, Christine Chinkin, and Shelley Wright. 'Feminist Approaches to International Law', *The American Journal of International Law*, 85 (1991), 613–645.

Etienne, Margareth, 'Addressing Gender-Based Violence in an International Context', *Harvard Women's Law Journal*, 18 (1995), 139–170.

Gardam, Judith, 'Women and the Law of Armed Conflict: Why the Silence', *The International and Comparative Law Quarterly*, 46 (1997), 55–80.

Goldstone, Richard., 'The United Nations' War Crimes Tribunals: An Assessment', *Connecticut Journal of International Law*, 12 (1997), 227–240.

Green, Jennifer, hondaCopelon, Patrick Cotter, and Beth Stephens, 'Affecting the Rules for the Prosecution of Rape and Other Gender-Based Violence Before the International Criminal Tribunal for the Former Yugoslavia: A Feminist Proposal and Critique', *Hastings Women's Law Journal*, 5 (1994), 171–221.

Grossman, Nienke, 'Sex Representation on the Bench and the Legitimacy of International Criminal Courts', *International Criminal Law Review*, 11 (2011), 643–653.

Halley, Janet, 'Rape at Rome: Feminist Interventions in the Criminalization of Sex-Related Violence in Positive International Criminal Law', *Michigan Journal of International Law*, 30 (2008), 1–123.

Keen, Maurice, *The Laws of War in the Late Middle Ages* (Aldershot, 1993).

Meron, Theodor, 'Rape as a Crime under International Humanitarian Law', *American Journal of International Law*, 87 (1993), 424–425.

'No Justice, No Peace Report: Accountability for Rape and Gender-Based Violence in the Former Yugoslavia: Based on a Mission of the Women in the Law Project of the International Human Rights Law Group', *Hastings Women's Law Journal*, 5, 89–128 (1994).

Reilly, Niamh ed., 'Testimonies of the Global Tribunal on Violations of Women's Human Rights at the United Nations World Conference on Human Rights, Vienna, June 1993', *Center for Women's Global Leadership*, 1994, available at http://www.nuigalway.ie/soc/documents/online_publications/reilly_testimonies_1994.pdf.

Sakamoto Rumi, 'The Women's International War Crimes Tribunal on Japan's Military Sexual Slavery: A Legal and Feminist Approach to the "Comfort Women" Issue', *New Zealand Journal of Asian Studies*, 3 (2001), 49–58.

Sellers, Patricia Viseur, 'The Prosecution of Sexual Violence in Conflict: The Importance of Human Rights as Means of Interpretation', *PeaceWomen Portal* (2007), https://www.peacewomen.org/node/89506.

INDEX

For the benefit of digital users, indexed terms that span two pages (e.g., 52–53) may, on occasion, appear on only one of those pages.

Note: Tables and figures are indicated by *t* and *f* following the page number